Marketing Information:
A Strategic Guide
for Business
and Finance Libraries

Marketing Information: A Strategic Guide for Business and Finance Libraries has been co-published simultaneously as *Journal of Business & Finance Librarianship*, Volume 9, Numbers 2/3 and 4 2004.

The *Journal of Business & Finance Librarianship* Monographic "Separates"

Below is a list of "separates," which in serials librarianship means a special issue simultaneously published as a special journal issue or double-issue *and* as a "separate" hardbound monograph. (This is a format which we also call a "DocuSerial.")

"Separates" are published because specialized libraries or professionals may wish to purchase a specific thematic issue by itself in a format which can be separately cataloged and shelved, as opposed to purchasing the journal on an on-going basis. Faculty members may also more easily consider a "separate" for classroom adoption.

"Separates" are carefully classified separately with the major book jobbers so that the journal tie-in can be noted on new book order slips to avoid duplicate purchasing.

You may wish to visit Haworth's Website at . . .

http://www.HaworthPress.com

. . . to search our online catalog for complete tables of contents of these separates and related publications.

You may also call 1-800-HAWORTH (outside US/Canada: 607-722-5857), or Fax 1-800-895-0582 (outside US/Canada: 607-771-0012), or e-mail at:

docdelivery@haworthpress.com

Marketing Information: A Strategic Guide for Business and Finance Libraries, by Wendy Diamond, MLIS, and Michael R. Oppenheim, MLIS, MA (Vol. 9, No (2/3)(4), 2004). *"Comprehensive. . . . Logically organized. . . . Simple to use and easy to consult when trying to identify a discrete resource to support a specific question. Library science graduate students in business research tracks will find this guide extremely useful. It has strong potential as a textbook at the undergraduate business/marketing student level as well. A valuable aspect of the book is its inclusion of contact information for most cited sources. This book should be on the 'resource shelf' of any business or marketing librarian. I know it will be on mine." (Sara B. Sluss, MLS, Business Librarian and Web Site Content Manager, California State University Long Beach Library)*

The Core Business Web: A Guide to Key Information Resources, edited by Gary W. White, MLS, MBA (Vol. 8, No. 2, 2002 and Vol. 8, No. 3/4, 2003). *"The reader will be led to the most relevant resources, thus eliminating much frustration and saving time." (Bobray Bordelon, MLIS, Economics/Finance Librarian, Princeton University Library)*

Library Services for Business Students in Distance Education: Issues and Trends, edited by Shari Buxbaum, MLS (Vol. 7, No. 2/3, 2002). *Explores approaches to providing library services for distance education business students; examines the standards and guidelines for measuring these services.*

Marketing Information: A Strategic Guide for Business and Finance Libraries

Wendy Diamond
Michael R. Oppenheim

Marketing Information: A Strategic Guide for Business and Finance Libraries has been co-published simultaneously as *Journal of Business & Finance Librarianship*, Volume 9, Numbers 2/3 and 4 2004.

Routledge
Taylor & Francis Group

NEW YORK AND LONDON

First Published by

The Haworth Information Press®, 10 Alice Street, Binghamton, NY 13904-1580 USA

The Haworth Information Press® is an imprint of The Haworth Press, Inc., 10 Alice Street, Binghamton, NY 13904-1580 USA.

Transferred to Digital Printing 2009 by Routledge
270 Madison Ave, New York NY 10016
2 Park Square, Milton Park, Abingdon, Oxon, OX14 4RN

Marketing Information: A Strategic Guide for Business and Finance Libraries has been co-published simultaneously as *Journal of Business & Finance Librarianship*™, Volume 9, Numbers 2/3 and 4 2004.

Cover design by Marylouise E. Doyle.

Library of Congress Cataloging-in-Publication Data

Diamond, Wendy, 1953-
    Marketing information : a strategic guide for business and finance libraries / Wendy Diamond, Michael R. Oppenheim.
        p. cm.
    Co-published simultaneously as Journal of Business & Finance Librarianship, volume 9, numbers 2/3 2004 and volume 9, number 4, 2004.
    Includes bibliographical references and index.
    ISBN 0-7890-2112-9 (hard cover : alk. paper) – ISBN 0-7890-6006-X (soft cover : alk. paper)
    1. Marketing research–Handbooks, manuals, etc. 2. Strategic planning–Handbooks, manuals, etc. I. Oppenheim, Michael R. II. Journal of business & finance librarianship. III. Title.
HF5415.2.D49 2004
658.8'3–dc22
                                                                        2003027319

Indexing, Abstracting & Website/Internet Coverage

Journal of Business & Finance Librarianship

This section provides you with a list of major indexing & abstracting services. That is to say, each service began covering this periodical during the year noted in the right column. Most Websites which are listed below have indicated that they will either post, disseminate, compile, archive, cite or alert their own Website users with research-based content from this work. (This list is as current as the copyright date of this publication.)

Abstracting, Website/Indexing Coverage . . . . Year When Coverage Began

- *Business Source Corporate: coverage of nearly 3,350 quality
  magazines and journals; designed to meet the diverse
  information needs of corporations; EBSCO Publishing
  <http://www.epnet.com/corporate/bsourcecorp.asp>* 2002

- *Business Source Elite: coverage of scholarly business,
  management and economics journals; EBSCO Publishing
  <http://www.epnet.com/academic/bussourceelite.asp>* 2002

- *Business Source Premier: coverage of scholarly journals and business
  periodicals covering management, economics, finance, accounting,
  international business, and much more; EBSCO Publishing
  <http://www.epnet.com/academic/bussourceprem.asp>* 2002

- *CNPIEC Reference Guide: Chinese National Directory
  of Foreign Periodicals* 1996

- *IBZ International Bibliography of Periodical Literature
  <http://www.saur.de>* 1996

- *Index Guide to College Journals (core list compiled by
  integrating 48 indexes frequently used to support
  undergraduate programs in small to medium sized libraries)* 1999

- *Index to Periodical Articles Related to Law* 1992

- *Information Science & Technology Abstracts: indexes journal articles
  from more than 450 publications as well as books, research reports,
  conference proceedings, and patents; EBSCO Publishing
  <http://www.infotoday.com>* 1992

(continued)

- *Informed Librarian, The <http://www.infosourcespub.com>*.............. 1993
- *INSPEC is the leading English-language bibliographic information service providing access to the world's scientific & technical literature in physics, electrical engineering, electronics, communications, control engineering, computers & computing, and information technology <http://www.iee.org.uk/publish/>* 1992
- *Journal of Academic Librarianship: Guide to Professional Literature, The* 1997
- *Konyvtari Figyelo (Library Review)* 2000
- *Library & Information Science Abstracts (LISA) <http://www.csa.com>* 1992
- *Library and Information Science Annual (LISCA) <http://www.lu.com>* 1998
- *Library Literature & Information Science* 1993
- *OCLC Public Affairs Information Service <http://www.pais.org>* 1997
- *Referativnyi Zhurnal (Abstracts Journal of the All-Russian Institute of Scientific and Technical Information– in Russian)* 1992
- *SwetsNet <http://www.swetsnet.com>* 2001
- *Technical Education & Training Abstracts* 1998

Special Bibliographic Notes related to special journal issues (separates) and indexing/abstracting:

- indexing/abstracting services in this list will also cover material in any "separate" that is co-published simultaneously with Haworth's special thematic journal issue or DocuSerial. Indexing/abstracting usually covers material at the article/chapter level.
- monographic co-editions are intended for either non-subscribers or libraries which intend to purchase a second copy for their circulating collections.
- monographic co-editions are reported to all jobbers/wholesalers/approval plans. The source journal is listed as the "series" to assist the prevention of duplicate purchasing in the same manner utilized for books-in-series.
- to facilitate user/access services all indexing/abstracting services are encouraged to utilize the co-indexing entry note indicated at the bottom of the first page of each article/chapter/contribution.
- this is intended to assist a library user of any reference tool (whether print, electronic, online, or CD-ROM) to locate the monographic version if the library has purchased this version but not a subscription to the source journal.
- individual articles/chapters in any Haworth publication are also available through the Haworth Document Delivery Service (HDDS).

To my parents, Rubin and Marion Diamond

Wendy Diamond

To my parents, Abe and Frances Oppenheim

Michael R. Oppenheim

Marketing Information: A Strategic Guide for Business and Finance Libraries

CONTENTS

Acknowledgments — xiii

Preface — xv

Where to Find It: A Checklist for Typical Marketing Concepts — xxi

PART I. INTRODUCTION

Chapter 1. Introduction to Sources and Strategies
for Research on Marketing — 3

PART II. RESEARCHING THE COMPETITIVE
ENVIRONMENT

Chapter 2. Sources for an Industry Scan — 41

Chapter 3. Sources About Companies, Brands,
and Competitors — 69

Chapter 4. Sources for Market Research Reports — 91

PART III. RESEARCH ABOUT CUSTOMERS

Chapter 5. Demographic, Geographic,
and Lifestyle Sources — 109

Chapter 6. Marketing Sources for Demographic Niches — 135

PART IV. RESEARCH FOR THE PROMOTIONAL
STRATEGY

Chapter 7. Advertising and Media Planning Sources — 157

Chapter 8. Public Relations Sources   189

PART V. RESEARCHING THE SALES STRATEGY

Chapter 9. Sales Management, Sales Promotion,
    and Retail Sources   205

Chapter 10. Direct Marketing and E-Commerce
    Sources   221

Chapter 11. International Marketing Sources   237

PART VI. RESEARCHING PRICE, PACKAGING,
    AND PLACE

Chapter 12. Product Development, Packaging,
    Pricing, and Place   269

PART VII. SPECIAL TOPICS

Chapter 13. Sources for Special Topics: Social Marketing,
    Nonprofit Organizations, Services Marketing,
    and Legal/Ethical Issues   287

APPENDIX: Selected Glossaries   301

Title Index   303

Subject Index   325

ABOUT THE AUTHORS

Wendy Diamond, MLIS, has been Business and Economics Librarian at California State University, Chico, since 1994. Currently, she also serves as Head of Reference Services. Previously, Ms. Diamond was Reference and Instructional Librarian at the Business and Economics Library, University of California, Berkeley.

Ms. Diamond is active in the American Library Association (ALA) and has held several positions in the Business Reference and Services Section (BRASS). She has presented programs at library conferences and workshops, co-designed an online business research skills course for undergraduates, and served as an advisor to a publisher of reference books. She has authored several reviews, articles, and book chapters, including "Serving Business Distance Education Students: A Checklist for Librarians" in *Reference & User Services Quarterly* (2001), "Investment Information in Academic Libraries: Faculty and Doctoral Students" in *RQ* (1996), and "Internal User Group: Reference & Instruction" in *Managing Business Collections in Libraries* (Greenwood Press, 1996).

Ms. Diamond holds a Masters of Library and Information Studies Degree (1988) from the University of California, Berkeley, and received the SLA Meckler Award for Innovation in Technology (1995). She is a member of Phi Beta Kappa.

Michael R. Oppenheim, MLIS, MA, has been Reference and Instructional Services Librarian at the Rosenfeld Management Library, Anderson School, University of California, Los Angeles, since 1997. Previously, he worked as Reference Librarian at both California State University, Los Angeles, and California State University, Dominguez Hills.

Mr. Oppenheim is active in the American Library Association (ALA) and has held various offices in the Business Reference and Services Section (BRASS), Government Documents Roundtable (GODORT), as well as in California Library Association (CLA), Business and Finance Division of Special Libraries Association (SLA), and California Academic and Research Libraries (CARL). He has contributed chapters on government information for business in *Government Online*

(Neal-Schuman, 2001) and *The Basic Business Library: Core Resources* (4th ed., Oryx Press, 2002). He has edited the "Local Publication and Resources" column for the annual Notable Documents issue of the *Journal of Government Information* since 1998. He has also written for *Current Biography* and Sage Publications' abstracting services.

Mr. Oppenheim holds a Master's Degree in English (1977) from the University of California, Los Angeles, and a Master of Science in Library and Information Science (1986) from the University of Southern California. He was the CARL Member of the Year in 1998.

Acknowledgments

I have the pleasant duty to express my gratitude and indebtedness to those without whose help this project would have faltered along the way.

My deepest appreciation goes to my co-author, Michael R. Oppenheim, who enhanced the book immeasurably with his professional contributions on numerous levels.

Thanks must go next to my librarian colleagues at California State University, Chico–particularly Carolyn Dusenbury, Director of Meriam Library, and Bill Post, Vice-Provost for Information Resources, for their continuing support of this project. I thank the University for granting me a four-month sabbatical which allowed me to concentrate on the book without the usual distractions.

Amelia Kassel, business and marketing information specialist, contributed her considerable insights at an early stage. I also wish to thank professors Dr. Lauren Wright, Dr. Daniel R. Toy, Dr. Kenneth J. Chapman, and Dr. Shekhar Misra, of California State University, Chico's College of Business, who each graciously consented to read various draft chapters. Along with the expected analysis and constructive criticism, I was also treated to encouragement.

I am especially appreciative of those "unsung heroes" of the library world, the gracious librarians and staff members of the various public and academic institutions whose collections I have utilized for background research. These generous institutions include San Francisco Public Library, Pasadena Public Library, Stanford University's Jackson Library, University of California, Berkeley's Haas School of Business' Library, and the Rosenfeld Library at the Anderson School at UCLA.

I owe a long-term debt of gratitude to my mentor and friend, Milton G. Ternberg, Head of Thomas J. Long Library of the Haas School of Business at the University of California, Berkeley. His insightful opinions and advice have always been a source of inspiration and guidance.

Last, but not least, thanks go to my family members for their patience and support. Particular love and appreciation go to my husband, Michael Mulcahy, who was always willing to help with his critical ear and excellent writing skills, and to my mother, Marion Diamond, who painstakingly proofread the manuscript.

Such failings that remain are mine alone.

Wendy Diamond

Preface

Marketing, as much as any other area, is a field that requires information for decision making. On a day-to-day basis, marketers find themselves involved with research, investigation, analysis, evaluation, comparisons, qualitative measures of psychology and emotion, and quantitative calculations about almost everything. Whether these activities are on a do-it-yourself or a hired-out basis, marketers need to determine what kind of information will best suit their needs, how and where to find it, and how they can utilize it. Poor information can lead to poor decision making, which can be very costly. Obviously, it is essential to have good information.

PURPOSE AND SCOPE

Although marketing has always been part of commerce and trade, modern marketing has evolved to such an extensive degree that an enormous and diversified body of literature has been developed by both practitioners and academics. Marketing is supported by a significant theoretical foundation, but it is nevertheless a practical discipline; its information sources are practical tools designed to solve real-world problems. Altogether, the literature comprises a very complex information landscape.

Marketing Information: A Strategic Guide for Business and Finance Libraries is intended as a resource for marketers and for those studying to be marketers. Its emphasis is on information, not on marketing itself. It is most assuredly not an encyclopedia or a handbook of marketing. Consider it a guided tour of the signposts and landmarks in the world of marketing information, highlighting the most important features but not covering everything.

[Haworth co-indexing entry note]: "Preface." Diamond, Wendy, and Michael R. Oppenheim. Co-published simultaneously in *Journal of Business & Finance Librarianship* (The Haworth Information Press, an imprint of The Haworth Press, Inc.) Vol. 9, No. 2/3, 2004, pp. xvii-xxi; and: *Marketing Information: A Strategic Guide for Business and Finance Libraries* (Wendy Diamond, and Michael R. Oppenheim) The Haworth Information Press, an imprint of The Haworth Press, Inc., 2004, pp. xv-xix. Single or multiple copies of this article are available for a fee from The Haworth Document Delivery Service [1-800-HAWORTH, 9:00 a.m. - 5:00 p.m. (EST). E-mail address: docdelivery@haworthpress.com].

The authors are academic business librarians with more than 25 years of combined experience advising many kinds of researchers in devising search strategies in order to find the right information. Their expertise has been honed in helping people at all stages of research: doctoral candidates and faculty researchers seeking empirical studies and statistical time series; MBA and undergraduate students applying fundamental theories to analyze case studies; marketing professionals seeking background intelligence on competitors; entrepreneurs preparing marketing plans for venture capitalists; and, of course, members of the general public wishing to learn about the businesses with which they trade.

The sources discussed were chosen to represent a selection of those most frequently used and recognized by seasoned experts, as well as a variety of sources less well known, with emphasis on those which offer unique information, perspectives, or services. This book is intended to serve working professionals and students. It will also open the world of the marketing specialist to marketers working outside their own specialty, professionals conducting marketing projects incidental to the primary purpose of their organization (such as hospitals or social service agencies), new entrepreneurs, educators, and the librarians who are called upon to assist them all. The authors hope it will also serve to provide librarians and scholarly researchers with leads to fresh sources, especially those newly available through such powerful information technologies as the World Wide Web. In so doing, it will help to strengthen the feedback loop between theoreticians and practitioners.

The book deals with the range of questions that is inevitably part of any research project: What do I need to know? Where can I find it? Where can I find the experts to advise me or are available for hire? How can I find out about the competition? Who collects current facts and figures? Are there time series of historical trend data and projections for the future? What calculation tools will work best? What are the rules of the road? How can I avoid reinventing the wheel, and how can I be sure I'm following established "best practices" and guidelines? Librarians will recognize these as reference questions, which are the kinds of questions this book will help to answer.

We focus on the needs of marketers in the United States. Most of the sources originate in the U.S., with a few exceptions. International marketing is covered from the perspective of the U.S. marketer seeking to incorporate an export component into a distribution plan.

Topics cover the major elements required for a marketing plan, ranging from industry and competitor environment, consumer demographics, advertising, sales, and public relations, to pricing, packaging, and distribution. Some ancillary subjects are included, such as international trade, e-commerce, law and ethics, services marketing, and social marketing, but the coverage is not intended to be comprehensive. Space and time do not permit us to cover everything, so it is important to note what is not covered: finance and budgeting, marketing management, sales forecasting, affiliate and relationship marketing, and sports marketing are some examples.

All publishing formats are included: print, CD-ROM, DVD, online subscriptions, free Web sites, and electronic texts–a list which reflects the complexity of the entire current information landscape. Historically, commercial publishers, university research centers, professional associations, and government agencies constituted the bulk of the business publishing industry. This guidebook contains those sources, as well as a significant amount of material originated by many types of producers beyond the traditional: commercial Web sites with no physical location, advertising and public relations agencies, market research firms, and software vendors. New technologies have enabled many types of disseminators, such as associations and agencies, to distribute materials online which were formerly unavailable to a wide audience (e.g., reports, white papers, data, statistics, glossaries, best practice guidelines, historical collections). While this is a boon to access by researchers and practitioners, it injects an undeniable challenge.

Further complicating the picture, products of traditional commercial publishers have also proliferated due to technology. It was clear from the start of this project that almost every traditional source has developed a Web-based adjunct or counterpart, usually not supplanting a print or CD-ROM source but complementing it. Furthermore, in order to produce any individual reference publication, publishers create a large database. They are now able to take various slices out of it to produce related products, publications, and databases. Thus, any individual title represents a "tip of the iceberg" out of a large underlying dataset. Because it is now harder to select any one single title as the best for all purposes, this book often highlights the publishers themselves (rather than source titles).

Taken together, all these changes represent a new dimension in marketing information. As information specialists and business librarians, we recognize that this proliferation of new disseminators, new formats, and new product families has created a growing need for guidance in finding, selecting, and pinpointing the right information.

Even beginners in marketing can no longer rely solely on print sources. In view of the enormous amount of information on the Web, this book assumes that the reader has basic computer knowledge and experience with using the Internet.

From the beginning, the authors were concerned that the dynamic nature of the publishing environment, particularly the Web, would make it nearly impossible to keep the information current, and in fact, that reality has become ever more apparent. The information for this book was collected between 2000 and 2003, with all Web-based material updated and verified from February through May of 2003. Given the certainty of more changes in the future, we have tried to help the reader gain enough understanding, so that even if an exact Web site, database title, or publisher name has changed, the reader knows what is needed for a particular purpose, and how to look for and find the latest permutation of a specific item. Additionally, it should be noted that many sources, both print and online, were described using publishers' brochures and/or publicity on the Web.

ORGANIZATION

The arrangement of this book into parts approximates the sequential elements of a marketing plan. In most cases, the marketing plan will begin with analyzing the industry environment and competitors, then define the target market, and devise promotion, pricing, and distribution strategies. The book is structured so that individual chapters can be consulted independently of other chapters. Within each chapter, the sources are generally listed starting with the most commonly known and widely available in libraries, underscoring the authority and practical value such titles tend to have. A discussion follows about those sources that tend to be more specialized, esoteric, or expensive.

The content of each chapter has been dictated by the nature of the topic, which means there is not an absolutely consistent amount or array of types of sources. Because the information needs differ, we have not attempted to force each discipline into a rigid template: the selection of sources is tailored for each sub-area of marketing (such as advertising, media planning, packaging, retailing, sales promotion). Clearly, the type of material included for pricing and packaging is more operations-oriented than the material for social marketing, and archival historical collections useful for advertising are not relevant for e-commerce. Many, but not all, discussions include important academic literature and policy-making issues. Tips which target a specific issue and short reading lists are highlighted and distributed throughout the book.

The introductory chapter lays the groundwork for the reader, whether novice or expert, to use the book to its best advantage. It provides an overview of business and marketing information, search strategies, and sources including basic reference tools, periodical indexes, and handy tools such as dictionaries and encyclopedias. Various research techniques for online searching are explained. In subsequent chapters, the standard pattern begins with a background discussion of concepts and issues, including relevant definitions and the context of that particular facet of marketing. This is followed by a discussion of the content and applications of major sources, so the reader can understand how to use them. Annotations for major sources describe the type of source and publisher, and explain features and organization. Heading styles for major sources vary according to whether it is a book, serial, publisher, professional association, or Web site. Alternative approaches and additional sources with unique features are also mentioned.

Pricing information is included where possible, but this has a high degree of volatility and variation. Many publishers provide tiered or negotiated pricing for electronic resources, and even books may be offered at various prices through different vendors. Therefore, prices in headings should be used as a "benchmarking" indicator which lets readers assess sources relative to each other. This can help determine whether a particular source is appropriate for their needs and, importantly, whether it is likely to be available in a local library or only in the most specialized environments.

We realize that this is probably not a book which will be read cover-to-cover. Some readers will browse through it to get a general overview of the whole picture. Others will zero in on one particular chapter or topic area to find a tool that meets the need of the moment. We trust that both kinds of readers will find it a worthwhile companion for their marketing research projects.

Wendy Diamond
Michael R. Oppenheim

Where to Find It: A Checklist for Typical Marketing Concepts

Marketing Concept	Chapter Discussion(s), generally . . .	Particularly these sources . . . - Check the Title Index for page numbers - Sources are arranged for usefulness and availability - Some titles are discussed in multiple chapters
Ad copy and campaigns	Chapter 7	*Ad*Access*; *Advertising Age Encyclopedia of Advertising*; *Encyclopedia of Major Marketing Campaigns*; *AdForum.com*; *AdReview.com*; *Commercial Closet*
Advertising agencies	Chapter 7	*Advertising Red Books*; *American Association of Advertising Agencies*; *Advertising Age Encyclopedia of Advertising*
Advertising industry	Chapter 7	*Advertising Age magazine*; *AdAge Data Center*; *Advertising Growth Trends*; *Advertising Ratios and Budgets*; *Bob Coen's Insider's Report*
Advertising law	Chapter 7	*Advertising Law*; *Advertising Law and Ethics*
Advertising rates	Chapter 7	SRDS (various titles); *SQAD Media Market Guide*; *Marketer's Guide to Media*; *International Media Guides*; WARC's *Pocket Books*; *Market & MediaFact Pocket Books*
Associations	Chapter 1 (and throughout)	*Encyclopedia of Business Information Sources*; *American Marketing Association*; *Statistical Reference Index (SRI)*; *Marketing Information: A Professional Guide*
Brand names	Chapter 3	*Companies and Their Brands*; *Brandchannel.com*; *World's Greatest Brands*; *Advertising Red Books (Advertisers)*; *Thomas Register of American Manufacturers*
Case studies	Chapter 1	*ABI/Inform*; *Emerald*; OrgScience Web Site "Resources on Using the Case Method in Business & Management Education"; *Google*; *Harvard Business Online*; World Advertising Research Center; *Encyclopedia of Major Marketing Campaigns*; *Adreview.com*; *E-Business Research Center*; *Product Manager's Handbook*; *Tools of Change*; NewProductWorks; Council of Logistics Management; *Marketer's Guide to Successful Package Design*

(continued)

Marketing Concept	Chapter Discussion(s), generally . . .	Particularly these sources . . . - Check the Title Index for page numbers - Sources are arranged for usefulness and availability - Some titles are discussed in multiple chapters
Children and marketing	Chapter 6	*Youth Research Sourcebook*; *American Demographics* magazine; *Youth University*; *Simmons Kids Study*; *Simmons Teen Study*; *Kids These Days*; *Roper Youth Report*; (See also periodical articles)
Company information and marketing strategy	Chapter 3, 7	*Advertising Age Encyclopedia of Advertising*; *Encyclopedia of Major Media Campaigns*; *International Directory of Company Histories*; *Companies and Their Brands*; *Advertising Red Books*; *Hoover's Handbooks*; *Mergent Online*; *Factiva*; *New Competitor Intelligence*; *Internet Intelligence Index*; (See also Annual Reports to Shareholders and periodical articles)
Consumer demographics	Chapter 5	*American FactFinder (Census of Population and Housing)*; New Strategist publications; *American Demographics* magazine; *TableBase*; *County & City Extra*; *Current Population Survey*; *Demographic Sourcebooks*; *Right Site*; PRIZM
Country information	Chapter 11	*World Factbook*; *Country Report*; *Country Study series*; *CountryWatch*; *Global Competitiveness Report*; *Political Risk Yearbook*; *CultureGrams*
Direct marketing	Chapter 10	*Statistical Factbook (DMA)*; *State of the List Industry Report*; *Direct Marketing List Sources*; *Direct Marketing Market Place*; *SRDS Direct Marketing List Source*
Distribution and logistics	Chapter 12	Council of Logistics Management; *LogisticsWorld*; *Loglinks*; *LogisticsZone*
Economic data	Chapter 2, 11	*Economic Census*; *Business Statistics of the U.S.*; *BizStats.com*; *TableBase*; *World Economic Outlook*; *World Economic and Social Survey*

Marketing Concept	Chapter Discussion(s), generally . . .	Particularly these sources . . . - Check the Title Index for page numbers - Sources are arranged for usefulness and availability - Some titles are discussed in multiple chapters
E-commerce	Chapter 10	*E-Stats*; *Gale Encyclopedia of E-Commerce*; *Plunkett's E-Commerce and Internet Business Almanac*; SRDS *Interactive Advertising Source*; *Ecommerce-guide.com*
Encyclopedias and Dictionaries	Chapter 1	*IEBM Encyclopedia of Marketing*; *Beacham's Marketing Reference*; *Marketing Glossary*; *Marketing: The Encyclopedic Dictionary*
Ethics of marketing	Chapter 13	*Advertising Law and Ethics*; *Marketing Ethics Web Sites*; *Marketing Ethics Guidelines for Managers*; *Marketing Ethics: An International Perspective*
Ethnic consumers	Chapter 6	*Marketing to the Emerging Minorities*; *Minority Buying Power in the New Century*; *Buying Power of Black America*; *Hispanic Media & Marketing Source*; *Hispanic Market Report*; *Ethnic Media Directory* (See also periodical articles)
Exporting	Chapter 11	*Exporters' Encyclopedia*; *U.S. Government Export Portal*; *Export Sales and Marketing Manual*; *Export Advantage*
Financial ratios for industries	Chapter 2	*BizStats.com*; *RMA Statement Studies*
Gay and lesbian consumers	Chapter 6	*Commercial Closet*; *GAYDAR*; *Gay Media Database*; *Gay/Lesbian Consumer Online Census*
Geographic target marketing	Chapter 5	*Survey of Buying Power & Media Markets*; *Demographic Sourcebooks*; *Rand McNally Commercial Atlas & Marketing Guide*; *Right Site*; *Places, Towns and Townships*; PRIZM
Handbooks	Chapter 1	*Handbook of Marketing* (Sage); Dartnell publications
Industry Information	Chapter 2	*Encyclopedia of American Industries*; *Industry Surveys* (S&P); *Value Line Investment Survey*; *Current Industrial Reports*; *Research Bank Web*; *U.S. Business Reporter*; *Economic Census*; *STAT-USA*; *Zapdata*
International advertising	Chapter 11	*Advertising Red Books–International Advertisers and Agencies*; *International Media Guides*;

(continued)

Marketing Concept	Chapter Discussion(s), generally . . .	Particularly these sources . . . - Check the Title Index for page numbers - Sources are arranged for usefulness and availability - Some titles are discussed in multiple chapters
		Euromonitor, *World Advertiser & Agency Database;* *World Advertising Trends;* WARC's *Pocket Books;* *Zenithmedia.com;* *More Advertising Worldwide*
International market research	Chapter 11	*Country Commercial Guides;* *Market Research Reports* (International Trade Administration); *STAT-USA;* *International Marketing Data and Statistics;* *Euromonitor,* *Global Market Information Database;* *World Marketing Data and Statistics*
Internet metrics and statistics	Chapter 10	*Internet Economic Indicators;* *CyberAtlas;* *E-Stats;* *Nua Surveys*
Legal issues	Chapters 7, 11, 13	*LexisNexis;* *AdLaw.com;* *Advertising Law;* *Advertising Law and Ethics;* *Advertising World;* Federal Trade Commission; *Uniform Commercial Code;* Robinson-Patman Act; *Exporters' Encyclopedia;* *U.S. Government Export Portal;* *Export Reference Library;* *International Trade Report;* *Investing, Licensing and Trade Conditions;* *How to Get Your Business on the Web*
Lifestyle information	Chapter 5	*Lifestyle Market Analyst;* ESRI BIS' *ACORN* (See also their *Demographic Sourcebooks*); PRIZM
Market research companies	Chapter 4	*GreenBook;* *Worldwide Directory of Market Research Companies and Services;* *Worldwide Directory of Focus Group Companies and Services*
Market research reports	Chapter 5	*MarketResearch.com;* *ECNext Knowledge Center,* *Mindbranch.com;* *Profound;* *Research Alert Yearbook;* *American Demographics* magazine (See also periodical articles)
Market segments	Chapter 2	*Encyclopedia of American Industries;* *Standard & Poor's Industry Surveys;* *Competia;* *Current Industrial Reports;* *U.S. Market Trends & Forecasts;* (See also periodical articles)

Marketing Concept	Chapter Discussion(s), generally . . .	Particularly these sources . . . - Check the Title Index for page numbers - Sources are arranged for usefulness and availability - Some titles are discussed in multiple chapters
Market share	Chapter 3	*TableBase*; *Market Share Reporter*; *U.S. Market Trends and Forecasts*; *Business Rankings Annual*; *SI: Special Issues*; *World Market Share Reporter*; *Global Market Share Planner*; *Market Share Tracker*
Media planning	Chapter 7	SRDS (various sources); WARC's *Pocket Books*
Media preferences of consumers	Chapters 5, 7	*Lifestyle Market Analyst*; *Simmons National Consumer Survey*; *Mediamark Reporter*; CMR (various services)
New product development	Chapter 12	*PDMA Handbook of New Product Development*; *NewProductWorks.com*; (See also books and periodical articles)
Outdoor Advertising	Chapter 7	SRDS' *Out-of-Home Advertising Source*; CMR (various services)
Packaging	Chapter 12	*Packaginginfo.com*; *Packexpo.com*; *Rauch Guide to the U.S. Packaging Industry*; *Handbook of Package Engineering*; (See also books and periodical articles)
Periodical articles	Chapter 1	*ABI/Inform*; *Business Source Premier*; *Business & Industry*; *Business Periodicals*; *Factiva*; *LexisNexis*
Pricing	Chapter 12	Professional Pricing Society; Export Institute USA; *Basic Guide to Exporting* (ITA); *Business Development Success Series* (See also books and periodical articles)
Psychographics	Chapter 5	*Lifestyle Market Analyst*; PRIZM; ESRI BIS' *ACORN*
Public relations	Chapter 8	Public Relations Society of America; *O'Dwyer's Directory of Public Relations Firms*; *Burrelle's Media Directory*; Bacon's Information Service
Retail Industry	Chapters 2, 9	*American Wholesalers & Distributors Directory*; *Manufacturing & Distribution USA*; *Editor & Publisher Market Guide*; *Plunkett's Retail Industry Almanac*; *Standard & Poor's Industry Surveys*; *Shopping Center Directory*; *Retail Tenant Directory*; *Sheldon's Major Stores, Chains & Resident Buying Offices*

(continued)

Marketing Concept	Chapter Discussion(s), generally . . .	Particularly these sources . . . - Check the Title Index for page numbers - Sources are arranged for usefulness and availability - Some titles are discussed in multiple chapters
Sales data for demographic groups	Chapter 5	*American Marketplace* (and other New Strategist publications); *Consumer Expenditure Survey*; *Consumer USA*
Sales data by geography	Chapters 2, 3, 5, 9	*Census of Retail Trade*; *Retail Sales Survey*; *County Business Patterns*; *Commodity Line Sales*; *Merchandise Line Sales (Economic Census)*; *Survey of Buying Power and Media Markets*; *Demographic Sourcebooks* (ESRI BIS); PRIZM
Sales data by industry and/or product	Chapters 5, 9	*Census of Retail Trade*; *Retail Sales Survey*; *County Business Patterns*; *Consumer USA*; *Market Share Reporter*; *Business Rankings Annual*; *TableBase*
Sales promotion	Chapter 9	*Directory of Premium, Incentive & Travel Buyers*
Sales management	Chapter 9	*Dartnell's Salesforce Compensation Survey*
Social marketing	Chapter 13	Social Marketing Institute; Social Marketing Network; *Tools of Change*
Services marketing	Chapter 13	*Handbook of Services Marketing and Management*; *Delivering Quality Service*; *Journal of Services Marketing*
Television commercials	Chapter 7	*Encyclopedia of Major Marketing Campaigns*; *Advertising Age Encyclopedia of Advertising*; AdReview.com; AdForum.com; *Commercial Closet*; *Television Commercial Monitoring Report*
Trade Shows	Chapter 9	TSNN.com; *Trade Show Week Online*; *International Tradeshow Directory*; *Trade Shows Worldwide*

PART I

INTRODUCTION

Chapter 1

Introduction to Sources and Strategies for Research on Marketing

Topics

Overview of Business Information
Business Libraries
Research Strategies
Copyright and Fair Use
Staying Current
Guides to Marketing Information Sources
Dictionaries
Encyclopedias
Finding Books and Articles
Searching Periodical Databases
General Business Periodical Databases
Specialized Business Search Systems
Statistics and Tables
World Wide Web
The Web and Professional Associations
Videos and DVDs
Classic Texts and Other Scholarly Materials

[Haworth co-indexing entry note]: "Introduction to Sources and Strategies for Research on Marketing." Diamond, Wendy, and Michael R. Oppenheim. Co-published simultaneously in *Journal of Business & Finance Librarianship* (The Haworth Information Press, an imprint of The Haworth Press, Inc.) Vol. 9, No. 2/3, 2004, pp. 3-37; and: *Marketing Information: A Strategic Guide for Business and Finance Libraries* (Wendy Diamond, and Michael R. Oppenheim) The Haworth Information Press, an imprint of The Haworth Press, Inc., 2004, pp. 3-37. Single or multiple copies of this article are available for a fee from The Haworth Document Delivery Service [1-800-HAWORTH, 9:00 a.m. - 5:00 p.m. (EST). E-mail address: docdelivery@haworthpress.com].

http://www.haworthpress.com/web/JBFL
© 2004 by The Haworth Press, Inc. All rights reserved.
Digital Object Identifier: 10.1300/J109v09n02_01

Sources

Encyclopedia of Business Information Sources
Marketing Information: A Professional Guide
Where to Go Who to Ask
Blackwell Encyclopedic Dictionary of Marketing
Marketing: The Encyclopedic Dictionary
Dictionary of Marketing and Advertising
The Marketing Glossary
IEBM Encyclopedia of Marketing
Beacham's Marketing Reference
ABI/Inform
Business Source Premier
Business & Industry
Business Periodicals
PROMT
Factiva
LexisNexis
Dialog
Datastar
.xls
World Advertising Research Center
TableBase
Statistical Reference Index
Marketing Classics: A Selection of Influential Articles
Marketing Science Institute. Working Paper Series

This chapter provides the foundation for the more specialized chapters that follow. It covers such basic reference tools as information guides, bibliographies, dictionaries, encyclopedias, periodical indexes, and the World Wide Web, and also explains fundamental research concepts and skills. It is assumed that users of this guide are "online" and "connected" to the World Wide Web. If not, it is possible to use public libraries or most local academic libraries to gain access. Many provide terminals and network connections, as well as librarians who can explain the basics of logging on, entering Web addresses ("URLs"), and searching. Increasingly, public libraries also offer workshops and seminars to teach these skills.

Marketing is a complex set of specific business functions, a strategy for profit making companies, a promotional tool for all kinds of organizations, and an academic discipline. Because it is all these things, and more, it has many definitions. The official definition used by the American Marketing Association (AMA) is: "Marketing is the process of planning and executing the conception, pricing, promotion, and distribution of ideas, goods, and services to create exchanges that satisfy individual and organizational goals." This definition first appeared in *Marketing News* on March 1, 1985, and was adopted by AMA's Board of Directors and published in its *Dictionary of Marketing Terms*, 2nd edition, edited by Peter D. Bennett (AMA 2002).

In the *IEBM International Encyclopedia of Marketing*, editor Michael J. Baker conceptualizes marketing as a "business philosophy, guiding an organization's direction and development, and as a business function, enhancing both efficiency and effectiveness in the execution of an organization's mission." Marketing is "a concept that is concerned with the creation of mutually satisfying exchange relationships" (Baker 1999, xii). Modern business has evolved from a traditional, company-centric focus on production and sales to a more customer-centric one, whereby companies seek to fulfill both explicit and implicit needs and wants. This customer relationship is the arena of marketing.

Modern marketing's strategic emphasis is expressed in the well-known "Four Ps" of the marketing mix. These define the primary functional areas as Promotion (communication with customers), Product (fulfilling needs and wants of customers), Pricing (exchanging with customers), and Place (distributing to customers). The complexity of modern marketing is revealed by the refraction of each of the "Ps" into multiple aspects and subtopics. "Promotion" includes everything from media buying to couponing to public relations; "place" includes everything from supply chain management to direct mail to e-commerce retailing; and "pricing" and "product management" encompass activities to maximize results with niche markets and relationships with customers. Each marketing specialty area has its own information needs, a body of literature, and a set of basic tools to which to refer.

TIP: "The Four Ps of the Marketing Mix"

The first use of the phrase was in 1960 by E. Jerome McCarthy in *Basic Marketing: A Managerial Approach* (Homewood, IL: Irwin). Neil H. Borden published an expanded checklist version in "The Concept of the Marketing Mix," published in the *Journal of Advertising Research* in 1964 (Borden 1964). Since that time, the Four Ps, Promotion, Product, Pricing, and Place, have been used as a paradigmatic definition of marketing in textbooks and teaching. The Four Ps have been expanded to include additional components, and current authors may speak of the Six Ps, Eight Ps ("process," "productivity"), the Rs ("relationships") and the Cs ("customer care"). Underscoring the complexity of today's marketing environment, these additional elements incorporate still greater focus on customers, service, and relationships (Kotler and Armstrong 2001, 68).

Most marketing specialties will require research, information, data, and analysis for decision-making and planning. Marketing research, like other categories of business research, can be a challenging and perplexing activity. Although it is not brain surgery or rocket science, sometimes finding the right answer can seem as urgent as a life-and-death situation, or as mysterious as sending a huge machine into outer space. After all, profits–the literal lifeblood of business enterprise–depend on it. The catch phrase "time is money" is never truer than when dealing with any kind of business information. Although timing can seem to be paramount, finding the *right* information is the key challenge. This book is an information guide that will both save you time and lead you to the right information, thereby improving your business decisions, planning, and problem-solving.

OVERVIEW OF BUSINESS INFORMATION

An understanding of the special forms and structure of business information will promote the effective utilization of it, whether for a marketing plan, term paper, competitive analysis, or any other research project. The very fact that business information is used as a profit-making tool is the driving force behind many publications. Often information is available simply because it is so saleable and desirable. As Michael Lavin puts it,

> Literally, any type of business information can be published, no matter how unlikely. Since information can be the key to business success, managers are usually willing to pay for it when the need arises. . . . Never assume information is unavailable just because its existence seems unreasonable. (Lavin 1992, 6-7)

However, as Lavin also points out, some information is proprietary, very expensive, and available only to bona-fide subscribers, citing two well-known examples in the Arbitron radio and television ratings and the Multiple Listing Service used by realtors (Lavin 1992, 5). Some information can also be *so* valuable that it is effectively unavailable to the average researcher. It helps to ask oneself: Why would someone provide a certain piece of information? What is its value to someone using it to make money? Is it particularly time- or labor-intensive to gather, valuable for profit making purposes, and/or competitive positioning? If so, it is likely to be expensive. At the other end of the spectrum, if it is likely to be useful to a government agency for economic or regulatory reasons, then it may be available at no charge.

The foregoing factors have important implications for the ease of locating and using business information. First and foremost, there is a huge volume of it. Second, its sources are fragmented, ranging from government agencies, to commercial publishers, to professional associations, to other advocacy groups. Frustratingly, the most valuable information may be proprietary, or at the least, very expensive (Butler and Diamond 2001).

Generally, business information is most useful when it is current and timely. There is a lifecycle to business information that dictates the type of "packet" in which it appears. Thinking about information in terms of its stage in the life cycle can be helpful in discovering where to look for a particular item. Both timeliness and reliability have a high value, and to some extent there is an inverse relationship between these two dimensions. At the earliest stages of the information life cycle, such as raw news and press releases, timeliness presents the greatest value but reliability may be low. With the Internet, raw data are disseminated continuously and easily but, as most people understand, with questionable reliability. As a piece of information moves along its life cycle, there is time for discussion and verification. At the next stage, the information appears in business newspapers, magazines, and newsletters, with added commentary and data (Ojala 1996, 79). Eventually, it may end up in a book, scholarly journal article, or published in a conference proceeding.

Another form of raw data is produced by government agencies. These sources are considered most reliable and authoritative, but they are often published in formats with limited features and convenience. Because almost all government information is in the public domain, it is common for private publishers to re-publish it with "value-added" features. Scholarly publications, such as journal articles and conference proceedings, are also known for high authority value, but they are generally lower on the timeliness scale. Books take the longest to research and produce, but they can range in authority depending on whether the work may be scholarly, published by a well-reputed firm, authored by an expert, or other factors.

It is important to note that all information "packages"–raw news, press releases, newspaper and magazine articles, proceedings, government reports, scholarly journal articles, and even books–may appear both in print and online. It is not the *physical* format per se that is crucial, but rather whether a format is appropriate for the information being conveyed.

The forms of business information "packages" are diverse. Though most are not unique to business, some forms are more common than they may be in other fields. The familiar, prosaic *list* is a basic form of information that is very commonly used in business. Directories of companies are a prime example of lists, and there are directory titles covering virtually every specialty. Because business is a competitive field, rankings, a form of list that offers a comparative measurement dimension, have a prominent role. The index number is another typical quantitative form which represents a "measure of relative value compared with a base quantity" (Shim and Siegel 1995, 180). The Consumer Price Index, issued by the federal Bureau of Labor Statistics, is the most well-known example, but marketers often use index numbers to express a relationship between ranked items, such as sales potential in geographic regions.

Qualitative, narrative forms that blend analysis, assessment, commentary, and review with charts, tables, graphs, and rankings are especially highly valued. Overviews are a common configuration that is used to present in-depth, detailed factual material in a concise form. The term "report" can be used in its most commonly-understood meaning, or it can convey a particular blend of narrative analysis and quantitative data, such as that found in investment analyst and market research reports. The "white paper," a term originally used by governments and later made popular in scientific communities, is another report form often used for lengthy reports, particularly those with a technical, investigative, or advocacy component.

Marketing is both a practitioner and an academic field, and there is a symbiotic relationship between the two perspectives. Academic researchers provide a theoretical foundation. Practitioners synthesize this theory with real-world applications to develop "best practices." Academic researchers, in turn, refer back to real world data and examples in the form of quantitative studies, case studies, and analysis in order to teach students to become professionals and to develop additional areas of research.

Case studies and handbooks are formats used to convey concrete concepts and practical applications of theoretical ideas. The former are often used in textbooks and courses to focus on company-level examples and real-world solutions to problems. Case studies also continue to be an important form of publication in the practitioner environment, and are often published as articles for professional audiences. Similarly practical in purpose, handbooks are a special type of reference book that combines some characteristics of articles, how-to guides, encyclopedias, and even statistical abstracts and directories. The best handbooks provide overview, background, in-depth discussion, and references to further reading in addition to hands-on, practical advice. They can be used by the novice to gain insight into the knowledge base of professional specialists, while at the same time guiding the expert to more detailed information. Many chapters throughout this book refer to excellent handbooks on a particular sub-specialty of marketing. In this introductory chapter we discuss some useful examples and provide strategies for locating others.

TIP: Fives Ways to Find Case Studies

1. *Books in online library catalogs*

- "Case Studies" is a Library of Congress subheading, typically used in most library catalogs. For example: "marketing–case studies" or "pricing–case studies."
- Use "case studies" (and variants) as a keyword combined with a topic term. For example: "sports marketing and case studies" *or* "sports marketing and cases."

2. *Periodical articles*

- *ABI/INFORM* (ProQuest; also available on Dialog, and other database systems).

ABI/INFORM is well known for its article treatment subject headings and classification codes: for example, "electronic commerce and case studies." In addition to subject headings, *ABI* also employs numeric codes to represent topics. The classification code ("cc") for "company specific/case studies" is 9110. An example is "brand management and cc(9110)." (Note that the exact format will vary depending on the database system.)

- *Business & Management Practices* (Gale Group; also available on OCLC First Search and other database systems). This index includes Article Type limits for "case study" and Department Phrase limits for "marketing and sales."

3. *On the Web for free*

- OrgScience Web Site. Charles Booth. 2002. *Resources on Using the Case Method in Business & Management Education.* Contact: http://www.geocities.com/orgscience/case.htm.
- Many companies put their own case studies on their Web pages in "portable document format" (PDF) as a promotional and/or training tool. A PDF document looks just like a typeset, printed version. *Google* (http://google.com) is one of the Web search engines that retrieves text formats, and it is possible to limit your results to items in this format: for example, "e-commerce case study pdf".

4. *On the Web for purchase*

- Emerald. Contact: http://www.emeraldinsight.com/partnerships/courseware.htm. (A subscription service for courseware and e-learning.)
- European Case Clearing House (ECCH). Contact: http://www.ecch.cranfield.ac.uk/. (Registration is required to place orders for cases.)
- Harvard Business Online. Contact: http://harvardbusinessonline.hbsp.harvard.edu. (This site sells Harvard Business School cases in online and print formats.)

5. *Monograph collections*

- Kerin, Roger A. and Robert A. Peterson. 2000. *Strategic Marketing Problems: Cases and Comments.* 9th Edition. Upper Saddle River, NJ: Prentice Hall.
- Bernhardt, Kenneth L. and Thomas C. Kinnear. 1997. *Cases in Marketing Management.* 7th Edition. New York: McGraw Hill.

TIP: Locating Handbooks

- For a keyword search in an online library catalog, combine "handbook" with a term describing your topic. For example, "handbook and relationship marketing."
- For a subject search in an online library catalog, use the subheading "handbooks, manuals, etc." For example, "marketing management-handbooks, manuals, etc."

TIP: Selected Marketing Handbook

Sage Publications has recently issued an overview of the field of marketing with contributions from leading scholars. Contact: http://www.sagepub.com. For example:

- Weitz, Barton A. and Robin Wensley. 2002. *Handbook of Marketing*. 582 pages.

Dartnell has published professional materials since 1917 and offers many handbooks geared to marketing and sales. Contact: http://www.dartnellcorp.com. For example:

- Block, Tamara Brezen and William A. Robinson.1994. *Sales Promotion Handbook*. 8th edition.
- Dilenschneider, Robert L. and Dan J. Forrestal. 1996. *Public Relations Handbook*. 4th edition.
- Levy, Sidney, Howard Gordon, and George Frerichs. 1994. *Marketing Manager's Handbook*. 3rd edition.
- Stansfield, Richard H. 1997. *Advertising Manager's Handbook*. 4th edition.

BUSINESS LIBRARIES

Business information cannot be discussed without including business libraries, a traditional "purveyor" of business information and still a locus for expert advice about this specialized area of research. Throughout this book, we refer to certain sources as "typically available in public and academic libraries." This phrase is intended to highlight sources which the authors, both of whom are academic business librarians, know to be commonly available in business departments of public libraries or in college and university libraries supporting degree programs in business. In the public library sector, there are only a very few entire libraries devoted exclusively to business. New York Public Library's Science, Industry and Business Library (SIBL) is the preeminent example. Throughout the rest of the United States, many large municipal or county library systems have a major reference department serving the business community. These are more likely than small neighborhood branches to own the most specialized sources. In any case, it is always worth calling a local branch to ask a librarian whether a specific resource may be available and, if not, what would be the best regional library for business information, or whether interlibrary borrowing is possible.

In some cases, the best local library will be an academic library serving students and faculty involved in learning and teaching business subjects. Within academic libraries, there are some distinctions. The most extensive collections are generally located in separate business libraries serving universities with MBA and doctoral programs. An important caveat is that some are private and not open to the public, or even if they are open, some resources may be restricted to currently enrolled students and faculty only. College libraries serving even undergraduate business programs will have many business reference resources, though again some may be restricted.

Another type of business library is known as the "special library." Often called "information centers," these are libraries that support the information needs of corporations, associations, or agencies. Because they are rarely open to the general public, they cannot be considered an access point, but nonetheless they play an important role. Many of the sources named in this book, as well as additional sources, are likely to be available in the marketing collections of corporate libraries, or in information centers of advertising agencies. Furthermore, special librarians are likely to be the most knowledgeable specialists in the intricacies of business research and the hundreds of available databases. If you are an employee of a corporation with a well-staffed library or information center, do not overlook this valuable resource.

RESEARCH STRATEGIES

In order to find the right information, you must start with defining a research problem. First, determine whether you are researching companies, or industries and products, or management theory and practice, or the general business climate. Each of these categories has particular business information tools. For company research, there are directories and annual reports; for industry research, there are industry overviews and statistics; for management practice, there are handbooks and "best practice" guidelines; and for the general business climate, there are economic reports from government and commercial analysts. Second, determine whether specific or comparative information is needed: do you need to find out about the marketing strategy of one particular company, or retrieve a ranked list of several apparel manufacturers?

The next useful question is whether quantitative or narrative information is needed: for example, do you need statistical data showing sales revenue in the retail apparel industry or do you need an analysis of retailing technologies? Next, determine the timeframe required. Are you seeking current information, or does the project require historical trend data? Do you also require projections and future forecasts?

You will also need to consider whether you require primary or secondary information. Primary information is information collected and generated directly, and might include personal telephone calls to experts or compiling a spreadsheet report of a company's sales. Secondary information is that which you gather from existing sources, such as company memos or commercial publishers. In *Business Information: How to Find It, How to Use It*, Michael Lavin (1992, 5) provides a useful matrix that distinguishes between internal or external and primary or secondary information. Lavin points out that secondary information is generally easier to acquire and less costly than primary data. In particular, understanding how to research and "mine" external secondary information is an often overlooked tool for business success.

After you have analyzed your business problem, and have determined whether you need comparative or specific information, narrative or quantitative, historical, current, or future data, you are ready to start looking for the right information. Using this book, review the discussion of the sources in each topic to find the type of information that meets your criteria. In addition, it is important not to overlook the general sources that do not focus on any one particular aspect of marketing, which are discussed in this chapter. Although these general sources might seem to be unfocused, they actually contain information about many different topics. Many of them will contain just the right nugget for your particular information need, but that can only be recognized at the moment that you need it.

The last crucial step in your research strategy is evaluating and critically assessing the information you have found for its currency, accuracy, and usefulness. This has always been true, but the Internet requires a slightly different set of criteria because anyone can publish anything on the Web. Without the usual controls and review processes of commercial or academic publication, the user must consciously consider some essential questions in order to determine the authority and reliability of the information, especially if it is to be used for decision making purposes. Is there a named author or producer? What is the primary purpose of the Web site–to sell or promote, to educate, or to advocate? Does the purpose alter the objectivity of the information provided? Is there a date of creation or revision? Can you ascertain whether the information is current or out-of-date? Is there a bibliography or list of sources cited where information can be verified and leads followed? Finally, is the Web site organized well with few typographical errors?

TIP: Criteria for Critically Evaluating Web Sites

If it is impossible or difficult to answer many of the following questions about a Web site, you need to be cautious in using the information found there.

- Authority: Is there an author, organization, or institution clearly identified with the Web site? Is there contact information provided, such as a physical address, telephone number, or e-mail? Does the producer of the Web site have credible qualifications of expertise on the topic?
- Objectivity: What is the main purpose of the Web site–to inform, educate, persuade, or sell? Is there a discernible opinion or point-of-view implicit in the presentation? If it is a commercial Web site, how does the site generate income? Are listings provided to companies as a form of advertising, and if so does this impact the legitimacy of the information?
- Currency: Is the information up-to-date? Is the date of creation and revision clearly given?
- Accuracy: How does the information at the Web site correlate with other known facts? Are sources of statistical data given? Is data cited in sources that can be accessed, such as secondary government information, or are only internal sources listed? How does this information compare with other sources?
- Organization and graphics: Is the Web site well-organized and easy to read? Are there typographical and spelling errors that can indicate a low standard of production quality?

TIP: Research Strategies in a Nutshell

Determining the answer to these questions helps define the research problem.

Step 1–What are you researching? Companies? Industries or products? Management theories or practices? General business climate?

Step 2–Do you need *specific* information about one particular company, product, or theory? Is *comparative* information needed about various companies, products, or theories?

Step 3–Does the project require *quantitative* (numerical, statistical) information or *qualitative* (narrative, analytical) information or both?

Step 4–What is the *time frame* required? Do you need historical trends, current data, or future projections?

Step 5–Do you need to perform you own *primary* research or can the information be gathered from *secondary* sources?

Step 6–Critically evaluate the information found for currency, accuracy, and usefulness.

COPYRIGHT AND FAIR USE

Copyright requires that you ascertain the owner of the information and get permission before reproducing or distributing it. Some business information providers are extremely strict about their proprietary material and it is wise to err on the side of caution should there be any doubt about the appropriate use of material. Nonprofit educational users may distribute material under the doctrine of "fair use," which requires adherence to certain standards of purpose, nature, amount and substantiality, and effect. However, according to the *Digital Millennium Copyright Act of 1998* (Public Law 105-304), known as the *DMCA*, the Internet is not necessarily considered the equivalent of a classroom. Although exemptions for distance education and nonprofit libraries and archives are mentioned in the law, it is not always entirely clear that educational fair use applies in the electronic environment. Again, it is wise to be cautious and request permission from copyright holders if there is any doubt.

TIP: More Information on Copyright, Fair Use, and the DMCA

Crews, Kenneth D. *Copyright Essentials for Librarians and Educators.* Chicago, IL: American Library Association, 2000.

Harper, Georgia K. University of Texas. *The Copyright Crash Course.* ©2001. http://www.utsystem.edu/ogc/intellectualproperty/cprtindx.htm.

Indiana University-Purdue University Indianapolis. Copyright Management Center. ©2002. http://www.iupui.edu/~copyinfo/fairuse.html.

Snowhill, Lucia. University of California, Santa Barbara. *Information Resources on Copyright.* http://www.library.ucsb.edu/subj/copyrt.html.

State University of New York at Albany. *Intellectual Property, Copyright, and Fair Use Resources.* Updated June 28, 2002. http://www.iupui.edu/~copyinfo/fairuse.html.

United States. Copyright Office Summary. *Digital Millennium Copyright Act of 1998.* http://www.loc.gov/copyright/legislation/dmca.pdf.

STAYING CURRENT

The time value of business information makes the issue of currency extremely important. The dynamism and volatility of the information landscape also makes currency even more challenging. No single route is right for all circumstances, but using information tools can help. Just as encyclopedias are an excellent means of exploring seminal literature in a field, newsletters are used by many professionals to keep up to date with current developments. The guides to marketing information sources given below are good places to start to identify newsletters in a particular field or specific area of interest. In addition, the Web offers electronic discussion lists ("listservs") and bulletin boards, such as those offered by professional associations and "vertical" business-to-business Web portals.

TIP: Staying Current with Business Information

If you are interested in tracking developments in the world of business information, these are a few of the tools used by professional searchers and business librarians.

- *Business Information Alert* (Chicago, IL: Alert Publications, Inc. Monthly. Print.) Contact: http://www.alertpub.com.
- *BusLib-L.* (Business librarians' electronic discussion). Contact: http://listserv.boisestate.edu/archives/buslib-l.html.

- *EContent Magazine* (Wilton, CT: Online, Inc. Monthly. Print or Online). Contact: http://www.ecmag.net.
- *The Information Advisor* (New York, NY: Find/SVP. Print. Monthly. Edited by Robert Berkman.) Contact: http://www.informationadvisor. com.
- *Link-Up.* (Medford, NJ: Information Today Inc. Six issues. Print.) Contact: http:www.infotoday.com.
- *Super Searchers* [book series]. (Medford, NJ: Information Today Inc.) Contact: http://www.infotoday.com/supersearchers.
- *Virtual Acquisition Shelf and News Desk.* (Compiled by Gary Price, MLIS. Online.) Contact: http://resourceshelf.freepint.com.

GUIDES TO MARKETING INFORMATION SOURCES

Like the book you are holding in your hand, the following sources are designed to lead you to essential and important information resources. They identify basic texts, subject-specific indexes and encyclopedias, special interest newsletters, major databases, statistical compendia, and more.

Encyclopedia of Business Information Sources. Annual. Farmington Hills, MI: Gale Group. Print $355. Contact: http://www.galegroup. com.

This well-reputed business reference tool identifies and describes directories, encyclopedias, databases, associations, trade journals, and newsletters in many business sub-specialties. In marketing, there are headings for retailing, sales and salesmanship, mature consumer market, etc.

Marketing Information: A Professional Guide. Hiram C. Barksdale and Jac L. Goldstucker. 3rd edition. Chicago: American Marketing Association, 1996. Print $150. 488 pages. Contact: http://www. marketingpower.com.

Written by two professors of marketing, this is an excellent guide to reference resources and major texts in marketing specialties. Despite the age of the book, its extensive and knowledgeable annotations guide the user to seminal and significant literature in the field.

***Where to Go Who to Ask (A Gale Ready Reference Handbook).* Carolyn A. Fischer, editor. Farmington Hills, MI: Gale Group, 2000. Print $145. Contact: http:/www.galegroup.com.**

This reference is designed for quick look-ups of contact information for thousands of associations, publications, databases, agencies, research centers, and organizations. Arranged by subject/keyword, it is especially useful for the list of specialized newsletters under the subject heading "marketing."

DICTIONARIES

Marketing is a dynamic and evolving field which generates a significant amount of "terms of art," jargon, and specialized uses of words so dictionaries have an obvious utility. Here are a few recently published works.

- *The Blackwell Encyclopedic Dictionary of Marketing* (Barbara R. Lewis and Dale Littler. Oxford, U.K.: Blackwell Publishers, 1999. 274 pages).
- *Marketing: The Encyclopedic Dictionary* (David Mercer. Oxford, U.K.: Blackwell Publishers, 1999. 422 pages).
- *Dictionary of Marketing and Advertising* (Jerry M. Rosenberg. New York: John Wiley, 1995. 371 pages).
- *The Marketing Glossary* (Mark N. Clemente. New York: AMACOM, 1992. 392 pages).

ENCYCLOPEDIAS

When encountering a topic for the first time, it is often useful to gain a background understanding of fundamental terminology and concepts that are well-known within the specialty. Subject-specific encyclopedias go beyond merely defining terms by explaining the development of major ideas and providing citations to further reading. The bibliographies found in encyclopedias guide the user to seminal literature and other important writing on the topic and can be an excellent means of starting a research project, especially in an unfamiliar area.

***IEBM Encyclopedia of Marketing.* Michael J. Baker, editor. Florence, KY: International Thomson Business Press, 1999. 865 pages. $150.**

Editor Michael J. Baker, emeritus faculty member of the University of Strathclyde, has gathered contributions from 75 authors for this recently revised reference book. It provides a "combination textbook and reference source" for "deep background" (Karel 2001, 97-98), and offers extensive bibliographies, charts, tables, and detailed explanations of marketing concepts and topics.

Beacham's Marketing Reference. Edited by Walton Beacham, Richard T. Hise, Hale N. Tongren. 2 volumes. Washington DC: Research Publishing, 1986.

Though dated, this encyclopedia is still a useful reference that explains the basic concepts and functions of marketing. Major topic areas include marketing organization and strategy, marketing research and information, consumer characteristics and behavior, target market development, product planning, packaging and branding, distribution, wholesaling, retailing, advertising, publicity and promotion, pricing, and social and ethical marketing. Each is broken down into specific sub-topics. However, other than for seminal literature, the sources cited in the reference bibliographies will need to be updated with current research. The software descriptions are particularly dated, and users should not rely on them for authoritative recommendations.

FINDING BOOKS AND ARTICLES

Books are often overlooked as a source of business information because they tend to be perceived as "out-of-date." However, trade books are still a predominant medium in publishing, and business is no exception. This fact resonates in many of the chapters in this book which include "short reading lists" because trade books are often the best source for background and advice on narrow topics.

Articles in magazines and journals are a highly sought form of business publishing and communication. Articles appear in a diverse variety of publications: newsletters, newspapers, industry trade journals, popular business magazines, and peer-reviewed (scholarly) journals. The diversity of article types is reflected in the diversity of finding tools for locating them.

The "full-text" content of books and articles is generally not available without charge on the Internet, at least not consistently so, though it is possible to find occasionally. Using our paradigm of business information, it should be evident that the production of information and digitizing text is a time-and-labor intensive, value-added activity that is performed by publishers for a fee. Even when fee-based, books are rarely found "full-text" with the exception of services like NetLibrary (see http://www.netlibrary.com) and a few others. Electronic books have yet to take hold and their potential is somewhat uncertain. On the other hand, full-text articles are widely available online in subscription databases, such as those described below.

The "finding tools" for both books and articles are emphatically electronic. Such structured databases as library catalogs and periodical indexes pre-date the Web and employ various features and capabilities. Computerized library catalogs are used to identify books on a particular topic or to locate a specific book by title or author. Most utilize the subject heading system defined by the Library of Congress (LCSH, for Library of Congress Subject Headings). Usually, there are options for "browsing" through an alphabetical list of subject headings and for "searching" using keywords.

TIP: Keyword Searches versus Subject Heading Searches

Search techniques utilizing keyword and defined subject headings can be used together to counteract the common problem of retrieving too much irrelevant material. First, try a keyword search using common language phrases to retrieve some relevant titles. Display the "full record" of the best of these titles and review them to identify the assigned Library of Congress subject heading, which can then be used for further searching. For example, the keyword search *consumer segmentation* would lead to books with assigned subject headings such as "target marketing," "marketing segmentation," and "consumer behavior."

In addition to searching in one's local library catalog, it may be helpful to identify books available in larger libraries. In most cases, a local library will be able to order your selections using Interlibrary Loan, a service, frequently free of charge, that can also be utilized to obtain materials identified in this book and in other guides to the literature.

TIP: Some Large Library Catalogs Available Free on the Web

- CATNYP. Contact: http:catnyp.nypl.org. (The library catalog of the Research Libraries of New York Public Library.)
- Melvyl Catalog (A division of the California Digital Library). Contact: http://www.melvyl.ucop.edu. (Contains the holdings of the nine University of California campuses and other California libraries.)
- Library of Congress Online Catalog. Contact: http://catalog.loc.gov/.
- Gateway to Library Catalogs. Contact: http://www.loc.gov/z3950/.

Sometimes it is more convenient to purchase books than to borrow them from libraries. Online services such as Amazon (http://amazon.com), Barnes and Noble (http:www.barnesandnoble.com), and Powells.com (http://powells.com) have revolutionized the world of bookselling by providing online users with evaluative tools on which to base their selection decisions. For many popular business books, these sites display sample pages, tables of content, indexes, and back cover blurbs. It is especially helpful to read reviews from well-known published sources and by knowledgeable fellow-readers. In addition, for many business-related books, Amazon provides experts' lists of favorite books, a feature that is particularly helpful for a dynamic topic like marketing. Interestingly, Amazon has also become a fulfillment service for the book sale sections of many professional Web sites, such as MarketingPower.com (http://marketingpower.com), the Web site of the American Marketing Association, and Business Nation's business book review service (http://www.businessnation.com/bookreviews/pages/index.html).

SEARCHING PERIODICAL DATABASES

A periodical index is a tool that enables the researcher to pinpoint relevant articles published in a wide array of different magazines and periodicals. Print versions of the *Reader's Guide to Periodical Literature* and *Business Periodicals Index* have saved researchers countless hours of time and frustration, but still required an additional step of retrieving the actual article itself. With computers, searching and retrieval can be combined into one process, and today's periodical databases have expanded to include the complete full text of many–sometimes all–of the cited articles in a database.

Many business libraries will have at least one of the following periodical databases which can be used as an index to locate articles on a specific topic. These are subscription databases that are usually too costly for individuals to consider. Independent researchers and professional information brokers often subscribe to search systems that offer numerous periodical databases at transactional pricing, such as those discussed below in the section "Specialized Business Search Systems."

Although each of the databases listed here has a different navigational system or "front-end software," most offer similar features. Like online library catalogs, they are structured databases that segment individual units of information about the article into "fields." This makes searching more reliable than it is on the Web, but it also requires some knowledge and skill to search effectively. Once learned, these search skills transfer readily to many different databases.

Features Found in Most Periodical Indexes

Keyword Searching

A "keyword" search finds all occurrences of a particular word in a title, subject heading, abstract/summary, or author name. This is useful when you are not sure of the correct subject term and just want to find some articles on your topic.

Subject Searching

Like library catalogs described previously, most periodical indexes employ a structured vocabulary of subject headings (sometimes known as a "thesaurus") in order to gather all similar articles together, thus reducing the need for trying different keyword variants. Many employ a thesaurus designed for the topic area covered by the database, enabling the researcher to perform very accurate searches. It is often possible to "browse" the alphabetical listing of subject headings in the thesaurus in order to select the term that best reflects your particular topic.

Field Searching

Field searching lets you target a search within a particular segment of the description of the article. For example, you could look for the words "niche marketing" in only the article title field. This is often a good way of retrieving the most relevant articles or of restricting your search when you get too many irrelevant "hits."

Truncation and Wildcards

This feature lets the searcher look for variations of words using only the word stem. For example, "advertis*" retrieves advertisement, advertising, advertiser, etc. Each database uses its own truncation symbols, and some have different ways of searching for one letter (useful for plurals) versus searching for unlimited additional letters. Some will also permit a wildcard character to be embedded *within* a word to be searched.

Boolean Combinations

The Boolean logic operators, AND, OR, NOT, allow the searcher to combine or exclude more than one word or phrase in a precise manner. Unlike many Web search engines, most structured databases are designed so that a two-word search is always executed as if the two words are next to each other, in the exact order as typed *unless* the searcher has joined them with AND or OR. Note the difference between these searches: "sports marketing" (no Boolean operator; searches as a phrase); "sports AND marketing" (retrieves articles that have both words in them); "sports OR marketing" (retrieves articles with either term or both). The first search would retrieve the fewest articles, probably those most relevant to sports marketing. The second would retrieve only articles that include *both* words, but not necessarily near each other; the third would retrieve all articles that include either the word sports or the word marketing, a result that would probably be neither manageable nor relevant. On the other hand, OR is useful when you want to include similar concepts or synonyms: for example, "game or toy."

Publication Searches

Periodical databases always include a list of the publications that are indexed. In a full-text database, this list can be used to retrieve a known article using the journal title, volume number, page, and date information, as with a citation from a bibliography or reading list.

GENERAL BUSINESS PERIODICAL DATABASES

One or more of the following databases is likely to be available in academic and public libraries that serve patrons interested in business.

ABI/INFORM. Ann Arbor, MI: ProQuest. 1971-present. Selected full-text and abstracts. Online subscription. Contact: http://www. umi.com/proquest/.

ABI/INFORM, considered the preeminent scholarly business database, is found in many academic and corporate libraries. Its scope of coverage includes peer-reviewed journal literature, trade journals, and the popular business press, including full-text articles from the *Wall Street Journal*. (However, it does not include other newspapers or conference proceedings.) The most complete version of the database includes over 1,800 periodical titles, of which 1,200 are current. Of these, more than 900 are full-text or page-image-with-graphics format. (There is also an Archive database which includes 100 full-text titles from 1918 to 1986 which may be found in some libraries.) In addition, the database has a significant international perspective and includes approximately 350 English language titles from outside the U.S.

The deep back file of older material is unusual in electronic databases, and *ABI/INFORM* is especially appreciated for its extensive and detailed vocabulary of business subject headings (including many related to marketing) and unique article treatment types. Using the latter, it is possible to limit results to articles containing a particular type of information, such as statistical data, case studies, guidelines, or empirical research.

Business Source Premier. Ipswich, MA: EBSCO Information Services. 1965-present. Selected full text and abstracts. Online subscription. Contact: http://www.epnet.com.

Like *ABI/INFORM*, EBSCO's *Business Source Premier* has excellent coverage of scholarly, peer-reviewed journal literature in combination with leading trade journals. According to the "Title Lists" available from the Web site noted above, the database contains 3,807 indexed journals, of which 3,031 are available in full text (and 1,018 of those are peer-reviewed). In the "Sales and Marketing" periodicals category, 108 of the 137 total titles are available in full text. Other content in *Business Source Premier* includes Business Wire News and country reports from the Economist Intelligence Unit, DRI-WEFA, and other well-known publishers (search results sort into the groupings "Scholarly Journals," "Magazine," "Monographs," and "Country Economic Data"). A "Company Profiles" section is separately browsable and searchable–covering both U.S. and international companies, these Datamonitor reports range in length from 20 to 35 pages. EBSCO also offers companion products with somewhat different date and content scope, such as *Business Source Corporate* (3,743 titles indexed and abstracted; 3,346 in full text) and *Business Source Elite* (1,763 titles indexed and abstracted; 1,109 in full text).

Business & Industry. Farmington Hills, MI: Gale Group. 1994-present. Selected full-text and abstracts. Online subscription. Contact: http://www.galegroup.com.

Available in a wide variety of libraries, this database covers approximately 1,300 sources with an emphasis on trade journals, the business press, newsletters, and international and national daily newspapers. It indexes the *Wall Street Journal*, though it is not full-text here. Its vocabulary of subject headings includes terms for such important concepts as market share, industry forecasts, market size, distribution channels, etc.

***Business Periodicals.* Bronx, NY: H.W.Wilson. 1982-present. Selected full text and abstracts. Online subscription. Contact: http://www.hwwilson.com.**

A popular periodical database, *Business Periodicals* covers 594 English-language titles, including trade journals, business magazines, academic journals, and newspapers. It includes indexing for the *Wall Street Journal* and *New York Times* business section. The database is also included on other information systems, such as Dialog, Ovid, Silver Platter, OCLC First Search, and others.

***PROMT–Predicast's Overview of Markets and Technology.* Farmington Hills, MI: Gale Group. Three-year back file plus current year. Full text and abstracts. Online subscription. Contact: http://www.galegroup.com.**

This longstanding database has always been known for its excellent coverage of market and industry information. This is a reliable source for finding market size and share, industry trends, product consumption patterns, and trade opportunities. Its scope is international, with indexing of trade and business journals, industry newsletters, and newspapers, plus it includes summaries from *Investext* investment research reports. *PROMT* is included as part of the suite of resources in Gale Group's *Business & Company Resource Center*, an online subscription service.

SPECIALIZED BUSINESS SEARCH SYSTEMS

The following are information services which provide access to a variety of different data products. They are generally available in many business libraries but may be restricted to affiliated users.

***Factiva.* New York: Dow Jones & Reuters. Date coverage varies. Full-text. Online subscription. Contact: http://www.factiva.com.**

Factiva, an alliance of Dow Jones and Reuters, provides news and business information from approximately 8,000 sources, including trade journals, newsletters, wire services, local and global newspapers, magazines, and broadcast transcripts. Part of the Dow Jones corporate family, it includes access to the full-text of the *Wall Street Journal* and *Barron's* and is the sole source for their online archive. The emphasis is on current, even same-day, news; back files vary for individual publications but most of the coverage begins in the mid 1980s. The searching software allows for industry and geographical limits, which are useful for targeting searches to specific markets, and its international coverage is extensive. *Factiva* offers both academic and corporate packages with various features.

LexisNexis*. Dayton, OH: LexisNexis Group. Online subscription search service. Contact: http://www.lexisnexis.com.

LexisNexis is a high-level online search service used in law offices, newsrooms, corporations, universities, and libraries. One of the publishing arms of Reed Elsevier, it provides access to many different types of information products, including journals and magazines, reference materials (including the *Red Book* advertising directories), legal cases, medical information, public records, and much more. The "nexis.com" service is the news component, including trade publications, magazines, and newspapers. It is international in scope and includes back files of older material. Different subscription packages are available, and there are options for credit card payment by one-time, "pay-as-you-go" searchers.

The following search services are online vendors of a wide array of databases, including indexes, full-text articles, and reference materials. They are aggregators of content provided from other producers and publishers, providing a uniform search interface for huge collections of materials. These systems are generally considered more specialized and are used by professional business searchers, special librarians, and corporate information analysts. In most cases, they are offered by subscription only, but increasingly there are options for one-time use by non-subscribers. In addition, access may be provided at top universities with MBA and doctoral programs in business and economics.

Dialog*. Cary, NC: Dialog. Contact: http:www.dialog.com.

Dialog aggregates hundreds of individual databases from numerous content providers that can be searched via one subscription plan. It is one of the subsidiaries of major information provider Thomson Corporation (also affiliated with Gale Group), and is used by many professional researchers who need a wide variety of specialized materials. It has a significant business component, and includes many of the periodical databases discussed previously, such as PROMT, *ABI/INFORM*, and *Business & Industry*, along with many others.

TIP: Get a Free Preview of the Potential of a *Dialog* Search

Go to: http://www.dialogweb.com/cgi/dwframe?context=databases& href=topics/All/. At this Web site, it is possible to select one of eight major database categories, including "Business," to browse its constituent databases to find out the extent of coverage a search topic–a company name, for example–may have in the databases. Categories within "Business" include company directories; company financials and reports; countries and regions; industries and markets; products; and other sources (such as procurement, or taxation). Once you see which databases (known in *Dialog* as "Files") contain hits for your topic, you can examine the *Dialog* "Blue Sheets" (fully detailed guides to each database) to find out which elements of records are searchable, and how much a particular search is likely to cost. The "Blue Sheets" are viewable on the Web at http://library.dialog.com/bluesheets/.

Datastar. Cary, NC: Dialog. Contact: http://products.dialog.com/ products/datastarweb/index.html.

Datastar is one of *Dialog*'s affiliated products. It specializes in European information and provides hundreds of databases, many focused on business and marketing.

.xls. New York: Alacra Inc. Contact: http://www.xls.com.

Introduced in 1997, *.xls* is a newcomer to the field but it has gained favor by aggregating content from 70 premier business database providers and by providing a means to export the quantitative data into spreadsheets. The emphasis is on financial and investment information, but there is also coverage of demographics and other marketing topics from such market research providers as the Economist Intelligence Unit. Related products include *PortalB*, an indexed, selective gateway to business Web sites, and *CompBook*, a search tool for company information.

World Advertising Research Center. Henley-on-Thames, Oxfordshire, U.K. Online subscription. Contact: http://www.warc.com.

For 40 years, the World Advertising Research Center (WARC) has been a provider of advertising and marketing information to trade associations, industry groups, and corporations through online information services, publishing, and conference planning. Its client base includes advertising agencies, media planners, advertisers, media companies, market research firms, and universities. Its online division provides subscription access to a database of articles, case studies, market research, and conference proceedings compiled from their own publications and those of content partners. These partners include publications like *International Journal of Advertising*, *International Journal of Market Research*, *Advertiser Magazine*, and several research series. The coverage of advertising and marketing topics is deep, with international coverage, particularly for English-speaking and European countries. Marketing topics include best practices, consumer target groups, advertising campaigns and advertisers, brand management, industry sectors, and more. The content providers include many outstanding research organizations in the U.S., U.K., Australia, and New Zealand. WARC itself produces worldwide ad spending data, and its Web site provides some summary tables in PDF format.

STATISTICS AND TABLES

Much business and economic information is quantitative and is best presented as tables, charts, graphs, rankings and the like. Economic data in particular is often reported in *time series* format, a term which refers to the fact that the information is presented in intervals arranged by some time-based frequency (e.g., daily, weekly, annually). Long time series of data are those that include historic depth, which are particularly valued because they enhance statistical certainty in spotting trends and making forecasts for the future.

Many of the databases discussed previously include articles from trade journals and industry newsletters that are likely to include tables and other graphics. In addition, there is a database that specializes in tables and other types of quantitative data.

TIP: Using Statistics and Tables

- Be aware of units of measurement in a table, especially when comparing data from multiple sources. Are figures reported as dollars, percentages, percent change, indexes, or whole numbers?
- Use source notes to identify leads to more detailed and in-depth information. For example, a table of market share data for the textbook publishing industry could lead to an annual special issue devoted to the topic in *Educational Marketer*, a trade journal.
- In his book *Business Information: How to Find It, How to Use It* (2nd edition; Phoenix, AZ: Oryx Press, 1991), Michael R. Lavin offers a comprehensive treatment of business statistics. In addition to defining basic concepts such as averages, percent change, ratios, index numbers, and rankings, there is discussion of advantages and disadvantages, logic, abuses and potential pitfalls of numeric data. This excellent overview is in his Chapter 13, "Introduction to Statistical Reasoning."

TableBase. **Farmington Hills, MI: Gale Group. Online subscription. Weekly updates. Contact: http://www.galegroup.com.**

TableBase is a unique database of tabular material from articles, market research, government reports, and other types of documents. It is extremely useful for researching such topics as market share, rankings, product usage data, and customer demographics. International in scope, it covers about 90 industries with material gleaned from trade journal articles, statistical annuals, investment research reports, trade associations and private research groups. Most tables are pulled from trade journals and newsletters from Gale's other products, particularly *Business & Industry*, and many are linked to the complete article. The strength of this database is its clear, nearly comprehensive indexing and "enhanced" table headings which make it easy to retrieve information with precision. *TableBase* is available through many online vendors, including Dialog (as File 93) and others.

TIP: Using Periodicals Databases to Find Articles Citing Statistics

- Use *ABI/INFORM*'s article treatment codes and headings to locate articles which include statistics, tables, and other quantitative data. For example, key in a search like this:

> - Sports marketing and cc(9140); or like this: sports marketing and statistical data.
> - *Business & Industry* offers document type terms like "industry overview" and "rankings," as well as concept terms like "market size" and "industry forecasts."
> - *Factiva* augments some headline fields with *Business & Industry*'s subject terms "industry overview" and "statistical data include." Thus, you can key in a search using these terms to retrieve excellent results for marketing topics. For example, key a search like this: hotel industry and statistical data; or like this: hotel industry and industry overview.

In addition to trade journals and industry newsletters, the publications of industry and professional associations, research organizations, and other similar entities can be statistical treasure troves. Frequently, a given trade association will be the *only* source of systematically collected and disseminated statistics for the goods or services in question. An easy way to mine such resources is provided by the *Statistical Reference Index (SRI)*, a selective though enormously wide-ranging guide to statistics which are *not* published by the U.S. government or by intergovernmental/nongovernmental organizations.

Statistical Reference Index. Bethesda, MD: LexisNexis Academic and Library Solutions. 1980-present. Monthly, with quarterly and annual cumulations. Print and online (pricing varies). Contact: http://www.cispubs.com.

The statistical publications of more than 1,000 leading trade associations and professional societies, universities and research centers, commercial publishers, and state government agencies are described and analyzed in *SRI*, which began publication in 1980. All types of publications are treated, including periodicals (*Advertising Age, Sales and Marketing Management*, etc.), annuals (*Trends in Advertising, U.S. Hispanic Market*, etc.) and other serials, and one-time publications; many of the titles covered are indexed in no source other than *SRI*. As the subject coverage tends to emphasize economics, business, and industry, *SRI* will usually be found in academic or public libraries serving a high demand for business information; however, the scope of the index encompasses many other fields as well.

The monthly issues and annual bound cumulations of *SRI* come in two parts: one provides the indexing, and the other the comprehensive bibliographic entries and detailed abstracts, including an exhaustive breakdown of all available tables and charts. Entries also provide *SRI*'s unique, recurring accession number for the item described, and note its availability status in the *SRI Microfiche Library* (described in the next paragraph). Indexing is thorough, with access offered by subject (*SRI* uses its own standardized indexing terminology), name, title, issuing source, and publication category. The abstracts are arranged in the following order, by type of publisher: associations; business organizations (such as banks, corporations, or consulting firms, and the like); commercial publishers; independent research organizations; state governments; and university research centers.

TIP: *SRI*'s Controlled Indexing Vocabulary for Advertising and Marketing Topics

The following subject indexing terms of interest to readers of this book are used in *SRI*: advertising; brands and brand names; competition; consumer market segments; customer service; direct marketing; electronic commerce; generic products; labeling; market research; marketing areas; packaging and containers; prices; public relations; retail trade; and sales promotion. Look under the heading "Business and industry" for still more relevant terms.

The *SRI* indexing and abstracting, deservedly renowned for its precision and detail, constitutes a uniquely valuable resource on its own as a discovery tool. The companion *SRI Microfiche Library* adds the value of handy microfiche reproductions of some 90% of the publications cited (due to copyright restrictions, not every item indexed can be reproduced). Each month, the publisher ships new microfiche to correspond to the companion issue of *SRI* (selected periodicals are shipped quarterly, as noted in their abstracts). Most of the filmed publications are reproduced in full; for publications that are not primarily statistical, the publisher films the available statistical tables, charts, and texts only. As alluded to in the preceding paragraph, the abstract entry shows whether a publication has been filmed, either partially or completely, and it provides the specific accession number by which the user will find it filed in the *SRI Microfiche Library*. Unless a publication changes title or issuing body, the same accession number will be used for it year after year.

On the Web, *SRI* is available as part of *LexisNexis Statistical*, formerly known as *Statistical Universe*. With *LexisNexis Statistical*, users can search *SRI* either alone or in combination with its companions, the *American Statistics Index* (*ASI*; comprehensive indexing of all statistics published by the U.S. government, from 1973 forward) and the *International Index of Statistics* (*ISI*; indexing of a wide-ranging selection of the major international and intergovernmental statistical publications, starting with 1983).

WORLD WIDE WEB

The World Wide Web ("the Web") has dramatically revolutionized information dissemination. In fields such as business, where there is a high premium on current information, the impact has been particularly powerful. In common parlance, the term "World Wide Web" is often used to indicate "online" or "electronic," implying that it is also freely available. There are also numerous fee-based sites and subscription databases, particularly in business, that use Web-based software; this content is not available to the general public without cost. Many of these online sources originated in other print or electronic formats (e.g., CD-ROM). Most now have at minimum an introductory Web page that *is* freely accessible to anyone with a network connection or an Internet Service Provider ("ISP"), such as AOL, and browser software such as Internet Explorer or Netscape. The fact that the Web makes it so easy to find information *about* other content is no less innovative than the provision of free information (which is notorious for its lack of accountability and authority). Because the Web is such an outstanding promotional and communication tool, professional associations, government agencies, university research centers, and commercial publishers all but universally use it to publicize themselves and their services.

In addition to the "free" Web and the fee-based online resources available through it, information professionals are also aware of a third component, the "invisible Web" or "deep Web." The invisible Web refers to materials that are not readily accessible–or findable at all–using standard searches in tools such as AltaVista, Yahoo, and Google. It is not that the information is not there, but rather it is not available at the strata closest to the surface. Increasing amounts of Web information are embedded within interactive databases, which must be are queried by the searcher in real-time. Product catalogs, glossaries, currency conversion calculators, and directories commonly take this form and are therefore important to business researchers. It is only when a "search form" is filled in that the request is executed and the information is retrieved. (This is the explanation for those often lengthy, garbled-looking Web addresses containing initials, numerals, and question marks; anything you cannot re-type easily is probably a "dynamic" URL.) These free, searchable databases may originate from government sources (e.g., a directory of contractor's license numbers or historical census data) or from private or commercial sources (e.g., company product catalogs or vendor directories).

Another type of deep Web information is lengthy textual material, such as that found in white papers, case studies, articles, reference books, and reports. These are often coded using software formats other than the usual Web software known as "HTML." Unless one has an exact title and Web address, these narrative documents can be difficult to locate except by scouring individual Web pages. The search engine Google (http://www.google.com) has made locating these documents easier by searching within the text of a variety of software formats, such as PDF, Microsoft Word, Microsoft Excel, PowerPoint, Postscript, and others. When you do a regular search in Google, your results list will include a notation of the format of the document. One way to locate case studies, white papers and other narrative documents is to restrict your search to one of the common textual file types.

TIP: Search Engines for Searching the Deep Web

- BrightPlanet. Contact: http://www.brightplanet.com.
  Offers fee-based search engines for searching the deep Web, including *Lexibot*, *CompletePlanet*, and *Data Query Manager (DQM)*.
- InvisibleWeb. Contact: http://www.invisibleweb.com.
  A free site offering categorized lists of interactive databases. The content includes business directories, legal case archives, product reviews, buyer's guides, expert directories, trademark databases, and more.
- Webdata.com. Contact: http://www.webdata.com.
  Describes and links to free Web databases on all subjects; it contains a good selection of marketing resources in its business category.

Web gateways are one of the most effective ways of finding useful material on the Internet. These are "entry portals" that organize a large amount of specialized material according to subject categories by providing a "mental map" of an entire field or discipline. There are examples from both commercial and academic producers. One of the best is *KnowThis.com "Marketing Virtual Library"* (http://www.knowthis.com) which was launched in 1999 by Dr. Paul Christ of West Chester University of Pennsylvania. It provides a classified list of Web resources on marketing topics such as advertising and promotions, marketing plans, principles of marketing, marketing research, media directories, Internet and Web site strategies and much more. Another excellent Web portal is entitled *Marketing Resource Gateway* (http://www.marketing.strath.ac. uk/rr-main.htm) from Strathclyde University's Department of Marketing. It includes many useful resources for U.S. marketers, as well as excellent coverage of U.K. and European materials.

TIP: Web Jargon and Acronyms

- HTML–Hyper Text Markup Language. The code in which Web documents are written. Thus, an "html-format" document is readable by any standard Web browser.
- ISP–Internet service provider. A service that provides access for individuals; AOL is a nationwide ISP.
- PDF–Portable Document Format. A typical text format used on the Web which is readable by Adobe Acrobat, a software program that encodes documents so they look as though typeset or printed when viewed on the Web. The reader software is available for free and has become the standard text format. Contact: http://www.adobe.com/products/acrobat/adobepdf.html.
- URL–Uniform Resource Locator. A Web address.
- XML–Extensible Markup Language. A text format that allows formatting of complex, specialized documents.

TIP: Searching for PDF Documents in Google

There are two ways to restrict your results to PDF or other textual formats in Google.

- Key in your search using the term "pdf." For example, "e-commerce case study pdf."
- Use the Advanced Search function and select the "file type" drop down menu to select from a list of available file formats.

THE WEB AND PROFESSIONAL ASSOCIATIONS

Professional and trade associations are in the business of providing practical support for their members and promotion of their industry to the general public, government, and others. These functions have long involved a range of information-gathering, knowledge-dissemination, and communication services, and the Web is a prime vehicle. There are numerous professional associations specializing in every aspect of marketing, many of which are named and described throughout this book. In particular, two general, broad-based associations should not be overlooked. These are the American Marketing Association (http://www. marketingpower.com) and Marketing Science Institute (http://www. msi.org).

To benefit from these association sites, the researcher can employ a simple but effective strategy. First, identify important professional organizations, trade groups, and research centers (perhaps using the guides to information sources listed previously). Then, thoroughly investigate their Web pages. Most Web pages have "site maps" which display the content in a hierarchical, non-distracting style–a big help for an overview of all available resources. Sections of Web sites are often titled with generic terms; it is only in the context of the actual Web page that the precise content becomes evident. For example, many detailed corporate annual reports are found under links entitled "investor relations" on the company Web site. Similarly, some of the most useful industry information is found under links called simply "research" or "statistics" on a trade association Web site.

TIP: Mouse Tracks for Web Discussions and Listservs

Mouse Tracks: The List of Marketing Lists has a comprehensive, up-to-date listing of marketing listservs and Web discussion groups. Contact: http://www.nsns.com/MouseTracks/tloml.html.

VIDEOS AND DVDs

Video and DVD are formats of modern publishing. Because they are best suited to group presentation, rather than individual research, these media are heavily used in classroom and work team settings. Dartnell (http://www.dartnellcorp.com) is a publisher which specializes in sales and customer service and offers many video titles. There are also providers of films for the educational market. For example, Films for the Humanities & Sciences (contact://www.films.com) and Insight Media (http://www.insight-media.com) distribute many videos and DVDs on marketing topics. *The Video Source Book* (Farmington Hills, MI: Gale Group, annual, print) is a comprehensive resource for videos on a variety of subjects.

CLASSIC TEXTS AND OTHER SCHOLARLY MATERIAL

Marketing professionals and scholars share a common literature of texts and articles regarded as "classics." There are times when the reader may wish to identify writings that are likely to be taught and discussed in marketing courses, and which are often referenced by those schooled in the discipline. Generally, one of the best methods for identifying important and respected literature is to use the bibliographies and reading lists in subject-specialized marketing encyclopedias, such as *IEBM Encyclopedia of Marketing*, described previously. In addition, there are subject encyclopedias on general business containing excellent articles on marketing topics and which include bibliographies of seminal literature. For example, the *International Encyclopedia of Business and Management* (IEBM 1996, 3198-3199) has an excellent bibliography under "marketing" in Volume Four. In addition to articles in peer-reviewed journals and books ("monographs"), research results are often distributed as "working papers," a form of scholarly publishing that is used in some disciplines, including marketing. Sources for both types of scholarly writing are given below.

Marketing Classics: A Selection of Influential Articles. Ben M. Enis and Keith K. Cox. 8th edition. Englewood Cliffs, NJ: Prentice Hall, 1994. Print $63. 578 pages.

This compilation presents reprints of classic articles that are cited regularly in textbooks and encyclopedias. It includes early classics that revolutionized and expanded the field such as "Marketing Myopia" (Levitt 1960), "The Concept of the Marketing Mix" (Borden 1964), and "Broadening the Concept of Marketing" (Kotler and Levy 1969), as well as important pieces on buyer behavior, marketing strategy, market share, psychographics, advertising research, and retail strategy. The book has name and subject indexes. There is a similar collection, with commentaries, entitled *Great Writings in Marketing: Selected Readings*

Together with the Authors' Own Retrospective Commentaries compiled by Howard A. Thompson (2nd Edition. Tulsa, OK: PennWell Publishing Co, 1981).

Marketing Science Institute. Working Paper Series. Cambridge, MA. Contact: http://www.msi.org/msi/publications.cfm.

The Marketing Science Institute (MSI) is a consortium of corporations and academics involved in the support of empirical research in marketing. MSI publications include working papers, monographs, and an executive newsletter. The Working Paper Series includes research reports, technical papers, commentaries, and conference summaries The Web site offers a searchable archive with listings for such topics as advertising, brand equity, pricing, promotion, international/global, social issues/public policy, services marketing, targeted marketing, and more. The average price for each working paper is $18.

REFERENCES

American Marketing Association (AMA). 2002. "About the AMA: Marketing Definitions." <http://www.marketingpower.com> (April 10, 2003).

Baker, Michael J. 1999. Preface to *The IEBM Encyclopedia of Marketing*. London: International Thomson Business Press.

Borden, Neil H. 1964. "The Concept of the Marketing Mix." *Journal of Advertising Research* 4, no 3: 2-7.

Butler, Barbara E. and Wendy Diamond. 2001. Business Research Skills Course. "Module 2.2: Business Information Environment." <http://www.csuchico.edu/~wd6/BRSC/course/module02/index.html> (June 6, 2002).

International Encyclopedia of Business and Management. (*IEBM*). 1996. Volume 4, s.v. "Marketing." New York: Routledge.

Karel, Thomas A. 2001. In *ARBA: American Reference Books Annual*. Englewood, CO: Libraries Unlimited.

Kotler, Philip and Gary Armstrong. 2001. *Principles of Marketing*. Upper Saddle River, NJ: Prentice Hall.

Kotler, Philip and Sidney J. Levy. 1969. "Broadening the Concept of Marketing." *Journal of Marketing* 33 (January): 10-15.

Lavin, Michael R. 1992. *Business Information: How to Find It, How to Use It*. 2nd edition. Phoenix, AZ: Oryx Press.

Levitt, Theodore. 1960. "Marketing Myopia." *Harvard Business Review* 58, no. 4 (July-August October): 45-56.

Ojala, Marydee. 1996. "The Life Cycle of Business Information." *Database* 19 (June/July): 79-80.

Shim, Jae K. and Joel G. Siegel. 1995. *Dictionary of Economics*. New York: John Wiley & Sons, Inc.

PART II

RESEARCHING THE COMPETITIVE ENVIRONMENT

Chapter 2

Sources for an Industry Scan

Topics

Industry Codes
Multi-Industry Overviews
Investment Research Reports
Statistics and Quantitative Data (market size, market share, financial ratios, etc.)
Industry Specific Information
Trade Journals
Trade Association and Other Web Sources
Government and Regulatory Information

Sources

Encyclopedia of American Industries
Industry Surveys
U.S. Business Reporter
Value Line Investment Survey
Research Bank Web
Economic Census
County Business Patterns
Current Industrial Reports
Annual Survey of Manufactures
Manufacturing & Distribution USA
Business Statistics of the United States

[Haworth co-indexing entry note]: "Sources for an Industry Scan." Diamond, Wendy, and Michael R. Oppenheim. Co-published simultaneously in *Journal of Business & Finance Librarianship* (The Haworth Information Press, an imprint of The Haworth Press, Inc.) Vol. 9, No. 2/3, 2004, pp. 41-67; and: *Marketing Information: A Strategic Guide for Business and Finance Libraries* (Wendy Diamond, and Michael R. Oppenheim) The Haworth Information Press, an imprint of The Haworth Press, Inc., 2004, pp. 41-67. Single or multiple copies of this article are available for a fee from The Haworth Document Delivery Service [1-800-HAWORTH, 9:00 a.m. - 5:00 p.m. (EST). E-mail address: docdelivery@haworthpress.com].

http://www.haworthpress.com/web/JBFL
Digital Object Identifier: 10.1300/J109v09n02_02   *41*

BizStats.com
SI: Special Issues.com
Industry Sector Notebooks

Whether tangible goods or beneficial services, the marketer has a *product* to sell. The initial focus of any marketing project is the product that will attract customers, be sold, generate profits, and garner new business. However, the product does not exist in isolation. It will be launched into a complex existing environment fraught with competitive constraints, social and political influences, and technological challenges. It is essential to understand the broader situational and environmental factors in the industry because they have direct impact on the ability to market a product or service effectively and thus sell it successfully.

Learning about the industry environment, often referred to as the "market," may seem at times to be far from the main goal of selling the product, but an in-depth analysis of the entire industry is an essential component of the overall marketing strategy. It can tell you whether you will be selling your product or service in a growing or contracting industry, whether there are a few large competitors or many small players, what new technologies may offer, whether the regulatory climate is benign or challenging, and whether the target customer base is growing. When the industry (or market) scan is complete, you will have an understanding of the current market size and the growth potential for your product or service.

TIP: Is It an Industry or Is It a Market?

Analyzing the "industry environment" results in a "market analysis." In this case, the word "industry" does not necessarily refer to manufacturing sectors or even a tangible product. It represents the surrounding forces impacting the potential of any product or service. It is variously called the industry or market environment.

This chapter describes an effective strategy for researching the market environment, the types of sources needed, and how to use them. One of the most challenging aspects of industry research is the simple fact that *each industry is different*. This fact has a large impact on both the ease of the process and the outcome of the finished research. For some industries, information is abundant, easy to find, and well targeted to the needs of marketers. For others, there is little available, and much of what is found may not seem to apply to the marketer's particular needs.

Like industries themselves, the sources of industry information are also diverse and widely differentiated. The ideal "industry overview" article, combining all the essential facts and in-depth analysis, could be published either in a trade journal, an investment analyst report, or on an association's Web site. Unfortunately, such an article does not *necessarily* exist for every industry. Likewise, there might be tables of sales data in an article, a company annual report, on a Web site, or in a governmental statistical report. Which source may be best is difficult to predict because some industry information may be reflected in all types of sources, some may appear only in one or two, and some may not be represented in any of them.

This combination of diversity and lack of predictability means that it is necessary to look at a variety of types of sources, each of which will provide a few pieces of the puzzle. For all industries, start with the widely available multi-industry sources containing succinct overviews. They offer an excellent background for trends, but may not be as current as you would like. Locate investment analyst or market research reports, if they are affordable or available at a library. Research and read trade journals, consult trade associations to see what data they have compiled, and check the Census Bureau and regulatory agencies (such as the Environmental Protection Agency) to see if the industry is within the government's scope of interest. As you inspect each source, try to keep the large picture in mind, filling in pieces of the puzzle as you go along. Maintain a list of questions about the industry and then, as you find a piece of information that answers a particular question, jot it down with the source noted.

Do not be discouraged by a few gaps in the emerging industry picture of recent trends, future forecasts, and marketing data. Even if it is not possible to answer all questions, an increasingly clear idea will emerge of what information is available about this particular industry. At the very least, you will be confident of what information *is* generally available and which factors *are not* widely known. It is important to be aware of the information that is generally available to your competitors, but even a "null answer," a lack of information, can be an important strategic tool in gaining advantage over a competitor.

To work efficiently through this complex and diversified information landscape, it is helpful to focus on the issues an industry research project can address. A completed industry analysis should answer the following questions, or at least have confirmed that the information is not generally available:

- Definition and scope of the industry

    Is it a component of a broader industry group?
    What are the relevant industry classification codes?

- Structure

    What are the major segments of the industry or market?
    Is it primarily a national, an international, or a regional presence?

- Historical development

    Is this a mature, established industry or a new, developing industry?

- Growth patterns

    What is the rate of growth?
    Is it cyclical or seasonal or steady?

- Present trends

    What current patterns are exhibited?
    What is the near-term forecast?

- Innovation

    How does the industry respond to change?

- Competitive environment in the industry

    Is there a concentration or dispersion of companies within the industry?
    Which companies are major competitors?

- Customer characteristics

    Which are the targeted demographic groups?
    What are the patterns of advertising, marketing, and selling?

- Product lines

  What are typical production and distribution patterns?
  Is the industry vertically or horizontally integrated?

- Environmental factors that impact the industry

  What is the macroeconomic climate?
  How do political, regulatory, or legal factors impact competitiveness?
  What important technological developments are forecast?
  How do general social and demographic trends impact this industry?

(Adapted from Porter 1980.)

Many of these questions will also be useful for other aspects of your marketing research. The difference here is that you will be researching these trends and customer characteristics for the entire industry, not just one particular product.

TIP: Using Industry Research for the SWOT Analysis

The term "SWOT" is used in marketing to indicate the process of assessing any venture's *S*trengths, *W*eaknesses, *O*pportunities, and *T*hreats. This process of analysis is fundamental to strategic marketing planning in order "to summarize the unit's present position in its market(s)" (McDonald 1999, 567). The sources for industry research given in this chapter will enable the marketer to carry out the SWOT analysis.

Because of the complexities of industry research, it is crucial to use a systematic, structured, multi-pronged strategy to deal with the diverse types of sources. As mentioned previously, it is useful to keep a checklist of questions, filling in analysis, facts, and figures as each source is consulted.

- *Step 1.* Consult sources for multi-industry overviews (discussed later in this chapter). Many are available in print or online by subscription, and will generally be found in libraries.

- *Step 2*. Determine whether investment analyst and/or market research reports are available in local libraries. These are expensive, but they may be available in many university and other specialized business libraries. (See Chapter 4 "Sources for Market Research Reports".)
- *Step 3*. Identify major professional and trade associations in the industry. Check Web sites for published data and research. While at the Web site, note any legislative or regulatory updates and any discussion of new technological developments.
- *Step 4*. Research business periodicals and trade journal articles. Using a periodical index, look for articles that include the name of your industry combined with typical subject headings used for industry overviews. Some typical headings are: "industry analysis," "industry overview," "industry forecasts," "industrywide conditions," "industry outlook," or "trends." For instance, search for *tourism* and *industry outlook*.
- *Step 5*. Identify major trade journals in your industry by using a directory or a listing of sources in the "For Further Research" section in one of the published overviews found in Step 1. Browse the tables of contents from recent years, looking for articles that cover trends, projections and forecasts. These are often "special features" titled "year in review" or "forecasts for the future." Scan regular features such as legislative updates, new technology, or advertising columns.
- *Step 6*. Consult federal statistical data or the secondary sources that republish government data for statistics on your industry. For example, look at the *Annual Survey of Manufactures* or *Current Industrial Reports* for manufacturing industries or data from the other *Economic Censuses* (such as *Census of Service Industries* or *Census of Retail Trade*) for other sectors.
- *Step 7*. Check relevant federal agencies, such as the Environmental Protection Agency (EPA), for narrative industry analysis and overviews.
- *Step 8*. Seek out available market share data using published secondary sources such as *Market Share Reporter* or *U.S. Market Trends and Forecasts*. (See Chapter 3 "Sources about Companies, Brands, and Competitors.)

(Adapted from Porter 1980, 368-382; Ojala 1996, 14-19.)

INDUSTRY CODES

When researching an industry, the marketer will encounter two common systems for classifying industries: the North American Industry Classification System (NAICS) and the Standard Industrial Classification (SIC). Both systems use a hierarchic, numeric scheme to define and distinguish one industry from another, helping to clarify whether the business is manufacturing, retail, wholesale, service-based, or commodity-based. As Michael Lavin puts it:

> It is vague to say a company is in the motion picture business. Is the speaker describing a film studio? A production company? A distributor? A casting service? . . . (Lavin 1992, 62)

The primary purpose of industry codes, such as NAICS and SIC, is to aid U.S. government agencies (and their North American counterparts) in collecting, tabulating, disseminating, and analyzing statistical data about business establishments and activity. The codes are also heavily used by information providers as a means of arranging many different types of information by industry, including company listings, narrative overviews, financial ratios, economic reports, and statistics.

NAICS officially replaced SIC codes in 1997, but SIC continues to be used in many commercial publications, and for historical data. Although the direct impetus for the revision was the adoption of the North American Free Trade Agreement (NAFTA), the SIC system had regularly been critiqued as out-of-date, and NAICS has indeed improved the definition of new and emerging sectors, especially technology, information, and service industries in general. Furthermore, regular revisions continue to keep it current.

While appreciating their usefulness, it is also important to recognize the limitations of industry codes as aids to research. Simply because there is a code for a particular industry, does not necessarily mean that there is a corresponding ability to capture a significant amount of information about it. For example, "bowling centers" has a NAICS code of 71395, but the researcher should not expect to find a great deal of published information about that particular enterprise. Instead, it might be necessary to look at the broader segment "Amusement, Gambling & Recreation Industries" (NAICS 713). Furthermore, many of the sources given below utilize their own industry names rather than the numerical, hierarchical NAICS or SIC systems.

NAICS is based on a six-digit code system whereby each industry can be broken down into finer distinguishing segments than was possible in the 4-digit SIC system. There are 20 major divisions, represented by the first two digits. After the initial two-digit category, the digits classify the industry more specifically in its sector. Thus, 71 represents Arts, Entertainment and Recreation; 713 is Amusement, Gambling and Recreation; 7139 is used for "Other Recreation"; 71391 is Golf Courses and Country Clubs, 71392 is Skiing, 71394 is Fitness and Recreational Sports Centers, 71395 is Bowling Centers, and so on.

NAICS Two-Digit Major Industry Sectors

11 Agriculture, Forestry, Fishing and Hunting	
21	Mining
22	Utilities
23	Construction
31-33	Manufacturing
42	Wholesale Trade
44-45	Retail Trade
48-49	Transportation and Warehousing
51	Information
52	Finance and Insurance
53	Real Estate and Rental and Leasing
55	Management of Companies and Enterprises
56	Administrative & Support & Waste Management & Remediation Services
61	Educational Services
62	Health Care and Social Assistance
71	Arts, Entertainment, and Recreation
72	Accommodation and Food Services
81	Other Services (exc. public administration)
92	Public Administration

(Source: U.S. Office of Management & Budget 1997: 26)

TIP: Where to Look Up a NAICS Code

- *American FactFinder Industry Quick Reports*. Contact: http://factfinder.census.gov.
- North American Industry Classification System (U.S. Census Bureau). Contact: http://www.census.gov/epcd/www/naics.html.
- *North American Industry Classification System–United States, 2002*. (U.S. Office of Management and Budget). Print and CD-ROM versions available from the National Technical Information Service (NTIS). Contact: http://www.ntis.gov or 1-800-553-6847.

TIP: More Information on NAICS Codes

Boettcher, Jennifer. 1999. "Challenges and Opportunities Presented by NAICS," *Journal of Business & Finance Librarianship* 5, no. 2: 3-13.

MULTI-INDUSTRY OVERVIEWS

A multi-industry overview is a collection of specific information about multiple industries across all sectors of the economy. These industry discussions generally give a snapshot review of the industry, and include narrative analysis together with facts, figures, and other data. Also included are sources for further leads, such as names of associations and trade journal titles. The value for the researcher is that these multi-industry overview sources integrate a tremendous amount of narrative analysis and statistics into one concise report.

Encyclopedia of American Industries. **Edited by Rebecca Marlow-Ferguson. 3rd edition. Farmington Hills, MI: Gale Group, 2001. Print. $560. 3,434 pages. Contact: http://www.galegroup.com.**

Due to its broad scope, the *Encyclopedia of American Industries (EAI)* is an excellent place to start an industry research project. According to its Introduction, *EAI* provides coverage on "every industry recognized by the U.S. Standard Industrial Classification (SIC) system," although sometimes the reports are not highly detailed or lengthy. The 3rd edition, published in two volumes, continues to be organized using the SIC system, but NAICS numbers are also given in each entry. Conversion tables for SIC and NAICS code comparisons are also provided.

Manufacturing Industries are covered in Volume 1 and Service Industries in Volume 2. In addition to discussions of current circumstances and future trends, *EAI*'s industry essays also treat historical events of consequence. This feature is useful for teachers and students of marketing because it offers opportunities to analyze outcomes and impacts of previous circumstances. The following issues are discussed in most industry entries (with some variation due to the idiosyncrasies of individual industries):

- Industry Snapshot–overview of key trends, issues and statistics
- Organization and Structure–configuration and functional aspects of the industry, including government regulation, sub-industry divisions, and interaction with other industries

- Background and Development–industry's genesis and history, including major technological advances, scandals, pioneers, major products, and other factors
- Current Conditions–status of the industry in the mid-to-late 1990s
- Industry Leaders–profiles major companies within the industry; includes discussion of financial performance
- Work Force–size, diversity and characteristics of the industry's work force
- America and the World–global marketplace factors
- Research and Technology–major technological advances and new areas of research that may have potential impact on the industry
- Further Reading–sources used to compile the articles and which can be used for further research

Industry Surveys. New York: Standard & Poor's. Weekly (boxed) or Quarterly (bound). Print or online (subscription). Price varies. Contact: http://www.standardandpoors.com.

Standard & Poor's (S&P's) *Industry Surveys* is an outstanding resource. S&P's fifty-two industry reports are comprehensive, detailed, and focused on the issues needed for any kind of industry assessment, whether for marketing or investment purposes. Standard & Poor's is an authoritative, well-respected company with an extensive history in the field of business publishing. However, its primary target is the investment advisory market, and therefore *Industry Surveys* only covers industries that have significant public company participation. Industries with mostly small and/or non-public companies are not included. Thus, there are excellent, in-depth reports on broadcasting and cable, computers, electric utilities, health care, biotechnology, and department stores, but not on photo processing, fitness centers, or music and concert performance. (For the latter types, use the *Encyclopedia of American Industries*.) This source will be found in larger academic and public libraries with specialized business collections and in corporate libraries.

Industry Surveys is issued in print, and is also available as part of Standard and Poor's Web-based subscription service, *NetAdvantage*. Various updating cycles are available to subscribers, including weekly loose-leaf or bound quarterly reports; weekly updates are loaded into *NetAdvantage* as soon as they are available. Each individual report, known as an "Industry Survey," is produced on its own internal bi-annual cycle and is time-stamped with the date of the most recent update.

Note that the quarterly volume, which is comprised of 52 individual industry surveys, may vary in currency by nearly a year.

Each report is presented in the same format, including current environment, industry profiles and trends, and company data. Included in the discussions are technological impacts, regulatory concerns, demographic trends, competitive climate, and the impact of the macroeconomic situation. "Current Environment" provides a succinct summary of major recent events and issues in the industry, including the economic context and company developments. The intent of the "Industry Profile" is to capture long-term industry trends, and there is usually some overlap and duplication in updates issued within a year or two of each other. For instance, the "Industry Trends" sections in the reports on "Retailing: General" dated May 24, 2001 and November 29, 2001 share certain identical material but each also reflects some changed and recent developments. This "carry-over" is also true of other sub-sections in the "Industry Profile" component. On the other hand, the details in the "Current Environment" section vary considerably, reflecting changes occurring in the six-month period that separates them.

In addition to industry information, *Industry Surveys* is also a source of public company information. A section of data tables entitled "Comparative Company Analysis" appears at the end of each report. Primarily useful for investment purposes, this section allows comparison of the financial performance of major competitors. Marketers will find some of these ratios helpful in assessing a competitor's position, although they do not reflect sales and market share. There is a helpful glossary of terms unique to the industry, and a section of "Industry References" that provides leads for other sources of information, such as major periodicals, trade associations, and government agencies.

U.S. Business Reporter. MetricMedia Group. San Diego, CA. ©2003. Online. $100/year. Contact: http://www.activemedia-guide.com/ index.htm.

Calling itself the "digital research tool of business," *U.S. Business Reporter* produces excellent industry overviews. Covering approximately 50 industry segments from aerospace to wholesaling, these reports include sections on overall environment, issues, employment, trends, outlook, characteristics, market share, and other statistics and data. Industry overviews are linked to a list of the sector's major companies, which are described in one-page snapshots focusing on investment performance, sometimes augmented with additional narrative profiles.

According to a company spokesperson, *U.S. Business Reporter* is produced by using a combination of internal primary research and external sources. The latter include International Data Corporation, Information Resources Inc., Gartner Group, and governmental sources such as the Federal Reserve Bank, U.S. Department of Commerce, and the U.S. Bureau of Economic Research, among others ("Brian" 2002). Much of the actual industry analysis is generated from the publisher's own research.

Value Line Investment Survey. New York. Weekly. Print or Online or CD-ROM. $598/year. Contact: http://www.valueline.com.

The *Value Line Investment Survey* is similar to Standard & Poor's *Industry Surveys* in that it is an investment resource with industry overviews that can be useful to marketers. *Value Line* also covers a limited number of industries, focusing on those with participation by public companies. Though briefer than the *Industry Surveys*, these succinct, one-page overviews are up-to-date and dense with valuable data and analysis. *Value Line* is widely available in most libraries serving individual investors and academic finance studies.

INVESTMENT RESEARCH REPORTS

Investment research reports are highly valued because they are written by expert analysts at investment banks, brokerage houses and consulting firms which closely follow particular industries and companies. Produced by financial services firms to guide investors, they focus on stock market buy-and-sell analysis and on individual companies. However, in addition to the company-level investment advice, many firms also produce broader reports about whole industries, which contain useful information for marketers.

The reports compile information from a variety of sources, some of which are unique. Thus, in addition to such standard sources as annual reports, business and trade press, and government sources, these investment research reports may also be based on one-on-one interviews, personal relationships with company management, company contracts, focus groups, and proprietary market forecasts.

One major problem is that analysts' reports can be somewhat difficult to access due to their high cost and specialized nature. Available both in print and through subscription Web sites, many specialized research-oriented business libraries may provide them, but smaller more general collections probably will not. In some cases, they may also be available in public libraries with large investment collections, and sometimes they can also be purchased individually through the investment company's Web site.

Research Bank Web. New York: Thomson Financial. Online subscription. Price varies. Contact: http://www.investext.com.

Research Bank Web is an online search system providing three content data sets that are highly useful for industry research: *Investext Investment Research*, *MarkIntel Market Research*, and *Industry Insider Trade Association Research*. The emphasis is on current material, though some historical reports as old as 1994 are available. The *Research Bank Web* interface is user-friendly, with excellent search and retrieval features and functions. It is possible to view tables of contents before purchasing and to selectively print required pages or sections. Documents can be viewed in PDF format so they appear just like the print originals. *Investext* and *MarkIntel* are also available through other vendors' online systems, such as Gale's *General Business File*, *Dialog*, *LexisNexis*, and others.

International in scope, *Investext* is a collection of analyst reports from over 630 brokerage, consulting, and investment firms, including Morgan Stanley Dean Witter, Merrill Lynch, Credit Suisse First Boston, Robertson Stephens, Lehman Brothers, and Salomon Smith Barney. These industry reports discuss trends, identify major players, disclose market share, and examine historical performance in an industry or region. *MarkIntel Market Research* covers 145 market research publishers including Datamonitor, GartnerGroup, and Economist Intelligence Unit. These reports offer coverage of public and private companies, including primary research and statistics, interviews with industry leaders, survey research, trends and forecasts, market size and share data, and market segment analysis. *Industry Insider Trade Association Research* is a unique online collection of professional association research. Reports cover approximately 200 trade organizations worldwide such as the Food Institute, the Personal Communications Industry Association, and Sporting Goods Manufacturers. These reports, often written by economists employed by the professional associations, contain growth trends, consumer spending habits, sales figures, export/import facts, manufacturing capacity, product development, market share, and news and analysis. Investment analyst reports are also available from broker-age firms themselves, especially to customers of the firm or through Web sites and other e-commerce gateways.

Multex (http://www.multexusa.com) is another source of online investment analyst reports. Registration is required, but the database can be accessed at no charge; in addition, institutional subscriptions are available. *Multex* software provides an easy method for limiting search results to industry reports only.

TIP: Industry Analysis in Market Research Reports

Industry-wide studies are also commonly published by market research firms and are available from many of the online aggregators discussed in Chapter 4, "Sources for Market Research Reports."

STATISTICS AND QUANTITATIVE DATA

All the multi-industry overviews and investment reports mentioned previously will include a wide variety of quantitative data to illustrate the points made in the narrative about production, sales, market share, profitability, and demographic information. Statistics give depth and add to the detail of industry reports. The following sources focus on numerical information. Most lack qualitative discussion, so it will be necessary to interpret the data in order to fit it into the context of a particular industry analysis.

***Economic Census*. Washington DC: U.S. Census Bureau. Every 5 years. Online (free). Print or CD-ROM (price varies). Contact: http://www.census.gov/econ/www/econ_cen.html.**

The *Economic Census* is a long-standing measure of business and industrial activity which takes place every five years with some annual updates. The *Economic Census* is comprised of the Censuses of Agriculture, Construction, Manufacturing, Retail, Wholesale, and Service Industries, and is one of the primary sources of original data for many of the economic measures developed and used by federal statisticians, agencies, and policymakers. In addition, the data are utilized by state and local governments to assess their tax base and to attract new businesses, by trade association analysts to study trends, and by individual businesses to locate potential markets and benchmark their own sales performance (U.S. Census Bureau, 1997 Economic Census: ZIP Code Statistics Introductory Text).

The data are found on the Census Bureau Web site, and have also traditionally been made available on CD-ROM and in print. As of this writing, data from the 1997 *Economic Census* are available at *American FactFinder* at http://factfinder.census.gov. Data from the 2002 *Economic Census* will become available in 2004 and 2005.

American FactFinder provides user-friendly access through the "Industry Quick Reports." The data categories are defined by the North American Industry Classification System (NAICS) which replaced the Standard Industrial Classification (SIC) system. NAICS uses codes to classify industries by Economic Sector, Sub-Sector, Industry Group, NAICS industry, and U.S. Industry. For instance, under Retail Trade, you might select "health and personal care stores," then "optical goods stores." You would find that optical goods stores fall under NAICS code 446130. Using the Industry Quick Reports, it is possible to retrieve a table that reports the number, size of establishments, and dollar amounts of shipments/sales/receipts for a specifically-defined industry sector for states, metropolitan statistical areas (MSAs), counties, and nationwide. The result is a tabular report with information showing number of establishments, number of employees, annual payroll, shipments/sales receipts, and population estimates. At each level, the appropriate level of NAICS code is provided, but it is not necessary to know it in order to do a search, because the site provides a handy way of looking up a NAICS code. Similarly, there is a Geography Quick Reports option, which can be useful for assessing the market valuation of a product segment in a particular region.

In addition to the pre-formatted "Quick Reports" option, *American FactFinder* offers a "Data Sets" option for building customized datasets For example, under Wholesale Trade, you could choose from datasets in the Geographic Area series, the Merchandise/Commodity/Receipt/Revenue Lines series, or the Establishment/Firm Size Statistics series. Options include selecting and sorting for industries and geographic regions until you have created customized a table meeting your unique circumstances and needs.

County Business Patterns. **Washington DC: U.S. Census Bureau. Annual. Online (free). Contact: http://www.census.gov/epcd/cbp/ view/cbpview.html.**

County Business Patterns (CBP) is another well-known and long-standing Census Bureau publication with marketing applications. The data are useful for analyzing market potential, setting sales quotas, measuring the effectiveness of ad campaigns, and comparing economic changes over time. For each United States county (plus District of Columbia and Puerto Rico), *CBP* reports the total number of establishments, the total number of employees, and the total payroll arranged by NAICS industry codes. Data are reported at the 6-digit level, so it is possible to be quite specific in the representation of a specific industry. If more detail is needed at the local geographic level, the user can consult *Zip Code Business Patterns* or *Metro Business Patterns*. Published on an annual basis since 1964 and at irregular intervals as far back as 1946, *County Business Patterns* is no longer issued in print or on CD-ROM. The Web site offers options for simple viewing and for downloading data in spreadsheet software format.

TIP: "How People Use Economic Census Data"

The Census Bureau has an excellent Web page describing the many marketing and business applications of the economic census data. For example, it can be used to locate business markets, calculate market share, design sales territories, and more. Contact: http://www.census.gov/epcd/www/ec97use2.htm.

TIP: Economic Census Data by ZIP Code

The 1997 *Economic Census* statistics are available for five-digit ZIP codes in 9 of the 18 NAICS sectors. These data are compiled as *Zip Code Business Patterns*, and are available on the Web at http://www.census.gov/epcd/www/zbp_base.html. In addition, more detailed data are also available in a 4-disk set on CD-ROM. The *1997 Economic Census (Volume 3) ZIP Code Statistics CD-ROM* has "establishment counts" for each detailed NAICS industry sector (with some limitations). For more information about ZIP Code data from the 1997 *Economic Census*, see http://www.census.gov/epcd/ec97zip/us/ US00000.HTM.

TIP: *Zapdata.com* **Industry Reports**

This free Web site (produced by Dun & Bradstreet) requires registration to obtain industry reports at the 4-digit SIC or NAICS level. Like *County Business Patterns* and other *Economic Census* reports, these data reports show total establishments, number of employees, and total sales for the entire industry at the national, state and city level. The site also provides prospecting lists and information on private companies. It is important to note that the Zapdata reports are not "time-stamped" so the user should determine if they are the most current data available from the U.S. Census Bureau. Contact: http://zapdata.com.

Current Industrial Reports **(*CIRs*). U.S. Census Bureau. Washington DC. Monthly, quarterly and annual. Print and online (free). Contact: http://www.census.gov/cir/www/index.html.**

The *Current Industrial Report (CIR)* program provides monthly, quarterly, and annual measures of manufacturing, construction, and mining activity. Unfortunately, data are not available for the agricultural, services, or retail sectors, so this source will have limited applicability for many marketing plan topics. As described by the Census Bureau, the *CIRs* are part of an "integrated statistical system" which also includes the *Census of Manufactures* and the *Annual Survey of Manufactures*. "The *CIR* surveys provide current statistics at a more detailed level than either of the other two statistical programs. A primary purpose is to produce timely data on production and shipment of selected products" (U.S. Census Bureau, Current Industrial Reports 2002). Reports include product descriptions, quantities of products manufactured, value of shipments, and numbers of companies in each manufacturing segment. The data in the CIRs are reported by 10-digit *product codes*, rather than by SIC or NAICS numbers, indicating the enhanced level of detail that the CIRs offer. (See "Product Codes and Descriptions for Selected Current Industrial Reports" at http://www. census.gov/prod/ec97/97numlist/apdxb.pdf.) Professionals involved in market analysis and forecasting are primary users of this information.

Annual Survey of Manufactures. **U.S. Census Bureau. Washington DC. Annual. Print and online (free). Contact: http://www.census. gov/econ/www/ma0300.html.**

The *Annual Survey of Manufactures* provides statistics on the location, activities and products of U.S. manufacturers. It includes all establishments (defined as company locations) that are classified in the "Manufacturing" part of the North American Industry Classification System (NAICS). These include plants, factories, mills and other mechanized operations that do not generally sell directly to the public (although some, such as bakeries and tailors, may include retail establishments). Topics covered are the same as in the *Census of Manufacturing*, including kind of business, location, ownership form, value of shipments, payroll, and employment. Marketers will also find other useful data, such as cost of materials, inventories, new capital expenditures, fuel and energy costs, hours worked, and payroll supplements. The *Survey* updates the quinquennial (every five years) *Census of Manufacturing*, which is issued as part of the *Economic Census*.

TIP: *STAT-USA* Is a Source for Industry Statistics from the U.S. Government

Industry statistics from the *Economic Census*, *Census of Manufacturing*, and *Current Industrial Reports* are also available in *STAT-USA*'s *State of the Nation (SOTN)* segment. Current material is available at the top-level under "Manufacturing and Industry." Historical time series are available in the "State of the Nation Library" under Industry Statistics. Regional economic information is available from the Federal Reserve's *Summary of Commentary on Current Economic Conditions* (known as the "Beige Book"), under the heading "Economic Policy." *STAT-USA* is an online subscription service provided by the U.S. Department of Commerce available in many public and academic libraries. Contact: http://www.stat-usa.gov/.

Manufacturing & Distribution USA. **Arsen J. Darney, Editor. Farmington Hills, MI: The Gale Group, 2000. 3,309 pages (3 volumes). $395. Contact: http://www.galegroup.com.**

Manufacturing & Distribution USA (*MDUSA*) presents essential statistical information from a number of government sources in a concise and convenient format. Its primary focus is on data from the *Economic Census*, but other information sources are incorporated. This title covers the manufacturing, retail, and wholesale sectors and updates the formerly separate volumes *Manufacturing USA* and *Wholesale and Retail Trade USA*. Published biannually, it is part of Gale Group's "USA" series, which also includes *Service Industries USA, Agriculture, Forestry, Fishing, Mining & Construction USA, Transportation and Public Utilities USA*, and *Finance, Insurance & Real Estate USA*.

MDUSA presents data on 856 industries, arranged by both SIC and NAICS codes in time series covering 1982 to 2001. Due to the fact that statistical data collection is still in a transitional stage, both SIC and NAICS systems are utilized. Some SIC codes have no direct NAICS equivalent, but are broken down and distributed into multiple NAICS categories. For NAICS categories, not enough data have yet been compiled to generate a time series. The editors have provided projections where available and reliable.

The publisher has enhanced the statistical graphs and tables with a number of additional features. There are tables showing general statistics, such as number of establishments, employment totals, compensation and hourly wages, value of shipments, cost of materials, and capital investment. For each industry, the same categories are reformulated to show indices of change, whether growth or contraction. Selected ratios are given for such variables as payroll, value added, investment, and sales per establishment and/or employee.

Additional features of special interest to marketers include data on material consumed and product share, which could be used for benchmarking supply chains, vendor contacts, and customer relationships. Maps allow the researcher to view the concentration and distribution of establishments in a state and regional framework, which could be used for sales planning. For developing mailing lists of new sales targets, there are also listings of top public and private companies for each industry. The indexes by company name, product/activity and SIC/NAICS codes enhance the usefulness of the work.

Business Statistics of the United States. Cornelia J. Strawser, editor. 8th edition. Lanham, MD: Bernan Press. 2002. $147. Contact: http://www.bernan.com.

Business Statistics of the United States is a desktop-size reference book providing current and historical data from the *Economic Census*, as well as from many other government agency sources. Offering 2,000 time series tables of statistics for major industry groups, including such essential facts as production, capacity utilization, shipments, consumer spending, sales, and inventories, this edition contains data from 1970 (and earlier for some major statistical series) through 2000.

At the beginning of each chapter, a graph and brief text depict some of the trends reflected in the data. Previous editions have featured expanded data on service industries and more detail on consumer spending by type. The extensive background notes containing definitions, descriptions of data, and references to additional information sources help the user apply the data and seek additional information from the source agencies. There is a well-formatted subject index.

BizStats.com. **Washington DC. ©2003. Online (free). Contact: http:// www.bizstats.com.**

BizStats.com is a free commercial Web site that offers access to financial ratios and other types of business statistics for the United States. The *BizStats.com* site is a convenient compilation of three types of industry data: "National Business Statistics" (similar to *Business Statistics* discussed previously); "Retail Benchmarks" (e.g., average annual sales by square foot); and "Small Business Industries" (e.g., financial ratios).

These financial ratios are needed for marketing and business plans developed for bank loan applications, venture financing partnerships, or internal company planning. Marketers are required to provide these operating and profitability ratios in order to make an objective comparison between their business and the industry average. Sometimes known as "industry norms," marketers may be familiar with several print sources for this data, such as *RMA Annual Statement Studies* and *Almanac of Business and Financial Ratios* (see below). *BizStats.com* is a convenient addition to this set of tools.

Compiled primarily from government and trade association sources, the site is easy to use and well-supported in its methodology, timeliness, and accuracy by a detailed "Disclosures" section. The top level page allows the user to select an industry (described in words, not by SIC or NAICS codes) and select a total business revenue. The site computes the data and reports average profitability and expense percentages for U.S. businesses. In addition to this interactive section, the user may also select from a wide range of links covering a variety of industry, business, and retail statistics. Along with standard government sources, some of the tables and charts are provided by *BizMinder.com*, a commercial provider of industry and market research.

TIP: Sources for Financial Ratios

In addition to *BizStats.com*, consult these sources for financial ratios. Several may be available in business libraries in print or electronic format.

- RMA Annual Statement Studies. Contact: http://www.rmahq.org/.
- *Industry Norms & Key Financial Ratios.* Contact: http://www.dnb.com.
- *Almanac of Business and Industrial Financial Ratios* by Leo Troy. Contact: http://www.aspenpublishers.com.
- *Financial Studies of the Small Business.* Contact: http://www.frafssb.com.

Additionally, most marketers will also need sales data in addition to ratios on an industry's profitability, operating ratios, production levels, and shipment values. Sales data for products, market segments, brand, and companies is often reported as *market share*. This market share information has traditionally been difficult to locate because it is expensive and time-consuming to produce. Nevertheless, market share and brand-level sales data are regularly reported in the trade press, and in recent years, reference tools have been developed that capture, synthesize, and republish data from these secondary sources. Examples are:

- *Market Share Reporter* (Farmington Hills, MI: Gale Group, Annual).
- *U.S. Market Trends and Forecasts* (Farmington Hills, MI: Gale Group, 3rd edition, 2002).
- *Global Market Share Planner* (Oxford, U.K.: Euromonitor, 2002).
- *World Market Share Reporter* (Farmington Hills, MI: Gale Group, 2001).

(For further discussion of market share sources, see Chapter 3, "Sources about Companies, Brands and Competitors.")

TIP: Use General Business Periodical Databases to Find Industry Data

As described in Chapter 1, "Introduction to Sources and Research Strategies," business periodical databases are excellent sources of all kinds of statistical information, including industry data. *TableBase*, *Business Source Premier*, and *ABI/INFORM* are particularly noteworthy.

INDUSTRY SPECIFIC INFORMATION

Following the investigation of multi-industry overviews and general statistical sources, the next step is locating information from *industry-specific* sources. Many industries produce a range of information specific to their own marketing and investment needs. Trade journals, business news and comment periodicals, and trade association Web sites are among the best means of finding this information.

TIP: Some Industry Specific Web Sites

- American Booksellers Association http://www.bookweb.org
- Food Marketing Institute http://www.fmi.org
- HAPPI Online (Household and Personal Products Industry) http://happi.com
- Hospitality Net http://www.hospitalitynet.org
- InfoTech Trends http://www.infotechntrends.com
- National Restaurant Association http://restaurant.org
- National Paint and Coatings Association http://www.paint.org
- National Sporting Goods Association http://www.nsga.org
- Outdoor Industry Association http://www.outdoorindustry.org
- Travel Industry Association of America http://www.tia.org

TRADE JOURNALS

Identifying the major trade journal titles for a particular field is a relatively simple task. You probably have already developed a list of them through your research in the sources discussed above. For example, the Standard & Poor's *Industry Surveys* and the *Encyclopedia of American Industries* include useful lists of trade journals and professional associations for each industry discussed. If you still need to find additional titles, here are some tools:

- The *Encyclopedia of Business Information Sources* (Farmington Hills, MI: Gale Group; annual) contains lists of important sources according to specific industries. Within each industry, sources are arranged in distinct categories, such as trade journals, trade association Web sites, databases, reference books, directories of industry professionals, etc. This reference book is available in general and business libraries of all sizes and types.

- *SRDS Business Publication Advertising Source* (Des Plaines, IL: Standard Rate and Data Service; annual). This publication, geared to the needs of advertising and media planning professionals, provides an extensive list of magazines and journals geared to specific industry environments and interests. For instance, trade magazines for baking, building management, travel, and printing are listed, along with those for manufacturers and retailers in toys, hobbies, restaurant supplies, and much more. *SRDS* directories will be found in academic and public libraries that specialize in business, and in the library collections of advertising agencies.

Trade journals offer many helpful features that augment industry research. Many include regular sections or columns on technology updates, legislative news, and statistical overviews. Others go even further and publish entire special issues focusing on specific, concentrated topics, much like a book or report does. For example, *Marketing News* publishes special issues throughout the year on topics ranging from industry forecasts ("The Year Ahead/Trends in Marketing") to various directories and listings ("Marketing Fact Book" or "Multicultural Marketing Directory").

SI: SpecialIssues.com. Houston, TX. Online subscription. Price varies. Contact: http://www.specialissues.com.

SI: SpecialIssues is an unusual tool for uncovering unique content of trade journals and professional magazines, usually only available and known to direct subscribers. It covers 2,773 trade journals, many of which are not indexed in other online periodical indexes. The database allows searching by journal name, industry grouping, subject headings, or keywords. Though *SI* itself is not a full-text provider, it offers multiple options for accessing content. These include a link to the Web site where a publication may be available in full text, selectively or otherwise; alternatively, telephone and fax numbers are provided to contact the editorial offices. *SI: SpecialIssues* is designed to meet the needs of researchers who regularly require industry information, such as those in the fields of competitive intelligence, business information consulting, and corporate librarians. It is also extremely useful as an index to trade journal collections and databases such as those found in public and academic libraries.

TIP: Finding Industry Overviews in Trade Journal Articles

When starting a new enterprise or job, it may be worthwhile to subscribe to one or two of the important trade journals in order to read them cover-to-cover over the course of a year or more. Simply to locate important articles in relevant trade journals and in general business magazines and newspapers, such as *Business Week, Fortune, Forbes*, or the *Wall Street Journal*, use a periodical index that specializes in business literature, such as one of those listed in Chapter One, "Introduction to Research Strategies and Sources."

Specific search terms for locating general industry-overview type articles will vary in each database, but the basic search strategy is the same: Construct a search using one term that represents an industry combined with another term that represents the "industry outlook" concept. Trial and error will help you retrieve the best results for the particular database available to you. For example, searches might be constructed thus:

- Tourism and industry-wide conditions
- Wireless and trends
- Sporting goods and forecasts
- Restaurants and industry overview

TRADE ASSOCIATION AND OTHER WEB SOURCES

The World Wide Web has become a premier source of industry information because it is so heavily used by professional and trade associations as an information dissemination tool. As advocates for and supporters of their respective industries, trade and professional associations are often the best–and sometimes the only–sources for specific research and data. Association Web sites cover news, legislative concerns, and, most productively for the researcher, general industry analysis, data, and trends. Although it is not a certainty, there is often a significant amount of highly usable data at association Web sites. They provide a wide variety of information that is useful in an industry research project: industry data and statistics, consumer survey results, state-of-the-industry trend reports, legislative tracking and updates, news of mergers, acquisitions, new product reports, and more. Although some associations restrict certain areas of their sites to members, there is often a great deal of information available to the general public, as well. However, keep in mind that each Web site varies and not every association produces or publishes a similar type or quality of research.

TIP: Selected Examples of Industry Facts, Figures, and Reports Available from Association Web Sites

- American Booksellers Association Research and Statistics http://www.bookweb.org/research/.
- Supermarket Facts: Industry Overview 2001 (Food Market Institute) http://www.fmi.org/facts_figs/superfact.htm.
- Five Technologies to Watch (Consumer Electronics Association) http://www.ce.org/publications/books_references/.
- State of the Industry Report (Outdoor Industry Association) http://www.outdoorindustry.org/.

TIP: Find Valuable Association Publications "Hidden" in a Library's Collection

A key statistical indexing and abstracting publication called *Statistical Reference Index (SRI)* covers a high percentage of industry and trade association publications. The famously detailed *SRI* indexing alone identifies key articles or trade association reports for you, but you may gain an added bonus if a library that carries the index also subscribes to *SRI*'s companion microfiche service. The full texts of approximately 75% of the titles annotated in *SRI* are reproduced on microfiche; these items are rarely if ever included in a library's catalog, but they are easily retrieved using *SRI*'s accession numbers. *SRI* and its sibling indices, the *American Statistics Index* (a comprehensive index of statistics published by the U.S. government) and the *Index to International Statistics* (covering the statistical publications of international intergovernmental organizations) are searchable jointly or individually in the LexisNexis database *Statistical Universe*, available in many large academic and public libraries.

There are several effective strategies for locating industry association Web sites. First, consult the reference lists at the end of each industry discussion in such sources as Standard & Poor's *Industry Surveys* and the *Encyclopedia of American Industries*. Second, use print and Web-based directories to find sources. The following sources are organized alphabetically with cross references and indexes by industry categories.

- *National Trade and Professional Associations of the United States* (Washington D.C.: Columbia Books; print; annual).
- *Encyclopedia of Associations* (Farmington Hills, MI: Gale Group; print; annual). It is also available as an online subscription under the title *Associations Unlimited* (http://www.galegroup.com).
- *American Society of Association Executives Gateway* (http://info. asaenet.org/gateway/OnlineAssocSlist.html).
- *Directory of Associations* (www.marketingsource.com/associations).

In addition to directories, there are other sources (again, in print and online formats) that are arranged by industry categories. These provide contact information and links to trade associations and other industry information:

- *Encyclopedia of Business Information Sources* (Farmington Hills, MI: Gale Group; print; annual). (Previously mentioned under "Trade Journals.")
- *Fuld & Company Competitive Intelligence Guide* (http://www.fuld. com/index.html). The Internet Intelligence Index (I^3) provides a free listing of industry Web sites in about 25 categories. Fuld & Company is a research firm specializing in "competitive intelligence" for clients. It provides this annotated list free on the Web, along with other resources, as a service and as a promotional tool.
- Competia (http://www.competia.com). Like Fuld & Company, Competia is a competitive intelligence research and consulting firm. The "Express" section of the Web site has a useful descriptive list of free links arranged in approximately 40 industry categories.
- Google Web Directory (http://directory.google.com/Top/Business). In its Business category, Google Web Directory lists over 30 industries from Accounting to Wholesale. Links to publications, associations, and organizations are given for most.

TIP: Finding Trade Associations Using Search Engines

When using search engines like Google, be sure to use quotation marks around words that need to be bound together as a phrase. Thus, if you search *"restaurant association"* with the quotation marks, you will find the National Restaurant Association. If you search without the quotation marks, you may get many irrelevant sites. At the association's home page, look for links called "research," "trends," "library," or other terms indicating data.

GOVERNMENT AND REGULATORY INFORMATION

In certain industries, legislative and regulatory issues are a significant concern. Even businesses in unregulated industries need to stay abreast of governmental policies that may impact profits and practices; for regulated industries such vigilance is vital. In some cases, the regulatory agencies themselves are a source of in-depth industry information. In others, the federal government provides industry information as a means to support U.S. businesses in exporting and marketing products overseas.

***Industry Sector Notebooks*. U.S. Environmental Protection Agency. Washington, DC. Online (free). Contact: http://www.epa.gov/ compliance/resources/publications/assistance/sectors/notebooks.**

These industry sector profiles from the Environmental Protection Agency (EPA) cover manufacturing industries with potential impact on air, water, and land resources. Examples include *Profile of the Dry Cleaning Industry*, *Profile of the Wood Furniture and Fixtures Industry*, *Profile of the Printing Industry*, *Profile of the Shipbuilding and Repair Industry*, and more. These lengthy reports include sections on industrial processes, summary of applicable statutes and regulations, and compliance and enforcement history. They are available for printing and downloading in a variety of file formats.

REFERENCES

"Brian." 2002. "Re: Industry Reports," personal e-mail correspondence. July 9, 2002.

Lavin, Michael. 1992. *Business Information: How to Find It, How To Use It*. Phoenix, AZ: Oryx Press.

McDonald, Malcolm H.B. 1999. "Developing and Implementing a Marketing Plan." In *The IEBM Encyclopedia of Marketing*, ed. Michael J. Baker. London: International Thomson Business Press.

Ojala, Marydee. 1996. "Industry Overviews: Turning Question Marks Into Answers." *Online User* (July/August): 14-19.

Porter, Michael E. 1980. *Competitive Strategy: Techniques for Analyzing Industries and Competitors*. New York: Free Press.

U.S. Office of Management and Budget. Executive Office of the President. 1997. *North American Industry Classification System*. Lanham, MD: Bernan Press.

U.S. Census Bureau. Washington D.C.

_____"Current Industrial Reports."

<http://www.census.gov/cir/www/index.html> (May 14, 2002).

_____"1997 Economic Census: ZIP Code Statistics Introductory Text." <http:// www.census.gov/epcd/ec97zip/introzip.htm> (July 2, 2002).

Chapter 3

Sources About Companies, Brands, and Competitors

Topics

Company Research Basics
Directories
Annual Reports and Form 10-Ks
Competitive Intelligence
Company Rankings and Market Share
Company History
Brand and Logo Information

Sources

Directory of Corporate Affiliations
Hoover's Handbook of American Business
Mergent Manuals
The Million Dollar Directory
Standard & Poor's Register of Corporations, Directors, and Executives
Thomas Register of American Manufacturers
Ward's Business Directory of U.S. Private and Public Companies
ReferenceUSA
The New Competitor Intelligence
Business Rankings Annual
Market Share Reporter

[Haworth co-indexing entry note]: "Sources About Companies, Brands, and Competitors." Diamond, Wendy, and Michael R. Oppenheim. Co-published simultaneously in *Journal of Business & Finance Librarianship* (The Haworth Information Press, an imprint of The Haworth Press, Inc.) Vol. 9, No. 2/3, 2004, pp. 69-89; and: *Marketing Information: A Strategic Guide for Business and Finance Libraries* (Wendy Diamond, and Michael R. Oppenheim) The Haworth Information Press, an imprint of The Haworth Press, Inc., 2004, pp. 69-89. Single or multiple copies of this article are available for a fee from The Haworth Document Delivery Service [1-800-HAWORTH, 9:00 a.m. - 5:00 p.m. (EST). E-mail address: docdelivery@haworthpress.com].

http://www.haworthpress.com/web/JBFL
© 2004 by The Haworth Press, Inc. All rights reserved.
Digital Object Identifier: 10.1300/J109v09n02_03

U.S. Market Trends and Forecasts
International Directory of Company Histories
Brands and Their Companies
Encyclopedia of Consumer Brands
World's Greatest Brands
Trade Name Origins
Brandchannel.com

Locating information about companies is fundamental to both business and marketing research, particularly when the marketer is seeking information about the competition. The researcher's primary concern is to define the character and dimensions of the environment in which a good or service will have to compete; that environment is defined by the activities and outputs of specific companies that are involved in the same market, or one similar to it.

COMPANY RESEARCH BASICS

The answers to certain questions at the start of a company research project will determine how it proceeds: is the company publicly-held, and traded on a stock exchange, or is it privately or closely-held? Information about publicly-held companies is very widely available–in fact, the larger and more prominent the company, the more difficult it will be to limit and focus research. Many information sources are available: directories; corporate and financial reports, such as Annual Reports to Shareholders and the various forms filed with the Securities and Exchange Commission; stock guides and other publications by investment analysts; and magazine and newspaper articles.

DIRECTORIES

The titles discussed below represent the national and international company directories most widely available in public and academic libraries.

Directory of Corporate Affiliations. New Providence, NJ: LexisNexis Group. Annual. Print $1,399. Contact: http://www.corporateaffiliations. com.

This eight-volume set is the first source to check to determine precisely what the ownership status of a company may be. Covering more than 170,000 major public and private companies in the U.S. and throughout the world, this directory documents "parent-offspring" relationships to the seventh level of corporate reporting, for (1) subsidiaries (chartered businesses, owned 50% or more by the parent company); (2) divisions (unincorporated internal units of companies); (3) joint ventures (businesses owned by two or more companies); and (4) affiliates (chartered businesses, less than 50% owned by the parent company). Some 19,500 private companies and 24,500 subsidiaries are listed. To be included, domestic companies must have revenues above $10 million, or "substantial assets/net worth," or 300 or more employees. Non-U.S. based companies must have revenues above $50 million. The Master Index (Volumes 1-2) lists all companies mentioned in volumes 3-6, regardless of their status as a parent company, subsidiary, division, etc. Also included is indexing by brand names, geography, Standard Industrial Classification (SIC) code, and "corporate responsibilities"–i.e., personnel arranged by function (e.g., CEO, corporate secretary, etc.). Volumes 3-4 cover U.S. public companies, Volumes 5-6 treat U.S. private companies, and Volumes 7-8 cover international public and private companies. Each category of volumes is arranged by parent company, and each volume has its own SIC code cross-index to the companies listed. Directory entries include such data as the following: addresses, telephone and fax numbers, e-mail and Web addresses, year founded, stock exchange and ticker symbol, assets, liabilities, number of employees, ownership percentage, key personnel, and more. The directory is available both on CD-ROM and in a Web version; the latter is updated weekly.

Hoover's Handbook of American Business. Austin, TX: Hoover's, Inc. Annual. Print $195. Contact: http://www.hoovers.com.

This two-volume guide, part of a four-title suite of Hoover's handbooks covering 2,550 companies in all, provides concise, information-packed profiles of 750 of the largest companies in the United States. Essentially a guide to public companies, the *Handbook* also includes coverage of more than 50 of the largest privately-owned corporations. Each two-page entry includes an overview of the company's current status, a thumbnail history, a statistical table of financial figures, and lists of officers, major products and trade names, key competitors, and geographical locations. The first part of Volume 1 contains an extensive collection of ranking lists. Volume 2 offers indexing by company name, headquarters, brands, and people discussed in the profiles.

A companion annual directory is *Hoover's Handbook of Emerging Companies* ($125). The 2003 edition of this directory covers some 600 "emerging" U.S. companies, all either publicly traded or expected soon to go public. "Emerging companies" are defined as those with sales between $10 million and $1 billion, at least three years of reported sales, no less than a 30% rate of sales growth during that time, and positive net income for their most recent fiscal year. Extensive profiles are provided for 200 of the companies. For 2003, *Hoover's Handbook of Private Companies* ($155) provides listings for some 900 U.S. "nonpublic" organizations, including private corporations; hospitals and health care organizations; government-owned corporations; charitable and membership organizations; major university systems; and more. The work's 200 in-depth, two-page profiles encompass the largest private companies; such basic information as officers, sales, and leading competitors is provided for the remaining 700 organizations covered (those with sales over $625 million). Finally, *Hoover's Handbook of World Business* ($165) covers 300 of the largest public, private, and state-owned companies based outside the United States. Each profile includes an overview of the company's current operations, a company history, a statistical table of financial figures, and lists of officers, major products and trade names, key competitors, and geographical locations.

These sources are amalgamated and expanded on the Web in *Hoover's Online* (http://www.hoovers.com), which covers some 14,000 public and private U.S. and international companies, nonprofit entities, and more. Much of *Hoover's Online* content is free; for a fee, subscribers can gain access to comprehensive profiles, in-depth financials, complete lists of key officers and other employees, expanded lists of competitors, competitive analysis, advanced searching/screening capabilities, downloadable contact information, and more.

Mergent Manuals. New York: Mergent, Inc. Annual. Print or online (subscription). Price varies. Contact: http://www.mergent.com.

This set of guides to corporate and governmental financial information is probably best known under its longtime original name, "Moody's Manuals." These manuals, geared primarily toward the information needs of investors, are especially renowned for the detailed and concise historical chronologies they provide for the entities covered. The two-volume *Mergent Industrial Manual* covers some 2,000 major industrial corporations listed on the New York Stock Exchange, the American

Stock Exchange, and regional U.S. exchanges. In addition to the company history, entries include a description of the business; listings of products, properties, and subsidiaries; names of company officers and directors; financial and income statements; balance sheets; debt ratings; and stock and bond activity. Another source of Mergent's/Moody's distinction is its provision of company financial information "as reported" (as opposed to other major resources, such as Thomson Research, which "regularize" and "standardize" such data). The other available manuals cover *Bank and Finance, International* companies (and the countries in which they are headquartered), *Municipal and Government* entities, *OTC Industrial* ("over-the-counter"), *OTC Unlisted, Public Utilities*, and *Transportation*. On the Web, all of this data, and much more (such as the full texts of corporate filings and annual reports to shareholders), is available as *Mergent Online*.

Million Dollar Directory. Short Hills, NJ: Dun & Bradstreet Information Services. Annual. Print $2,200 or online (price varies). Contact: http://www.dnb.com.

This well-known source covers more than 160,000 U.S. and Canadian companies, including over 136,000 that are privately owned. Companies which meet one of the following criteria are included: (1) 180 or more employees if the company is a headquarters or a single location, or 900 or more employees if the location is a branch; or (2) $9 million or more in sales. Subsidiaries and, obviously, branches are included if they meet the listing criteria; divisions are not. A typical entry includes such elements as headquarters location, contact information, total sales, number of employees, brief executive biographies, business description, and more. Volumes 1-3, the "alphabetical volumes," provide the company entries. Volume 4, the first of the two "Cross Reference Volumes," indexes the companies by Standard Industrial Classification (SIC) code, and Volume 5 is a geographical index, arranged by state and then alphabetically by city within state. D & B offers six Web versions of the "Million Dollar Database" (http://mddi.dnb.com/mddi/last_update.aspx), ranging from the "Million Dollar Database Lite," covering about 81,000 of the leading U.S. public and private companies with 200 or more employees, to the top-of-the-line "Million Dollar Database Premier," covering 1,362,000 companies with one million dollars or more in sales, or 20 or more employees, or branches with 50 or more employees.

***Standard & Poor's Register of Corporations, Directors and Executives.*
New York: Standard & Poor's Corporation. Annual. Print or online
(subscription). Price varies. Contact: http://www.standardandpoors.com.**

This well-known guide covers more than 75,000 public and private
U.S. and foreign corporations. Entries in Volume 1 provide names of
officers and directors, primary and secondary North American Industry
Classification System (NAICS) codes, business description or products
made, year of incorporation, ticker symbol and stock exchange (if applicable), names of primary bank, law, and accounting firm, sales, number
of employees, and subsidiaries. (Entries in the Web version also indicate whether a company's "Market Regions" are national or international, or both.) Volume 2 lists over 71,000 officers, directors, and other
personnel, with brief biographical information (e-mail addresses are
sometimes included). Volume 3 provides indexing by NAICS code (on
pink pages), geography–either state or country (on yellow pages), and
corporate family structures (on blue pages). On the Web, the *Register* is
available as part of S&P's *Net Advantage.*

***Thomas Register of American Manufacturers.* New York: Thomas
Publishing Co. Annual. Print, CD-ROM, or DVD (free except for
shipping charges). Online (free with registration). Contact: http://
www.thomasregister.com.**

This comprehensive directory of more than 189,000 American and
Canadian manufacturing firms, currently published in 27 volumes, is
made accessible by a minutely-detailed "Index to Products & Services
Section Headings," which uses some 75,000 product and services headings. Also available is "The American Trademark Index," an alphabetical arrangement of both trademarks and brand names. Manufacturers
are listed geographically, by state, within the product listings. Company
listings provide a brief address, tangible asset size, telephone and/or fax
numbers, and often such additional information as subsidiaries, sales
offices, and corporate affiliations. Two or three volumes per annual edition consist of company product catalogs. It is also available on the
Web, and access is free following registration. Searching on the Web is
by product or service, company name, or brand name, and entries include links to product catalogs, when those are available on the Web.
The print, CD-ROM, or DVD versions of the directory are free to
U.S. and Canadian companies (who must pay shipping and handling
charges).

Ward's Business Directory of U.S. Private and Public Companies.
Farmington Hills, MI: Gale Group. Annual. Print $2,830. Contact:
http://www.galegroup.com.

In the 2003 edition, volumes 1, 2, and 3 provide entries (arranged alphabetically by company name) for approximately 100,000 companies (90% of which are private), including address; telephone and fax numbers; number of employees; company status, whether public (including ticker symbol and stock exchange), private, division, or subsidiary; up to five officers' names and titles; year founded; SIC and NAICS codes; financial size designated by either sales, total assets, operating revenue, or gross billings; immediate parent company name; import/export designation; and, when available, e-mail addresses and Web addresses. There is no minimum financial qualification for inclusion.

Volume 4 covers "Special Features" ("top 1,000"-type rankings, such as the 1,000 largest privately held companies; 1,000 largest publicly traded companies; 1,000 largest employers; analysis of private and public companies by state; and an analysis of private and public companies by 4-digit SIC code), and provides a geographic listing of the companies by ZIP code within state. Volume 5 ranks companies by sales within 4-digit SIC categories. Volumes 6 and 7 rank companies within states by sales within 4-digit SIC categories. Volume 8 ranks companies by sales within 6-digit NAICS (North American Industry Classification System) codes.

Because public and private companies are ranked together, the researcher can develop a truer picture of the competitive landscape within a NAICS or SIC designation than that offered by most other rankings, which tend either to be focused on public companies, or to separate public and private companies. *Ward's* is available on the Web as part of Gale's *Business & Company Resource Center.*

According to the type of company information required, the researcher may need to consult state, regional, or other specialized business directories. Perhaps the researcher needs a detailed picture of the local competitive landscape. For that type of need–for example, how many greeting card stores there are within three contiguous ZIP codes, or how many Hallmark gift shops there are within a county–the following tool will be able to provide an answer.

ReferenceUSA. Omaha, NE: InfoUSA, 1999- . Online (subscription
price varies). Contact: http://www.infousa.com.

This Web-based database (also known, as a CD-ROM product, as *American Business* Disc) provides detailed information in five modules covering (1) more than 12 million U.S. businesses, both public and (overwhelmingly) private; (2) 120 million U.S. residents (90 million U.S. households); (3) 683,000 U.S. health-care providers; (4) one million Canadian businesses; and (5) 11 million Canadian residents. Because libraries may customize the product by purchasing one module alone, or a combination, the researcher may be most likely to find the U.S. businesses version available.

The sources for the *ReferenceUSA* database are extensive: more than 5,200 yellow page, business white page, and white page telephone directories; annual reports to shareholders, 10-K forms, and other SEC filings; federal, state, and municipal government data, including Census Bureau data; information from Donnelley Marketing (owned by InfoUSA); data from Chambers of Commerce; regional business magazines, trade publications, newsletters, and 350 major newspapers; and the U.S. Postal Service, including national change of address updates.

ReferenceUSA is essentially a considerably enhanced telephone directory. Through the "Custom Search" mode, searches may be conducted on the following fields: company–by company name, executive name, or ticker symbol; company description ("Yellow Pages")–by *ReferenceUSA* "Yellow Pages" heading (these expand SIC code headings to six digits, making it possible to identify businesses devoted to a specific segment of a broader product or service), Primary SIC Code, NAICS Code, or major industry; location ("Geography Selects")–by state, county, metropolitan area, area code, city, ZIP code, street address; by telephone number; by business size–number of employees, or sales volume; and by *ReferenceUSA* "Special Selects," which are executive title; headquarters/branch (i.e., one or the other only, or both); government offices; public company status and/or stock exchanges; and years in the database/yellow pages ad size.

In search results, each of the above elements appears in a detailed listing display, along with a credit rating (the calculation of which is explained onscreen); one or more contact names; and, depending on availability or applicability, a fax number, a toll-free telephone number, a Web site address, and ranking within the Fortune 1000. Results, which cannot be ranked, also provide maps and corporate hierarchy, to trace the relationships between parent companies, subsidiaries, and branches. Another feature available in the "Detailed Listing" display for a single business makes it possible to retrieve either "all" surrounding businesses, or nearby businesses by one or more SIC codes, located within a radius ranging from one-tenth of a mile up to 20 miles.

ANNUAL REPORTS AND FORM 10-Ks

Many researchers often overlook the company itself as, quite literally, a primary source of valuable information. For public companies, the Annual Report to Shareholders (ARS) and the Form 10-K filed with the Securities and Exchange Commission (SEC) should always be reviewed to learn what a company has to say about its competitive position and strategies for maintaining or improving it. Market share may be specifically mentioned, for example, if the company is especially proud of it.

The most universal free access to 10-K forms is through the SEC's *EDGAR* database (http://www.sec.gov/edgar/searchedgar/webusers. htm), which allows searching by company name, state, or SIC code. (The *"EDGAR"* acronym stands for "Electronic Data Gathering, Analysis, and Retrieval.") From a list of search results, click on the link "text" to call up a report, and then use the Web browser's "find in page" function to search for specific words, or character strings. A search for the character string "competi," for example, will find every occurrence in the text of competition, competitive, competitors, etc.

A public company's annual report to shareholders, often found most readily within the "Investor Relations" section of the company's Web site, will tend to be reproduced in PDF (portable document format). Use the "binoculars icon" function in PDF to search for occurrences of specific words or character strings.

TIP: Free Web Sites for Company Annual Reports

- *Annual Report Gallery.* Contact: http://www.reportgallery. com/.
- *CAROL: Company Annual Reports Online.* Contact: http://www. carol.co.uk/. (Contains European and U.S. annual reports.)
- *Corporate Annual Reports.* Lippincott Library of the Wharton School. Contact: http://oldsite.library.upenn.edu/etext/collections/ lippincott/index.html. (Contains facsimile copies of historic annual reports.)
- *CorporateInformation.* Contact: http://www.corporateinformation. com/. (Free; registration is required.)

TIP: More on Unearthing Competitive Intelligence in Public Corporate Filings

Henry, David and Christopher H. Schmitt. 2001. "The Numbers Game," *Business Week* No. 3732 (May 14): 100-110.
Scherreik, Susan. 2002. "Unlocking the Secrets of a Proxy Statement," *Business Week* No. 3772 (March 4): 108-109.

Unfortunately, there are no annual reports or Form 10-Ks for private companies. With privately-held companies, the problem–especially with smaller, non-newsworthy companies–will frequently be finding any information at all. Although more than a few directories, such as those discussed previously, identify private companies, any additional information provided may often be no more than the directory publisher's estimate of annual sales, and "ballpark" figures (e.g., "20 to 50") for number of employees. Whereas public companies are required by law to file a wide range of disclosure forms with the U.S. Securities and Exchange Commission, with the objective of enabling the general public to make informed investment decisions, private companies are under no such legal obligation. Even for companies that are subsidiaries or divisions of a public company, any detailed information will often be extremely limited, if available at all.

TIP: Free Web Resources for Private Company Information

- *Forbes 500 Largest Private Companies.* Contact: http://www.forbes.com/private500/.
- *Inc. Magazine.* Contact: http://www.inc.com/inc500/. (Gives its latest *Inc. 500* annual ranking of "America's Fastest-Growing Private Companies.")

COMPETITIVE INTELLIGENCE

As the research into the company proceeds, a storehouse of "competitive intelligence" (CI) will begin to take shape. CI is systematically gathered and "processed" information about the characteristics and activities of competitors that must be considered as crucial to marketing success. What are the competing company's product lines, prices, market share, finances, goals and objectives, strategies for the future? And how does the marketer's good or service fit into that environment?

The New Competitor Intelligence: The Complete Resource for Finding, Analyzing, and Using Information About Your Competitors. Leonard M. Fuld. New York: John Wiley & Sons, 1995. Print $135. 482 pages.

This is a revised and updated edition of Fuld's 1985 work, *Competitor Intelligence: How to Get It, How to Use It,* one of the best-known handbooks on competitive intelligence. No reader should miss the "Strategic Intelligence Index" at the start of the book (pages 4-19), in which the author provides a taxonomy of the concepts and related subjects (including specific industries and countries overseas) that are, in his professional experience, "the most often requested types of intelligence." The book also has a conventional index, but it is much briefer and far less detailed. Fuld's five major CI categories, or "super concepts," are cost/financials (example: trade show analysis reveals pricing strategy); management (example: basic sources for company history); process (example: evaluating environmental filings to discern production methods); strategy/marketing (example: the best ways to use trade associations to learn market trends); and technology/R&D (example: analyzing help-wanted advertisements for clues about new products and technologies). Although clearly written in a "pre-World Wide Web" context, the book illuminates concepts that have enduring application. Even if many of the databases Fuld cites have changed names or ownership–or both–at least several times over since publication, his searching tips and discussion of database limitations retain their relevance.

TIP: More on Mining for Competitive Intelligence

At the Fuld & Co. Web site, "CI Strategies and Tools," the "Internet Intelligence Index" provides pithily annotated links to more than 600 business intelligence-related Internet sites. The links are arranged in three broad categories, covering general business, industry-specific, and international business sites. Contact: http://www.fuld.com/i3/index.html.

TIP: A Concise Competitive Intelligence Reading List

Fleisher, Craig S. and Babette E. Bensoussan. 2003. *Strategic and Competitive Analysis: Methods and Techniques for Analyzing Business Competition.* Upper Saddle River, NJ: Prentice-Hall.

Hussey, David E. and Per Jenster. 1999. *Competitor Intelligence: Turning Analysis into Success.* New York: John Wiley & Sons.

Porter, Michael E. *Competitive Strategy: Techniques for Analyzing Industries and Competitors: With a New Introduction.* 1998. New York: Free Press. (Originally published in 1980. Note in particular Appendix B, "How to Conduct an Industry Analysis.")

COMPANY RANKINGS AND MARKET SHARE

Rankings can be very useful for comparing companies' strengths and weaknesses, and indicating a company's relative position within its industry. Companies are most often ranked, not surprisingly, on their financial performance: such factors as their sales volume or revenues are popular benchmarks. Rankings by production level or number of employees are also fairly common. Rankings may also be specific to a particular industry, such as ranking of airlines on their on-time performance, or the ranking of manufacturers based on their "environmental friendliness." The following resource provides an excellent starting-point for identifying rankings.

***Business Rankings Annual*. Farmington Hills, MI: Gale Group. Annual. Print $325. Contact: http://www.galegroup.com.**

This is a finding guide for thousands of ranked lists, frequently in "top 10" format, of companies, goods, services, and other subjects that are published in more than 1,000 sources such as periodicals and newspapers. Particularly well represented are rankings related to marketing, retailing, and market share, making this work an excellent source for competitive company information. Entries–the rankings–are arranged alphabetically by subject, and the master index shows all rankings in which a company or brand name appears. *Business Rankings Annual* has been published since 1989, and is widely available in public and academic libraries that serve business information seekers. It is among the resources included in Gale's Web-based *Business and Company Resource Center*. A *Cumulative Index 1989-2002* to *Business Rankings Annual* is also available. It includes references to all listings in every edition.

TIP: Updating Information Found in *Business Rankings Annual*

- Using the Source notes given for each entry in the book, look for the same ranking in more recent issues of the cited journal. (Many trade journals publish regular ranking features in the same monthly issue from year to year.)
- Using ProQuest's *ABI/INFORM* database, search by the Subject term "ratings and rankings" in combination with a subject term for an industry, a good, or a service, or SIC/NAICS code. (EbscoHost's *Business Source Premier* does not use a similar Subject term.)
- Using Gale's *Business and Industry* or *TableBase* databases, search by the "Business Subject" term "ranking" in combination with a search by Company Name, Industry Name, Product Name/Code, or some other class of item(s) indexed in the databases.

Market share, another form of ranking, is a major indicator of competitor strength. It may be described as the percentage of total sales of a given market held by each competitor in that market. When consulting published market share figures, the researcher needs to be aware of how broadly or narrowly a given market may be defined: is the "universe" the top three competitors, or *every* manufacturer or provider of a service within a particular classification? Market share information, whether found in a full-text article database or compiled in a reference work, most frequently can be found in trade and industry periodicals. Sometimes the industry, or good or service, may be so specialized or esoteric that market share data can be found only in commercially-produced market research reports, a much more difficult type of resource for the average information-seeker to access (see Chapter 4, "Sources for Market Research Reports").

Market Share Reporter: An Annual Compilation of Reported Market Share Data on Companies, Goods, and Services. **Farmington Hills, MI: Gale Group. Annual. Print $285. Contact: http://www. galegroup.com.**

This is a compilation of reported market share data for North American companies, goods, and services. The volume contains over 2,000 entries, giving corporate, brand, product, service, and commodity market shares, reproduced (generally listing the "top ten") from magazines, trade journals, and other periodical literature. (The "Annotated Source List" in the back provides complete contact information for each publication; most entries also include publication frequency and price.)

Market Share Reporter is organized into sections by 2-digit Standard Industrial Classification (SIC) code categories, representing broad industry groups. Within each section, entries are shown by 4-digit SIC codes, with the original source fully cited. Indexing is by company name, by place name, by source, and by "products, services, names and issues." The Source Index in particular is an excellent tool for identifying more current rankings and uncovering further information. It is divided into "primary sources" (publications where the market shares were found) and "original sources" (original sources cited in the primary sources). These can provide many leads to more in-depth discussion of the market characteristics of products and services.

U.S. Market Trends and Forecasts. **Farmington Hills, MI: Gale Group. Annual. Print $325. Contact: http://www.galegroup.com.**

The marketer will probably want to develop an idea of the recent market status and projected outlook for the product or service. The forecast may be included among the 400 significant markets covered in this handbook, which is organized by SIC code, and cross referenced to the North American Industry Classification System (NAICS). Each SIC Code is given a three- or four-page entry, in which graphs and tables sequentially depict market value (of the industry, over a five-year period), market sectors (segmentation by product type), market shares (by company), and market forecasts (forecasting dollar value and growth rate, for a five-year period). Entries often cite the top three competitors in an industry (expressed by SIC code), and specify the one which accounts for the largest share of the market in question. Overall arrangement is by approximately 30 broad industry groups, such as apparel, automotive, business services, consumer goods, and retailing and wholesaling; as few as 3 and as many as 25 specific goods or services are covered within each group. Within "Retailing and Wholesaling," for example, the following are included: book stores; clothing retailing; consumer electronics wholesaling; do-it-yourself retailing; drinks retailing; food wholesaling; mail order and home shopping; pharmacies; and sports equipment. The General Index cites companies, products, associations, personal names, government agencies, specific legislation, and other terminology appearing in the text. The well-respected market research firm Datamonitor is the primary source for the information.

COMPANY HISTORY

Knowing the history of a company aids the researcher in placing the company analysis in context. Historical performance may provide clues to the rationale for more recent corporate strategies and policies. History can also shed light on a particular corporate culture or image. Additionally, it may be useful for those seeking employment in a specific company.

***International Directory of Company Histories*. Farmington Hills, MI: Gale Group. Irregular. Print $199. Contact: http://www. galegroup.com.**

This source, which began publication in 1988, has earned a reputation as one of the best sources of company history for U.S. and international firms. As of 2003, this ongoing set is comprised of 57 volumes. Most of the companies covered have annual sales of at least $100 million, and are the "major players" in either their industries or geographical locations. The majority by far are also public companies, although a few private and non-profit corporations are included. The company profiles, ranging from three to ten pages in length, include brief bibliographies for "further reading." Frequently, a company's history is updated in a later volume. As each new volume appears, the index in the back, by company name and by industry, is recumulated for the entire set. The index usefully covers all mentions of the companies throughout the series, even in another company's profile. A geographical index to companies, sorted by the country location of the head office, began with Volume 37 of the series. Gale includes this resource in its Web-based *Business and Company Resource Center.*

TIP: Additional Key Sources of Company History

- *"Mergent Manuals."* Contact: http://www.mergent.com.

As noted near the beginning of this chapter, this longstanding collection of eight reference books, formerly known as "Moody's Manuals," provides directory, descriptive, and financial information for some 25,000 U.S.-based and foreign public companies, and also for 15,000 U.S. governmental bodies. A special feature of the company entries is the concise history, in which each major event in the company's history, by month and year, is presented chronologically in a sentence or two. This feature is retained in *Mergent Online*, the Web-based version.

- *Notable Corporate Chronologies.* Farmington Hills, MI: Gale Group, 2001. 3rd edition. Print $465.

This two-volume reference work provides a timeline of the key dates and major events in the histories of more than 1,500 companies. On the Web, it is available as a component of the Gale Group's *Business and Company Resource Center.*

- *Capital Changes Reports.* Riverwoods, IL: CCH Inc. Contact: http://www.cch.com.

Geared to the needs of tax attorneys and accountants, this service tracks capitalization changes such as stock splits, dividends, and reorganizations for 58,000 U.S. public companies. The entire database spans over 100 years and is available in print (loose-leaf with weekly updates), CD-ROM (monthly updates) or online (biweekly updates). There are also companion products for non-U.S. companies.

BRAND AND LOGO INFORMATION

The story behind a company's logo and its product brand(s) are clearly a major part of its history. The logo serves as a company's constant, visual presence in the marketplace–a symbol that instantly connotes a product or service, and, most desirably, a positive emotional response in consumers. The brand name is another "shorthand" by which a company is known, and may become a lasting presence in the lives of consumers. The marketer also has certain practical concerns: Does a brand name under consideration for a product or service already exist? Was it ever used before? What are the characteristics of successful brand names? Why are a brand name and associated logo so important to marketing success?

***Brands and Their Companies.* Farmington Hills, MI: Gale Group. Annual. Print $895. Contact: http://www.galegroup.com.**

More than 115,000 companies (manufacturers, distributors, importers) and 420,000 U.S. consumer brands are listed in this directory, as much a company history resource as it is a guide to brands. Information sources used for the entries include company literature, trade journals, and the United States Patent and Trade Office (PTO). Historical brands (those no longer in production, or now considered generic) are also included, along with cross-references for corporate name changes. The directory, currently in its 24th edition, is published in three volumes. The bulk of the work is devoted to an alphabetical listing of brand names. The rest consists of a separate directory of company names and addresses. Each entry for brand names includes a concise product description, the company name, and the source of the information. In a companion set, the two-volume *Companies and Their Brands* ($595), product names appear directly under the company name. A separately published companion set, *International Brands and Their Companies/International Companies and Their Brands* ($365), last issued in 1996, covers some 75,000 trade names, trademarks, and brand names for consumer products manufactured in countries other than the United States. *Brands and Their Companies* is included in Gale's Web-based *Business and Company Resource Center. Brands and Their Companies*, with both the domestic and international versions, is also available online via Dialog, as File 116 (see Chapter 1, "Introduction to Sources and Strategies for Research on Marketing").

***Encyclopedia of Consumer Brands.* Farmington Hills, MI: Gale Group, 1993. Print $300. Contact: http://www.galegroup.com.**

In three volumes covering approximately 600 of the most popular brand names in America, this work focuses on those which first gained prominence in the 1950s, or later, and which have come to attain "household word" status. Also included are some notorious if historically instructive flops, such as the Edsel, and some other once very popular goods whose stars dimmed considerably (e.g., Cabbage Patch dolls, WordPerfect). Those items are somewhat indicative of the aging status of this source, but they remain historically important.

Volume I covers "Consumable Products" (food; pet food; non-alcoholic beverages; alcoholic beverages; and tobacco); Volume II covers "Personal Products" (apparel and accessories; cosmetics and fragrances; health and beauty aids; household cleaning and paper products; miscellaneous household products; over-the-counter drugs; and stationery and office supply); and Volume III covers "Durable Goods" (appliances; automobiles and related products; computers, electronics, and office equipment; home furnishing and building supplies; musical instruments; photographic equipment; sporting goods; and toys and games).

Here the marketer learns how a company devised its brand name, how it was leveraged in the marketplace, how advertising was built around it, and how the rest of the market responded to the presence of the brand. In addition to this valuable analysis, entries include the product logo. For the vast majority, the current logo (as of the early 1990s) is shown, though selected entries also include an older version of the logo and a photograph of the product. Indexing is by brand name, companies and persons, and brand categories (e.g., automobiles, showing at a glance all the makes covered, or breakfast food, showing all the brands covered).

The World's Greatest Brands. **Edited by Nicholas Kochan. 2nd ed. Washington, NY: New York University Press, 1997. Print $55. 200 pages.**

The origins of more than 300 of the most successful international brands and trademarks, arranged alphabetically, are discussed and fully illustrated in this information-packed, if deceptively slender, volume. The introduction covers the origins of branding, goes on to discuss the "values and visions" that are embodied in brands, and concludes with a discussion of the future of brands. An intriguing prediction is that some companies will begin to include a "statement of value" as part of their balance sheet, to cover such intangibles as the value of their brand(s) and the value of their technology and databases (Kochan 1997, xv).

For this study, Interbrand devised specific measures of "Brand Power" as a means of assessing a brand's marketing and financial strengths and potential. The four components of Brand Power are (1) brand weight not "merely" market share, but instead the influence or dominance that the brand exerts over its product category or market; (2) brand length–the "stretch" or "extension" that the brand has already achieved, or is expected to achieve in the future; (3) brand breadth–the level of authority or "presence" a brand has achieved, internationally and among different types and ages of consumers; and (4) brand depth–the extent to which the brand has captured and sustained customer loyalty. By these measures, McDonald's is ranked first in weight, Disney first in length, Coca-Cola first in breadth, and Apple Computer first in depth (positions #2-#9 are also listed for each measure). "At-a-glance" graphics are also provided for "The World's Top 100 Brands" and "The World's Top Brands by Sector" (alcohol, automotive and oil, beer, non-alcoholic beverages, tobacco and accessories, fashion and luxury goods, financial services, food, household, leisure/travel, media, personal care, retail, technology, and toys).

TIP: Additional Logo Sources

All these titles were edited by David E. Carter, a prolific author of works on trademarks, logos, and corporate images.

- *Logos of America's Fastest Growing Corporations.* 1992. New York, NY: Art Direction Book Co.
- *Logos of American's Largest Companies.* 1988. New York, NY: Art Direction Book Co.
- *Logos of Major World Corporations.* 1989. New York, NY: Art Direction Book Co.

Trade Name Origins. Adrian Room. Lincolnwood, IL: NTC Publishing Group, 1997. Print $12.95. Contact: http://www.ntc-cb. com.

Previously, and perhaps more familiarly, known as *NTC's Dictionary of Trade Name Origins*, this source alphabetically lists well over 700 renowned trade names and details the derivation and history of each name, as well as the name's connotations and associations. For selected entries, the logo for a brand or trade name is reproduced in the left margin. Although the most prominent U.S. trade names/manufacturers are covered (e.g., Coca-Cola, Polaroid), the emphasis here is distinctly Western European, and especially British (the work was originally published in Great Britain). The rather lengthy introduction is an excellent essay on the lexicography of trade names. The three appendices deal with letters and suffixes (such as the many uses of the terminal vowel "o"); "computer-devised names," all consisting of four letters–a curiosity; and a brief listing of "unexplained names," such as "Dry Sack" sherry and "Tabasco" sauce, for which the author is eager to receive any leads.

TIP: Another Source for Product and Company Names Origins

Encyclopedia of Corporate Names Worldwide. Jefferson, N.C.: McFarland, 2002. Print $75.

Noted name historian Adrian Room, who produced the resource described previously, is also responsible for this volume of company and product or brand name origins. The approximately 3,500 entries cover American and British names mostly; some French, German, Italian, and Japanese corporate names are also included. One appendix lists about 175 advertising slogans; another recounts the story of how nylon got its name. Contact: http://www. macfarlandpub.com.

TIP: Finding Brand Names in Other Business Directories

- *Thomas Register of American Manufacturers*. New York: Thomas Publishing Co. Annual. Print or Online. Contact: http:// thomasregister.com. (Has a brand name index for U.S. and Canadian firms.)
- *Directory of Corporate Affiliations*. New Providence, NJ: Lexis-Nexis Group. Annual. Print or online. Contact: http://www. corporateaffiliations.com. (Has a brand name index.)

Brandchannel.com. Interbrand. London. Online (free). Contact: http://www.brandchannel.com.

Interbrand, promulgator of *The World's Greatest Brands* (described above), is a worldwide brand consulting firm, headquartered in London. The company calls its Web site "the world's only online exchange about branding," and offers detailed brand profiles, with links to related articles; book reviews; a glossary of branding terms; job postings; a directory of branding professionals' Web sites; and a schedule of industry conferences. Also available are free "brandpapers," 2-page to 13-page essays, chiefly in PDF format. Recent titles include "1-2-3 Success! Build Your Personal Brand and Expand Your Success," "A View on the Future of Branding," and "Best Practice: The Principles of Effective Advertising for Dotcoms." Interbrand is also well-known for its annual ranking of the world's most valuable brands. Starting in 2001, *Business Week* joined Interbrand in creating the ranking, which may be found at http://www.finfacts.com/brands.htm.

REFERENCE

Kochan, Nicholas. 1997. Introduction. In *The World's Greatest Brands*. 2nd ed. Washington Square, NY: New York University Press.

Chapter 4

Sources for Market Research Reports

Topics

About Market Research Reports
Primary and Secondary Research
Selecting a Market Research Report
Role of the Web in Market Research
Print Directories
Free Web Aggregators
Subscription Web Aggregators
Investment Research Reports
Customized Research on the Web
Directories of Market Research Firms
Using the Web for Primary Research

Sources

Findex
Research Alert Yearbook
MarketResearch.com
ECNext Knowledge Center
Mindbranch.com
Profound
MarketResearch.com Academic
*GreenBook: Worldwide Directory of Market Research Companies
    and Services*
Worldwide Directory of Focus Group Companies and Services

[Haworth co-indexing entry note]: "Sources for Market Research Reports." Diamond, Wendy, and Michael R. Oppenheim. Co-published simultaneously in *Journal of Business & Finance Librarianship* (The Haworth Information Press, an imprint of The Haworth Press, Inc.) Vol. 9, No. 2/3, 2004, pp. 91-106; and: *Marketing Information: A Strategic Guide for Business and Finance Libraries* (Wendy Diamond, and Michael R. Oppenheim) The Haworth Information Press, an imprint of The Haworth Press, Inc., 2004, pp. 91-106. Single or multiple copies of this article are available for a fee from The Haworth Document Delivery Service [1-800-HAWORTH, 9:00 a.m. - 5:00 p.m. (EST). E-mail address: docdelivery@haworthpress.com].

http://www.haworthpress.com/web/JBFL
© 2004 by The Haworth Press, Inc. All rights reserved.
Digital Object Identifier: 10.1300/J109v09n02_04

Quirks.com
QuickTake.com

Marketing involves decisions; decisions require information; information is generated by research and analysis. The "market research report" is a unique form of documentation that is extensive, detailed, and intended to yield data and insight to address a particular marketing question, such as the effect of a new brand name, or an advertising slogan, or new packaging, or some variable about a *specific* product, service, advertising campaign, or packaging decision.

ABOUT MARKET RESEARCH REPORTS

Marketers have two options when it comes to market research reports: (1) locating and utilizing completed reports published by others; or (2) generating new, custom reports to meet the specific needs. The bulk of this chapter focuses on understanding the purposes and content of published reports, and how best to find, evaluate, and utilize them. The marketer may need to determine whether an individualized, custom report would be preferable. The chapter closes with a discussion of Web options for conducting customized research and directories for locating market research firms for hire.

Let's suppose you are selling cookies and want to know how your caramel cream will sell with a new packaging design in upscale food stores. Industry analysis and demographic research will give you the general trends in baked goods, but they will not answer specific questions about the most popular flavors and successful package designs in the cookie segment. A market research report on "Cookies," might contain charts, tables, graphs and narrative on such topics as "Retail Cookie Sales and Demographics," "Industry Pricing and Profit Situation," and "Purchaser Demographics for Major Branded Cookie Products."

At one time, market research was considered an "extra step," reserved for the most sophisticated, elaborate marketing plans. However, that is no longer the case; searching out published market research reports is now a relatively routine step in the marketing planning process, and fortunately, they have also become easier to obtain. The reports themselves are still quite expensive, but some of the upfront costs, such as subscription fees, have dropped. In addition, because "off the shelf" market research reports are now more accessible than ever before, many marketers rarely find it necessary to hire consultants to develop an expensive, customized market research project from scratch. However, a published market research report will not give you the actual responses of real people to the taste of your cookie and the look of the package. For that kind of response measurement, it will still be necessary to hire a market research firm to carry out primary research using a taste-panel, focus group, survey, or interviews to assess response to your own product and its package.

The term market research can refer to several different types of studies. The reported data may be quantitative (numerical and statistical), or it may be qualitative (subjective and emotional). Reports may cover an entire industry, a specific segment of an industry, an individual product, or a series of related products. They are usually highly detailed, specific, and full of quantitative data in the form of charts, tables, and graphs, along with expert, in-depth analysis. Narrative sections may include discussions of "nitty-gritty" aspects of the marketing process, including competitor strengths and weaknesses, market share, sales volume, pricing issues, distributors, suppliers, and customer segments. Published market research reports cover consumer or industrial studies, syndicated and multi-client studies (e.g., Nielsen ratings for television), circulation audits, or subscription research services. In some cases, market research is the only source of information for some types of industrial, technological, and international products or services. The wide range of topics covered by market research reports is indicated by this group of sample titles:

- Commercial Refrigeration Equipment
- Golf Equipment and Accessories
- World Markets for WINTEL and RISC/UNIX Workstations
- Cookies

TIP: Dictionaries and Glossaries of Market Research Terminology

- *Glossary of Market Research Terms.* Contact: http://www.imriresearch.com/www/gloss-en.htm.
- Koschnick, Wolfgang J. 1996. *Dictionary of Social and Marketing Research.* Brookfield, VT: Gower.
- Van Minden, Jack J. R. 1987. *Dictionary of Marketing Research.* Chicago: St. James Press.

PRIMARY AND SECONDARY RESEARCH

The terms primary and secondary research are essential concepts in market research. Robert Irving Berkman and Arthur Hammond-Tooke provide an excellent definition of primary and secondary research in their book *Finding Market Research on the Web* (1999, 20-22). *Primary research* refers to information which is gathered "first-hand," that is, data from direct sampling of individual consumers through a survey, questionnaire, focus group, telephone interview, taste panel, or shopping observation. Designing and carrying out such a project can be time and labor intensive, and therefore very costly, especially if large samples and statistical expertise is needed. On the other hand, a simple primary research project might consist of a short questionnaire enclosed with a customer's billing statement. Though time and labor intensive, direct, customized, primary research is invaluable in its ability to prevent a costly marketing mistake. Primary research is particularly useful when trying to measure potential customer response to a discrete event, such as a new product, a new technology, new packaging, or an advertising campaign. It may be qualitative, such as when focus groups or interviews are used to measure the subjective responses to a new brand name or advertising slogan or flavor. In other instances, hard, quantitative data are needed, and a large, statistically valid sample may be desired.

Because primary research is expensive, it is practical to begin a project by exploring existing secondary research sources. *Secondary research* refers to data that are available "second-hand," that is, information that has already been reported elsewhere. It was probably collected and analyzed for a different reason or for a different "client," but now it may be beneficially applied to a new purpose. Sometimes known as "desk research," it consists largely of ferreting out and synthesizing published information from articles, databases, statistical tables, government reports, company annual reports, etc. As an example, the sources for industry and customer research discussed in Chapters 2 and 5 of this book consist wholly of "secondary" research.

In fact, the best market research reports combine primary and secondary research. By purchasing an existing report, marketers can take advantage of primary research gathered by market research firms in the course of other projects. These published reports are expensive, especially when compared to regular trade books and magazines, but not nearly as costly as contracting for a primary research project or as making a bad marketing decision due to not having the right information.

SELECTING A MARKET RESEARCH REPORT

The selection of the best report is a critical step. Consider the business objective and specific questions about competitors, groups of consumers, emerging technologies, geographical areas, and the utility of small versus large samples. Look for reports that combine primary research (found in questionnaires and surveys) with extensive secondary research (using trade associations, articles, government sources, etc.). Select the most specific report you can, but remember that even broad coverage may yield excellent information. If the search service provides a listing of companies mentioned in the report, this can be an important clue. When selecting among a group of reports, compare other reports written by the market research firm to see which specialize in your industry.

ROLE OF THE WEB IN MARKET RESEARCH

Since the advent of the Web, there has been an explosion of market research sites, resulting in significant improvements in the availability of reports on the secondary market, as well as a significant reduction in the cost when compared to contracting for primary research. There are now a number of free Web databases (discussed below) that aggregate reports from hundreds of different publishers. Although the reports themselves are anything but free (ranging from a few hundred to several thousand dollars), the researcher can now readily locate a current report and order it instantly. Furthermore, these sites offer such service improvements as the ability to preview the table of contents or sample pages, thus minimizing costly mistakes in ordering an inadequate report. Improving cost effectiveness further, many also offer "slice and dice" pricing, so that it is possible to purchase just the relevant pages out of a lengthy report.

In addition to free aggregator sites, there are also a number of Web-based subscription services which compile reports from numerous publishers. Although these sites require a fee in order to search them, they are still an improvement in currency and turnaround time over a print directory. Subscription services offer decided advantages, such as the ability to set up a custom profile and receive notification of new reports.

Despite the increased availability of published market research reports, many projects will still require primary, customized research. The Web has also made it easier to locate a marketing research firm and even to perform a "do-it-yourself" project. There are Web-based directories of market research firms, and the Web also offers additional ways to sample a customer base and distribute questionnaires and surveys.

TIP: *Finding Market Research on the Web* **by Robert Irving Berkman and Arthur Hammond Tooke.**

The ideas and concepts used in the previous discussion are based on the book entitled *Finding Market Research on the Web*, by Robert Irving Berkman and Arthur Hammond-Tooke (New York: Kalorama Information LLC, 1999). The authors provide many excellent tips for evaluating and selecting market research reports. A 2001 update is available from *MarketResearch.com.*

PRINT DIRECTORIES FOR MARKET RESEARCH REPORTS

Although traditional, print tools for locating market research are not thought of as "aggregators," this is essentially what they do.

FINDEX. **Rockville, MD: MarketResearch.com. 2002. Print $399. Online $399. 500+ pages. Contact: http://marketresearch.com.**

FINDEX 2002 is the 23rd edition of this longstanding reference tool which was formerly entitled *FINDEX: The Worldwide Directory of Market Research Reports, Studies and Surveys*. It is now part of the MarketResearch.com product line. This version, available in both print and online, contains descriptions of 8,000 reports, surveys, and studies from 350 publishers. Reports are listed by category and by publisher. There are 20 subject categories, in which the entry for each report includes publisher, date, purchase options, and subject category cross-references. The section of "reports by publisher" includes all publishers in the *MarketResearch.com* collection. There is also a directory of publishers with contact information. There are two indexes: an alphabetical list of reports for each category, and a listing of reports by country.

Research Alert Yearbook. **New York: EPM Communications. Annual. Print $295. Contact: http://www.epmcom.com.**

Research Alert Yearbook is published by EPM Communications, a publisher specializing in target marketing. In one handy volume, it compiles data from over 1,000 studies, reports, polls, and focus groups. Unlike *Findex* and most of the Web-based aggregators, it does not cover industrial, technology, or international markets. Organized into 40 subject categories, it provides an annual update of published market research on consumer products and demographic segments. Just as re-searchers use the source notes in tables in the *Statistical Abstract of the United States*, they can use the abstracted data in this compendium to provide leads to worthwhile "off-the-shelf" reports.

FREE WEB AGGREGATORS

The proliferation of market research sites on the Web provides the opportunity to survey hundreds of current reports at no cost, and then purchase individual reports as needed. No subscription fees are in-volved, though sometimes registration is required. Most services pro-vide various payment and delivery options, including instant online delivery.

Some of the best-known free Web aggregator services are *MarketResearch. com* and *Mindbranch.com*. Most share similar, though not identical, search functionality and customer service features, so it is worthwhile to explore a few possibilities. Even within one site, reports from various producers may vary; in some cases, the report may reside on the site's own server; in others it will arrive from the report producer's own data-base. When reviewing a site, look for options that help in report selec-tion: viewing sample pages, tables of contents, or contact with a sales representative who will tell you if the report in question contains the in-formation you need. Those that offer "slice-and-dice" pricing for pur-chase of selected pages or chapters help reduce the cost considerably.

MarketResearch.com. **Rockville, MD. ©2002. Online (free). Con-tact: http://www.MarketResearch.com.**

Initially formed in 1998 as Kalorama Information LLC, *MarketResearch. com* claims to be the leading provider of market research products, in-cluding over 40,000 publications from more than 350 originators. In its relatively short history, it has acquired numerous market research firms, including the published products division of FIND/SVP and *Findex: The Worldwide Directory of Market Research Reports, Studies and Surveys*. It has also entered partnerships with other information provid-ers like ProQuest (for exclusive distribution of *MarketResearch.com Academic*), Simmons Market Research Bureau, and Hoover's Inc.

Updated daily, *MarketResearch.com* serves as a gateway for locating reports from all major producers. No fees or registration are required to search the site. *MarketResearch.com* offers options for purchasing just one chapter, or section, or sub-section of a very expensive report, so that costs can be controlled. However, these segments are sometimes priced in such a way that it soon becomes more cost effective to purchase the whole report. Many reports are available immediately online, though a few are available only in hardcopy and must be faxed or shipped.

The search engine is one of the most flexible. There are options for browsing within categories for industries and topics, as well as searching with keywords, Boolean operators, proximity operators, and word stemming (truncation). A search may be further refined by focusing within a set of results, or filtering by geography, and then sorted by relevancy, title, date, or price. The *MarketResearch.com* results screen also provides a great many options to help with selecting the best report. There is a full abstract and, in most cases, a table of contents, as well as a handy link to a question form where more information about any specific report can be requested.

Especially worth noting is the unique STAT ("search-term-and-text") feature, which enables a preview of a report by displaying how many times and on what page a particular search term appears. Further, each term is hyperlinked to a window of text which reveals the exact context. For example, a search on "caramel cream" reveals four reports containing that term. Selecting the STAT feature on each report makes it easy to choose those that offer the most relevant discussion. The site also has a "Fast Find" feature with direct links to over 5,000 country reports and 2,000 company reports.

ECNext Knowledge Center. ECNext Inc. Powell, OH. ©2002. Online (free). Contact: http://www.ecnext.com/commercial/knowledgecenter.shtml.

ECNext Knowledge Center is the current permutation of *IMRMall.com* which started as a market research search site in 1997. It is similar in scope to the other aggregators and similarly provides access to market research reports from a number of different originators. Unlike the others, this Web site contains more than market research reports, as it also includes commercial newsletters, country profiles, financial reports, investment research, tables, and trade journals. Its periodical content is derived from a set of Gale Group databases, including *TableBase, Business & Industry*, and *Business Management Practices*. Market research suppliers include such major names as Euromonitor, Roper ASW, and Freedonia. Searching is free and full citations are provided as the result.

"Slice-and-dice" pricing is a primary feature, and purchases can be made at the chapter or article level. The reports are all delivered in electronic format.

As noted in a 2002 review in the *Information Advisor, ECNext Knowledge Center* has a number of advantages. "In addition to its superb interface, excellent help tutorials and customer service, the database offers high quality sourcing, powerful search capabilities, and subject indexing." The major drawbacks noted were the lack of an option to sort results and the ability to view introductory matter for free (Berkman 2002, 2).

Users can search by subject, publication type categories (e.g., market research, investment reports, tables, trade journals), industry categories, countries, publishers, and titles. Advanced techniques using Boolean connectors, word expansion (stemming), and field searching are available. The results list provides full citations but not access to tables of contents or sample pages.

Mindbranch.com. MindBranch, Inc. Williamstown, MA. ©2002. Online (free). Contact: http://mindbranch.com.

Mindbranch.com provides many of the same search features as *ECNext Knowledge Center* and *MarketResearch.com*. It offers custom research services as well as access to market research reports and newsletters from other originators. Searching and viewing report descriptions are free; registering allows you to set up a user profile, but is not required in order to use the site. A "Personal Research Assistant" is available, free-of-charge, to help clients find research. Another distinguishing feature is the access to real-time, live help using chat room technology. While online, customer support experts will describe a report and its contents, making it more likely that you will be able to select the best report for your purposes.

Although the scope and content of *Mindbranch.com* is not as extensive as the previous services discussed, it provides several useful features. Searches can be done within a single industry category or refined and sorted by date, price, product, and region. Results are provided in categorized levels which indicate the focus of the particular report. For example, a search on "juice drinks" provides a result of 148 reports in the Consumer Products category, further broken down into 20 sub-categories such as demographics or product specific. Selection is made easier by an enhanced results display that features a healthy amount of description and tables of contents.

TIP: Some Well-Known Market Research Firms

- Burke Inc. http://www.burke.com/bmr/
- DataMonitor http://www.datamonitor.com
- Euromonitor http://www.euromonitor.com
- FIND/SVP http://www.findsvp.com
- Freedonia (Packaging research specialists) http://www.freedoniagroup. com
- Frost & Sullivan (Manufactured goods) http://www.frost.com
- Gartner Group (Information Technology) http://www4.gartner.com
- Insight Research Corporation (Telecommunications) http://www. insight-corp.com/
- Jupiter Communications (Emerging technology) http://www. jup.com
- Forrester http://www.forrester.com
- Synovate http://www.marketfacts.com
- USDATA.com (Brand names and geographic research) http://www.usdata.com

---

SUBSCRIPTION WEB AGGREGATORS

This section discusses a few of the Web-based services that require a monthly or annual fee in order to search their databases of market research reports. With the number of free search engines available, why would someone select this option? The advantage is the extra services provided and the availability of more current material. Sometimes subscribers are eligible for automatic updates to reports they have purchased, or access to reports three to six months before they are offered for sale on the open market. Many services provide access to the content of reports for the cost of the subscription fee.

Examples of subscription based search services include *Investext's Research Bank Web*, Profound's *ResearchLine*, and Dialog's *MARKETFULL*. Two will be discussed here; one is used heavily by major corporations and professionals, and the other is geared to the academic market.

Profound. Cary, NC: The Dialog Corporation. Online. Subscription (price varies). Contact: http://www.profound.com.

The *Profound* service has long been highly valued among professional information and marketing specialists. A subscription fee is required to access the database, but in return it offers streamlined and sophisticated features designed for executives and experienced analysts. Along with being a source for market research reports, it also includes update and alert services as well as other types of information: these include *BrandLine* for trademark and brand information, *BrokerLine* for investment research reports (from the *Investext* database), *NewsLine* for newspaper articles, *WireLine* for wire service stories, *CountryLine* for global economic data, and *CompanyLine* for private and public company accounts information.

The market research component is called *ResearchLine*, which is a comprehensive offering of over 130,000 full-text market research reports from 100 originators. *Profound* has structured its database to allow for precision retrieval, with proximity and keyword-in-context features. Every item of data is indexed according to an established, sophisticated thesaurus of terminology and scope terms. This is a true subject taxonomy, with broader, narrower, and related terms defined. This feature facilitates speedy and accurate retrieval because the user can set the criteria used for indexing and searching. *Profound's Market Briefings* offer a snapshot overview of markets from which you can also access news and research. These overviews are graphically-rich with numerous tables, charts and "bullet-points." They allow the user to drill down to specific discussions, such as market size, market sectors, market share, or consumer profile. Reports are displayed in PDF, making them easy to read and print.

In summary, *Profound* is an excellent search tool for corporate marketing departments or information consultants, but the annual subscription fee probably puts it out of reach for the occasional research project.

MarketResearch.com Academic. MarketResearch.com. Rockville, MD. ©2000. Online. Subscription (price varies). Contact: http:// academic.marketresearch.com.

Formerly *Kalorama Academic*, this database is a subset of *MarketResearch.com's* full commercial catalog of market research which is available exclusively through ProQuest, a major database vendor (http://www.proquest.com). Designed and priced for academic libraries and business schools, the database is not comprehensive and contains a substantial number of somewhat older reports. Starting in 2002, the "currency" of the content increased dramatically. The reports are all full-text and they cover such categories as demographics, consumer products, telecommunications, financial services, transportation and shipping, and more.

MarketResearch.com Academic can be searched by keyword or browsed within categories. Most reports are full-text in PDF format, some are in PowerPoint, and all contain the desirable but elusive features unique to market research, such as major industry competitors, sales figures, and market share. The reports in PowerPoint belong to the *MarketLooks* series, which consists of concise, graphics-rich, 15-30 page summaries of full-length market research reports. Reports that cover more than one market segment are split into individual *MarketLooks*; their PowerPoint format facilitates easy extraction of text, charts, and tables for use in presentations.

INVESTMENT RESEARCH REPORTS

The primary purpose of investment research, also known as brokerage house or investment analyst reports, is to provide stock market and financial advice to investors. When analysts evaluate the investment potential and market performance of companies, they often discuss a company's marketing strategy and decisions because investment potential is inextricably related to a company's industry and marketing environment. Thus, many stock analysts and brokerage houses produce reports that are an outstanding source of market research.

The best source for locating these reports is Thomson's *Investext* database, which aggregates reports from many different firms, such as Morgan Stanley Dean Witter, Credit Suisse First Boston, Merrill Lynch, and hundreds of others. *Investext* is available both from its own Web site called *Research Bank Web* (http://www.investext.com), and from a number of subscription-based online vendors, such as *LexisNexis*, *Factiva*, and others. Sometimes a business library affiliated with a large university or major city provides access to the *Investext* database. Reports are available for search and retrieval on a one-time transactional basis, making *Investext* a good option for the occasional user who may not want to subscribe to an online service. Nevertheless, the reports can be quite expensive, varying from several hundred to over a thousand dollars.

Multex (http://www.multex.com) is another search option that provides access to a database of investment research reports from many brokerage houses and analysts. It is also a subscription service with excellent search functionality and deep content, and it is becoming increasingly available in university libraries serving advanced degree programs in business and finance.

CUSTOMIZED RESEARCH ON THE WEB

Despite the thousands of reports from hundreds of publishers that are available through free and subscription Web sites, they represent only a relatively small percentage of all market research. Sometimes marketing demands a custom-designed, primary research project targeted to a specific need. There are hundreds of market research firms that may be retained to perform custom research. Many of these firms specialize in a niche industry ("high tech"), or function ("packaging"), or area of business ("international"). In fact, for some industrial research projects, these specialists may be the only ones who retain staff with experience and expertise in a particular business segment.

This section describes sources for identifying market research firms and also discusses the use of the Web itself for certain types of primary research, especially direct polling of consumers.

DIRECTORIES OF MARKET RESEARCH FIRMS

Directories identify sources for locating market research firms when you have a specialized need or wish to find a firm to convene a focus group, distribute a questionnaire, or observe shoppers.

***GreenBook: The Worldwide Directory of Market Research Companies and Services* (Volume 1) and *Worldwide Directory of Focus Group Companies and Services* (Volume 2). Bradenton, FL: New York AMA Communications Services Inc. ©2002. Print (Volume 1 $250; Volume 2 $100). Online (free). Contact: http://www.greenbook.org.**

For 30 years, people have turned to the *GreenBook* to locate market research firms. Currently available as two volumes in print and as a free online database, it offers specialized categories to help the user pinpoint the precise type of firm needed. Market research firms pay for their basic listing and definition of their own specialties. Users should note that the "Top 3" firms listed in each category represent firms that have paid for a "premium listing."

The Worldwide Directory of Marketing Research Companies and Services (Volume 1) is arranged alphabetically by company name. Entries include services offered, audiences covered, and markets served. There are eight indexes, including research specialties, computer programs utilized, audiences services, online research tools, etc. *The Worldwide Directory of Focus Group Companies and Services* (Volume II) is arranged geographically. Its category indexes include video-conferencing, Internet broadcasting, usability testing, recruiting, and moderating. Together the two print volumes list more than 2,000 firms and over 400 types of services.

On the Web, the *GreenBook* is especially flexible because it is searchable using multiple criteria. These include detailed specialties in research services, audience and markets served, computer programs, geographic locations, and more. It is also possible to browse within certain categories. For instance, you might select the Audiences/Industries/Market Specialties listing. More than 180 categories are available, ranging from acquisitions to yellow pages; geographical and lifestyle segments are also included. Searching is simple and the results are organized by the stipulated criteria, though the "Top 3" are always listed first.

***Quirks.com.* Quirk's Marketing Research Review. Minneapolis, MN. ©2002. Online (free) or print ($35/year). Contact: http://www. quirks.com.**

The *Quirks.com* site provides free online access to the publisher's annual *Research Sourcebook*, a directory of market research providers. The database of 7,300 firms is provided on the Web site and is searchable by company name, by geography, or by industry or research specialization, such as "mystery shopper," "focus group facilities," "ethnic research," and others. *Quirks.com* also provides access to a searchable archive of articles published in the journal, *Quirk's Marketing Research Review*, between 1986-2001. More than 1,000 full-text articles are available, with added options to facilitate printing or e-mailing. The site also features a Glossary which lists "over 650 common and uncommon marketing research words and phrases."

An alternative market research directory is located at *ResearchInfo. com* (http://www.researchinfo.com). It is also a free site. The listings can be browsed alphabetically or searched using four categories: Full Service (industry sectors, social policy, political/election), Qualitative

Field Service (geographic), Quantitative Data Collection (phone, mail, online), and Other (suppliers, associations).

A print directory called *Little Black Book of Research Resources* (EPM Communications. New York, NY. 2001. $80) contains nearly 500 alphabetically-arranged company listings. Each listing includes brief descriptive blurbs and full contact information for each company; the directory is indexed by subject.

Web search engines are another good means of identifying market research firms. For example, *Google Directory* (http://directory.google.com) provides an extensive listing in the Business/Marketing/Market Research Suppliers category.

USING THE WEB FOR PRIMARY RESEARCH

As discussed earlier, primary research refers to the "first-hand" investigation of a market research question, usually by direct contact with customers. The interactive, discursive nature of bulletin boards, listservs, and other Web activities has great potential for assembling a focus group or posting a questionnaire. In most cases, it is preferable to hire professionals because primary research usually involves decisions about sampling methodologies and statistical analysis. However, the quick turn-around and straightforward logistics of carrying out polls using Web-based forms or "live chat" technology means that it can be done less expensively than ever before. In addition, sites such as *Quicktake.com* have introduced a new way of doing primary market research.

QuickTake.com. Greenfield Online Inc. Wilton, CT. ©2001. Online (fee varies). Contact: http://quicktake.com.

QuickTake.com is a service and software provider that carries out online polling, sampling, and surveying of consumers who use the Internet. It provides "real-time feedback" for marketing and public policy decision-makers about ideas, products, concepts, packaging, and anything else. For marketers, its primary use is to gather data directly for a market research project, but it offers some other useful features. Data can be cross tabulated, and results displayed in colorful charts and graphs. Survey groups can be selected by gender and age, geographical location, occupation, and special interests. Pricing is based on the number of respondents, but the cost may be less than hiring a market research consultant.

Despite the obvious attraction of direct, low cost access to consumers, combined with speedy results, it is important to be cautious. People responding to *Quicktake.com* are a self-selected group, with all the variables attached to unseen, unverified, and possibly unreliable Internet users. Whether they are truly representative of desired statistical characteristics cannot be determined. So, in the long run, it may be best to return to the tried and true, if expensive, solution of purchasing an existing market research report or retaining a professional market research firm.

TIP: *Quicktake.com*'s Guides and Templates

At *Quicktake.com*, there are two helpful handbooks: "Survey Writing Tips Guide" and a set of "Survey Templates." Composed by market research professionals, these are helpful tools for the design of any survey or questionnaire.

REFERENCES

Berkman, Robert I. and Arthur Hammond-Tooke. 1999. *Finding Market Research on the Web*. New York: Kalorama Information LLC.

Berkman, Robert I. 2002. "ECNext's Knowledge Center: New and–Yes–Improved!" *Information Advisor* 14: 4 (April).

PART III

RESEARCH
ABOUT CUSTOMERS

Chapter 5

Demographic, Geographic, and Lifestyle Sources

Topics

Demographic Data from the U.S. Census
Demographic Sources with Enhanced Marketing Features
Specialized Lifestyle and Psychographic Sources

Sources

Census of Population and *Housing*
U.S. Census Bureau Web Site
Current Population Survey
American Community Survey
County and City Extra: Annual Metro, City, and County Data Book
Consumer Expenditure Survey
Survey of Buying Power and Media Markets
New Strategist Publications
Right Site
Lifestyle Market Analyst
1999 National Consumer Survey for College and Universities
VALS Survey
Demographic Sourcebooks
PRIZM

[Haworth co-indexing entry note]: "Demographic, Geographic, and Lifestyle Sources." Diamond, Wendy, and Michael R. Oppenheim. Co-published simultaneously in *Journal of Business & Finance Librarianship* (The Haworth Information Press, an imprint of The Haworth Press, Inc.) Vol. 9, No. 2/3, 2004, pp. 109-134; and: *Marketing Information: A Strategic Guide for Business and Finance Libraries* (Wendy Diamond, and Michael R. Oppenheim) The Haworth Information Press, an imprint of The Haworth Press, Inc., 2004, pp. 109-134. Single or multiple copies of this article are available for a fee from The Haworth Document Delivery Service [1-800-HAWORTH, 9:00 a.m. - 5:00 p.m. (EST). E-mail address: docdelivery@haworthpress.com].

http://www.haworthpress.com/web/JBFL
Digital Object Identifier: 10.1300/J109v09n02_05

Every marketer knows that in order to sell successfully, one must identify, find, understand, and connect with the customer. The marketer must conceive the buying process from the point of view of the customer. To do this, many marketers rely on a model of consumer behavior that incorporates population demographics, social class, culture, family, interests and hobbies, stage of life, values, and other characteristics (Hawkins, Best and Coney 1996, 609).

The sources in this chapter focus on describing current and potential buyers in several ways: as members of social groups, as residents of geographic locations, and as individuals with unique identities and lifestyles. To gain an understanding of customers, marketers turn to demography, a field of study with both statistical and social science components. This has given modern marketers access to many specialized marketing sources that incorporate lifestyle, buying habits, and values information. Altogether these varied sources offer an understanding of the broad sweep of society as well as detail about local regions and neighborhoods. Some of these sources are inexpensive and widely available in libraries, but others are highly specialized and therefore costly to access.

Although demographic analysis is used extensively for many different business functions, marketing professionals are probably the primary business users of demographic tools and data (Pol and Thomas 1997, 240-251). Major functions such as retail site analysis, market valuations, finding customers, developing new products, setting sales targets, and target marketing could not be performed without demography. In a strict sense, demography involves the statistical description of populations and their locations, using baseline data such as age, gender, ethnicity, income, and location. However, the needs of marketers have generated a number of sources to help them understand the "softer" side of their customers, such as buying habits, lifestyles, values, and psychology. The sum of characteristics that marketers consider are: demographic (age, income, marital status, ethnicity, education), geographic (country, region, city, neighborhood), psychographic (beliefs and values), and lifestyle (activities, hobbies, recreational interests).

Since marketing encompasses all activities linking a product or service with *customers*, understanding and describing the target audience becomes paramount in designing a marketing plan. This has become an increasingly important part of the marketing mix. Segmentation defines customers into distinct groups in order to enable the marketer to select, or target, the right customers. Where once mass marketing was adequate, our increasingly diversified society comprised of distinctive ethnicities, regions, and lifestyles, makes it essential to specifically define and understand a narrowed target market. *Target marketing* and *segmentation* mean that a marketing plan will take into account a specific set of customers and try to understand what motivates their purchases.

Marketing is not only the largest user of demographic data within the business community, but it is also certainly one of the largest of all non-governmental uses of U.S. census products (Lavin 1996, 38). Although the census is mandated by the U.S. Constitution for the primary purpose of establishing congressional districts, its applications have expanded exponentially. Census data are unique because information is given at the macro level of the nation as a whole, as well as at the micro, local level of individual neighborhoods and even blocks. Thus, in addition to demographic profiling and customer segmentation, companies also consult census data in order to carry out many routine business activities like locating retail stores and distribution centers, buying radio and television advertising time, determining how much of a specific product to ship to individual stores, identifying regions with characteristics similar to an existing successful sales area, and delineating sales territories. Companies also rely on census data for those marketing applications that require a social scientist's understanding of population shifts and demographic trends, to help in designing new products or creating advertising campaigns. The aging of the baby boomer generation, the growth in single parent households, and the move to the suburbs are some examples of social changes that have had direct impacts on business decisions.

Our discussion will focus on many different kinds of sources that describe customers in these various ways. Most are secondary sources of data that either originate from, or are based largely, on data generated by government agencies, especially that produced by the U.S. Census Bureau. Although the originating governmental information is inexpensive, it is sometimes less current and more cumbersome to use than the demographic data available from private publishers in repackaged, re-formatted and augmented forms. Many non-profit advocacy organizations and research firms also compile unique data which are used by private publishers to augment fundamental census products.

DEMOGRAPHIC DATA FROM THE U.S. CENSUS

The United States Census Bureau, a division of the Department of Commerce, generates and publishes an extensive variety of reports, tables, databases, and summaries of potential usefulness to marketers (Lavin 1996, 20). These include the *Census of Population and Housing*, the *Current Population Survey*, the *American Community Survey*, the *Consumer Expenditure Survey*, the *American Housing Survey*, the *Census of Retail Trade*, the *Census of Wholesale Trade*, the *Retail Trade Survey*, and the *Household Food Consumption Survey*. This section does describe every one of these, but it is useful for marketers to be aware of the varied information available from easily accessed government sources. (Many types of Census data are discussed throughout this book.)

At this writing, only partial data from Census 2000 have been released, and while some new terminology and user-friendly Web-based software have been adopted, the underlying issues and publication structure are similar to the 1990 Census, as explained below.

TIP: Sampling versus Complete Counts in Census Data

Some census data represent *sampling* surveys and others are *complete counts*. When comparing data, be sure not to mix "apples and oranges" by confusing the two types. In his book *Understanding the Census: A Guide for Marketers, Planners, Grant Writers and Other Data Users*, Michael Lavin recommends choosing the correct geographic level, checking table titles and footnotes, and determining the unit of measurement, which may be persons or households (Lavin 1996, 369).

Census of Population and Housing. **Washington DC: U.S. Census Bureau. Decennial. Online (free). Contact: http://www.census.gov.**

The "granddaddies" of census publications are the *Census of Population* and *Housing* series. Once issued as separate reports, the Census 2000 designation is *"PHC"* for Population and Housing Count/Characteristics. This report provides the majority of demographic information describing the population in terms of gender, age, income, race or ethnicity, language group, housing, and geographic location. The census is useful for target marketing because data are available for 54 separate states (and state-like entities), as well as nationwide. The United States Summary Reports are useful because they tabulate data at the national and regional levels and provide tables which make "nationwide comparisons extremely easy" (Lavin 1996, 277).

While national, regional, and state data are essential, especially for marketing projects involving major social trends, census data are also available for smaller geographic units. Most sales and marketing planners find the county-level and sub-county level data to be the most useful. Although the Census Bureau has an elaborate and detailed scheme for designating these smaller geographic areas, marketers will generally utilize those describing cities, counties and their respective sub-areas. Cities and counties are combined into areas known in census publications as Metropolitan Statistical Areas (MSAs) and Consolidated Metropolitan Statistical Areas (CMSAs). Generally speaking, MSAs are urban areas of fewer than 1 million people. CMSAs have larger populations, and are comprised of a number of separate MSAs, sometimes called "primary metropolitan statistical areas" (PMSAs). For example, Los Angeles-Long Beach is one of the MSAs (or PMSAs) which make up the Los Angles-Riverside-Orange County CMSA. Thus, MSAs are usually one or more cities with close economic ties; CMSAs and PMSAs are larger regional areas, often comprised of more than one county and multiple cities.

The census information for smaller entities within cities and counties is classified as tracts, block groups, and blocks. The data available for these smaller areas enable analysis of highly specific localities such as neighborhoods. It is also possible to target the ZIP code level by using either U.S. Census or privately published data, described later in this chapter. Often these smaller geographic levels provide less detail because some information is omitted to preclude the identification of individuals and the violation of confidentiality (Lavin 1996, 285). Where detail is available, it is not issued in printed reports but can be accessed as Summary Files. For instance, at the Census Block level, marketers will need to consult the Web site or CD-ROM. Fortunately, improved software has made it relatively easy to retrieve information using pull-down menus and sub-menus.

The greatest level of detail is available in the Public Use Microdata Sample (PUMS) files. The Census Bureau is distributing PUMS files with national and state-level characteristics, in one-percent and five-percent samplings respectively. With sample sizes broad enough to protect confidentiality, these files contain the responses to census questionnaires without names and addresses. As of April 2003, these data are available over the Internet using FTP (file transfer protocol) or CD-ROM/DVD format.

TIP: Introduction to CENSUS 2000 Data Products

The Census Bureau provides an excellent short overview of Census geography, report forms, and data products (issued in June 2001). Contact: http://www.census.gov/prod/2001pubs/mso-01icdp.pdf.

TIP: The Census Bureau's Public Use Presentation Library

This is a collection of PowerPoint presentations prepared by the Census Bureau which may be downloaded, viewed, and duplicated. The topics cover the American Community Survey and many Census 2000 topics such as geographic concepts, data products, and race, ethnicity, age, and gender information. Contact: http://www.census.gov/mso/www/pres_lib/index2.html.

U.S. Census Bureau. Washington, DC. Online (free). Contact: http://www.census.gov.

The Census Bureau's Web site makes it ever easier to retrieve data. Due to the convenience of desktop computers and the Internet, users can retrieve a huge amount of information without leaving their homes or offices. From the Census 2000 Web page (http://www.census.gov/main/www/cen2000.html), there is a link to *American FactFinder (AFF)* (http://factfinder.census.gov), a flexible and simple navigational tool making it easy to extract, manipulate, print, and save data. Researchers can seamlessly create custom tables from the Summary Files by selecting database variables and geography from nested and pull-down menus. Based on these customized data sets, maps can be created and tables displayed while online, or extracted for later use in statistical software.

At the Census Web site, there are several different pathways to basic demographic information. There are links to "People," "Housing," "Income," and a helpful A-Z subject list. Census categories for people and housing include age, sex, family characteristics, group quarters population, ethnicity and race, household characteristics, age of householder, household type, household size, occupancy/vacancy status, number of occupants in unit, race of householder, whether owners or renters, etc. The information is arranged by geographic area, down to the MSA level. As mentioned previously, MSAs represent towns, cities or communities, but since they usually combine two or more cities they may not be refined enough for some marketing projects like locating a retail store or targeting customers for a mail campaign.

Numerous private publishers and educational institutions made 1990 Census data available in searchable formats on the Web and there are some similar packagings for Census 2000. The Census Bureau itself also issues numerous publications and databases that go beyond statistics on population and housing. In addition to the decennial census, the Bureau is responsible for other sampling projects which are conducted for various purposes and are generally more current. The following sources are some of those that are most useful for marketing purposes.

Current Population Survey. **Washington DC: United States Census Bureau. Bi-annual. Print. Online (free). Contact: http://www.census. gov/main/www/cprs.html.**

A joint project of the Bureau of Labor Statistics (BLS) and the Census Bureau, the Current Population Survey (CPS) is a sampling of about 50,000 U.S. households which measures unemployment and labor force characteristics, capturing important population shifts and social trends. The survey is conducted monthly and is therefore quite up-to-date. It serves as a baseline for many ancillary studies such as BLS' own *Employment and Earnings* and much of the commercial lifestyle information described later in this chapter. The raw data are available at the BLS Web site at http://www.bls.census.gov/cps/cpsmain.htm.

The Census Bureau itself issues the *Current Population Reports* series as a byproduct of the survey: *P20 Population Characteristics*, *P23 Special Studies*, and *P60 Consumer Income and Poverty*. Each has potential applications for marketing purposes, and individual documents are available in PDF format at http://www.census.gov/main/www/cprs. html.

P20 Population Characteristics contains information on geographic residence and mobility, school enrollment, marital status, living arrangements, households and families, and ethnic populations. Printed reports are currently issued every other year, and may be accessed in PDF format at http://www.census.gov/main/www/cprs.html. The reports contain numerous tables, graphs and charts with narrative explanations, and vary from a few pages to book length. Sample documents in the *P20* series include "Geographical Mobility," "Fertility of American Women," and "Marital Status and Living Arrangements." Some sample sub-sections in the 1997-1998 Geographical Mobility report include "moving rates have never been lower," "westerners move the most," "rates of moving vary with ethnic groups," and other topics of interest to marketers for understanding general population shifts and social trends, which might be especially useful to those selling relocation services, baby products, or single-serving foods.

The *P23 Special Studies* series is geared to one-time special topics. Sample topics include "How We Are Changing: The Demographic State of the Nation," "Home Computers and Internet Use," and "65+ in the United States Current Population Report." These reports document important social changes of great use for developing, selling, and advertising any number of products and services.

The third series in the *Current Population Survey* is *P60 Consumer Income and Poverty*, which primarily addresses economic issues. It is probably not as generally useful for marketers as the previous two, but reports such as "Health Insurance Coverage" and "Money Income in the United States" may have particular application for certain industries. It is important for all marketers to be aware of them because these reports provide the raw data for many of the commercial customer segmentation tools discussed later in this chapter.

American Community Survey. **Washington DC. U.S. Census Bureau. Online (free) or CD-ROM. Contact: http://www.census.gov/acs/www.**

Unlike the *Census of Population* and *Census of Housing*, which are conducted once every decade, the *American Community Survey (ACS)* is an ongoing study conducted annually by the U.S. Census Bureau for states, cities, counties, metropolitan areas, and smaller population centers. The *ACS* is designed to provide more up-to-date and accurate demographic profiles of communities every year. Business people, local governments, and other data users have long requested more timely indicators for communities and population subgroups than were available in the decennial census. Indeed, many of the commercial products discussed later in this chapter developed their own proprietary methodologies in response to marketers' needs for more currency and accuracy. The *ACS* is the Census Bureau's own response to these needs. It is fully implemented for every county in 2003.

Intended to replace the decennial census' long form, which collects data for federal programs and does not require a literal population count, the *ACS* utilizes technology and sampling techniques that are widely used by academicians and market researchers. A sample of the population will be surveyed every year, with no single household receiving the questionnaire more than once in any five-year period. For cities and population groups greater than 65,000 people, this sample size will be sufficient to provide annual data immediately. For smaller areas, it will take two-to-five years to accumulate a sufficient sample to produce data. Annual sampling, re-calculating, and updating are intended to make the *ACS* data more reliable then the decennial censuses. Based on three methods of data collection (self-enumeration through the mail, Computer Assisted Telephone Interviewing and Computer Assisted Personal Interviewing, plus follow-up by Census Bureau employees), *ACS* data will be available within six months of a collection period or calendar year.

Data from the *ACS* are available for counties, cities, and places under 25,000 population using the Web and also on CD-ROM or DVD. The Web site is user-friendly and easily navigated with tabs for Data Profiles, Ranking Tables, PUMS (e.g., Public Use Microdata Samples), and Detailed Tables. The Data Profiles tab provides basic tabular and narrative data on general demographic, social, economic, and housing characteristics. In addition to the primary American Community Survey itself, additional data are derived from several experimental programs, such as Continuous Measurement and Census 2000 Supplementary Survey.

Some marketers may also find the PUMS data useful for special projects. This data shows the complete survey responses of one household or household member to the questions about occupation, place of work, or travel time. (As is usual with the Census, identifying information is removed to ensure confidentiality.) The microdata samples let the user create a table based on a customized set of variables rather than using predefined tables. Although some basic statistical and computer knowledge is required, PUMS data can be readily accessed over the Web without sophisticated software or skills.

TIP: ACS Narrative Profiles

The American Community Survey's *narrative profiles* are "plain-language descriptions with representational graphs to complement the standard tabular profiles." They are designed for easy use by newspaper reporters, grant writers, loan applicants, and students (U.S. Census Bureau 2002). Contact: http://www.census.gov/acs/www ("Data Profiles" tab), or http://www.census.gov/acs/www/Products/Profiles/index.htm.

County and City Extra: Annual Metro, City, and County Data Book. Katherine A. DeBrandt and Deirdre A. Gaquin. Lanham, MD: Bernan Press, 2002. 11th edition. $120. 1,300 pages. Contact: http://www.bernan.com.

Bernan Press is one of the largest private publishers of U.S. government-related information. This title, together with its companion, *Places, Towns and Townships*, is an excellent source of demographic data available in many types of libraries. Both titles are regularly updated with recent data from the Economic Censuses and Current Population Surveys, and also incorporate statistics published by other federal agencies. Bernan also offers *County and City Extra: Special Decennial Census Edition* (2002) with updated data from the 2000 Census. In addition, the Census Bureau itself publishes its *County and City Data Book: A Statistical Abstract Supplement (2000)*, which is also distributed by Bernan.

County and City Extra (CCE) provides a summary of statistical information for every state, county, metropolitan area, congressional district and city with at least 25,000 population. The companion volume *Places, Towns and Townships (PTT)* provides data for "places" with less than 25,000 population as of the 1990 Census. Consisting primarily of data tables, *CCE* contains some other very useful features. For instance, the Highlights section provides both a narrative summary and maps of population changes for "States, Counties and Places in the Late 1990s." Much like an executive summary, the narrative encapsulates the most important changes reflected in the hundreds of detailed tables that follow. Population growth, land area use, labor force changes, income and poverty levels are discussed in a straightforward way, with full-color maps graphically illustrating changes from 1990-1997.

Though varying in depth, currency and detail, these two reference books can be used to great advantage, especially when a project is at the early stages of site selection, market evaluation, or customer segmentation. They contain statistics on many standard demographic measures, plus information on health, crime, education, taxes paid, housing construction, transportation and some industries.

There are some limitations to the usefulness of these sources for marketing and local planning projects requiring data at smaller geographic scales. In *CCE*, more data elements are available for states than for counties and cities, including population projections, health insurance coverage, homeownership rates, number of immigrants, and expanded employment information. Because these are books in print format, *CCE* and *PTT* do not offer the degree of customization and sorting options available from electronic databases. On the other hand, they are easier to use and often more suited to the purpose at hand. They are a good way to get an overview, enabling marketers to perform the preliminary steps for customer segmentation, target marketing, site analysis and market valuation. State and county totals can be found quickly and compared easily using these efficient and concise reference tools.

DEMOGRAPHIC SOURCES WITH ENHANCED MARKETING FEATURES

The following sources augment basic demographic information with enhancements for marketing purposes. These sources are distinguished from those discussed in the next section, "Specialized Lifestyle and Psychographic Sources," because they are more widely available in many public and academic business library collections, or are free on the Web. They may not offer as much in-depth detail as more specialized sources, especially on topics like buying habits and lifestyles, but they are relatively inexpensive and therefore more accessible.

Consumer Expenditure Survey. **Washington DC: U.S. Bureau of Labor Statistics. Online and print (free). PUMS data on CD-ROM (price varies). Contact: http://www.bls.gov/cex/home.htm.**

Produced by the Bureau of Labor Statistics, the *Consumer Expenditure Survey (CES)* collects and disseminates information on the buying habits of American consumers. The *CES* is designed primarily to update the "market basket of goods" that provides the data for the Consumer Price Index. It is also directly applicable to market research and consumer analysis. By providing a benchmark of expenditure patterns according to socioeconomic characteristics, the *CES* is fundamental to marketing projects involving lifestyle and buying habits research. Like the socioeconomic information collected in the *Current Population Survey* and other Census Bureau reports, this information is used by commercial publishers and analysts as a baseline for their proprietary publications and statistical analyses of buying habits. The data generated by market researchers via focus groups, personal interviews, and mail questionnaires would be much less meaningful without the comparative nationwide sample provided by the government.

The *CES* data are actually two surveys carried out in over 100 areas of the United States. The quarterly Interview survey samples respondents on a rotating basis about large-scale expenditures for items like housing, apparel, transportation, health care, insurance and entertainment. The Diary survey provides data about items that are more frequently purchased, like food, tobacco, personal care products, and nonprescription drugs. By including baseline demographic, household, and socioeconomic characteristics, the survey provides a wealth of data about real-world demand for goods and services.

The *Consumer Expenditure Survey* uses the term "consumer units" for its sampling instead of the "Households" term used by the Census Bureau. They are not exactly the same, since households may contain more than one consumer unit, which is largely defined by financial independence. Due to the definition of BLS' Consumer Units versus Census Households, the former outnumbers the latter by several million, most of whom are young adults. It is important to be aware of this significant factor when comparing data from the Bureau of Census and the Consumer Expenditure Survey (Russell and Mitchell 1999, 685-687).

TIP: Four Ways to Access Consumer Expenditure Data

- *Tables Created by BLS*. Offers pre-formatted tables for 1984 through 2000 in current, two-year, and multi-year series. These are available in text (HTML) or PDF directly on the Web and include cross-tabulations of expenditure data by age and geography. See http://www.bls.gov/cex/home.htm.
- *Get Detailed Statistics*. Formerly called "Public Data Query," lets the user create customized tables using selected variables. This requires java-enabled browser software. See http://www.bls.gov/cex/home.htm.
- *Public Use Microdata (PUMS)*. Interview and Diary Survey data for the years 1972 through 2000 are available for purchase on CD-ROM. For more information, see http://www.bls.gov/cex/csxmicro.htm.
- Russell, Cheryl and Susan Mitchell. 2001. *Best Customers: Demographics of Consumer Demand*. 2nd edition. Ithaca, NY: New Strategist. (Offers a handy, well-formatted, printed compilation of the 1997 Consumer Expenditure Survey.)

***Survey of Buying Power and Media Markets*. New York: Sales and Marketing Management. Annual special issue. Print and online ($48/year). Contact: http://www.salesandmarketing.com.**

Published for over 70 years, the *Survey of Buying Power (SBP)* is an annual special issue of the trade journal *Sales and Marketing Manage-*

ment. Describing itself as a "reference guide to American purchasing influence" and geared to marketing and sales managers, its primary purpose is to provide demographic and retail spending data and growth projections for cities, counties and states.

SBP generates two unique, proprietary measures designed specifically for marketing needs. The *effective buying income* (EBI) indicator was developed by *Sales & Marketing Management* magazine to measure disposable or "after tax" income, using the formula of money-income minus tax-payments. Their second indicator is called the *buying power index* (BPI), which is a weighted measure of spending power that quantifies a community's "ability to buy" by incorporating demographic factors (population), economic factors (income) and distribution factors (retail sales) (Galea and Lorge 1999, 214). ". . . BPI is to consumer spending what the wind-chill factor is to the weatherman . . . Just as the combination of the temperature and the wind make a day feel colder than it really is, so too is the BPI a truer measure of an area's potential to buy . . ." (Ibid., 1999, 6). Businesses use the EBI and BPI measures for a variety of marketing purposes: developers use the data to determine where new retail stores are needed; fundraisers use it to set goals for metropolitan areas; marketing managers use it to plan sales territories and set sales goals; newspaper advertising salespeople use it to generate local retail advertising.

The *SBP* defines geographic areas in two ways: the Census Bureau's Metropolitan Statistical Areas (MSAs) and Nielsen Media Research's Media Markets, also referred to as "designated market areas" (DMAs). The *SBP* provides local-level MSA and Media Market data in four sections: (1) Market Ranking Tables, (2) Market Totals, (3) Five-Year Market Projections, (4) Merchandise Line Sales.

In the first section, 321 Metropolitan Markets and 210 Media Markets are ranked in 21 categories for demographics, economics, and sales. The categories include ethnic population, median age, median household EBI, total retail sales, apparel store sales, drugstore sales, eating and drinking place sales, hardware sales, general merchandise sales, and the community's BPI. For example, Chicago ranks at the top for Total Retail Sales, Los Angeles ranks at the top for Food Store and Gasoline Service Station Sales, and New York ranks at the top for Apparel and Accessory Store Sales. Thus, using the Media Market Rankings, a marketer might decide how and where to spend the advertising budget for various kinds of merchandise, whether drugstore items, car accessories, or shoes.

The second section, Metro and Media Market Totals, is the lengthiest and most extensive in the SBP. It provides information on population, effective buying income (EBI), retail sales, and BPI for every state, regional Metro markets, county and major city in the U.S. The same categories are covered for the 210 Media Markets, which are categorized by state; information is also provided for selected cities fitting certain size criteria (Galea and Lorge 1999, 57). Here, a marketer can look up a specific city or county, find its population broken down by age, and the dollar volume of retail sales in designated categories (food, eating and drinking places, general merchandise, furniture, and automotive). For each city or county, the tables provide the total EBI in thousands-of-dollars and percentage-of-households with that income in each community.

Each Media Market is also analyzed for ethnic population, age, retail sales, EBP and the buying power index. This information might be used to determine what kind of retail establishments may be under-represented relative to the buying potential in a particular area, thus identifying competitive opportunities for marketers.

The projections in the third section help the marketer plan for growth in population, effective buying income, retail sales and buying power in the next five years. In section four, Merchandise Line Sales, communities are ranked by retail sales in 10 merchandise categories, and data are organized according to the type of retail enterprise, such as grocery, drug, clothing, footwear, household appliances, hardware, furniture, television equipment, and computers. The tables include a typographical marker which indicates the "total top 50, 100, or 200" in each category, making it easy to pick out the best prospects.

TIP: *Rand McNally Commercial Atlas & Marketing Guide*

The *Rand McNally Commercial Atlas & Marketing Guide* has a 132-year history of publishing marketing data in a graphic, accessible format. It is found in most libraries and has many special features:

- Defines "major trading areas" and "principal business centers" in addition to MSAs and counties;
- Lists major U.S. corporations with headquarters cities;
- Maps major population centers for military installations, college population, manufacturing, and retail sales;
- Rates cities based on their relative importance as national, regional, local, and suburban business centers;

- Provides highway, airline, railroad, telephone, and postal maps;
- Locates air and rail services, banks, post offices, colleges, hospitals and prisons;
- Offers Census Bureau population and economic data;
- Offers retail sales data at numerous levels, including "basic trading areas," states, MSAs, counties, "principal business centers," and ZIP Codes;
- Provides retail sales data from Market Statistics, a division of Claritas.

TIP: The Geography of Marketing Terms

MSAs = Metropolitan Statistical Areas (U.S. Census Bureau)

ZIP Codes = "neighborhoods" (U.S. Postal Service)

FIPS = Federal Information Processing Standard (cities & counties)

Media Markets = "reached by the same TV signal"

DMAs = Designated Market Areas (a media market defined by Nielsen Media Research)

ADI = Areas of Dominant Influence (a media market defined by Arbitron)

Ranally Metro Area (RMA) = developed areas around cities irrespective of county boundaries, including suburbs (Rand McNally)

New Strategist Publications. Ithaca, NY. Contact: http://www. newstrategist.com.

New Strategist Publications specializes in books that re-organize, abstract, synthesize, and re-format a huge amount of statistical data, making it easy for the marketer to glean needed facts and figures. New Strategist publishes neatrly 20 individual titles that are categorized into four series: "American Consumer," "American Generations," "American Money," and "Politics Behind the Numbers." Synthesizing the demographic, lifestyle and buying habits components of the customer segmentation process, each one specializes in a specific demographic or product-purchase aspect.

Gathered from numerous governmental and private sources, the information is presented in an understandable, graphically pleasing, and even entertaining manner. Sample titles include: *Racial and Ethnic Diversity: Asians, Blacks, Hispanics, Native Americans and Whites*; *American Men: Who They Are and How They Live*; *The Millennials: Americans Under Age 25*; and *Best Customers: Demographics of Consumer Demand.* These books are especially helpful for students learning the target marketing process and for the experienced professional seeking an overview of salient trends.

A primary example, *American Marketplace: Demographics and Spending Patterns (AM)*, focuses on correlating demographics to spending habits. The 2001 edition is divided into chapters covering topics like education, health, housing, income, living arrangements, spending, population, and wealth. Major national demographic trends are emphasized, and each chapter includes a "Highlights" section that succinctly summarizes the significant points presented in the statistics. Tables and bar graphs follow under topical categories like "Americans are Moving Less," "Early Retirement Trend to End," and "Spending is Highest in the West." Narrative comments and analyses, plus source notes for further research accompany each table and chart. Other titles focus on the statistical portrait of a single generation, the differences between generations, or the demographics of consumer behavior. For example, *Best Customers* provides profiles of purchasers of specific products, like alcoholic beverages, computers, food at home, reading material, and transportation.

Thus, a marketer who is developing a new snack food can target the age, income, and ethnicity characteristics of likely consumers of that particular product. By identifying the targeted customer, focus groups can be formed, advertising and packaging can be designed, and the product can be tested in he most appropriate settings.

TIP: New Strategist Web Site Offers Content from Its Print Publications in Electronic Formats (PDF or Excel)

As an alternative to purchasing the hardbound publications, it is also possible to download complete books or even individual chapters with "pay as you go" options. This makes the data available to researchers who only need a portion of a printed work or who wish to analyze data using spreadsheet programs. In addition, the publishers offer some free material on the Web site under the link "Data about American Consumers." Contact: http://www.newstrategist.com.

As an alternative to the individual titles issued by New Strategist, the *EPM Consumer Segmentation Survey* (EPM Communications. New York, NY, 2002) provides 60 segmentation profiles derived from market research firms, advertising agencies, and others. The content covers all generation and demographic groups and includes consumer habits, buying patterns, and lifestyle data in five sections. Numerous charts, tables, and graphs are included in each section.

Right Site. Bellmawr, NJ: Easy Demographics Software Inc. Online (price varies). Contact: http://www.easidemographics.com.

The *Right Sight* Web site provides demographic analysis and selected "quality of life" information for specific localities. Though primarily in the business of selling software analysis tools and customized databases, the publisher issues several ready-made free reports on the Web that require only online registration. The database incorporates 2000 Census data, as well as updates where available. The user can gather basic demographic profiles for ZIP codes, MSAs, TV markets, counties, and states. In addition, it is possible to perform an unlimited number of "ring studies" which determine the population and demographic profile of people living within the circumference of a designated location. Data for smaller geographic units, such as census tracts and media markets are also available at the Web site, but those require a fee. Nevertheless, even the limited amount of free data makes this site an excellent tool for site analysis and setting sales territories.

TIP: *American Demographics* **Magazine**

One of the best sources for demographic data combined with purchasing habits and lifestyle factors is the magazine *American Demographics*. Articles typically include a discussion of population characteristics, social trends and the resulting impact on shopping and purchasing. Contact: http://www.inside.com/default.asp?entity=AmericanDemo.

American Demographics is included in most business periodical databases, such as *ABI/INFORM, Business & Industry, Business Source Premier, TableBase*, and others. A simple strategy for finding articles in this magazine is to search with keywords representing the topic and the journal title. For example: "swimming and demographics" retrieves an article from August 2001 about population trends impacting children's recreational activities.

SPECIALIZED LIFESTYLE AND PSYCHOGRAPHIC SOURCES

As marketers know, people select products and services for many complex reasons that go beyond simple demographic identity of gender, age, race, income, and location. In our sophisticated marketplace, buying decisions have as much to do with sense of self, psychology, values, status, class, and group identity as with filling simple physical needs. To reach the right customers and fully understand why they act the way they do, marketers must include lifestyle and psychographic components in their target marketing strategies.

There are more and more sources that tie lifestyles, values, and psychological factors to basic demographic and geographic measures (such as the New Strategist publications listed in the previous section). However, because lifestyles and psychographics research is complex and labor intensive, many of the most specialized sources are fairly expensive. Even the printed reference tools are not cheap, and customized reports derived from the electronic databases are available to marketers for an even steeper fee. Nonetheless, some marketing projects require more specialized, customized data and for those purposes, the following sources will prove helpful.

Lifestyle Market Analyst: A Reference Guide for Consumer Market Analysis. Des Plaines, IL: SRDS. Annual. Print $411. Contact: http://www.srds.com.

Lifestyle Market Analyst (LMA) is co-published by SRDS, the well-known producer of reference materials for media planning professionals, and Equifax, a credit reporting, database marketing, and information services firm. The Equifax proprietary database of demographic, lifestyle, and buying habit data is created from consumers' product registration cards for purchases of appliances, clothing, electronics, sporting goods, etc. This book is the most available version of this specialized database, and is found in many academic and public business libraries. As such, *LMA* is a happy medium between the less specialized sources listed previously and the more expensive databases that follow.

LMA correlates baseline demographic and geographic data and enhances it with the lifestyle component. In a marketing context, *lifestyle* refers to interests, hobbies, and activities: how adults spend their free time and, by implication, their discretionary income, which taken together, represents their buying habits. *LMA* is especially useful for uncovering new markets, estimating the buying power of customer segments and regions, and targeting ideal customers at the local, regional, and national levels. Standard statistical procedures enable Equifax to extrapolate data using the 1990 U.S. Census as a baseline. The data in the 2002 edition of *LMA* is drawn from questionnaires collected in two periods between 1999 and 2001.

The book is organized into four sections: "Market Areas," "Lifestyle Profiles," "Consumer Segments," and "Consumer Magazine and Direct Marketing Lists." The first section, "Market Profiles," is organized by 210 geographic market areas, called "designated market areas" (DMAs), which can be cities, counties, or Census MSAs. This section is used to analyze geographic regions in terms of demographics and lifestyle interests. The user can look up a specific place and find its percentages of people in various age, race/ethnicity, income, and occupational categories. For each DMA, household characteristics like marital status, presence of children, home ownership, credit card usage, and "stage in family lifecycle" are quantified, as well as the percentage of households participating in various lifestyle activities and interests. The rate of participation in each metropolitan region is compared to the rest of the U.S. population.

In the second section, 76 of the most popular "Lifestyle Profiles" are analyzed in terms of the type of household likely to participate. Each lifestyle has a name and is described according to its household demographics and description, then compared to the U.S. population as a whole. The lifestyle tables are divided into seven categories: home life, the good life, investing and money, great outdoors, sports-fitness-health, hobbies, and high-tech activities. For each activity, estimates are provided for household count, percent household distribution, and household index comparison. As an example, for planning a sales promotion of photographic equipment, the marketer could identify the types of households and localities of people who might be likely to utilize photography by looking at the lifestyle profiles of those who like the outdoors, travel, or spending time with grandchildren.

This section also enables the marketer to assess secondary lifestyle activities of the target market. For each primary Lifestyle, there are rankings of other preferred activities, and the top ten are highlighted. This enables the marketer to determine which additional activities are likely to be popular among households which regularly attend Cultural/Arts Events, or participate in Community/Civic Activities, or Self-Improvement, or Real Estate Investments, etc. In addition, each geographic area is ranked for its degree of participation in the particular lifestyle profile. For easy reference, the top ten DMA markets are typographically highlighted so it is easy to see which regions have the heaviest participation. This section can be used for targeting a likely geographic market, identifying its key consumer segments that make up each lifestyle audience, and developing new products based on their related interests.

The third section, "Consumer Segment Profiles," analyzes the characteristics of households fitting certain demographic and economic criteria. These demographic categories are profiled by lifestyle interests and their prevalence is ranked geographically. For instance, you might want to look at the group of Marrieds, 34-44 years old and identify household characteristics, hobbies, interests, and where they are concentrated geographically. However, because the segments are defined using *household* characteristics rather than *individual* characteristics, certain characteristics are not included (race/ethnicity, occupation, education, and credit card usage). But it is possible to determine that this population group is more likely to have an income of over $50,000 and have children in their teens than the U.S. population as a whole, and that the top ten lifestyles for this group includes owning a camcorder, playing video games, owning a dog, and traveling on business. This section can be helpful for identifying consumer segments most likely to purchase certain products and services, developing advertising that relates to their lifestyle behavior, and discovering where specific consumer groups are concentrated geographically.

Finally, section four provides a listing of consumer magazines and mailing lists targeted to each lifestyle profile. These are provided by and arranged in SRDS' classifications from its publications *Consumer Magazine Advertising Source* and *Direct Marketing List Source.*

1999 National Consumer Survey for Colleges and Universities. **Deerfield Beach, FL: Simmons Market Research Bureau Inc. CD-ROM. Price varies ($1,000 to $2,500). Contact: http://www. smrb.com or 888-909-7672.**

Simmons' *National Consumer Survey* (*NCS*), formerly known as the *Study of Media and Markets*, is a comprehensive, ongoing sample of approximately 25,000 adults in the United States. It is a syndicated study used by many major corporations for target marketing of products, brands, and media. The College Program makes 3-year-old data available to schools at an affordable price. Two software versions are offered: Choices II or Choices III, an upgrade with increased functionality and features.

Simmons *NCS* answers questions such as "What age group of females is most likely to purchase frozen dinners?" "What is the demographic profile of late night TV viewers?" or "What age group of women are loyal to brand names of toothpaste?" Almost 8,000 brands are measured in approximately 50 product and service categories including finance, hair care, mini-cycles and mopeds, ailments and remedies, cats and dogs, and more. Detailed lifestyle descriptors and demographic variables can be specified, using brand names, TV programs, magazine titles, or media use patterns. The software performs cross-tabulations, media rankings, reach and frequency reports. For example, the searcher might want to determine the demographic profile and media habits of purchasers of "gum and snacks." After selecting a product category, the searcher could define the demographic target according to gender, age, income, and other variables using the table format function. This resulting report might have a list of snack foods (tortilla chips, potato chips, popcorn, etc.) as column headings and the demographic variables (sex, age, education, etc.) as rows. The cross-tabulation function compares the two types of data and locates a target audience, providing lifestyle segments. Another feature, the media ranking report can be used to find the preferred media choices of these target customers. The results can also be graphed and reports can be saved in Excel, Lotus, and many other formats.

TIP: Using Simmons' *National Consumer Survey* **Data**

It is important to remember that the Simmons data are actually a probability sample. Results are reported as Totals, Projected, Index, and Percentages of specific column and row headings. Each of these is precisely defined, and it may be necessary to understand the underlying formulas to make full use of the data. The cross tabulation function can result in samples that are unstable or too small for reliability. In these cases, it may be necessary to broaden a search.

In addition to Simmons' National Consumer Survey with Choices software, there is a similar product from *Mediamark Research Inc.* (New York: Mediamark Research Inc., semiannual, CD-ROM, contact: http://www.mediamark.com). Their MEMRI database, like Simmons, is based on a large national consumer survey and is used to create customized tables for target marketing and media planning decisions. It contains brand names and offers psychographics and lifestyle variables.

The *Mediamark* CD-ROM is used in several academic libraries. Like Simmons, it is available in a reduced-price academic version with dated material varying from 2 to 5 years old.

TIP: Detailed Guides to Using Simmons (Choices II) and Mediamark Reporter

- Boetccher, Jennifer. Georgetown University. Lauinger Library. "Simmons Choices II CD-ROM Tutorial." Contact: http://www. library.georgetown.edu/swr/ref/simmain.htm (Revised January 2002).
- De Santis, Karen. Pace University Library. "Choices II: Simmons Study of Media and Markets." Contact: http://www.pace.edu/ library/instruct/guides/simmonschoicesii.html (Revised August 2001).
- Higgins, Sarah. Pace University Library. "Using MRI *Mediamark Reporter.*" Contact: http://www.pace.edu/library/instruct/guides/ mri.html (Revised May 2002).

VALS Survey. **Menlo Park, CA: SRI Consulting Business Intelligence. Contact: http://www.sric-bi.com/VALS.**

The *VALS (Values and Lifestyles) Survey* is a market research tool that offers a psychological-demographic profile of consumers, enabling the marketer to assess the self-perception, motivations, and values that impact an individual's buying decisions. The data from the survey are not published as a whole, but must be purchased on a customized basis. However, the survey questions and psychographic segment definitions are available free on the Web. Though costly, a customized report may be a worthwhile purchase for the marketer who is designing a new product, repositioning an existing one, or designing a major media or direct marketing campaign.

SRI Consulting Business Intelligence, a market research firm, developed the *VALS Survey* in the 1970s and refined it in 1989. It defines U.S. adult consumers according to a psychological and demographic profile. The company claims that it uniquely incorporates psychological and motivational factors into consumer buying behavior, rather than relying solely on geographic and demographic factors.

The *VALS Survey* itself is a questionnaire of about 40 simple attitude statements that the company's research has shown to correlate with consumers' product and media choices. For example, the respondent "agrees" or "disagrees" with statements such as "I like a lot of variety in my life" and "I would rather make something than buy it." The Survey uses these responses to sort people into an eight-part typology, constructed along two primary dimensions: s*elf-orientation* and *resources*. The self-orientation dimension represents motivations based on principle, status, and action. That is, "principle-oriented consumers are guided in their choices by abstract, idealized criteria rather than feelings, events, or desire for approval and opinions of others. Status-oriented consumers look for products and services that demonstrate [their] success to their peers. Action-oriented consumers are guided by a desire for social or physical activity, variety and risk-taking" (SRI Consulting Business Intelligence 2001-2002).

The Resources dimension refers to the range of "psychological, physical, demographic, means, and capacities people have to draw upon. It encompasses education, self-confidence, health, eagerness to buy things, intelligence, and energy level . . ." (Ibid.). This dimension can be directly tied to demographics because "resources" generally vary with stage of lifecycle, increasing from adolescence through middle age but then decreasing again with old age.

SRI also offers a product called *GeoVALS* that correlates psychographics with a geographic component. Unlike some other studies, *GeoVALS* does not assume that people in the same neighborhood think, behave, and buy alike. This tool would be useful in selecting site locations or designing a direct mail campaign to find ZIP codes with the highest concentration of a particular VALS segment, thus allowing a small mailing to have a bigger impact in reaching desired households.

Demographic Sourcebooks. Vienna, VA: ESRI Business Information Solutions. Annual. Print $900. CD-ROM $995. Print and CD-ROM set $1,300. Contact: http://www.esribis.com.

This reference tool was published for nearly fifteen years by CACI Marketing Systems, a company which was acquired by ESRI BIS in 2002. The series adds considerable value and ease-of-use to basic census data at the tract and block levels by translating it into more familiar ZIP codes and counties. Use the *Sourcebooks* to evaluate a customer base and how it is changing, forecast demand for products and services, explore the potential of new opportunities, compare trade zones and sales territories, plan targeted mailings and media campaigns, and sites, or otherwise analyze a given market. Providing detailed information by ZIP codes and counties, the two print titles in the *Demographic Sourcebooks* series are *Sourcebook of ZIP Code Demographics* and *Sourcebook of County Demographics* (books). The CD-ROM, entitled *Sourcebook-America* (CD-ROM), includes the data from both print titles.

Like the other publishers discussed in this section, ESRI BIS is a provider of specialized marketing data blending demographics and geographics with values, lifestyles and buying habits. Specializing in customer information at very specific and customized levels, the company maintains extensive proprietary databases, from which a variety of products, publications, online tools, and reports in a wide variety of print and electronic formats can be generated.

The *Sourcebooks* provide current-year updates and five-year forecasts, covering 73 data variables from the full array of databases. As part of a large set of underlying databases, the information includes demographics, geographics, lifestyle data, business data, and consumer expenditures. For example, the data elements available for an individual zip code include population details, households and families, race and age distribution, household income distribution, per capita and average disposable income, and the number of business establishments in categories like financial services, home, entertainment, and personal care.

The lifestyle segmentation component is called *ACORN* ("A Classification of Residential Neighborhoods"), which segments customers according to a system of 43 neighborhood clusters. While selected data are included in the *Sourcebooks*, customized output is also available in other formats, such as printed and PDF reports, CD-ROM, maps, and in PC-Desktop analytical tools. Because counties cannot be refined to the neighborhood level, *ACORN* segments are included only in the *Sourcebook of ZIP Code Demographics* and the CD-ROM.

The 43 *ACORN* segment clusters are derived from 9 general groups. For instance, the Upscale Households group includes clusters like "urban professional couples" and "older settled married couples." Each cluster is associated with lifestyle and purchasing habits. Comments that convey the gist of the cluster's consumption patterns include "they spend on theater and concerts and dining out . . ." or "emphasis on savings . . . spending is home-oriented." Some clusters are defined by regional or housing type, such as "southwestern families," "heartland communities," "rural resort dwellers," or "high rise renters."

Another underlying database contributing to the *Sourcebooks* is called *Consumer Expenditures*. Consumer Expenditures data measure the likely expenditure for a product or service in a county, ZIP Code, or other trade area. The file includes the average expenditure per consumer household, total expenditures, and a Spending Potential Index (SPI). This index number is similar to the Buying Power Index (BPI), utilized in the *Survey of Buying Power* discussed previously. The index compares the average expenditure for a product or service locally to the average amount spent for it nationally. Thus, an index number higher than 100 shows greater spending in a particular county or neighborhood relative to the U.S. average. This information can help determine how much the people in an area spend on a specific kind of product and assess whether they have enough discretionary income to buy yours.

PRIZM. San Diego, CA: Claritas Inc. Online (subscription). Contact: http://www.claritas.com/index.html.

PRIZM is also a lifestyle segmentation system defining neighborhoods in terms of 62 demographic and lifestyle characteristics. Created in the 1970s, it is one of the most detailed and comprehensive systems available and proportionately expensive. In addition to the basic PRIZM database, Claritas offers many other data products, such as *Workplace Population*, which gives marketers the ability to segment and target non-residential daytime populations, such as that found in a downtown area. Claritas products are expensive, subscription-based, and not generally available in public and academic libraries. (However, Claritas is affiliated with *Sales & Marketing Management* magazine, so a small portion of its data is incorporated into the *Survey of Buying Power*. It is also a source of sales data in *Rand McNally's Commercial Atlas and Marketing Guide*.)

As marketing trends have led to more focus on the customer, marketers have come to rely heavily on demographics, geographic distribution, psychographics, and lifestyle characteristics to understand how to turn consumers into customers. It is therefore not surprising that marketing is one of the largest non-governmental users of data products from the U.S. Census and other federal agencies. With an enormously broad range and considerable detail, it provides both nationwide and local level information for marketers. Because census information is so basic, inexpensive, and readily available in print and online, it is important to understand its potential applications and how it is collected and presented. The value of census data is reflected by the large number of publishers which specialize in compiling, analyzing, and re-packaging it. Although sometimes expensive, these sources can provide marketers with specialized features and additional flexibility to support target marketing efforts.

TIP: A Short Reading List on Demographics and Customer Segmentation

Hawkins, Del I., Roger J. Best, and Kenneth A. Coney. 1996. rev. ed. *Consumer Behavior: Implications for Marketing Strategy.* Plano, TX: Business Publications.

Kahle, Lynn R. and Larry Chiagouris, Larry. 1997. *Values, Lifestyles and Psychographics.* Mahwah, NJ: Lawrence Erlbaum Associates.

Michael R. Lavin. 1990. *Understanding the Census: A Guide for Marketers, Planners, Grant Writers and Other Data Users.* Phoenix, AZ: Oryx Press.

Pol, Louis G. and Richard K. Thomas. 1997. *Demography for Business Decision-Making.* Westport, CT: Quorum Books.

White, Gary W. and Peter Linberger. 1999. "Demographic Data Sources on the Internet: A Selective Guide." *Journal of Business & Finance Librarianship* 5, no. 2: 15-37.

REFERENCES

Galea, Christine and Sarah Lorge. 1999. "The Power of the Survey," *Sales & Marketing Management. Survey of Buying Power & Media Markets* (September).

Hawkins, Del I., Roger J. Best and Kenneth A. Cooney. 1996. *Consumer Behavior: Implications for Marketing Strategy.* Revised edition. Plano, TX: Business Publications.

Lavin, Michael R. 1996. *Understanding the Census.* Phoenix, AZ: Oryx Press.

Pol, Louis G. and Rickard K. Thomas. 1997. *Demography for Business Decision Making.* Westport, CT: Quorum Books.

Russell, Cheryl and Susan Mitchell. 1999. *Best Customers: Demographics of Consumer Demand.* Ithaca, NY: New Strategist Publications.

SRI Consulting Business Intelligence. 2001-2002. "The VALS Types." <http://www.sric_bi.com/VALS//types.shtml> (June 1, 2002).

U.S. Census Bureau. American Community Survey. 2002. "Profiles Produced by Survey by Year." <http://www.census.gov/acs/www/Products/Profiles/index.htm> (March 11, 2003).

Chapter 6

Marketing Sources
for Demographic Niches

Topics

Marketing to Multicultural and Ethnic Groups
Marketing to Children and Youth
Marketing to Gays & Lesbians

Sources

*Racial and Ethnic Diversity: Asians, Blacks, Hispanics, Native
   Americans, and Whites*
Source Book of Multicultural Experts
Ethnic Media Directory
Minority Buying Power in the New Century
The Buying Power of Black America
Hispanic Media & Market Source
U.S. Hispanic Market Report
Marketing to the Emerging Majorities
Marketing to Ethnic Consumers: An Annotated Bibliography
2001 Youth Research Sourcebook
Roper Youth Report
Simmons Kids Study and *Simmons Teen Study*
*Kids These Days '99: What Americans Really Think about the Next
   Generation*
*Bibliography of Research and Writings on Marketing and Advertis-
   ing to Children*

[Haworth co-indexing entry note]: "Marketing Sources for Demographic Niches." Diamond, Wendy,
and Michael R. Oppenheim. Co-published simultaneously in *Journal of Business & Finance Librarianship*
(The Haworth Information Press, an imprint of The Haworth Press, Inc.) Vol. 9, No. 2/3, 2004, pp. 135-153;
and: *Marketing Information: A Strategic Guide for Business and Finance Libraries* (Wendy Diamond, and
Michael R. Oppenheim) The Haworth Information Press, an imprint of The Haworth Press, Inc., 2004, pp.
135-153. Single or multiple copies of this article are available for a fee from The Haworth Document Delivery Service [1-800-HAWORTH, 9:00 a.m. - 5:00 p.m. (EST). E-mail address: docdelivery@haworthpress.com].

Digital Object Identifier: 10.1300/J109v09n02_06   *135*

> *Children and Adolescents in the Market Place: Twenty-Five Years of*
>   *Academic Research*
> *Gay Media Database*
> *GAYDAR: Gay Directory of Authoritative Resources*
> *Commercial Closet: The World's Largest Collection of Gay Adver-*
>   *tising*
> National Gay Newspaper Guild
> *2001 Gay/Lesbian Consumer Online Census*

In Chapter 5, "Demographic, Geographic and Lifestyle Sources," we discussed many general sources that are available for identifying and targeting customers regionally, demographically, and psychographically. Niche marketing goes one step further and focuses on one specific customer segment. Niche strategies are used when segments can be defined that are "of sufficient size to be profitable while at the same time are of less interest to the major competitors" (Bennett 1995, 189). Sometimes products or services are developed specifically for the niche segment, but often the marketer simply creates a specially targeted advertising and promotion campaign for a product which has very broad appeal.

Certain demographic and lifestyle groups, such as women and the affluent, have always been considered niche markets of interest due to their spending power. Current trends mean there are also many sources about marketing to Children and Youth, but fewer for other demographic groups. The importance of Gays and Lesbians as a market segment has increased, especially since the groundbreaking 1994 Yankelovich MONITOR Perspective on Gays/Lesbians identified the group as "distinct, highly-influential, and well-identified" (Luckinbill 1999, 80).

However, the marketer should not overlook the broader sources discussed throughout this book; many also contain valuable information on marketing to niche segments. For instance, the *Advertising Red Book* for advertising agencies (discussed in Chapter 7, "Advertising and Media Planning Sources") has an index which guides the user to agencies specializing in African-Americans, Hispanics, Asians, and other groups. Information on these topics and more (e.g., marketing to affluent consumers, women, seniors) will also be found by searching in subscription databases such as *MarketResearch.com*, *TableBase*, *ABI/INFORM*, *Business and Industry*, or *Business Source Premier* available at local public or academic libraries.

The sources discussed in this chapter will help the marketer target promotional efforts to major ethnic, lifestyle, and demographic groups.

MARKETING TO MULTICULTURAL AND ETHNIC GROUPS

There are more specific sources for certain ethnic and lifestyle groups than there are for others. For example, the marketer will find a large variety of tools and resources for target marketing to Hispanics and African Americans, but little or none for most other ethnic groups. However, Asian Americans and Native Americans are usually covered in sources that address minority and multicultural issues as a whole. As the world has become more globalized and the U.S. more culturally diversified, the amount of literature on multicultural marketing is expanding.

***Racial and Ethnic Diversity: Asians, Blacks, Hispanics, Native Americans, and Whites.* Cheryl Russell. 4th edition. Ithaca, NY: New Strategist Publications, 2002. Print $99. Contact: http:// www.newstrategist.com/.**

This is the latest update in a series from New Strategist Publications, which specializes in demographic publishing for business and marketing. Based on data from various government agencies, the book draws heavily from the 2000 Census, in which not only were single races and ethnicities identified, but also approximately 7 million people identified themselves as multiracial. There is a chapter for each of the eight major racial/ethnic groups, including narrative and statistical tables on business, income, spending, wealth, labor force, education, housing, and living arrangements. A separate chapter provides comparative statistics with the total U.S. population. Data on minority-owned businesses from the 1997 *Economic Census* is included. There is also a chapter entitled "Attitudes and Behavior," covering such issues as affirmative action and group stereotypes.

The book is well-indexed, and includes a glossary, a bibliography of data sources, and a list of government specialists and Web sites.

TIP: *Mapping Census 2000: The Geography of U.S. Diversity*

This Census Bureau Special Report (Series CENSR/01-1) presents an overview of ethnic diversity in the United States. Authored by Cynthia A. Brewer and Trudy A. Suchan, it is available on the Web. Contact: http://www.census.gov/population/www/cen2000/atlas.html.

***Source Book of Multicultural Experts.* New York: Multicultural Marketing Resources. Annual. Print $60. Contact: http://www. multiculturalmarketingresources.com.**

The *Source Book of Multicultural Experts*, published by a public relations and marketing firm, is a directory designed to aid journalists and publicists seeking knowledgeable and reliable sources for stories. Marketing executives also increasingly need to contact experts to help them reach ethnic customers. Listings in the *Sourcebook* are categorized by market sections (e.g., African American, Gay & Lesbian), by business type (e.g., ad agencies, large corporations, professional associations, seminars, research firms), and by industry area (e.g., financial services, entertainment, telecommunications). Each market section is sponsored by a leading advertising agency which focuses on that segment, and contains an introductory article that provides an overview with statistical profiles and other highlights.

Many of the companies listed in the *Source Book* have previously appeared in the bimonthly newsletter *Multicultural Marketing News*, also published by Multicultural Marketing Resources Inc. This firm also maintains a Library and Knowledge Center which serves as a resource for companies wishing to target Hispanic, Asian-American, African-American, gay/lesbian, and other cultural and lifestyle groups. Located in New York City, the Library offers research services and is available by a fee-based subscription.

***Ethnic Media Directory.* New California Media (NCM). San Francisco. Online (free). Contact: http://www.ncmonline.com.**

The *Ethnic Media Directory* is a 30-page listing of California media outlets and sources produced by New California Media (NCM), an association of over 400 print, broadcast, and online ethnic media organizations. The Web site is sponsored by Pacific News Service as a means of promoting an inter-ethnic editorial exchange and increasing the visibility of ethnic media. The directory is searchable in four media format categories (print, radio, television, online), but it is not possible to search by ethnicity or region. Most entries include the title of the publication, station, or Web site, the contact name and addresses, and a brief description.

Although it includes only California media, the listings are useful in other geographic regions because of the size and diversity of the state's population. There are other similar localized directories in print, such as *The Ultimate 2000: Directory of Ethnic Organizations, Ethnic Media and Scholars for the Chicago Metropolitan Area* (Chicago, IL: Illinois Ethnic Coalition, 2000).

TIP: Public Relations for Multicultural Communications

The Public Relations Society of America (PRSA) has a Professional Interest Section for practitioners responsible for Multicultural Communications. Areas of concern include programs, employment, career development, etc. PRSA also publishes a *Directory of Multicultural Relations Professionals and Firms*. Compiled by Howard University, it includes contact information for PR firms owned by minorities. Contact: http://www.prsa.org.

Minority Buying Power in the New Century **(The Multicultural Economy 2002). University of Georgia, Terry College of Business, Selig Center for Economic Growth. Athens, GA. CD-ROM ($100) or Online (free). Contact: http://www.selig.uga.edu/.**

Developed by Jeffrey M. Humphries, this unique report focuses on minority group buying power in the United States and fills a major gap in the data for consumer research. As discussed in Chapter 5, "buying power" (commonly defined as after-tax, disposable personal income) is an important measure used in retail planning and target marketing, and this report reflects the growing economic power of minorities in terms of both individual ethnic groups and the minority segment as a whole.

The Web version offers statistics for the nation as a whole and for individual states for the years 1990 and 2000, plus forecasts for 2002 and 2007. The report is comprised of tables and analyses covering expenditures, market share, and buying power measures for whites and four ethnic groups: African Americans, Hispanics, Asians, Native Americans. There is also a section of rankings and indices of change for these groups and for minority buying power as a whole.

The complete dataset covering the period from 1990-2007 is available on CD-ROM. In addition to detailed data in expenditure categories for the major ethnic groups, it also offers county-level data for Georgia and Florida.

The Buying Power of Black America. **Chicago: Target Market News. Annual. Print $99. Contact: http://www.targetmarketnews.com/.**

The Buying Power of Black America 2002 is the ninth annual report on the spending habits of African Americans. Published by Target Market News, Inc., a market research firm, the report offers an analysis of data compiled by the U.S. Department of Commerce, based on surveys of black consumers. It presents detailed data on black consumer household expenditures for apparel, entertainment, food, beverages, toys, computers, cosmetics, automobiles, travel, and more. Organized in five major sections, the 2001 edition includes black income, city-by-city data for 30 metropolitan areas, expenditure trend data, and demographic data. There is a special section listing items for which African Americans out-spent white consumers. Online, the publisher's free Web site contains a summary report of demographics and expenditures for black consumers, as well as full-text articles about trends in marketing to this ethnic group.

For another source of information on this customer segment, see *The African American Market* (Packaged Facts 2000, $2,750), available from *MarketResearch.com.*

Hispanic Media & Market Source. Des Plaines, IL: SRDS. Quarterly. Print $284. Contact: http://www.srds.com.

This print source covers a cross-section across all media for one specific consumer market defined by language and ethnicity. Like the other Standard Rate and Data Service (SRDS) tools described in Chapter 7, "Advertising and Media Planning Sources," it is designed to help professional media buyers select venues and place ads. An annual subscription includes four quarterly issues, with 2,300 listings covering all media geared to the Spanish-speaking audience, such as radio, television, daily and weekly newspapers, consumer and business publications, out-of-home advertising companies, and direct marketing lists. Listings are organized by DMAs (direct marketing areas) and media type, making it easy to locate advertising venues that either reach a specific geographic region or have a broad reach. Listings include important contact information, rate scales, technical specifications, and other essential information. There is also a separate section of suppliers and service providers that specialize in Hispanic advertising and marketing.

Some of the alternative media sources listed in Chapter 7 also contain sections devoted to Hispanic media. For example, *Marketer's Guide to Media* (http://www.vnubusinessmedia.com/box/bp/div_mmr_dir_marketerg.html) is a directory that can be used to access contact information.

U.S. Hispanic Market Report. Miami, FL: Strategy Research Corporation, 2002. Print $600. CD-ROM (with supplementary graphs) $150. Contact: http://www.synovate.com.

The *U.S. Hispanic Market Report* has been published by Strategy Research Corporation (SRC) since 1980. It contains up-to-date population estimates and projections through the year 2050, with demographic, household buying power, and household survey data for the nation and for the top 50 U.S. Hispanic metropolitan markets. In addition, the report addresses buyer behavior and such cultural issues as acculturation, language use, e-commerce use, ownership and use of products and services, with sections on media, sports, and social and political issues. The marketer can use this book for fundamental marketing and advertising functions such as distribution, media buying, sales projections, and market research.

SRC also offers related products such as *Tele-Nacion*, a monthly market research survey of Hispanic consumers. Prices vary depending on the sample size and regions selected; more information is available at http://www.src.com/tele.html.

There are other valuable sources of market research on this customer segment. Simmons Market Research produces a report called the *Hispanic Study* (http://www.smrb.com/). Using a sample of 10,000 consumers, it contains a great deal of specific data but, like all market research, it is costly. Additionally, researchers can consult an academic or public library for relevant material from databases such as *MarketResearch.com*, *TableBase*, *ABI/INFORM*, and *Business Source Premier.*

Marketing to the Emerging Majorities. New York: EPM Communications. 12 issues/year $295. Online archive (price varies). Contact: http://www.epmcom.com/html/target.html.

This is a trade newsletter focused on marketing to African Americans, Hispanics, Asian Americans, and Native Peoples–the "emerging majorities." Its emphasis is on articles that present facts, overviews, projections, and forecasts; numerous graphs and charts are included. Articles typically cover consumer behavior, niche marketing, and spending patterns. For example, the January 2002 issue included topics such as "American Indian and Alaska Natives–an Untapped Emerging Majority Market," a calendar of diverse cultural holidays, and reports of targeted promotions from major corporations. The Web site provides a free index to archived articles from 1998 to the present, but there is a charge for article retrieval. (Costs vary on a tiered basis, with single-article, 30-day, or one-year plans.) In addition, full-text articles are included in a number of online subscription databases, such as *Factiva* and *Business & Industry*, available in many public and academic libraries.

EPM also publishes other target marketing newsletters such as *Marketing to Women* (12 issues/$337) and *Youth Markets Alert* (12 issues/ $349). For broader coverage of numerous demographic and lifestyle groups, EPM's desktop reference, *Research Alert Yearbook* (Annual, $295), contains summarized findings from thousands of reports, studies, polls, and focus groups.

Marketing to Ethnic Consumers: An Annotated Bibliography. **Geng Cui and Pravat Choudhury. Chicago: American Marketing Association, 2000. $30. 111 pages.**

Defining ethnic marketing as "the deliberate effort by marketers to reach a group of consumers on the basis of their unique ethnic characteristics" (Cui and Choudhury 2000, vi), this bibliography provides an overview of published research from 1932 through 1999. The topical coverage includes target marketing, advertising, promotion, and retailing as they relate to major U.S. ethnic and racial groups like African Americans, Hispanics, Asian Americans, and Native Americans. Entries are annotated with a summary of findings, theories, concepts, and issues. The bibliography is organized alphabetically by author and a subject index provides cross-references for specific ethnicities, consumer behavior, marketing functions, and concepts.

The authors have defined their objectives and scope clearly. Noting the need for integrated reviews of the literature on the specifically *marketing*-related aspects of ethnicity, they have excluded country studies and anthropological or cross-cultural material. Furthermore, they include only scholarly works that have made "adequate contribution to knowledge development" and which incorporate theory, methodology, or data analysis (Ibid., vi). A primary purpose of the bibliography is to provide a tool which marketing academics and professionals can use to bring the topic into their curricula, research, and practice.

TIP: Use *Ethnic NewsWatch* for Background Articles

Ethnic NewsWatch, a subscription periodical database from ProQuest, contains articles from over 200 ethnic, minority, and native press publications. It includes coverage of the following groups: African American/Caribbean, Arab/Middle Eastern, Asian/Pacific Islander, Europe/Eastern Europe, Hispanic, Jewish, Native People, and a catchall "multi-ethnic" category. Use keywords combined with your selected ethnic category (e.g., target marketing and Asian/Pacific Islander). Check availability at your local public or academic library. Contact: http://home.softlineweb.com/.

TIP: Selected Web Sites with News, Media Research, and Consumer Data About Ethnic and Lifestyle Markets

- Africana.com. Contact: http://www.africana.com.
- AdNoir.com. Contact: http://www.adnoir.com.
- BlackPressUSA Network. Contact: http://www.blackpressusa.com.
- CAB Multicultural Marketing Resource Center. Contact: http://www.cabletvadbureau.com/MMRC/.
- HispanicAd.com. Contact: http://www.hispanicad.com.
- HispanicTrends.com. Contact: http://www.hispanictrends.com.
- DiversityInc.com. Emerging Markets. Contact: http://www. diversityinc.com/public/department8.cfm (requires registration).

TIP: A Short Book List for Multicultural Marketers

American Advertising Federation. *Principles and Recommended Practices for Effective Advertising in the American Multicultural Marketplace.* [n.d.]. <http://www.aaf.org/multi/principles.pdf> (April 28, 2003).

Davila, Arlene. 2001. *Latinos Inc.: The Marketing and Making of a People.* Berkeley, CA: University of California Press.

Rao, C.P. *Marketing and Multicultural Diversity.* 2002. Westport, CT: Quorum Books.

Tharp, Marye C. 2001. *Marketing and Consumer Identity in Multicultural America.* Thousand Oaks, CA: Sage.

Schreiber, Alfred L. and Barry Lenson. 2000. *Multicultural Marketing: Selling to the New America.* Ithaca, NY: Paramount Market Publishers.

Wong, Angi Ma. 1994. *Target the U.S. Asian Market: A Practical Guide to Doing Business.* 2nd edition. Palos Verdes, CA: Pacific Heritage Books.

MARKETING TO CHILDREN AND YOUTH

The affluence of our society has been accompanied by a growing awareness of the influence and importance of children and youth in the marketplace. This section includes sources for the practitioner, the researcher, and the policy-maker. In the marketing field, a significant body of studies and reports has been developed to guide marketers in reaching this demographic segment. Psychologists and sociologists who study children from their perspectives are also concerned with this topic. Because there are ethical concerns unique to this area of marketing, we have also listed some resources for parents and caretakers who wish to counteract the commercialization of childhood.

2001 Youth Research Sourcebook. **New York: Advertising Research Foundation. Annual. Online (free). Contact: http://www.arfsite.org.**

The *2001 ARF Youth Research Sourcebook* is a directory of Advertising Research Foundation (ARF) member companies that conduct market research among children. The *Sourcebook* is provided as a service to the industry by the ARF Youth Research Council. Available as a PDF document on the Web, it is 38 pages long and lists 26 firms. Entries, which appear to have been written by the market research firms themselves, are extensively annotated with detailed product descriptions and specific areas of expertise. This source provides an excellent complement to general directories of market research firms, such as the *Green Book* (see Chapter 4, "Market Research Reports"), which contains more listings but less extensive descriptions.

Roper Youth Report. **New York: RoperASW. Quarterly. Multi-part subscription including print report, newsletter, and CD-ROM $18,500. Contact: http://www.roperasw.com.**

The *Roper Youth Report* is an ongoing research study that is part of the Roper Reports Consumer Insights program. RoperASW is part of NOP World, a global market research firm that also owns Mediamark Research Inc. (MRI) and other information providers. RoperASW has also developed customer segmentation systems called MONITOR and VALUESCOPE which are similar to the ACORN and PRIZM systems discussed in Chapter 5.

The steep annual subscription price includes quarterly updates with two major print reports, a newsletter, electronic access to statistical data, and in-person briefing. This is a product geared to corporate environments and it is not available in public and academic libraries. However, it is a worthwhile lead for researchers of all types, including students and practitioners in small firms, because Roper data are often quoted in market research reports and trade journals. Using the report name as a search term in such databases as *Factiva*, *ABI/NFORM*, or *LexisNexis*, or in other business periodical indexes will often result in articles that quote recent data from this major research effort. The same search can be done in *MarketResearch.com* to locate reports for purchase.

The *Roper Youth Report* helps marketers create new products, understand young consumers, plan advertising and distribution strategies, and "start a lifelong relationship with new customers" according to a company brochure (Pares 2002). Based on in-home, in-person interviews using a sample of 1,000 young people between the ages of 8 and 17, the report emphasizes mood, consumer behavior, attitudes and opinions, lifestyles, media, technology, and relationships of kids and teens. Also included are long-term trend analyses from over a decade of annual studies.

***Simmons Kids Study* and *Simmons Teen Study*. New York: Simmons Market Research Bureau. Irregular. Format varies. Price upon request. Contact: http://www.smrb.com.**

Based on Simmons' National Consumer Survey, the *Kids Study* and the *Teen Study* are used by corporations and other marketers. Simmons is a respected market research originator with over 40 years of experience. Like many market research studies, these reports are costly. The *Kids Study* questionnaire is a booklet designed to appeal to children in order to reduce the likelihood that adults in the household will fill it out in lieu of direct responses from children. The report covers product use and brand preference as well as psychographic measures. The *Teen Study* offers measures such as demographics, media exposure, lifestyle, brand use, grocery products, and lifestyle and psychographic factors. This report emphasizes grocery products, electronics, fashion, and entertainment choices.

TIP: "Data-Mining" to Obtain (Otherwise) Expensive Market Research Data

Summaries of data from major market research firms often can be obtained from articles published in trade journals, press releases, and from market research reports. Use standard periodical indexes and market research databases found in academic and public libraries (e.g., *ABI/INFORM*, *Business Source Premier*, *Business & Industry*, *TableBase*, *Factiva*, or *MarketResearch.com*) and search by the name of the producer or report.

Examples: "roper youth report" or "roper green gauge report" or "simmons national consumer survey," etc.

Kids These Days '99: What Americans Really Think About the Next Generation. **New York: Public Agenda, 1999. Online (free). Contact: http://www.publicagenda.org/specials/kids/kids.htm.**

This five-year tracking study was first conducted in 1997 by Public Agenda, a policy think tank for citizen education. The second report was published in 1999 and it is scheduled for an update in 2002. The Advertising Council, producer of public service advertising, was one of the sponsors as part of its 10-year initiative focusing on improving the lives of children. The findings show that the majority of Americans are troubled about the character of the next generation. This study provides background information that puts marketing data in a sociological context.

The full 12-page 1999 report is available online in HTML or PDF formats from Public Agenda. It is also available in print from the Ad Council (http://www.adcouncil.org). The 50 page 1997 report is available in print from Public Agenda.

Bibliography of Research and Writings on Marketing and Advertising to Children. **James U. McNeal. New York: Lexington Books, 1991. Print. 168 pages.**

James McNeal is a renowned expert on marketing to children; as a professor of marketing at Texas A&M University, he has focused his research on this area since the 1960s. This bibliography is the result of his work over a 30-year period. The subject scope is the consumer behavior and market targeting of children between the ages of four and 12, with only limited materials about pre-schoolers and adolescents.

The bibliography includes academic journals, books, and conference proceedings from the marketing, psychology, sociology, and consumer education disciplines. Unlike many academic reference books, it also includes citations from popular business and household magazines and newspapers, such as the *Wall Street Journal, Advertising Age, Parenting,* and *Newsweek.* Newsletters are the only type of material specifically excluded. Social and economic historians will especially appreciate the coverage of articles from the popular business press that report on product introductions and advertising campaigns geared to children. Marketers will benefit from the citations to articles noting successes and failures, and from studies of children's consumer behavior. Policy makers will gain from its broad scope and coverage.

Containing 621 annotations for the period from 1960 through 1990, it includes international material, though all cited works are in English. Entries are arranged in alphabetical order, and annotated with brief summaries. A Major Topic Index categorizes the 621 entries into 20 topics (brands, clothing industry, research guidelines, etc.). This classification enables academic researchers to identify areas for which topics have received extensive treatment (such as advertising), and those which have little (such as pricing and packaging) (McNeal 1991, 12).

Children and Adolescents in the Market Place: Twenty-Five Years of Academic Research. **Tomasita M. Chandler and Barbara M. Heinzerling. Ann Arbor, MI: The Pierian Press, 1999. Print $145. 669 pages.**

This extensively annotated bibliography includes articles from academic journals and proceedings from 1970 through 1995, focusing on children ages three through 18 as consumers or otherwise in the market place. Most of the 836 summaries describe empirical research works, with few literature reviews or policy-oriented articles cited. The authors are a child development professional and a consumer educator.

Entries are alphabetized by author's name within six major subject categories: learning the consumer role; economic and financial behavior; expenditures, shopping behavior, and brand preferences; consumer behavior determinants; public policy; and related research. Like McNeal's bibliography, this arrangement points up which areas have received relatively more or less research attention. Lengthy summaries provide detail about research findings, methodologies, data collection instruments, and about the children studied. There are author and title indexes.

TIP: A Short Reading List About Marketing to Children and Teens

Acuff, Daniel S. 1997. *What Kids Buy and Why: The Psychology of Marketing to Kids.* Daniel S. Acuff and Robert H. Reiher. New York: Free Press.

Frontline. *Merchants of Cool: A Report on the Creators and Marketers of Popular Culture for Teenagers.* 2001. <http://www.pbs.org/wgbh/pages/frontline/shows/cool> (April 28, 2003).

McNeal, James. 1998. "Child's Play," *Marketing Tools* 5, no. 1 (January): 20-24.

_____*Kids as Customers: A Handbook of Marketing to Children.* 1992. New York: Lexington Books.

_____*The Kids' Market: Myths and Realities.* 1999. Ithaca, NY: Paramount Market Publishing.

_____"Tapping the Three Kids' Markets," *American Demographics* (April 1998): 36-41.

Sinatt, Jacqui. "Targeting Kids Is a Fickle Business," *Brand Strategy* 153 (November 2001): 15.

Youth University. Monthly e-mail newsletter. Cincinnati, OH: WonderGroup. <http://youthuniversity.com> (April 28, 2003).

Zollo, Peter. 1999. *Wise Up to Teens: Insights into Marketing and Advertising to Teenagers.* 2nd ed. Ithaca, NY: New Strategist Publications, Inc.

TIP: Resources for Policy and Ethical Issues on Marketing to Children and Youth

- *Business Partnerships with Schools: Policy Guidelines for Schools Seeking to Establish and Maintain Productive and Ethical Relationships with Corporations.* "Ethical Concerns." ERIC Clearinghouse on Education Management. College of Education, University of Oregon, Eugene. Contact://http://eric.uoregon.edu/publications/policy_reports/business_partnerships/ethical_concerns.html.
- *Kids and Commercialism.* Center for a New American Dream. Contact: http://www.newdream.org/campaign/kids/index.html.
- *Media in the Home.* Annenberg Public Policy Center. Contact: http://www.appcpenn.org/mediainhome/.
- *National Institute on the Media and the Family.* Contact: http://www.mediaandthefamily.org/index.shtml.
- McNeal, James U. 1991. "Preface." In *Bibliography of Research and Writings on Marketing and Advertising to Children.* New York: Lexington Books.
- Presents a positive viewpoint on the legitimacy of marketing to children and the "growing economic power" and "market maturity" of children (McNeal 1991, v-vi).
- *Self-Regulatory Guidelines for Children's Advertising.* (Revised December 2001). Better Business Bureau. Childrens Advertising Review Unit. Contact: http://www.caru.org/carusubpgs/guidepg.asp.

MARKETING TO GAYS AND LESBIANS

A generally accepted principle in consumer behavior literature is that there is a "congruency between the self-concept and products people buy" (Kates 1998, 3). Marketers, therefore, seek to reach groups that express a particular set of preferences, tastes, and values. Furthermore, the "common wisdom" in market research is that certain groups, such as gay men, tend to have significantly higher income levels than society in general. Like marketing to children, there is also controversy surrounding the topic of marketing to gay people. Some in the gay community have been concerned that the affluence of gay consumers has been overestimated for marketing purposes and has been used by anti-gay political groups to show that gays have undue influence in society (see http://www.noglstp.org/economic.html). In any case, this demographic group, like others with a distinctive profile, is an increasing focus of marketers' attention.

***Gay Media Database.* GLINN Media Corporation. Key West, FL. ©2002. Online (free). Contact: http://www.gaydata.com.**

This Web site provides directories of publications and media with an editorial focus on gay and lesbian consumers. Listings provide contact information, format, and frequency in several categories. There are selections for major national publications, local publications, broadcast media, directory publishers, Web resources, and others. The database of publications is not searchable and the Web site design is somewhat lacking in sophistication, but there are available links to gay and lesbian publications.

***GAYDAR: Gay Directory of Authoritative Resources.* Amherst, MA: Institute for Gay and Lesbian Strategic Studies. 1999-2000. Online (free). Contact: http://www.iglss.org/pubs/gaydar/gaydar.php.**

The *Gay Directory of Authoritative Sources* (GAYDAR) is a publication of the Institute for Gay and Lesbian Strategic Studies (IGLSS), which identifies itself as an independent think tank answering questions that affect the lesbian, gay, bisexual, and transgender communities. Subtitled *Experts on Gay, Lesbian, Bisexual, Transsexual, and Transgendered Policy-relevant Research*, the *Directory* is intended to facilitate connections between social scientists and other expert researchers and those needing research findings, such as elected officials, judges, journalists, and the general public (Institute of Gay and Lesbian Strategic Studies 1997-2002).

The first edition of *GAYDAR* is dated 1999-2000, and easily downloaded in PDF from the IGLSS Web site. The full entry for each expert is given in the Alphabetical Index, which contains contact information, academic discipline, and area of expertise. The General Subject Index groups the specific areas of expertise into 11 broad subject areas, including discrimination, health, politics, and workplace issues. A Geographical Index lists researchers by state and country. Although the primary focus of the *GAYDAR* is policy-related, marketers may find some researchers listed in the "Workplace and Economic Issues" and "Culture/Media" areas who have expertise worth tapping for marketing-related topics.

TIP: IGLSS Web Site

In addition to the Gay *Directory of Authoritative Resources* (DAR), the IGLSS Web site offers the following sources.

- *Income Inflation: The Myth of Affluence Among Gay, Lesbian, and Bisexual Americans* by M.V. Lee Badgett (PDF)
- *Angles: The Policy Journal of the Institute*
- *IGLSS Abstracts*, an electronic subscription service summarizing recent scholarly works
- *IGLSS Technical Reports*

***Commercial Closet: The World's Largest Collection of Gay Advertising.* Commercial Closet Association. New York. ©2001-2002. Online (free). Contact: http://www.commercialcloset.org.**

The Commercial Closet Association is a non-profit education and journalism organization that seeks to encourage positive, inclusive images of lesbian, gay, transgender, and bisexual people in advertising. The Web site is a "virtual museum" of 800 advertising images that can be retrieved according to various criteria. Spanning over 30 years of print and broadcast advertising, the ads are categorized using a thesaurus of 50 Themes (e.g., situations such as "mistaken identities" or "in the bar"; identities such as "couples" or "lipstick lesbians"; ad industry related, such as "ad parodies" or "oldest ads"). In addition, each ad is rated according to its type of "portrayal," that is, whether it conveys a positive, negative, neutral, or vague impression of gay life. It is possible to search directly for a specific ad according to various criteria, such as business category, medium, target audience, and region. Each ad is described and cataloged, including brand name and company, air date, country, and industry, and can be viewed using QuickTime video, or as a still storyboard. For research and study, the site also contains a list of publications under the link "Gay Marketing Resources."

National Gay Newspaper Guild. Rivendell Marketing Company Inc. Online (free). Contact: http://www.rivendellmarketing.com/ngng/ngng_set.html.

The National Gay Newspaper Guild (NGNG) is a consortium of gay publications which, with the help of Rivendell Marketing Company, contracts with Simmons Market Research to survey their joint readership every four years. Although the full report is available only to members of the NGNG, the Web site provides a "Reader's Profile" section with summary demographic data. Here there is a percentage breakdown in the categories of gender, age, employment, education, and income. Because they represent only the readership of the NGNG's member publications, these statistics do not necessarily represent a reliable sample of the entire gay population.

2001 Gay/Lesbian Consumer Online Census. **GLCensus Partners. 2001. CD-ROM $32,000 (Parts 1&2), $18,250 (Part 1 only), $1,625 (individual industry sections). Contact: http://www.glcensus.com.**

Responding to the lack of detailed data on this consumer group, this study describes worldwide gay and lesbian communities. It is a joint project of Zogby International (a public opinion and market research firm), OpusComm Group (a market research and public relations firm), the S.I. Newhouse School of Communications at Syracuse University, and GSociety (a media/entertainment company). Using the Internet to mount an outreach and public relations campaign, the research was conducted among 6,451 participants in a 40-minute online survey originally administered between July 9 and August 29, 2001. New polls are conducted on a periodic basis. The complete report is obviously costly and geared to a corporate clientele, but, again, some summary data may be found in trade journal articles and market research reports. In addition, the press releases issued by OpusComm Group contain useful overviews, facts, and figures. For example, available at the Web site under the link "Media Kit," the press release entitled "Gay Purchasing

Power a Significant Force, Major Study Reveals" issued on October 17, 2001, offers summary data on gay income levels.

The complete report has two major sections. Part I covers demographics and deals with such topics as age, ethnicity, geographic representation (U.S. and worldwide), economic status, education level, occupation, self-identification, parenting and children, residence profile, and politics and religion. Media usage comprises a large sub-section: the data are detailed and broken down quite specifically as to preferences for newspapers, TV shows, and radio formats. Part Two reveals purchasing patterns and behavior in such categories as Automotive, Apparel, Child Care, Computers, Electronics, Entertainment, Food & Beverage, Personal Hygiene and Health, Sports, and Fitness and Travel. Customized reports for specific industry categories are also available.

TIP: A Short Reading List for Marketing to Gays and Lesbians

Badgett, M.V. Lee. "Income Inflation: The Myth of Affluence Among Gay, Lesbian, and Bisexual Americans." 1998. New York: Policy Institute–National Gay and Lesbian Task Force. <http://www.iglss.org/pubs/publications.html> (June 27, 2002).

Gardyn, Rebecca. 2001. "A Market Kept in the Closet," *American Demographics* 23 no.11 (November): 36-43.

Kates, Steven M. *1998. Twenty Million New Customers! Understanding Gay Men's Consumer Behavior.* (Haworth Gay & Lesbian Studies). New York: Harrington Park Press.

Lukenbill, Grant. 1999. *Untold Millions: Secret Truths About Marketing to Gay and Lesbian Consumers.* 2nd edition. (Haworth Gay & Lesbian Studies). New York: Harrington Park Press. (This book incorporates data from Yankelovich's *MONITOR*, an ongoing study of consumer segments. See http://www.yankelovich.com/.)

Wardlow, David L. 1996. *Gays, Lesbians, and Consumer Behavior: Theory, Practice and Research Issues in Marketing.* New York: Harrington Park Press. (Simultaneously issued by the Haworth Press under the same title, as a special issue of *Journal of Homosexuality* 1996, 31 no.1/2.)

Yankelovich. 1994. *Gay/Lesbian/Bisexual MONITOR Survey.* New York: Yankelovich and Associates.

TIP: These Publishers and Market Research Firms Focus on Niche Markets and Provide a Wide Range of Books, Newsletters, Statistical Reports, and Studies

- Target Market News. Contact: http://www.targetmarketnews.com.
- EPM Communications. Contact: http://www.epmcom.com/.
- Paramount Market Publishing. Contact: http://www.paramountbooks.com/defaultmain.cfm.
- Mediamark Research (MRI). Contact: http://www.mediamark.com/.
- Simmons Market Research Bureau. Contact: http://www.smrb.com.
- RoperASW. Contact: http://www.roperasw.com/.
- Yankelovich. Contact: http://www.yankelovich.com/.
- Gallup Organization. Contact: http://www.gallup.com.

REFERENCES

Bennett, Peter D. 1995. *Dictionary of Marketing Terms.* 2d ed. Chicago: American Marketing Association and Lincolnwood, IL: NTC Books.

Cui, Geng and Pravat Choudhury. 2000. *Marketing to Ethnic Consumers: An Annotated Bibliography.* (Bibliography series). Chicago: American Marketing Association.

Institute of Gay and Lesbian Strategic Studies. 1997-2002. *Gay Directory of Authoritative Resources.* <http://www.iglss.org/iglss/pubs/gaydar/gaydar.asp> (July 31, 2002).

Kates, Steven M. 1998. *Twenty Million New Customers! Understanding Gay Men's Consumer Behavior.* (Haworth Gay & Lesbian Studies). New York: Harrington Park Press.

McNeal, James U. 1991. *Bibliography of Research and Writings on Marketing and Advertising to Children.* New York: Lexington Books, 1991.

Luckinbill Grant. 1999. *Untold Millions: Secret Truths About Marketing to Gay and Lesbian Consumers.* New York: Harrington Park Press.

Pares. 2002. "Pricing for Roper Reports," May 3, 2002. Company brochure received via e-mail.

PART IV

RESEARCH
FOR THE PROMOTIONAL
STRATEGY

Chapter 7

Advertising and Media Planning Sources

Topics

Locating Advertisers and Agencies
Media Planning and Buying
Advertising Expenditures, Ratios, and Industry Data
Current Tracking Services
Historical Advertisements and Campaigns
Advertising Research and Measurement
Advertising Law
Handbooks and Web Gateways

Sources

Advertising Red Books
Standard Rate and Data Service (SRDS)
Television Commercial Monitoring Report
Advertising Ratios and Budgets
Advertising Growth Trends
Bob Coen's Insider's Report
AdAge Data Center
CMR, A Taylor Nelson Sofres Company
Ad*Access
Encyclopedia of Major Marketing Campaigns
Advertising Age Encyclopedia of Advertising
AdForum.com

[Haworth co-indexing entry note]: "Advertising and Media Planning Sources." Diamond, Wendy, and Michael R. Oppenheim. Co-published simultaneously in *Journal of Business & Finance Librarianship* (The Haworth Information Press, an imprint of The Haworth Press, Inc.) Vol. 9, No. 2/3, 2004, pp. 157-187; and: *Marketing Information: A Strategic Guide for Business and Finance Libraries* (Wendy Diamond, and Michael R. Oppenheim) The Haworth Information Press, an imprint of The Haworth Press, Inc., 2004, pp. 157-187. Single or multiple copies of this article are available for a fee from The Haworth Document Delivery Service [1-800-HAWORTH, 9:00 a.m. - 5:00 p.m. (EST). E-mail address: docdelivery@haworthpress.com].

AdReview.com
Advertising Research Foundation
Magazine Publishers of America
ARS Group
AdLaw
Advertising Law
Dartnell's Advertising Manager's Handbook
American Association of Advertising Agencies
Advertising World

Advertising may be the most important component of the overall marketing plan for consumer goods. Although packaging, pricing, promotions, and public relations all play a part in establishing the product or service in the consumer's mind, nothing is as powerful as advertising. Defined as "any paid form of nonpersonal presentation and promotion of ideas, goods, or services by an identified sponsor" (Kotler and Armstrong 2001, G-1), advertising is the best opportunity for companies to proclaim their attributes and strengths. In our communication-rich world, advertising incorporates print, broadcast, visual, and interactive media.

Advertising in America has a long history. It is estimated that by 1800 advertising expenditures were already $1 million. The first U.S. advertising agency was established in 1849. By 1861, there were 20 agencies in New York City, and in the 1870s outdoor advertising was so ubiquitous that states began to impose limitations to protect natural scenery (John W. Hartman Center for Sales, Advertising, and Marketing 2000). Advertising has evolved into a large and influential industry throughout the world. In the United States, it involves four major types of organizations: advertisers themselves, advertising media, advertising agencies, and support services (Beacham, Hise and Tongren 1986, 10).

The advertisers are the companies that seek to promote and sell their goods or services, functions which may be handled in-house or contracted out to an advertising agency. "Agencies usually have four departments: *creative*, which develops and produces ads; *media*, which selects media and places ads; *research*, which studies audience characteristics and wants; and *business*, which handles the agency's business activities. Each account is supervised by an account executive, and people in each department are usually assigned to work on one or more accounts" (Kotler and Armstrong 2001, 557).

Each part of the industry has a unique set of information needs, but all share a pool of questions in common. This chapter covers a selection of sources to address both needs. We discuss the important information tools used by professionals working within advertising, as well as those outside the industry who are researching, teaching, or analyzing it. The topics in this chapter range from basic tools, such as directories and industry data sources (easily found in many public and academic libraries) to those that are more specialized, such as tracking services and measurement studies (more likely available only in large corporate or research settings.) Sources of historical advertisements and campaigns and advertising law are included because they are important to all segments. Finally, this chapter includes some "gateway" Web sites and handbooks that provide general information on all topics.

LOCATING ADVERTISERS AND AGENCIES

Because of the visibility of advertising itself, there is considerable concurrent publicity about advertising agencies. Focused, subject-specific directories are the best way to locate and identify them. In addition to providing information-packed listings, the best directories usually include bonus features in the form of cross-referenced indexes, rankings, lists, articles, and more. Because of the demand for this information, these directories are commonly found in public and academic libraries, and there is increasing availability on the Web.

***The Advertising Red Books* (*Agencies edition* and *Advertisers edition*). New Providence, NJ: LexisNexis Group. Bi-Annual with supplements. Print $1,796. CD-ROM $1,495. Online $1,495. Contact: http://www.redbooks.com.**

Published for nearly 100 years, "The Red Books" are a mainstay of information about the advertising industry. If you need to know which advertising agency a corporation uses, who is in charge of an advertising agency, what other corporations it represents, or the size of a company's advertising budget, these directories answer those questions. The two companion editions of *The Red Books*, currently designated the *Agencies edition* and *Advertisers edition*, were formerly titled *Standard Directory of Advertising Agencies* and *Standard Directory of Advertisers*, respectively. They are published separately in January and July of each year, with supplements issued in April and October. These may be purchased separately with or without the International edition (i.e., *The Advertising Red Books–International Advertisers and Agencies edi-*

tion). The content is also available with more frequent updates in electronic form in CD-ROM, on the Web, and is also available via the Dialog information service (as Files 177 and 178). In addition to basic directory information, the *Red Books* offer "bonus" information in the form of rankings, indexes, and lists. The publisher's long experience with these directories results in a wealth of detailed information presented in a compact and highly useable form.

The Advertising Red Books–Agencies is a compendium of facts about advertising agencies. The 2003 edition lists over 13,000 based on information compiled from questionnaires or gathered from business publications. To qualify for a listing, an agency must either report a minimum of $200,000 in gross annual billings, or be the agency of record for one of the companies listed in its companion title, *The Advertising Red Books–Advertisers.* All agencies listed originate in the United States or Canada, or have at least one U.S. or Canadian branch. Agencies originating in other countries are included in a separate section called "Geographic Index–Non-U.S."

Agencies are arranged according to five types: Advertising Agencies, House Agencies, Media Buying Services, Sales Promotion Agencies, and Public Relations Firms. Most are listed alphabetically by parent company names, but some large branches are listed separately. In addition to name and address, a typical entry includes key personnel with contact information, agency specializations, amount of annual billings, breakdown of gross billings by media, names of account supervisors, and accounts served. Some listings are enhanced with a paid "Agency Profile," describing achievements, awards, and expertise. A list of "Mergers, Acquisitions and Name Changes" provides a succinct snapshot of change within the industry.

Four indexes provide cross-referencing within this single print volume: Geographic, Special Markets, Personnel, and Agency Responsibility indexes. The Geographic index is arranged by state and is useful for finding an agency in a particular locale. The Special Markets index identifies advertising agencies that focus on certain industries, ethnic markets, or media. For example, this index makes it a simple matter to find an agency that specializes in fashion, or African-American media, or business-to-business services.

The indexes devoted to Personnel and Agency Responsibilities locate individuals within each agency. When a name is known, use the Personnel index, which gives affiliations and official titles. For example, this index, in either print or electronic format, can be useful when one encounters a name in a news report or meets someone at a conference. The Agency Responsibilities index, which is arranged by firm name, lists by name people working as account executives, art directors, media buyers, and so on. Either print or electronic versions can be used to locate the person responsible for a specific function within an agency, but the electronic version also makes it possible to generate lists of all Art Directors, Account Executives and the like.

The *Agencies* edition also offers a wealth of bonus information in the form of rankings, lists, and a section of "Services and Suppliers." For example, there are lists of U.S. Agency Brands Ranked by Gross Income, Top 10 Agencies by U.S. Media Billings, and the World's Top 50 Advertising Organizations. In addition, there are lists of Associations, membership of the American Association of Advertising Agencies, winners of the industry's prestigious awards, and Who Owns Whom. The "Services and Suppliers" section, provides a business-to-business directory of specialized firms serving advertising agencies (e.g., copywriters, photographers, fulfillment centers, mailing list brokers, etc.).

TIP: Finding Agency Rankings

Agency rankings in the *Red Books* are provided by Crain Communications. They are also published in a special issue of *Advertising Age* magazine, usually in April. The information is also available free at the Web site (http://www.adage.com/datacenter.cms).

Its companion title, entitled *The Advertising Red Books–Advertisers*, is more extensive in content and indexing. Essential to advertising professionals, it is valuable to anyone looking for information about the marketing strategies of "companies that advertise," that is, "advertisers." Like its companion, it covers companies in the U.S. and Canada, and includes data on more than 14,000 companies which spend at least $200,000 on national and regional advertising; information is supplied by the companies themselves and/or gathered from trade journals. Data are verified.

The *Advertisers* edition is issued in two volumes, one arranged by geography and entitled *Advertising Red Book–Geographic*; the other arranged by business classifications and called *Advertising Red Book–Advertisers Business Classifications*. Here the data about companies are listed according to 55 categories (hardware, schools & colleges, shoes, internet/online, etc.) This lets the user easily compare levels of advertising activity and spending of all companies within an industry. In the geographic volumes, headquarters and major branches are listed by state (or province) and city. Both editions have an auxiliary section of rankings and tables supplied by CMR, a market research firm specializing in advertising. An industry snapshot is provided by listings of Leading Advertisers with dollar amounts of expenditures, and tables listing the Top 25 Advertisers in various categories, such as consumer magazines, newspapers, Sunday magazines, television, radio, etc. In addition, there are lists of companies not previously covered, and a breakdown of total numbers of companies by business classification and by location.

In both *Business Classifications* and *Geographic*, the main sections are comprised of entries containing information about companies and their advertising activities. In most cases, the company's advertising agency and advertised products are listed, along with the name of the person in charge of each account. Entries usually include other significant personnel as well as approximate sales totals, year founded, number of employees, trade names, and business description. Each company entry has a report of its advertising budget, including a breakdown by type of media. This feature is useful in many contexts. For example, a media sales representative can discover which media are underutilized by a particular firm, in what month they set their advertising budget, and whether products are distributed nationally, by direct mail, or by other means. The various types of media (TV, outdoor billboards, radio, newspaper, magazines, etc.) are symbolized by numbers that are keyed on every page of the directory. This system allows a tremendous amount of information to be included in a condensed space, and yet it remains easy to use.

In addition, there are tabbed sub-sections with listings of companies that have in-house advertising agencies, recent mergers, acquisitions and name changes, and new entries. There is a separate volume of indexes for both *Business Classifications* and *Geographic*. Each index volume contains four cross-referencing lists (Product Categories by State, Brand Name, Standard Industrial Classification, Personnel). The indexes are actually identical, but there are two sets of page references for each entry. The first, in italic type, references the company's listing in the *Business Classification* edition; page references in regular type lead to the *Geographic* edition. Thus, for 2003 the brand name "Born Blonde" will be found on page 343 (Connecticut) in the *Geographic* edition and page 476 (Cosmetics & Toiletries) in the *Business Classification* edition.

TIP: Use the Brand Name Indexes in the Advertisers *Red Books* to locate the name of the company affiliated with a brand or trade name.

TIP: In the listings, company names that begin with a person's name are alphabetized according to the last name.

TIP: If you can't find a business classification that precisely fits the description of the type of company you are trying to find, consult the Index to Product Categories which provides page references to 750 narrow subdivisions that are covered within the 55 business classifications.

A subscription to the set of two *Red Books* is costly. Print subscriptions can be augmented with online access for an additional fee (currently $99 per year for print subscribers). The Web version (http://www.redbooks.com) offers more online advertisers, continuous updates, and flexible navigational capabilities for 17 search criteria. For a less expensive alternative, there is Schonfeld & Associates' *U.S. Sourcebook of Advertisers* (Riverwoods, IL. Annual. $345 print, $495 print and database), which is similar in purpose to the *Red Books–Advertisers*. The *U.S. Sourcebook of Advertisers*' entries similarly include contact information, executive titles, and advertising budgets, but its scope is considerably more limited because it excludes privately held companies (i.e., those that do not sell shares or file reports with the Securities and Exchange Commission).

TIP: The *Red Books* Contain Lots of "Bonus" Information

- Ranked lists of Leading Advertisers
- New Listings
- Mergers, Acquisitions & Name Changes
- Services & Suppliers to the Advertising Industry
- Number of Companies by Business Classification
- Number of Companies by Location

For advertising agencies, there are less costly directories as well, but they also do not cover as many firms or include as much bonus information as the *Red Books* do. For example, *Adweek Directory* (New York: AdWeek Directories. Annual. Online $700; http://www.adweek.com/aw/directories/index.jsp) is a listing of approximately 6,400 U.S. advertising agencies, public relations firms, media buying services, and related organizations. Arranged alphabetically by company name, with separate entries for branches, entry data includes: contact information, services offered, industries served, billings, fee income, key personnel, and major accounts. There are indexes by geography, by organization type, by parent company, and by ethnic specialty. Overall, *Adweek Directory* has less depth and scope than the *Agency Redbook*, covering about half as many firms and not including the useful media breakdown of gross billings or any of the personnel indexes. Additionally, the only agency specialization it indexes is ethnic focus.

There are three Web sites which similarly contain advertising agency listings. The *AAAAgency Search* (http://www.aaaagencysearch.com), a service of the American Association of Advertising Agencies, is a Web directory which provides its membership roster free to non-members. Listings include specialties and location information with a direct link to the agency's site. In some cases, the names of clients and billing amounts are included. *Agency CompPile.com* (http://www.agencycompile.com), which can be accessed for free with registration, is a Web directory of U.S. advertising agencies, public relations firms, and services for sales promotion, design, interactive, and media buying services. It also provides several useful links to specialized associations and services, such as a database of sample legal contract forms from *AdLaw.com*. *AdForum.com* (http://www.adforum.com) is an international, subscription-based directory of over 16,000 agencies in 137 countries. In addition to several free news features, this site offers fee-based services for advertising agencies, advertisers, and production companies. These include: (1) "Ad Folio," a searchable database of creative work, containing 14,500 broadcast production ads from over 2,500 production companies; (2) "BizSector Creative Reviews," a database of reviews of business-to-business advertisements; and (3) "Agency Preview," a service for advertisers which allows users to search for agencies which meet specific criteria. In addition, *AdForum* offers Custom Research for locating agencies and CD-on-demand services for obtaining hard copies of creative work.

TIP: Other Directories for Media Buying Services, Sales Promotion and Public Relations

Alternatives to the *Red Books'* sections on media buying services, sales promotion agencies, and public relations firms are discussed in the sections on Media Planning and Buying (in this chapter), Promotion (Chapter 9), and Public Relations (Chapter 8).

MEDIA PLANNING AND BUYING

For advertising to be effective, media planners and buyers must identify and select the best magazine, newspaper, Web site, radio station, TV channel, or mailing list for the purpose at hand. Decision making requires consideration of both operational and qualitative factors, such as editorial and geographical scope, circulation, audience size and composition, interactivity, seasonality, technical and design requirements, and cost. The final step in the media planning and buying process is making the contacts to carry out the advertising program.

This section covers a selection of sources useful to media planners and buyers for making choices in today's communications-rich environment.

Standard Rate and Data Service (SRDS). Des Plaines, IL. Contact: http://www.srds.com.

For over 80 years, the publisher Standard Rate and Data Service (SRDS) has provided media planning information in an extensive suite of specialized titles. These titles cover advertising rates for consumer magazines, trade publications, newspapers, TV and radio, mailing lists, billboards, other out-of-home venues, and the Internet, for U.S. and international markets. As part of the monthly print subscription cost, SRDS offers access to online versions, including such major titles as *Consumer Magazine Advertising Source, Business Publication Advertising Source, Interactive Advertising Source, Radio Advertising Source, Direct Marketing List Source*, as well as a number of others. Overall, SRDS catalogs more than 100,000 advertising sources (media properties or publications) and maintains currency with "more than 21,000 listing updates every month." It claims that 95 percent of all advertising agencies rely on its products (SRDS 2002). In the fast moving worlds of media and advertising, SRDS publications have a good reputation as reliable and authoritative. SRDS is a subsidiary of VNU, which also owns A.C. Nielsen Media Research and BPI Communications, a magazine publisher.

SRDS' content consists of listings of individual media venues or resources, i.e., publications, radio stations, television channels, and other vehicles in which advertising appears. Each listing contains a descriptive editorial profile provided by the publisher/owner, names of company officials, and contact information for branch offices and advertising sales representatives. Printed magazines and newspapers are the most ubiquitous media venue, and they comprise the largest proportion of total SRDS content. In its publications covering print media, entries provide three components: (1) audited circulation and audience figures (as available) for subscription and single issues so the media buyer can ascertain the potential "reach"; (2) general and specific rate policies for black/white, color, covers, inserts, and special issues of various dimensions, lengths, and frequencies; and (3) printing and layout requirements, binding style, trim sizes, and issue closing dates. The SRDS listings for non-print media (radio, TV, cable and Internet) vary more in content; broadcast and electronics formats are diverse and rate information is variable because negotiated rather than standardized prices are the norm. These listings generally include programming, special features (e.g., stereo availability), infomercial time slots, types of facilities, wattage power, interactivity, etc.

Both the print and online versions offer features and utilities that enhance their usefulness. For example, the print format offers several "bonus" features such as a three-year Media Buying Calendar, a glossary of media terms, and lists of representatives. The print format makes it easy to identify new or deleted titles and media venues, or to locate magazines that offer special geographic and/or demographic editions. Print is also an easier format for use in a working group, or when a simple telephone number or address is needed quickly.

However the online versions have other unique strengths. With the electronic format comes additional flexibility, timeliness, and many features well suited to the needs of media buyers. Using the Web versions, it is possible to create and print custom reports, copy and paste logos from SRDS listings into reports and presentations, and output data into spreadsheets and other planning software. Each entry provides direct links to publisher/owner Web sites, e-mail addresses, and media kits containing editorial calendars, audience research data, and full-text audit statements which independently verify circulation. Updates are continual and access is available "24/7," which is convenient for business travelers.

The complete SRDS series consists of over 10 individual titles, but only one is discussed here. *Consumer Magazine Advertising Source* is published monthly in print, including access to the online format, for $691 per year. The print version provides a myriad of indexes which organize the listings in various ways. Users can easily review lists by magazine title, classification groups, publication location, group buying opportunities, split runs, and more. In both versions, source entries are organized into 85 topical classifications, such as "babies," "opinion, thought & commentary," "home office/small business," etc. This feature allows the user to locate and analyze all comparable publications targeted to a certain market. There are several component databases (Domestic, International, Farm, business-to-business Card Decks, etc.) which are listed in separate sections in both the print and Web versions of this particular title.

The online version offers additional flexibility. Here one can search for keywords within publication titles, classifications, editorial profiles, publisher's name, special features, and analysis of circulation. It is possible to limit results to those titles that are professionally audited by one of the circulation verification bureaus. Data such as ad rates, issue and closing dates, circulation figures, editorial profiles, and contact personnel can be viewed and printed in two ways: "profile" format for quick scanning and top-level evaluation and "detailed" format for in-depth analysis.

TIP: Glossaries of Media Buying and Magazine Publishing Terms

- SRDS publications include a useful glossary in the front of the print volumes which includes technical "terms of art" related to printing, publishing, media buying, marketing, and advertising.
- *Marketer's Guide to Media.* VNU Business Publications. Contact: http://www.vnu.com.
- The Magazine Publishers of America (MPA) Web site has two glossaries at http://www.magazine.org/resources/top_requests. html entitled "Magazine Research Terminology" and "Circulation Terminology."

TIP: Media Planning and Buying Calculators from *SRDS*

The SRDS Web site offers free access to non-proprietary information for media planning decisions. Students and industry professionals alike will benefit from the standard formulas and how-to manuals. At the "support services" section, there are media buying guides, calculators, and definitions of technical tools such as Cost-Per-Thousand (CPM), Cost-Per-Rating-Point (CPP), Brand Development Index, Category Development Index (CDI), and more. Contact: http://www.srds.com/.

Few other tools provide the same reliability, excellent reputation, depth of coverage, and extensive scope as SRDS. Clearly, the ability to keep pace with the fast-changing advertising and media industries explains why SRDS claims its products and service are utilized by 95% of advertising agencies (SRDS 2002). However, for some, a subscription to SRDS is too costly. Small libraries and marketing departments might consider some other options. *Publist* (http://publist.com) is a free Web service that provides basic contact, frequency, and editorial descriptive information. However, it does not contain editorial calendars, demographic or advertising rates. *MediaPost* (http://www.mediapost.com) is a subscription Web site that offers a directory of 60,000 media contacts covering radio, TV, cable, Internet, magazines, newspapers and agencies. As a "portal" serving media buyers and planners, it offers other resources such as "rate and data" services, research, ratings, productivity tools, and industry news.

There are also several print publications that may serve in lieu of SRDS. The *Mediaweek Multimedia Directory* (New York: VNU Publications. Annual. Online $700; http://www.adweek.com/aw/directories/about.jsp) lists contact information for traditional and digital media outlets but the entries do not include rates or demographic breakdowns. It covers the top U.S. markets for radio, broadcast and cable TV, newspapers, consumer and trade magazines, interactive agencies, Web developers, online information sites, and more. Also published by VNU, the *Marketers Guide to Media* (New York: VNU Publications. Annual. Print. $125) is a portable, digest-sized source for cost and demographic information. It covers the top 100 U.S. markets for broadcast and cable TV, radio, newspapers, plus information on 450 consumer and trade magazines.

The *SQAD Media Market Guide* (Tarrytown, NY: SQAD Inc. Quarterly. Print. $260-$375) is an excellent adjunct to SRDS because it includes TV and radio advertising rate trends. Published quarterly, it contains cost projections for advertising with TV and radio, cable, newspapers, magazines, and outdoor media. Local markets and national networks are ranked by cost-per-rating-point (CPP) and cost-per-thousand (CPM), and data is included for 26 demographic categories. TV and radio dayparts (e.g., prime time, PM drive time), children's programs, cable stations, Neilsen's Direct Market Areas, and circulation rates are covered in simple tables with auxiliary explanatory pages. Annual subscription, single issues, and college library pricing are available.

Another alternative for media planning is available from Mediamark Research Inc. Their online Web-based product *MRI+* (http://www. mriplus.com) offers circulation data, audience data, editorial information, rates, and subscriber studies for 6,000 consumer and trade magazines. The database is available for trial use by registering at the Web site.

TIP: Advertising Rates and Cost Data for TV, Radio, and Outdoor Advertising

SRDS' publications formerly provided advertising rates and cost data for broadcast television networks, cable, and radio stations, but no longer do. There are two alternative sources for this data.

- *SQUAD Media Market Guide* is a quarterly print source containing projections of advertising cost data for TV, cable, radio, newspapers, magazines and outdoor media. Local and network markets, plus 26 demographic categories, are covered in tables with accompanying explanations. The *Guide* is available at reduced prices to colleges and libraries. Contact http://www/squad.com.

- *Marketer's Guide to Media* is a print directory published by VNU Publications. It gives advertising cost data for the top 100 U.S. markets and for major television networks (Harrington 2000-01). Contact http://www.vnu.com.

***Television Commercial Monitoring Report*. New York: American Association of Advertising Agencies (AAAA) and Association of National Advertisers (ANA). Annual. Print $35. Online (free) at http:// www.ana.net/com/ta/clutter.pdf. Contact: http://www.ana.net/.**

Like anything else, the cost of television advertising is related to supply and demand. In television advertising, "supply" is the number and desirability of available commercials and "demand" is the competition for viewers' attention, which is directly impacted by proliferation of non-program material. In order to keep buyers and sellers informed of the amount of non-program material, known in the industry as "clutter," the American Association of Advertising Agencies (AAAA) and the Association of National Advertisers (ANA) jointly sponsor the *Television Commercial Monitoring Report* (colloquially known as the "Clutter Study"). This annual study reports the non-program content of six major broadcast networks, 19 syndicated shows, and 19 cable networks, including network commercials, local commercials, public service announcements (PSAs), program credits, and network and station announcements ("promos"). The data are collected by CMR, a market research firm and provider of tracking services discussed elsewhere in this chapter.

The "Clutter Study" monitors television programming measured during specific time periods in selected places. Categorized into prime time, daytime, early morning, and late night, the data cover commercials and other non-program minutes aired on broadcast, network, syndication, and cable television. Other data segments cover Network Evening News and Local Evening News. The study provides an objective picture of what is actually broadcast, and it is used by media planners and buyers when negotiating contracts for commercials. For instance, the 2001 report finds that "non-program minutes appear to have reached an all time high" and recommends that "programmers should make clear, in advance, the maximum amount of non-program material that each program will carry" (ANA and AAAA 2001, 3). For social scientists, policy-makers, researchers, and students, this report provides a unique view of the realities of television content beyond what appears in program schedules.

ADVERTISING EXPENDITURES, RATIOS, AND INDUSTRY DATA

Because it is one of the most far-reaching service industries in the economy, advertising industry data are regularly sought by economists, investment analysts, policy makers, researchers, and students. Advertising professionals themselves also need aggregated and comparative data as benchmarks to gauge their effectiveness. The sources in this section answer questions about market size, recent growth, future trends, and other quantitative information about the advertising industry.

***Advertising Ratios & Budgets*. Riverwoods, IL: Schonfeld & Associates. Annual. Print $345. Print and disk combination $495. Contact: http://www.saibooks.com.**

Advertising Ratios & Budgets (ARB) is an annual report that tracks advertising expenditures for over 6,000 companies and 400 industries. Excerpts and summaries from the report are published and quoted in the business and trade press because advertising expenditures are considered an indicator of general corporate well being, which in turn represents trends in the overall economy. For those inside the industry itself, such as advertising agencies and marketing professionals who plan to sell services, this report provides essential information for many functions, such as tracking competition, gaining new ad agency clients, justifying ad budgets, selling media space and time, and planning for new media ventures and products.

TIP: *Advertising Age* **Is a Source for Schonfeld's Data**

Data from Schonfeld's *Advertising Ratios & Budgets* are reported in a special issue of *Advertising Age* magazine, usually in a July, August, or September issue. (See *Advertising Age*, September 16, 2002.)

For each company and industry, the report contains the previous year's advertising budgets, current year data for ad-to-sales ratios and ad-to-gross margin ratios, forecasts, and growth rates for the next two years' budgets. Because *ARB* is such a comprehensive and detailed report containing extensive quantitative data, users should be aware of how the data are gathered in order to understand their applicability and limitations. The report offers only ad spending totals; it does not provide a breakdown by media. Furthermore, because the data on companies' advertising expenditures are derived primarily from financial statements in 10-Ks and other Securities and Exchange Commission (SEC) filings, users should be aware that there can be some variation in what is defined as "advertising." Not all "customer acquisition activities" are treated as bona fide advertising costs in the financial statement of a public company. In an article discussing the then-new accounting standard for advertising costs (known as Statement of Principle SOP 93-7, issued by the *American Institute of Certified Public Accountants*),

Munter and Ratcliffe point out that there are certain activities, such as coupons, contest prizes, gifts, and discounts that are not legitimately included (Munter and Ratcliffe 1994). Furthermore, because companies designate their own Standard Industrial Classification (SIC) or North American Industry Classification Systems (NAICS) codes when filing financial statements with the SEC, and only one SIC or NAICS can be selected, the reports of industrial totals can be somewhat skewed. For instance, Johnson & Johnson is a pharmaceutical company according to its SIC, but most of its advertising budget is used in support of its cosmetic and personal care products. This is not immediately evident from the data (Gottesman 1998, 14).

***Advertising Growth Trends: Inflation Adjusted Analysis of Ad Spending.* Riverwoods, IL: Schonfeld & Associates. Annual. Print $345. Print and disk $495. Contact: http://www.saibooks.com.**

Schonfeld & Associates also produces a companion publication from the same dataset. *Advertising Growth Trends* (*AGT*) tracks 5-year trends in advertising spending for public companies. This information is useful for measuring profitability and effectiveness of a company's advertising expenditures; *AGT* also offers insight into market share and competition within industries. Listed within SICs, each company's historical information includes: annual advertising spending over five years; percent of advertising in relation to spending by all companies within the same SIC; and the average annual percent change within the five-year period in ad spending and sales. Some of this material duplicates what may be found in *Advertising Ratios and Budgets*, which also provides tables with industry averages. However, because of the longer time series it presents, *AGT* provides a superior tool for analysis of macro trends in the economy.

***Bob Coen's Insider's Report.* Universal McCann (division of McCann-Erickson WorldGroup). New York. Online (free). Contact: http:// www.mccann.com/insight/bobcoen.html.**

Produced by Robert J. Coen, Senior Vice President and Director of Forecasting for Universal McCann, the *Insider's Report* is published irregularly and made available at the McCann-Erickson WorldGroup Web site. This online newsletter provides a periodic overview of current trends in the advertising industry, with particular emphasis on macro-economic and social forces that impact the fortunes of advertising. The *Insider's Report* analyzes worldwide and national level advertising data to forecast growth and demand in the industry. It provides prior-year performance and next-year projections for advertising in newspaper, radio, TV, direct mail, Yellow Pages, Internet, and national and local media.

The newsletter Web site also offers access to an unusual time series of historical advertising expenditures of particular interest to market analysts, economists, social historians, and similar researchers. Covering advertising expenditures for the United States, the time series begins with abbreviated and estimated data as far back as 1776, and extends to the current period, with increasingly detailed data. By 1998 the data are extensive and, for the U.S., broken down by media type. Also reported is a time series entitled "Advertising as a Percent of U.S. GDP" which starts with 1929. Although not formatted for flexible searching or direct downloading, users are allowed to reprint portions as long as they give proper credit to Universal McCann (McCann-Erickson WorldGroup 2001).

AdAge Data Center. **Crain Communications. New York. ©2003. Online (free). Contact: http://www.adage.com/datacenter.cms.**

This Web site from *Advertising Age* magazine is another source for industry data such as statistics, surveys, and rankings of advertisers, marketers, media, agencies, brands, and salaries. The data is published throughout the year in various special features of the print magazine, and compiled, updated and archived at the AdAge Data Center. The content presented at the Web site may vary, but additional data can be requested are requested through contacts listed at the Web page.

The information is presented in four categories: Marketers, Media, Agencies, and Salary Surveys. For Marketers, the site features rankings for ad spending and estimates for leading national and international advertisers and markets. For Media, the largest U.S. media companies, magazines and newspapers are ranked and listed with circulation, ad linage, and revenues. For Agencies, the site offers *Ad Age*'s annual Agency Report, which has been published for over 50 years. The 2002 issue features the Agency Income Report, which provides a global look at the agency business. In the category of Salary Surveys, *Ad Age* reports the compensation of agency executives, which is handy for job changers, human resource personnel, and those engaged in salary negotiations.

TIP: More Advertising Industry Data

- Aggregated data on the magazine advertising industry are available at the Magazine Publishers of America (MPA) Web site. From the home page, select "Resources" or "Publisher Information Bureau," or go directly to http://www.magazine.org/pib/index. html. Contact: http://www.magazine.org.
- To look up national-level, aggregated advertising industry data, access the *Industry Quick Reports* under Economic Census at http://factfinder.census.gov/. Select sector "54: Professional, scientific & technical services." Advertising begins at NAICS code 5418.

CURRENT TRACKING SERVICES

As described in the previous section, analysts seek data about the advertising industry because it is seen as a "canary in the mine," portending macro-economic changes by reflecting a reluctance on the part of companies to spend money in uncertain times. Now, moving away from the macro-level, this section discusses sources that contain information pertaining to individual advertisements or campaigns.

After media planners have decided on ad placement, agency professionals need to verify that ads have actually run in the designated time slot, magazine issue, or on the channel or outdoor venue for which the advertiser has paid. There is also a need to monitor ads produced by competitors, and to keep up with trends and creative developments in the ad business itself. Given the large number of media venues which are simultaneously displaying ads, advertisers and agencies often require professional services to track their own and others' ad occurrence and expenditures.

CMR, A Taylor Nelson Sofres Company. New York. Contact: http://www.cmr.com.

Although there are other companies in this business, CMR is the best-known and largest source of competitive advertising data and customized tracking services. The company was formed in 1992 with the conglomeration of Broadcast Advertisers Reports (BAR), Leading National Advertisers (LNA), Radio Expenditure Reports (RER), and Radio TV Reports (RTV). Currently a member of Taylor Nelson Sofres' media monitoring network, CMR tracks "$100+ billion in advertising and more than 100 million advertising occurrences a year." Using centralized data collection sites, the company claims to have built an advertising database covering 900,000 brands (CMR 2001-2002). In addition, recent partnerships with such firms as Mediamark Research, Inc. enable CMR to incorporate demographic data into their advertising occurrence reports. Reports are available by subscription or can be compiled to meet customized needs.

Issued through a number of services and in a variety of standard formats, CMR's portfolio covers two basic variables: advertising expenditures and advertising occurrences. Some products combine expenditures, occurrences, and ratings in highly detailed incident-level reports (*Stradegy2*); some are summary reports of expenditures (*Ad$pender*); some are focused on particular media (*AdNetTrackUS* for the Internet, *Target2* for consumer magazines, *AdTelligence* for television and newspapers).

The *Stradegy2* report offers broad and deep coverage across many media for individual brands and company names. It tracks advertising occurrences and expenditures in a variety of different venues: print (magazines, local newspapers, national newspapers, Sunday magazines, etc.); television (network, cable, syndicated, spot); radio (network, national spot); and outdoor (posters, billboards, painted walls, bus shelters). National and local media are available in one report, updates are posted weekly, and year-to-date summaries are included. Clients can customize reports with over 1,000 data elements and create customized spreadsheets and flowcharts. Ad agencies and product managers subscribe to *Stradegy2* to confirm that ads for their own products have actually run, and also to keep up with the competition. It answers such questions as "Which publications are my competitors currently buying for their ads?" "How much are my competitors spending?" "When and where did my competitor's brand first appear?" (CMR 2001-2002). Too expensive and detailed to be available in most public or academic libraries, *Stradegy2* reports are usually accessed by clients over phone lines or the Internet.

Every business, whether small entrepreneur or large corporation, finds it useful to have some information about competitors' advertising records. However, most libraries and many companies cannot afford customized tracking services, so these users turn to CMR's summary-level reports in order to find out what products are being advertised. Formerly the resource most commonly found in libraries, *Ad $ Sum-*

mary, which was published in print by LNA, a CMR affiliate, is no longer issued in print; instead, it is now part of CMR's quarterly electronic Multi-Media Service together with its companion titles, *Company/ Brand $* and *Class/Brand $*. CMR offers a related product called *Ad $ Spender*, a monthly CD-ROM that reports summary data on advertising expenditures for 100,000 brands across all media for the past five years. It ranks top spenders, identifies the media mix within industries, and shows trends. Marketers use *Ad $ Spender* to answer such questions as "What is the media mix for the beverage industry?" "Who are the top magazine advertisers?" "Is Levi's spending more or less this year?"

Other companies besides CMR provide fee-based competitive tracking of advertisements and press publicity. Users may wish to consult the following: *Competitrack* (http://www.competitrack.com) which covers broadcast and print but is available only to authorized corporate advertisers and their agencies; *National System Ad Tracking* (http://www.nationalsystem.com/frames.cfm) which covers traditional newspapers; *Adfacts* (http://www.adfacts.com) which offers publicity tracking of press reports useful for both public relations and competitive intelligence purposes; and VMS *Video Monitoring Services* (http://www.vidmon.com/index.html) which monitors TV and radio news in top U.S. and international markets.

HISTORICAL ADVERTISEMENTS AND CAMPAIGNS

Marketing students, graphic designers, and social historians often need to retrieve examples of old advertisements and campaigns. Many professionals in the advertising industry also turn to historic archives for inspiration and study.

Ad*Access. **Duke University. John W. Harman Center for Sales, Advertising, and Marketing History. Durham, NC. ©1999. Online (free). Contact: http://scriptorium.lib.duke.edu/adaccess.**

The *Ad*Access* project provides Web access to images and descriptive information for over 7,000 historical advertisements printed in U.S. and Canadian newspapers and magazines between 1911 and 1955. Funded by a Duke University endowment, it is intended to make available a rich source of social and cultural history and to support study of the history of technology, new product development, and social trends. The value of this collection is that it offers virtual access to primary material that is usually ephemeral and discarded, even by those companies and agencies that pay for and produce it. Its 7,000 images provide enough scope and depth to study the advertising of a single product over an extended period, or the development of a whole technology, or historical retailing practices. The database content has been selected, designed, and categorized to represent significant social, cultural, business, and technological developments in North American history.

Images are derived from the "Competitive Advertisements Collection" from the J. Walter Thompson Company Archives. Before there were tracking services such as those discussed in the previous section, advertising agencies clipped competitors' advertising from newspapers and magazines for use as a working reference. These images are useful to graphics professionals, as well as to students of social history.

The *Ad*Access* site is well designed and user friendly, with both Browse and Search options. It is possible to scan for an image within a category, or search directly for an ad for "cold cream" or "Pontiac." In the Browse section, the ads are arranged in five major categories: Beauty and Hygiene, Radio, Television, Transportation, and World War II, and then further narrowed by subcategory, date, or decade. For example, within *Transportation*, there are sub-categories for Airlines, for pre- and post-World War II periods; within *Beauty & Hygiene*, there are subcategories for Deodorant from 1925-1952, and for Hair Preparations for each decade from 1920s on. The site also includes a Timeline feature that puts the ads into a social and political context.

The options from the Search page are sophisticated and also well designed. A simple keyword search is the best choice for looking for a specific television program, company, brand, or publication name. For precision searching, there are also defined fields and pre-formatted searches for locating specific advertising content, types, styles, or media venues, such as *testimonial, radio program, target audience, minorities, children, coupons, famous people*, and more. The database also provides Boolean and truncation options, a thesaurus of Database Terms and Descriptions, and extensive Help screens and examples.

The result of a search of the main database is an advertising image with descriptive cataloging and two size choices for viewing and printing. When using this site, it is necessary to be aware of copyright issues. For the most part, Duke University does not hold the copyright and, if the images are to be published, the advertiser (i.e., the company named in the ad) must be contacted. For most educational purposes, the Web site images may be printed, or slides and photocopies may be requested for a fee (John W. Hartman Center for Sales, Advertising and Marketing History 2000).

TIP: Other Collections of Historical Advertisements

- Advertising Educational Foundation. "Advertising Collections and Museums" provides a list of advertising collections. Contact: http://www.aded.org.
- D'Arcy Collection and Advertising Council Archives at University of Illinois at Urbana-Champaign. Contact: http://web.library.uiuc.edu/ahx/adcouncil/default.asp.
- Mass Communications History Collections at the State Historical Society of Wisconsin. Contact: http://www.shsw.wisc.edu/archives/readroom/masscol.html.
- N. W. Ayer and Warshaw Collections at the National Museum of American History. Contact: http://americanhistory.si.edu/archives/d-7.htm.

***Encyclopedia of Major Marketing Campaigns*. Edited by Thomas Riggs. Farmington Hills, MI: Gale Group, 2000. Print $285. 2,063 pages.**

The *Encyclopedia of Major Marketing Campaigns (EMMC)* provides a historical perspective on important advertising campaigns of the 20th century. Based on the related series called *Major Marketing Campaigns Annual*, the encyclopedia compiles 500 notable campaigns, such as Apple Computer's "1984," Nike's "Just Do It," and the U.S. Government's "Uncle Sam." This encyclopedia is a useful compilation of an important part of 20th century social history and popular culture.

Selection of campaigns is based on any of a number of factors: historical or social significance, extraordinary sales effectiveness, advertising industry innovation, impact on consumer products and lifestyles, or simply the reputation and size of the company. Because the campaigns represent a cross section of effectiveness (such as Avis' "We Try Harder"), failure (such as "New Coke"), technique (such as product endorsement), and strategy (such as branding and comparative advertising), *EMMC* not only offers facts and context, but also offers case studies for teaching and learning.

As is usual with Gale Group products, this source is well designed and easy to navigate. The major section is arranged by company name, augmented by a General Index, which lists advertising agencies and people, with cross-referenced product names and brands. The Subject Index makes it easy to identify entries that provide examples of particular ad types or content, such as negative campaigning, image advertising, humorous ads, relationship marketing, etc. Each entry follows the same pattern and provides essential information for analysis: Head (company's name and addresses); Overview (campaign summary); Historical Context (historical and social facts needed to understand the campaign); Target Market (audience toward which the campaign was directed and why); Competition (competitors' products, market share, and advertising campaigns); Marketing Strategy (how and when the campaign was designed, plus its goals and objectives); and Outcome (campaign's success in sales, awards, etc.). Each entry also provides a list of Further Reading, and most include at least one small photo or other graphic, plus a sidebar with intriguing anecdotes.

***Advertising Age Encyclopedia of Advertising*. Edited by John McDonough and Karen Egolf. New York: Fitzroy Dearborn, 2003. 3 volumes. Print $385. 1,958 pages. Contact: http://www.routledge.co.uk/.**

The *Encyclopedia of Advertising* is an important contribution to the historical literature on advertising. With substantive coverage of campaigns, slogans, logos, brands, advertisers, social and cultural issues, methodology, and theories, this encyclopedia offers fresh perspectives on the development of the worldwide advertising industry from its beginning through the end of the 20th century. It is unique in its presentation of research on the "agency side of the advertising business," many aspects of which have "never before been researched" (McDonough 2003, vii, ix). It was written and compiled using the combined resources of the Museum of Broadcast Communications, Duke University's Hartman Center for Sales, Advertising, and Marketing History, and *Advertising Age* magazine.

Its nearly 600 entries are arranged in alphabetical order and fall into four basic categories: agency histories; advertiser, brand, market histories; biographies; and entries on theoretical and practical aspects of advertising. Essays are well-written and enhanced with considerable detail, and each includes further references. Where relevant, many also include chronologies and lists of principal agencies. The visual side of advertising has not been overlooked and the set is filled with over 500 illustrations, many of which are full-page and in color. The glossy paper quality and good binding make it appealing for browsing. There is a comprehensive index that covers subjects, ads, advertisers, agencies, people, illustrations, and slogans. Appendixes list top advertisers, agencies, award-winners, and degree programs.

As E. Truax says in a review: ". . . delightfully rich detail can be found: the General Motors essay prints the lyrics of 'Baseball, Hot Dogs, Apple Pie, and Chevrolet,' and the 'History' of advertising begins with the ancient Egyptian marketplace and concludes with coverage for each decade of the 20th century" (Truax 2003).

***AdForum.com.* Hoboken, NJ. Online (Primarily subscription based; some areas free). Contact: http://www.adforum.com.**

As a service of Maydream, a global information provider, AdForum is designed to bring advertising agencies together with potential customers. By providing an Internet location where advertisers can view agency portfolios and other creative work provided directly by agencies, AdForum has built a collection of ads in all media and industries. The Web site offers tiered access. The daily showcase of ads and directory of over 17,000 worldwide advertising agencies can be viewed by casual users without registration. Its extensive database of video clips and images of 23,000 contemporary ads from all over the world is available to subscribers or to those who register as bonafide industry professionals.

***AdReview.com.* Crain Publications. New York. ©2003. Online (free). Contact: http://AdReview.com.**

AdReview.com is a service of Ad Age Group and Crain Publications, publisher of *Advertising Age* magazine. Aimed at a professional industry audience, the site reviews the creation and use of U.S. and international television advertising. It also has potential value for review of case studies in educational settings. Treating television ads as business documents, the site presents analysis and discussion of content, production methods, technological innovations, audience impact, and controversies. It also contains an Ad Review column by Bob Garfield, a writer for *Advertising Age.*

TIP: Advertising World

Advertising World's "Ads" section offers a list of Web sites with examples of print, radio and TV ads. Some are free, some are fee-based. Contact: http://advertising.utexas.edu/world/Ads.asp.

ADVERTISING RESEARCH AND MEASUREMENT

Given that advertising is expected to show tangible results, professionals have always been daunted by the need to "prove" the of effectiveness advertising. "Because advertising's contribution to sales has long been believed to be too complex to measure, it has traditionally managed to escape close scrutiny" (Bushko 1997, 49). Even today, executives and academics are unwilling to accept the inherent value of advertising without positive proof. In fact, attempts to measure advertising effectiveness have existed in some form since the 1920s (Lipstein 1984/1985, 12). Return-on-investment (ROI), total quality management (TQM), and benchmarking have made the study of advertising effectiveness even more important, while the technological and methodological means have also improved. The marketer will find the following selection of sources useful starting points for a general understanding of research metrics, techniques, and concepts.

Advertising Research Foundation (ARF). New York. Contact: http://www.arfsite.org.

The Advertising Research Foundation (ARF) supports its membership of advertising agencies, media companies, corporate advertisers, and universities with activities to "improve the practice of advertising, marketing and media research in pursuit of more effective marketing and advertising communications" (ARF 1996-2002). It provides a financial and administrative umbrella for significant primary research serving the advertising industry as a whole. It publishes reports, organizes conferences, and sponsors awards; ARF's major contribution is its ability to bring together competitors for the purpose of conducting research. Organized into 14 specialized research units (such as Multicultural Research Council, Radio Research Council, Digital Media Measurement, and the Media Accountability Council), ARF has undertaken numerous qualitative, quantitative, methodological, and survey studies. Examples are described at the Web site at http://www.arfsite.org/Webpages/PrimaryPages/programs.htm.

Corporate and institutional members receive access to published results automatically, and their employees also have access to the ARF Info Center, a comprehensive library collection of advertising, media, and marketing research books and periodicals. Non-members can gain access to published findings, conference proceedings, and workshop transcripts at many public and academic libraries, or by purchasing them through the ARF Web site.

TIP: For Further Reading on the Copy Research Validity Project

One of the best-known ARF efforts was the "Copy Research Validity Project," completed in 1990, which tested standard dimensions such as recall, persuasion, and likability. For more information, see the following.

- "Copy Testing." 1994. *Journal of Advertising Research* (Special Issue) 34 no. 3 (May/June).
- Hell, Russell I. and Allan L. Baldinger. 2000. "The ARF Copy Research Validity Project," *Journal of Advertising Research* 40 no. 6 (November/December), 114-135.

Magazine Publishers of America (MPA). New York. ©2003. Contact: http://www.magazine.org.

The Magazine Publishers of America (MPA), established in 1919, is the industry association for consumer magazine publishers. The MPA represents more than 200 U.S. publishing companies, 75 international companies, and over 90 associates providing services to the industry. In addition to advocacy and promotional roles in support of members, MPA's mission includes being "the primary source of information . . . about the publishing industry for both its members and the community at large" (MPA 2002).

The MPA Web site contains a huge amount of free information in the form of guidelines, handbooks, research studies, a glossary, and research data. For example, in the area of research and measurement, there are the following useful reports: "Measuring the Mix: Quantifying the Sales Impact of Magazine Advertising" (commissioned by the MPA and conducted by Media Marketing Assessment); the "Advertising Effectiveness Survey" (Millward Brown); and "ACNielsen Sales Scan."

In addition, the site provides a link to the Publishers Information Bureau (PIB), an organization administered by MPA that tracks the type and amount of advertising in consumer magazines. PIB is a valuable tool for advertisers and agencies needing statistical industry data for planning, competitive analysis, and budgeting.

ARS Group. Evansville, IN. ©2001-2003. Contact: http://www. ars-group.com.

In the field of advertising effectiveness and return-on-investment (ROI) measures, there are several important for-profit organizations that have made significant contributions. One important firm is ARS Group, also known by its alternate name rsc [sic] which has over 25 years of experience in pioneering methodologies to study how and why advertising works. One of its metric tools, *ARS Persuasion* (a pre-market test of sales potential) has been utilized and validated by thousands of advertisers and academics, and has become the "world standard" (ARS Group 2001-2002). Similarly, the company has developed some other well-known measures, such as recall and memorability, effective visual elements, and consumer diagnostics.

TIP: For Further Reading on Advertising Measurement

Bushko, David and Richard H. Stansfield. 1997. Advertising Research. Chap. 2 in *Dartnell's Advertising Manager's Handbook.* Chicago: Dartnell Corporation.

Dutka, Solomon. 1995. *DAGMAR, Defining Advertising Goals for Measured Advertising Results.* 2nd Edition. Lincolnwood, IL: NTC Business Books.

Fletcher, Alan D. and Thomas A. Bowers. 1983. *Fundamentals of Advertising Research.* 2nd Edition. Columbus, OH: Grid Publishing.

Jones, John Philip. 1998. *How Advertising Works: The Role of Research.* Thousand Oaks, CA: Sage Publications.

The ARS Group packages these measurement tools and offers them in a range of fee-based services and products. Their *Best Practice Tools* is a set of decision support software for global market intelligence, advertising planning, brand-building, real-time consumer insight, and more. Registered members can interact with research staff at the "Empirical Knowledge Library" in order to query ARS Groups' massive databases.

Although the ARS Group Web site is not a direct information source–primarily, it serves as a promotional device for the company's products and services–we include it here because it is important for practitioners and academics to be aware of commercial advertising research services. Other firms also have developed well-reputed measurement tools and have Web sites which may contain summaries or copies of research reports, newsletters, and methodologies. These include ASI Market Research (http://www.asientertainment.com/index.html), MSW Research (http://mswresearch.com/msw_group_main.htm) and Millward Brown International (http://www.millwardbrown.com/html/overview/).

ADVERTISING LAW

Because advertising takes place in the public arena, advertising law cannot be ignored. This section is not intended to substitute for a complete legal library, but it should serve to familiarize practitioners, researchers, and students with basic issues and enable them to find further information.

AdLaw. **Hall, Dickler, Kent, Goldstein, & Wood LLP. New York. ©2002. Online (free). Contact: http://www.adlaw.com/.**

Calling itself "the premier source of legal information for advertising and marketing professionals" (Hall Dickler Kent Goldstein & Wood 2002), *AdLaw* is a commercially sponsored site of advertising and marketing law that is well organized and easy to use. Researchers will find the "Resource Files" section especially useful. There is a handbook of key issues in advertising law, contract forms, case files, cyber law advertising materials, and links to other advertising law Web sites.

Advertising Law. **Arent Fox Attorneys at Law. Washington DC. Online (free). Contact: http://www.arentfox.com/quickGuide/businessLines/advert/advertisingLaw/advertisinglaw.html.**

Arent Fox is an advertising and trade regulation law firm representing clients before federal and state agencies in the advertising industry's self regulatory proceedings. "Arent Fox also is recognized as a leader in the use of the Internet in connection with the practice of law, and maintains the Advertising Law Internet Site, the only Web site on the Internet devoted solely to advertising law issues" (Arent Fox, n.d.).

The Advertising Law site contains news and alerts, Federal Trade Commission (FTC) updates, related articles, and the full text of FTC regulations and rules (including such specialized materials as the full text of the FTC's Advertising Guidelines and Enforcement Policy statements). These FTC regulations and guidelines cover such detailed topic areas as environmental marketing claims, deceptive pricing, endorsements and testimonials, composition of shoes, tires, mail order insurance, and many more. In addition to federal regulatory documents, the site provides a review of the decisions of the National Advertising Division (NAD) of the Better Business Bureau. These self-regulatory documents cover such topics as children's Web sites and general Internet marketing practices.

HANDBOOKS AND WEB GATEWAYS

The sources listed here are general in nature and cover a variety of advertising topics. Handbooks are reference works which give a broad perspective and offer practical information, introductory overviews, guidelines, and reading lists. Web gateways are collections of Web sites on many different aspects of a topic, and they are especially useful for locating further information.

Dartnell's Advertising Manager's Handbook. Edited by David Bushko. 4th edition. Chicago: Dartnell, 1997. 484 pages.

This handbook provides a practical summary of all aspects of advertising. It will be useful to the students who need background and analysis of fundamental concepts, and a handy reference tool for the working professional. In twelve chapters, many fundamental functions are given full yet succinct treatment, including references to information sources, companies, and professional associations that can be used as starting points for further research. Indicating the breadth of this handbook, there are chapters on advertising research, media planning, persuasive copywriting, sales promotion techniques, international audits, and managing creative resources. Charts, tables, checklists, illustrations, appendices, and citation lists are distributed throughout, and it is fully indexed.

Another handbook on this topic is the *Advertising Manager's Handbook* by Robert W. Bly (Paramus, NJ: Prentice Hall, 1999).

American Association of Advertising Agencies. New York. Online (free). Contact: http://www.aaaa.org.

The Web site for this major professional association contains the *Standards of Practice for Advertising Agencies*, a searchable roster of member agencies, and links to sites for further research. There are also links to related industry associations, government agencies, and legislative and regulatory reports relevant to media and communication.

***Advertising World*. Department of Advertising, University of Texas Austin. ©1995-2002. Online (free) Contact: http://advertising.utexas. edu/world/.**

The Web site of the Department of Advertising at the University of Texas, Austin, *Advertising World*, is a comprehensive compendium of advertising resources. Funded by a gift from Leo Burnett Worldwide, the agency whose heritage includes such brand icons as the Jolly Green Giant and the Pillsbury Doughboy, the site provides a comprehensive set of resources for advertising and marketing professionals, students, and teachers. From "account planning" to "word of mouth," this is one of the most extensive directories of advertising-related links on the Web. In addition to *Advertising World*, the Department of Advertising also provides significant material at its "Research Resources" page (http://advertising.utexas.edu/research/Topics.html). This site contains archives of white papers on the future of advertising, full-text articles and papers, and online bibliographies on such essential topics as research methods, social impact, advertising law and ethics, psychology of advertising, agency practices, and more. On the lighter side, there are links for advertising humor, quotations, biographies, famous slogans, and reading lists. Additionally, sources that help advertising practitioners and students acquire basic awareness of legal and regulatory requirements are included.

REFERENCES

ANA and AAAA. 2001. *Television Commercial Monitoring Report.* New York: Association of National Advertisers (ANA) and American Association of Advertising Agencies (AAAA).

ARF. 1996-2002. "About the ARF." <http://www.arfsite.org/Webpages/PrimaryPages/arfinfo.htm> (May 19, 2002).

ARS Group. 2001-2002. "Advertising Measurement" <http://www.ars-group.com/admeas/arspersuasion.htm> (May 20, 2002).

Arent Fox Attorneys at Law. "Practice Areas: Advertising and Trade Law." <http://www.arentfox.com/quickGuide/businessLines/advert/advert.html> (May 26, 2002).

Beacham, Walton, Richard T. Hise, and Hale N. Tongren. 1986. *Beacham's Marketing Reference.* Washington DC: Research Publishing.

Bushko, David. 1997. *Dartnell's Advertising Manager's Handbook*, 4th edition. Chicago: Dartnell Corporation.

CMR. 2001-2002. "About CMR." <http://www.cmr.com/about/coverage.html> (May 19, 2002).

"Products." <http://www.cmr.com/products/stradegy2.html> (April 30, 2002).

"Products." <http://www.cmr.com/products/adspender.html> (May 19, 2002).

Gottesman, Alan. 1998. "Who Advertises?" *Adweek* 39 no. 2 (August 10).

Hall Dickler Kent Goldstein & Wood L.L.P. 2002. "AdLaw." <http://www.adlaw.com> (May 19, 2002).

Harrington, Deborah Lynn. 2000-01. "Advertising FAQs: Selected Sources." Texas A&M University Libraries. <http://library.tamu.edu/wcl/buguides/advertising/intro.htm> (May 30, 2002).

John W. Hartman Center for Sales, Advertising, and Marketing History. 2000. "Emergence of Advertising in America: 1850-1920." <http://scriptorium.lib.duke.edu/eaa/timeline.html> (May 20, 2002).

1999. "Ad Access: Frequently Asked Questions About the Ad*Access Project." <http://scriptorium.lib.duke.edu/adaccess/faq.html> (May 19, 2002).

Kotler, Philip and Gary Armstrong. 2001. *Principles of Marketing*. 9th edition. Upper Saddle River, NJ: Prentice Hall.

Lipstein, Benjamin. 1984/1985. "An Historical Retrospective of Copy Research." *Journal of Advertising Research* 24, no. 6 (December/January): 11-14.

MPA. 2001. "About MPA: Mission." <http://www.magazine.org/aboutMPA/mission.html> (May 26, 2002).

McCann-Erickson WorldGroup. 2001. *Bob Coen's Insider's Report.* <http://www.mccann.com/insight/bobcoen.html> (May 17, 2002).

McDonough, John and Karen Egolf. 2003. *Advertising Age Encyclopedia of Advertising.* New York: Fitzroy Dearborn.

Munter, Paul and Thomas A. Ratcliffe. 1994. "Accounting and Reporting of Advertising Costs." *Ohio CPA Journal 53*, no. 6 (December): 23-29.

SRDS. 2002. "Company Overview." <http://www.srds.com/frontMatter/about/index.html> (May 20, 2002).

Truax, E. "The Advertising Age Encyclopedia of Advertising (review)." 2003. *Choice* (April). <http://www.choicereview.org> (April 1, 2003).

Chapter 8

Public Relations Sources

Topics

> Directories of Media and Press Contacts
> Media Monitoring and Press Clipping Services
> Locating PR Firms
> Professional Associations

Sources

> *Burrelle's Media Directory*
> *Working Press of the Nation*
> Burrelle's Information Service
> *O'Dwyer's Directory of Public Relations Firms*
> American Marketing Association
> Council of Public Relations Firms
> Public Relations Society of America
> International Association of Business Communicators
> Institute for Public Relations

It has been said that advertising involves what a company says about itself, and public relations involves what others say about the company. Certainly, public relations (PR) is intrinsically connected with the promotion and advertising, but they are not equivalents. The concept of PR applies to many areas such as crisis management, political influence, and labor relations, but it is also an essential component of any marketing

[Haworth co-indexing entry note]: "Public Relations Sources." Diamond, Wendy, and Michael R. Oppenheim. Co-published simultaneously in *Journal of Business & Finance Librarianship* (The Haworth Information Press, an imprint of The Haworth Press, Inc.) Vol. 9, No. 2/3, 2004, pp. 189-202; and: *Marketing Information: A Strategic Guide for Business and Finance Libraries* (Wendy Diamond, and Michael R. Oppenheim) The Haworth Information Press, an imprint of The Haworth Press, Inc., 2004, pp. 189-202. Single or multiple copies of this article are available for a fee from The Haworth Document Delivery Service [1-800-HAWORTH, 9:00 a.m. - 5:00 p.m. (EST). E-mail address: docdelivery@haworthpress.com].

Digital Object Identifier: 10.1300/J109v09n02_08

plan which is designed to promote products and services to customers. Good publicity and image enhancement are the desired end products of successful public relations efforts, and a "marketing program devoid of publicity forfeits opportunities for placing marketing messages in the editorial space and broadcast programming that the competition is getting" (Bergen 1994, 1197).

Both advertising and PR involve influencing and persuading, but advertising focuses on paid media, whereas public relations focuses primarily on gaining media coverage in the public arena, in the so-called "free" media, i.e., the news. The marketing aspect of PR involves the generation of publicity to influence underlying attitudes of potential customers about the company and its saleable products and services.

> Each of these disciplines, after all, is an element of the all-encompassing term "marketing." Yet each remains distinct. They blend not as in a melting pot, but as in a salad. Everything goes well together, but you can still distinguish the lettuce from the tomatoes. The skilled "marketer" understands these differences and can apply them appropriately. (Rich 1991, 255)

Another distinction between advertising and public relations is that the publicity campaign is subject to delivery by an external messenger, and therefore cannot be completely controlled. Good publicity can support a paid advertising and promotion campaign, but cannot rescue a bad marketing decision. A classic example of the latter is the well-known failed introduction of "New Coke." On the other hand, good public relations can prevent a marketing disaster, as exemplified by the control of rumors about Tylenol poisoning.

In order to distribute a message to the media, publicists and marketers write and distribute press releases, how-to articles, captioned photographs, and success stories. In addition, they may produce events and spokesperson's tours (Bergen 1994, 1200). For all of these activities, the publicist or marketer needs to establish contacts with the press, often seeking out the person responsible for a specific editorial area. They must also monitor and track the media in order to assess the impact of their efforts, and to ensure they are aware of all mentions, whether good or bad, of their product, service, or company. Professionals also seek sources about the PR industry itself: they need extensive professional development and career building materials ranging from best practices and guidelines and codes of conduct, to research studies and articles, news and updates, and continuing education resources. This chapter presents an array of sources to meet these information needs, and includes directories of press sources and media contacts, monitoring and tracking services, press release distribution services, and professional associations.

DIRECTORIES OF MEDIA AND PRESS CONTACTS

Burrelle's Media Directory. New York: Burrelle's Information Services. Annual. Print directory ($995) or online subscription ($1,895). Contact: http://www.burrelles.com.

Designed for the public relations professional who regularly distributes press releases, *Burrelle's Media Directory* is a list of sources compiled from 300,000 media contacts and 60,000 media outlets. Burrelle's, whose history dates to the late 19th century origins of the public relations industry, is one of the oldest publishers providing services to the industry.

The annual print edition of the *Media Directory* is a five-volume set covering daily and non-daily newspapers, radio, television and cable, magazines, and newsletters. Entries include addresses and e-mail, telephone and fax numbers, and Web sites. Subscribers to the directory are provided with access to electronic updates.

In addition to the national version, Burrelle's also provides ten regional editions. The East Coast is well-represented with separate volumes for New York, Pennsylvania, New England, and Chesapeake, etc., while only a few individual states outside of the East have a dedicated volume. The West Coast, Midwest, and Southeast are covered in regional volumes. Format and cost vary; some regional editions are available in CD-ROM only, and prices range from $145 to $200.

The database is also available online. Known as MDOL ("Media Directory Online"), it is updated daily. Designed with special features and tools, the electronic version can be used to develop customized lists (e.g., Top 100 Dailies by Circulation) and to create address labels for mailings. A free trial is available at Burrelle's Web site.

Working Press of the Nation. New York: Bowker. Annual. Print or Diskette ($530). Contact: http://www.bowker.com.

The 2002 edition of *Working Press of the Nation (WPN)* is the 52nd edition of this reliable and well-known reference tool. Entries include descriptive information about publications and stations, and the guide is especially useful for locating contact information about individuals working within the media industry. Bowker is one of the oldest publishers specializing in materials for libraries, booksellers, and the publishing industry.

Issued in three volumes, *WPN* covers approximately 8,000 newspapers (including feature syndicates and photo services), 5,700 magazines (including consumer, farm, trade, professional, and industrial publications), 1,700 newsletters (including internal corporate publications), and 14,000 TV and radio stations (including information on programming and market descriptions). Information is compiled from questionnaires and each volume is arranged in categories unique to its subject area.

The "Newspaper Directory" (Volume 1) lists newspapers in various sections that make it easy for the publicist to locate publications targeting a particular customer base. There is an alphabetic listing of all titles, with daily and weekly newspapers listed geographically. There are separate listings for newspapers and news services of all types, such as special interest (e.g., military, college and alumni), religious, ethnic, foreign language, national newspapers, feature syndicates, and news and photo services. For media buyers and other marketers who typically use Areas of Dominant Influence (ADIs) to define metropolitan regions, there is an "Index of Newspapers by ADI." In addition, there are subject indexes of syndicates and editorial personnel (feature editor, motion picture editor, etc.). Entries contain useful detail that define the longevity, frequency, size, distribution, subscription rates and pay scale, deadline requirements, and contact information for each newspaper.

Volume 2 is the "Magazine and Internal Publications Directory," which includes newsletters. The categories unique to this subject area are: business magazines, farm and agricultural magazines, consumer magazines, newsletters, and internal publications. The volume is indexed by subject, title, and internal publication sponsor. Because few other directories provide detailed information on newsletters and internal publications, this is a very useful source.

Volume 3, the "TV and Radio Directory," similarly provides useful categories and indexes. As in other volumes, the listings are extensive and full of descriptive and contact information enabling the media buyer, publicist, or marketer to select a target market for a publicity campaign or press release.

WPN is the premier source for this type of information, but there are a number of similar sources. Among those is Gebbie Press' *All-in-One Media Directory* (New Paltz, NY. Annual. Print $105, Diskette $295, CD-ROM $540), which provides 22,000 total listings of newspapers, consumer and trade magazines, and TV and radio outlets. Listings are less detailed, and there are fewer special interest categories and indexes, than in *Working Press of the Nation. Gebbie's* (as it is known) does include Hispanic and African American newspapers, but there are no listings for newsletters or internal publications. Its smaller size and spiral-bound format is handy, but e-mail and Web addresses are available only in the electronic versions. Gebbie's Web site (http://www.gebbieinc.com/) has a helpful article on "how to write a news release," which outlines the structure, style, and protocol familiar to news directors and editors.

Bacon's Information Inc. (http://www.bacons.com/directories/maindirectories.asp), a firm with a 50-year history of providing information to the PR industry, also produces a set of popular media directories. Together, they cover nearly 70,000 media outlets, 500,000 editorial contacts, and 100,000 editorial profiles. Individual titles focus on media types (newspaper/magazine, radio/TV/cable), geographic areas (New York, Metro California), or industry-specific media (computer/high tech, medical/health). The entries contain several features useful to PR professionals, including preferred contact methods, best days and times, beat specialties, and deadlines. These are annual print or CD-ROM volumes, costing approximately $325 per title or $2,095 for the set.

MEDIA MONITORING AND PRESS CLIPPING SERVICES

Also known as "tracking services," media monitoring and press clipping services inform marketers whenever their product, service, or company is mentioned in the press or media. As the size of the media industry has grown, there is a greater need than ever before to utilize these specialized firms in order to capitalize on positive publicity and to counteract negative images as they develop.

Burrelle's Information Service. New York. Contact: http://www.burrelles.com.

In addition to publishing its media directories, as described previously, Burrelle's also offers a media monitoring service for clients interested in tracking the news about any subject. Burrelle's covers national, international, and regional levels including newspapers, wire services, magazines, trade journals, radio and TV broadcasts and the Internet. Primarily designed for publicists who want to keep track of the results of their publicity efforts, Burrelle's service is also used in marketing departments for current awareness and updates about the general corporate and industry image. This information helps advertising professionals design campaigns that are appropriate for the current marketplace and social climate. Burrelle's offers a number of different service options. Known as "clips," media monitoring reports can be delivered in print, electronically, or as summarized lists. High-end options include same-day monitoring services. According to the Web site, a new Spanish-language version is planned (Burrelle's 2002).

TIP: Business Wire and PR Newswire

Business Wire and *PR Newswire* are press release distribution services used by most major corporations. Each service compiles a database of previous press releases which provide the researcher with a rich source of unique information in the form of "raw news" emanating from corporate public relations departments. This can include announcements of new products, new advertising campaigns, joint ventures, and management changes, some or all of which may never appear in newspapers, magazines, or on broadcasts simply for lack of space and time. The savvy marketer will take advantage of the publicity urge of competitors to locate relevant reports using these two databases. The Web sites of *Business Wire* and *PR Newswire* both contain current and archived press releases, plus they are each included in many aggregated search systems such as *Factiva*, *LexisNexis*, and *Dialog*. Contacts: http://www. businesswire.com/ps/index.html and http://www.prnewswire.com/ news/.

TIP: eReleases for Press Release Services

A partner of PR Newswire, eReleases.com, provides small businesses with flat-fee services including writing and targeted distribution of news releases. The Web site includes advice on writing and submitting press releases. Contact: http://www.ereleases.com.

LOCATING PR FIRMS

As is the case with advertising, a business or its marketing department may decide to utilize an agency rather than handle PR functions in-house. The principle is the same, but the terminology is slightly different. In advertising, the outside consultants are known as "agencies." In PR, they are usually called "firms." Some firms specialize in a specific industry segment or area of PR, such as corporate communications, product placement, investor relations, or political candidates; others may offer many specializations within a single firm.

O'Dwyer's Directory of Public Relations Firms. **New York: O'Dwyer's. Annual. Print and CD-ROM $175. Contact: http://www.odwyerpr. com.**

Since 1970, O'Dwyer's has been one of the major publishers in the field of public relations. Their *Directory of Public Relations Firms* is used by those seeking the services of a PR organization to analyze, advise, plan, budget, write, and supervise publicity activities. The 2002 edition lists 2,900 large and small public relations companies worldwide, of which 2,200 are located in the U.S. Firms cover all facets of PR, from investor relations to political lobbying to product publicity. In the main section of the directory, firms are listed in alphabetical order, followed by indexes by geography, size, and PR specialty. The "Cross-Client Index" provides a way of looking up a particular company and determining its outside public relations consultant. In addition, there are industry rankings, with leaders given in 11 specializations: agriculture, beauty, entertainment, environmental, financial, food, healthcare, high-tech, home furnishings, sports, and travel. The directory also includes two "bonus" articles which describe how to hire and utilize a PR firm.

In addition to the annual print volume, there is a Web-based version which contains a selected list of companies that have paid for highlighted listings in the print version. The online directory can be searched alphabetically, geographically, and by specialty. The Web site also offers ranked lists, such as the "top 50 U.S. firms," "U.S. revenue and employee levels," and "top worldwide fees of independent firms with major U.S. Operations."

O'Dwyer's also publishes a set of companion print directories, such as *O'Dwyer's Directory of Corporate Communications* and *O'Dwyer's Directory of Public Relations Executives.* Their series of newsletters, reports, and special reports provide additional background and guidance, such as *PR Buyer's Guide* and *Media Placement Guide: How to Work with Editors and Enjoy It.*

A free alternative online directory exists at the Council of Public Relations Firms Web site (http://www.prfirms.org), under the link "Find a PR Firm." The Council screens its membership of 122 firms, including the "top ten," to assess their standards of client service, fiscal accountability, ethical conduct with clients, employees, media, and commitment to the Council's standards of practice. The directory of member firms is designed to accommodate potential clients as well as career seekers. Users can search by state, city, size category, industry sector expertise (e.g., Consumer/Retail: Home Furnishings), and service area expertise (multicultural marketing, business-to-business, sports/event marketing, etc.). Entries for each firm include standard contact information and sometimes a recruiting contact for prospective employees, number of employees, annual revenue, cities and regions of operation, and industries covered. Additional information about the Council of Public Relations Firms is in the following section of this chapter.

PROFESSIONAL ASSOCIATIONS

As is evident throughout this book, professional associations are frequently established to assist practitioners in their daily work and in professional development, and also to maintain high standards in their specialized areas. PR is no exception, and professional associations are among the best providers of information for the everyday practice of public relations. As is to be expected, much information is limited to members only, but the majority of professional groups allow access by non-members to some resources as well. The Web sites of professional organizations should be consulted by anyone looking for immediate tips or guidelines on a particular issue, or wishing merely to browse.

Associations generally offer "best practices" information and other types of how-to materials, such as guides to creating and distributing press releases or dealing with the media; sometimes there are specialized sections for particular interests. Some conduct an assessment or certification procedure, to designate individuals who meet certain educational and professional standards. Many have developed their own standards of professional behavior and codes of ethics. Web sites include publication lists, news reports, and sometimes online articles about recent research and trends. Almost all provide networking opportunities, and job and career information; some have separate sections for students. Most associations issue directories listing their members, and some issue supplementary directories as well. Professional associations can also be a source of data and statistics related to the PR industry.

American Marketing Association. Marketing Power.com. Chicago. ©2002. Contact: http://www.marketingpower.com.

The American Marketing Association is one of the largest umbrella organizations in marketing, and it is mentioned throughout this book. In the field of public relations, it is an excellent resource for keeping up with news and trends, as well as for finding practical tools and career information. The Association's Web site requires registration, but there is no charge for nonmembers to access news, tutorials, best practices links, and articles. From the home page, click on "Topics" and select Public Relations from the drop-down menu. This results in a convenient one-page summary of a wide variety of PR resources. For example, there are links to such topics as Press Release Distribution; Marketing Services Directory; Generate Client Leads; Resume Writing and Distribution; Choosing a Public Relations Agency; and several articles from the AMA publication *Marketing News*.

Additional information about fee-based PR services is found under "Toolkit." There is a link providing descriptive and cost information for "Press Release Distribution," but the user must register to get detailed information about most of the other services, including International News Distribution, E-Watch Internet Monitoring, Online Trade Show Press Kit, etc.

Council of Public Relations Firms (CPRF). New York. Contact: http://www.prfirms.org/.

In addition to its "Find a PR Firm" directory discussed previously, the Council of Public Relations Firms Web site offers an extensive repository of full text materials about the public relations industry, including industry statistics, how-to articles, and white papers. "A primary objective of the Council of Public Relations is to become the authoritative source of information about the public relations industry," and therefore it promulgates research that helps "build the case for public relations as a strategic business tool" (CPRF 2002).

Although certain features are password protected for members only, the Web site provides many resources for free to non-members; most of the free material is found under the "Industry Resources" section of the Web site. Under "Research" there are reports, surveys, and presentations on a variety of topics, including building a corporate reputation, the value of public relations, industry and media research, advertising, corporate social responsibility, and research from other PR organizations. In particular, there are studies and presentations on PR return on investment, white papers on building corporate reputation, a survey on brand building, and PowerPoint slide presentations on a number of topics.

Another link under "Industry Resources" is the "Innovation Center," which also provides fulltext and PDF versions of studies and white papers. For example, there are articles entitled "Six Online Services PR Firms Should Provide for Every Client" (from the *Holmes Report,* July 30, 2001) and "The Impact of the Internet on Public Relations and Business Communication." The Innovation Center is the result of a partnership between the Council and Mainsail Interactive Services and is designed to help PR firms maximize new communications technologies such as the Internet. Council publications are also available in various electronic formats, some for free and some for a fee from the Industry Resources section. The Council Annual Report is available, as well as studies entitled "Building Corporate Reputation," and "Hiring a Public Relations Firm: A Guide for Clients."

There is a useful collection of quantitative statistics about the PR industry entitled "2001 Industry Documentation and Rankings" (http://www.prfirms.org/resources/rankings/2001_rankings.asp). This industry overview gives aggregated figures for U.S. and worldwide revenues, including market share, acquisitions, industry size, staff levels, and growth. There are two measures for growth: *pro forma* growth represents total annualized revenues, and is considered most relevant for a "forward-looking snapshot of the size of a firm or an industry"; *organic growth* is calculated by removing all revenues attributable to new acquisitions, and is most important as a measure of the success of client development and vitality in the PR industry (CPRF 2002). There are also tables and charts giving rankings in industry sectors (technology, healthcare, industrial), practice areas (consumer marketing, employee communications, public affairs), U.S. cities, and by global markets. Under "Career Seekers," there are links to labor statistics, a PR salary survey, an employee satisfaction survey, articles, recruiting tools, and more.

Public Relations Society of America. New York. Contact: http://www. prsa.org.

The Public Relations Society of America (PRSA) was chartered in 1947 and now claims, with nearly 20,000 members, to be the largest professional PR society in the world (PRSA). There is also an adjunct society for students called Public Relations Student Society of America (PRSSA), with chapters at over 200 college campuses. The Society includes 15 "Professional Interest Sections," including Educators Academy, Environment, Food and Beverage, Health Academy, International, Multicultural, Technology, Travel and Tourism. Since 1989, it has conducted a certification review process for university undergraduate programs. Placing major emphasis on its Code of Ethics and Statement of Professional Values, PRSA provides a wide range of professional development services to its members, as well as useful information online available to the public.

PRSA publishes three separate annual directories, including two which can be accessed by non-members online at no charge. The *PRSA Blue Book* lists all its members with details about addresses and business affiliations. It is in print format only, and free to members; the price for others is different for individual or institutions. The *PRSA Red Book: A Directory of the PRSA Counselor Academy* lists public relations firms and is available in both print and online at no charge. In addition to offering advice on selecting a PR firm, it contains an alphabetical listing of member firms who abide by PRSA's Code of Professional Standards for the Practice of Public Relations. It is indexed by area of practice specialization (integrated marketing, government relations/public affairs, media relations/training, product publicity, etc.), and has cross-references for geography and industry specializations. The content of the PRSA *Red Book* is available at the Web site in order to enable "members to contact one another, and for visitors in search of public relations counsel" (PRSA).

The Green Book: A Select Guide to Industry Services is also available free online. It covers more than 50 specialized services and suppliers for PR, such as Celebrity Placement, Executive Media Training, Government Testimony Preparation, Live Event/Satellite Services, and Translation Services.

PRSA also publishes two periodicals. *PR Tactics*, a monthly tabloid-style newspaper, features PR trends and how-to information for practitioners. Highlighted articles from recent issues and archives can be viewed online, and an annual subscription to the newspaper is available to non-members. *The Strategist*, a quarterly magazine, is geared to the management level, stressing fresh perspectives on the importance of effective public relations. Lead articles from recent issues and archives are available free online. Additional resources are available free at the Web site for the general public. These include a PR salary survey, tips and techniques, best practices, a career reading room, and a national credibility index. Members may access such additional resources for e-learning via Web casts.

International Association of Business Communicators. San Francisco. ©2002. Contact: http://www.iabc.com.

The International Association of Business Communicators (IABC) began in 1970 and describes itself as "the premier international knowledge network for professionals engaged in strategic business communications management" (IABC 2002). Like other professional associations, its main purposes are to serve as an information source for its members, and to support high standards of professional practice. The IABC has a membership of over 13,000 in more than 100 chapters worldwide.

The IABC Research Foundation is its non-profit research and development entity, but the Web site provides only minimal information for non-members. There are brief notes on current in-progress projects, and reports on completed studies which may be ordered for a fee. In July 2002, the report entitled "The Communication Function in Small Businesses," by Dixie Evatt, was available free online, as was a 1999 report on high performing organizations and strong business communications. Fees vary for other reports that may be ordered in print or online (PDF). The IABC also publishes *Communications World*, a monthly journal, available to members only.

The IABC conducts an unusual accreditation program that allows business communicators to validate their high level of achievement. Based on a combination of education and years of experience, evaluation of work samples, and an extensive written and oral examination process, applicants may become designated as an Accredited Business Communicator.

Institute of Public Relations. University of Florida. College of Journalism and Communications. Gainesville, FL. ©2002. Contact: http://www.instituteforpr.com/index.phtml.

The Institute of Public Relations (IPR), a research institute, offers a wide variety of articles and reports at its Web site. It was originally established in 1956 by a group of experienced PR practitioners, and it continues to focus on PR education and non-proprietary research; the intent is to inform and assist students, educators, and practitioners. IPR has conducted over 200 research projects on topics like student curricula and the effect of new technologies on the PR profession.

The "Research" section of the Web site contains links to full-text reports on a variety of topics. Subject areas include Best Practices, Internet/New Technology, Law, Career Development, and more. The reports include an abstract or summary and may be accessed in PDF. "Measurement and Evaluation" is one of the Institute's largest areas of investigation. Examples of recent report titles include "Guidelines and Standards for Measuring the Effectiveness of PR Programs" and "How to Measure Your Results in a Crisis."

TIP: A Short Reading List on Marketing and Public Relations

Dilenschneider, Robert L. 1996. *Dartnell's Public Relations Handbook.* 4th edition. Chicago: Dartnell Corporation.

Harris, Thomas. 1991. *The Marketer's Guide to Public Relations.* New York: John Wiley and Sons.

_____1999. *Value-Added Public Relations: The Secret Weapon of Integrated Marketing.* Lincolnwood, IL: NTC Business.

Marconi, Joe. 1999. *Complete Guide to Publicity: Maximize Visibility for your Product, Service or Organization.* Lincolnwood, IL: NTC.

Yale, David R. and Andrew J. Carothers. 1995. *The Publicity Handbook.* New edition. Chicago, IL: NTC Business Books.

REFERENCES

Bergen, Harold A. Public Relations. 1994. In *Dartnell's Marketing Manager's Handbook*, ed. Sidney J. Levy, George R. Frerichs, Howard L. Gordon. 3rd edition. Chicago: Dartnell Corporation.

Burelle's Information Service. 2002. <http://www.burrelles.com> (April 18, 2003).

Council of Public Relations Firms (CPRF). 2002. "Research and White Papers." <http://www.prfirms.org> (May 22, 2002).

"2001 Industry Documentation and Rankings." <http://www.prfirms.org/docs/2001rankings/factsheet2002.doc> (August 15, 2002).

International Association of Business Communicators (IABC). 2002. "Welcome." <http://www.iabc.com> (July 5, 2002).

Public Relations Society of America (PRSA). [n.d.]
"About PRSA." <http://www.prsa.org/_About/main/> (April 25, 2003).
"The Red Book." <http://www.prsa.org> (July 3, 2002).
Rich, Judith. 1991. Public Relations and Marketing. In *Lesly's Handbook of Public Relations and Communications*, edited by Philip Lesly. 4th edition. New York: AMACOM.

PART V

RESEARCHING
THE SALES STRATEGY

Chapter 9

Sales Management, Sales Promotion, and Retail Sources

Topics

Sales Management, Promotion and Selling
Trade Shows
Basic Wholesale and Retail Data
Getting the Product to Market

Sources

Dartnell's Salesforce Compensation Survey
Directory of Premium, Incentive, & Travel Buyers
Incentive Magazine
International Tradeshow Directory
Trade Shows Worldwide: An International Directory of Events, Facilities and Suppliers
Tradeshow Week Online
TSNN.com
Economic Census–Wholesale and Retail Trade Sectors
Retail Trade Survey
National Retail Federation
Plunkett's Retail Industry Almanac
American Wholesalers & Distributors Directory
Sheldon's Major Stores & Chains & Resident Buying Offices

[Haworth co-indexing entry note]: "Sales Management, Sales Promotion, and Retail Sources." Diamond, Wendy, and Michael R. Oppenheim. Co-published simultaneously in *Journal of Business & Finance Librarianship* (The Haworth Information Press, an imprint of The Haworth Press, Inc.) Vol. 9, No. 4, 2004, pp. 205-220; and: *Marketing Information: A Strategic Guide for Business and Finance Libraries* (Wendy Diamond, and Michael R. Oppenheim) The Haworth Information Press, an imprint of The Haworth Press, Inc., 2004, pp. 205-220. Single or multiple copies of this article are available for a fee from The Haworth Document Delivery Service [1-800-HAWORTH, 9:00 a.m. - 5:00 p.m. (EST). E-mail address: docdelivery@haworth press.com].

http://www.haworthpress.com/web/JBFL
© 2004 by The Haworth Press, Inc. All rights reserved.
Digital Object Identifier: 10.1300/J109v09n04_01

Shopping Center Directory
Retail Tenant Directory

In the marketing mix established by the "Four Ps of Marketing (product, price, place, promotion), *sales* relates both to Place (the how and where of the physical distribution of goods, expressed in terms of wholesale and retail) and to Promotion (sales incentives and promotions, trade shows). Sources discussed here deal with "place" by identifying middlemen and the types and physical locations of sales locations. Other sources address the needs of the professional salesperson and sales manager.

Sales promotion is specifically defined as "short-term incentives to encourage the purchase or sale of a product or service" (Kotler and Armstrong 2001, 559). It is also a very big business: in late 2000, the Incentive Federation conducted "A Study of the Incentive Merchandise and Travel Marketplace." Some 8,000 sales, marketing, and human resources executives responded that their total expenditure for merchandise and travel items used for incentive programs rose from 22.8 billion in 1996 to $26.9 billion in 2000. The Federation's study also found a 6% increase in the number of responding companies who report using incentives–from 26% in 1996 to 32% in 2000 (Incentive Performance Center 2002).

Much of sales promotion is focused on making an "instant" impact. The objective is to make the purchase happen immediately, by offering an incentive to stimulate the consumer. Examples of such incentives include free product samples, cents-off coupons, rebates (offers of cash refunds), premiums (some desirable item that comes with an item being sold), advertising specialties (a coffee mug with the advertiser's name, for example), purchase reward or "loyalty" programs (discussed below), point of purchase promotions, and contests, sweepstakes, and games. Individual consumers are not the only audience for sales promotions; they are also designed for business customers, retailers and wholesalers (think of trade shows), and sales force members.

In addition to prompting quick sales to consumers, sales promotions are also used to build long-term relationships with them, as in the use of loyalty marketing programs. Among the best and most recognizable examples of this kind of promotion are airlines' "frequent flyer" programs or a chain bookstore's "frequent reader" program. Consumers earn points and other benefits as a reward for their loyalty–their repeated purchase or use–of a particular product or service. Loyalty programs are designed to boost sales by giving customers an added incentive to make a particular purchase or book a flight on a particular airline–and the seller derives even more benefit from being able to create a database of those customers containing a record of their consuming habits.

> . . . [C]reating fun and excitement, and providing instant gratification at the point of sale helps to keep customers coming back to your stores again and again. A desire to rapidly accrue reward points, earn instant rewards and bolster the chance to win special prizes gives your customers a strong incentive to drive past a competitor's site to stop at yours. (Lewis 2002, 68)

In recent years, the rigorous, computerized analysis of that customer information, popularly known as "data mining," has become one of the most powerful tools in the marketer's arsenal. As a database grows over time, specially designed sales promotions can be targeted toward particular customers, based on the predictable consumer habits and behaviors they share.

Trade shows are used to induce the retailers themselves to expand their existing inventories, to add new products, and to increase their advertising expenditures. Travel and trade shows unite all the key "players" in an industry–suppliers, carriers, intermediaries, and destination marketing organizations–at one location to showcase their services. Exhibitors get the benefit of a highly specialized target audience, and spare themselves the time and energy of making sales calls to innumerable individual prospects.

The sources discussed here range from the highly specialized (e.g., the *Directory of Premium, Incentive & Travel Buyers*) to those which are also specialized (focusing on wholesaling and retailing) but nevertheless widely available in the business reference collections of larger public and academic libraries.

SALES MANAGEMENT, PROMOTION, AND SELLING

***Dartnell's 30th Sales Force Compensation Survey 1998-1999.* By Christen P. Heide. Chicago, IL: Dartnell. Biennial. Print $159. Contact: http://www.dartnellcorp.com.**

This is the source to consult for benchmarks of sales productivity and compensation levels. This edition covers more than 800 companies that each employ at least 90,000 or more salespeople. More than 30 industries are represented. The information provided includes base salary/incentive split and bonuses paid to ten different levels of salespeople in over 30 industries; number of sales calls per day and number of calls to close a sale; training expenses; levels of sales volume by industry, experience, and performance; trends in compensation; turnover rates; and more.

TIP: National Customer Service Week

In addition to being a long-time publisher of a variety of well-known handbooks in marketing (such as Dartnell's *Public Relations Handbook, Sales Manager's Handbook, Sales Promotion Handbook*, and more), the Dartnell Corporation is also responsible for the Web site for "National Customer Service Week." This commemoration, which always takes place the first week of October, was initiated in 1988 by the International Customer Service Association. In October 1992, Congress made the designation official (Senate Joint Resolution 166). Sponsored by Dartnell Corporation, the Customer Service Week Web site offers a fully illustrated collection of incentives and awards that may be ordered online, free service tips, celebration tips, games and puzzles, and links to recommended customer service resources sites. Contact: http://www.customerserviceweek.com/.

***Directory of Premium, Incentive & Travel Buyers.* Richmond, VA: Douglas Publications, Inc., The Salesman's Guide Directories. Annual. Print $329. CD-ROM ("Unlimited Use") $1,299. Contact: http://www.douglaspublications.com.**

This directory profiles the business market for promotions, covering some 18,000 buyers of premiums, incentives, and travel programs used to motivate sales personnel at more than 12,000 companies. Retailers or service providers who use sales forces have a vital stake in "incentivizing" them to attract customers and gain new accounts. Listings show the company's annual budget for premiums and incentives, as well as the size and destination of incentive trips. Some entries also provide otherwise hard-to-find contact names for such positions as manager of meetings and conventions, or manager of merchandising services; any marketer who has access to this directory could find such contacts useful.

TIP: A Free Web Source for Creating Sales Prospect Lists

Zapdata, an Internet service of Dun & Bradstreet Sales and Marketing Solutions, is a well-known source for business sales leads, mailing lists, and market analysis. Following registration at the site, which is free, it is possible to build a list of company sales prospects based on location, industries, demographics of the targeted companies, specialty data item (e.g., area code, primary telephone exchange, fax number, and many more), and/or job functions (through 20 broad occupational or professional categories, which are further broken down with increasing specificity). On the prospect list results page, the searcher may choose to download the five Free Leads only, or opt instead to get the Free Leads deducted from the price of the entire list. Five different types of records are offered: mailing (the least expensive), telemarketing, enhanced telemarketing, prospecting, and strategic marketing (the most expensive). Contact: http://www.zapdata.com/index.asp.

Incentive Magazine. **New York, NY: Bill Communications, Inc. Monthly. Print $55. Contact: http://www.incentivemag.com.**

Incentive Magazine is "the only publication devoted exclusively to motivation and performance improvement through the use of incentive programs and consumer promotions" (Incentive.com 2003). The Web version offers full-text articles from the current issue. The "Reports and Analysis" section provides the full texts of recent in-depth feature articles. With the free online Buyers Guide, the marketer can search for product and service providers using company names, 66 major product categories, or product keywords. Search results are displayed with the most comprehensive results first, followed by other providers that match the search criteria.

TIP: For Further Reading on Sales Management

Fred, Charles. L. 2002. *Breakaway: Deliver Value to Your Customers–Fast!* San Francisco, CA: Jossey-Bass.

Garofalo, Gene. 1997. *Sales Manager's Portable Answer Book.* Englewood Cliffs, NJ: Prentice Hall.

Kulik, Todd. 1999. *Forging an Effective Sales Organization.* New York: The Conference Board.

Spiro, Rosann L., William J. Stanton, and Gregory A. Rich. 2002. *Management of a Sales Force.* 11th ed. New York: McGraw-Hill.

TRADE SHOWS

Trade shows represent "the major sales promotion strategy for firms marketing industrial products." Companies exhibit their products at regional, national, or international venues, with a likelihood of reaching as many as 50% to 60% of their prospects. Those prospects, in turn, have an excellent opportunity to view the competition (as do the sellers). Trade shows are also sales generators; as many as half the visitors to a given trade show will eventually buy a product they first learned about at the show (Hise 1986, 981-982).

***International Tradeshow Directory*. Frankfurt, West Germany: M + A Verlag fuer Messen, Ausstellungen und Kongresse GmbH. Semi-Annual. Print $172. Contact: http://www.m-averlag.com/home-english/home-english.html.**

This directory provides detailed information for over 9,000 events held in more than 115 countries. The main organization is geographical, by country. Entries for trade fairs (as they are referred to in Europe) include the following information: the official abbreviated fair name; the fair title; exhibition dates for the next three to four years; registration deadline for exhibitors; frequency; location and site of the show; the main product groups or sectors; admission restrictions (i.e., whether the show is open to the public, or to professionals only); the rented exhibition area of the previous event; a profile of the event's previous exhibitors and visitors; conventions and meetings held in conjunction with the exhibition; address of the show management; name of the project and operations manager; membership in fair associations; and the address of the fair's official representative.

Other ways of accessing the information are provided. One section of the directory lists the fairs and shows in chronological order, starting with the date, city, and country, followed by the acronym and fair title. Another categorizes the events into 150 business and trade classifications, beginning with country and city and followed by the acronym and fair title. An italicized cross-reference number is used to provide easy access to the full entry that appears in the main body of the directory. Finally, a fourth section lists all the trade fairs by their abbreviated names, again using the italicized cross-reference number for access to the main listing. The directory is also available on CD-ROM.

***Trade Shows Worldwide: An International Directory of Events, Facilities, and Suppliers*. Farmington Hills, MI: Gale Group. Annual. Print $355. Contact: http://www.galegroup.com.**

Detailed entries are provided in this well-known, widely available annual directory of more than 10,000 trade shows and exhibitions held in the United States and throughout the world, some 7,000 trade show sponsoring organizations, and over 5,000 facilities, services, and additional sources of exhibiting information. Part One provides contact information, sponsoring organizations, show statistics, and fees for admission and booth rental. Part Two consists of a separate alphabetical listing of show organizers and sponsors. Part Three contains about 200 pages of listings on "Trade Show Facilities, Services, and Information Sources," and also includes a "Rankings" section detailing the amounts of exhibition space and number of hotel rooms needed for the shows and facilities, along with the amount of space that is available. The directory is indexed by show date, geographical location, and industry.

***Tradeshow Week Online*. Los Angeles, CA: Reed Business Information. Contact: http://www.tradeshowweek.com.**

This is the Web version of *Tradeshow Week* magazine, since 1971 the weekly "bible" of the trade show industry. From the home page, called the "main lobby," the nonsubscribing viewer may access a substantial array of content. The "Tradeshow Trends" section provides fact-filled excerpts from *Tradeshow Week*'s many surveys and reports, which include such titles as the *Quarterly Report of Tradeshow Statistics*, the *Annual Consumer Show Report*, the *Semiannual Computer Show and Electronics Report*, and the *Semiannual Medical Show Report*. The free "Tradeshow Directory" permits searching for all trade shows alphabetically or by keyword, as well as by focusing searches according to any combination of industry category, country, state or province, city, month, or year. Search results may be sorted, either alphabetically, or chronologically (by month and year), and they include complete contact information for the show(s). The *Tradeshow Week* "Article Archives" is searchable by keyword, month and year (from 1996 forward), and by article category (e.g., awards, case studies, news about shows, promotions that work, and many more). Text of the articles is not provided. The "Buyers' Guide" is searchable by company name (all companies listed are *Tradeshow Week* advertisers), industry category (for trade show services), and city.

***TSNN.com*. Needham, MA. Contact: http://www.tsnn.com/.**

This Internet repository for trade show data provides a substantial amount of free information–and still more, for paying subscribers–covering more than 30,000 trade shows, conferences, and seminars, 5,000 service providers, and 5,000 venues and facilities around the world. Searching for events by industry category, part of the event name, city, state, country, or month is free. Typically, a result will provide the full name of the event, the location name and dates, the number of exhibitors, the exhibition floor size (in square feet), and the address for the organizer of the event. Subscribers receive additional details relating to the contact information, the event organizer and any related shows. Basic searches for event suppliers and venues are also available at no charge; results include an organizational name, address, telephone number, and Web address.

TSNN.com is a quick and easy way to learn the names and cities for event venues throughout the United States and around the world. Calling itself "the ultimate tradeshow resource," it culls from other trade show information resources on the Web to offer the best of these resources organized into sections by topic. There are sections offering trade show events' and industry press releases and links to related news sources, information on event management, exhibitor sales and marketing, trade show marketing itself, and more. Within the latter, the subsection on "Direct Marketing" includes such useful texts as "37 Ways to Improve Your User Conference Brochure," "Developing Your E-Mail Marketing Lists," and "Ten Attention-Getting Ways to Use E-mail Lists."

BASIC WHOLESALE AND RETAIL DATA

***Economic Census–Wholesale and Retail Trade Sectors*. Washington, DC: U.S. Census Bureau. Online (free) or Print on Demand (price varies). Contact: http://www.census.gov/epcd/www/econ97.html.**

As part of the *Economic Census*, every five years (in those years ending in "2" and "7"), the Census Bureau surveys wholesale and retail establishments that sell merchandise for business, personal, or household use. These surveys cover the United States as a whole: states, metropolitan areas, counties, places, and ZIP codes.

Wholesale trade comprises "... establishments engaged in wholesaling merchandise, generally without transformation, and rendering services incidental to the sale of merchandise" (U.S. Census Bureau 2002). With the implementation of the North American Industry Classification System (NAICS) in the late 1990s, "Wholesale Trade" became industry sector 42. The Census Bureau identifies three main types of wholesalers: those that sell goods on their own account (e.g., wholesale merchants, distributors, jobbers, and others); those that sell goods made in the United States by a parent company; and those that arrange sales and purchases for others–such as agents and brokers who receive commissions or fees.

"Retail Trade" became industry sectors 44-45, which "comprise establishments engaged in retailing merchandise, generally without transformation, and rendering services incidental to the sale of merchandise" (U.S. Census Bureau 2002). The two main types of retailers are store and nonstore. The reported data are based on the retail outlets themselves, as types of establishments.

An *establishment*, as defined by the Census Bureau, should not be confused with a company: it is "a physical location where business is conducted, or business or industrial operations take place" (U.S. Census Bureau 2003). A company may consist of one or more establishments; examples include sales offices, industrial production plants, assembly operations, and support operations (such as administrative offices, warehouses, customer service centers, or regional headquarters).

Additionally, a variety of "Subject Series" reports are published: *Merchandise Line Sales* (retail); *Commodity Line Sales* (wholesale); *Establishment and Firm Size* (available for retail or wholesale); and *Miscellaneous Subjects*. Despite its generic title, the latter offers considerable detail. The "wholesale" *Miscellaneous Subjects* report includes sales by class of customer; end-of-year inventories; type of operation; sales and commissions received; and gross margins and gross profits. The "retail" *Miscellaneous Subjects* report includes floor space by selected kind of business and class of customer by kind of business. Finally, a *Summary* report consolidates the most widely-used statistics among the previous topics.

For product-level information (as classified by NAICS), the researcher should consult two reports in particular. *Merchandise Line Sales* (http://www.census.gov/prod/ec97/97r44-ls.pdf) provides information on the type of merchandise handled by various retailers. This can reveal surprising information about competitors or potential channels of distribution (for example, men's apparel is also sold in hardware stores). Information about wholesalers is found in *Commodity Line Sales* (http://www.census.gov/prod/ec97/97w42-ls.pdf). It can answer such questions as "What lines of commodities does a particular type of wholesaler handle?" and "How much of their business is involved with that particular commodity line?" There is considerable detail, such as data on the number of establishments handling a specific line and the percentage of total sales of the type of business. Additional specific product-based information, such as value and quantity of shipments, is also available in the "Manufacturing" industries series component of the *Economic Census* (http://www.census.gov/prod/www/abs/ecmani.html).

For the years *between* those ending in "2" or "7," the Retail and Wholesale Trade section of the Census Bureau's Web site (http://www.census.gov/econ/www/retmenu.html) provides monthly retail and wholesale sales and inventory data, annual survey data from the past 10 years or more, detailed county-by-county data for every state in the U.S. as reported in the *Census of Retail Trade* and *Census of Wholesale Trade* for 1992, and a link to the 1997 *Economic Census* home page (http://www.census.gov/epcd/www/econ97.html). Reports are presented in a variety of formats, including HTML, spreadsheet and PDF. (Different formats may be available for different data series.)

TIP: Geographic Coverage of the *Economic Census*

For the 1997 *Economic Census*, the print publications (which are also available in PDF from the Web site) show national-level data only. For more detailed state- and metropolitan area-level data, see *American FactFinder* (http://factfinder.census.gov) or the *Economic Census* on CD-ROM. (Formats may change when the 2002 *Economic Census* is released in 2003 or 2004.) Contact: http://www.census.gov/epcd/www/econ97.html.

***Retail Trade Survey.* Washington, DC: U.S. Census Bureau. Annual and monthly. Online (free) or Print on Demand (price varies). Contact: http://www.census.gov/econ/www/re0200.html.**

The *Retail Trade Survey* provides detailed statistical data about stores that sell goods and services to final consumers. According to the Census Bureau, consumers inject trillions of dollars into the economy and knowing the state of the retail trade sector is therefore vital to the federal government. A byproduct of the government's investment in data collection is that market researchers gain a useful analytical tool.

The *Retail Trade Survey* is conducted monthly, cumulated annually, and issued each spring in a combined monthly and annual report. On a national basis, the reports contain estimates of annual sales, per capita sales, gross margins, monthly and year-end inventories, inventory/sales ratios, merchandise purchased, gross margin/sales ratios, and accounts receivable balances by kind of business. Comparable statistics are shown for the previous year, along with year-to-year percentage changes. Monthly data for the most recent 10 years are also presented.

No brand name information is included, and market share is not directly reported per se. However, the survey provides an essential benchmark for developing market share figures, particularly for nationwide retailers. For example, a national chain of home improvement stores gains a better perspective toward a drop in its own sales volume by viewing the totals in the category "building materials group stores." The data can also be used to spot trends in specific purchase categories. A marketer of bicycle accessories would need to know the rate of increase in bicycle sales to write a marketing plan, embark on a major sales campaign, or apply for a loan to fund development of a new product.

In summary, the U.S. Census Bureau provides a wealth of varied, general, and detailed data that has great potential to serve the needs of the marketing professional. Improvements in electronic access and software make it easier than ever for marketers to ensure that baseline demographic analysis is included in planning. Despite these advances, the sheer number and variety of different Census publications and databases make the process of locating and retrieving the right information seem somewhat daunting. Understanding how different publications relate to each other and knowing what is available should help the marketer take competitive advantage of this surfeit of riches.

National Retail Federation (NRF). Washington, DC. Contact: http://www.nrf.com.

The National Retail Federation (NRF) is the preeminent umbrella retail organization in the United States, representing various other state and national associations, along with corporate members both large and small. The Association is involved in research, education, and training to advance the retail industry. Its Web site offers industry news, directories, links to retailing resources on the Web (including the most current federal government statistics for retail activity), information on governmental affairs and legislative activity important to the retail industry, and more. The "Advocacy" section offers the most current two years of *Washington Retail Insight*, a weekly newsletter, and the full texts of the NRF's *Congressional Voting Scorecards* for the most recent three sessions of Congress. The "Headlines" section covers recent retail industry news, and is gathered from such sources as the Associated Press, Business Wire, Dow Jones Business News, PR Newswire, and Reuters.

***Plunkett's Retail Industry Almanac.* Houston, TX: Plunkett Research, Ltd. Biennial. Print $200. Contact: http://www. Plunkettresearch.com/index.htm.**

"Retail" is defined in this guide to include retail store chains, retail services companies, and non-store retailers (the latter includes companies that sell through catalogs or other forms of direct mail, or via the Internet). The bulk of the text consists of full-page profiles of the 433 largest and most successful U.S. retailers, arranged alphabetically by company name. Each entry typically includes the company's URL; store data, including typical size in square feet and number of stores; type of business; brands, divisions, and affiliates; a narrative description of growth plans and any special features of the company; contact names; telephone and fax numbers; sales and profits ranks; number of employees; and brief financial data for the most recent five years. Entries are indexed by such access points as geography, industry, brand names, subsidiary names, and more.

Additional content includes a glossary of retail industry terms and chapters on such topics as major trends affecting retailing; important retail industry contacts, both domestic and international; online retailing and non-store retailing; trends in malls and shopping centers; and careers in retailing. A CD-ROM representing the "core database" of the almanac's company profiles is included with the purchase of the book. The Web site also provides free access to a repository called the "Retail Industry Channel" (http://www.plunkettresearch.com/retail/index. htm). Four information-packed sections are available: (1) a glossary of retail terms; (2) "Retail Industry Trends/Retail Trade Analysis," a narrative with some statistics; (3) a section devoted to "Retail Industry Statistics"; and (4) a section of "Retail Industry Contact Information," encompassing advertising/marketing, business associations, general retail information, government and trade organizations, real estate shopping centers, retail magazines, and store security/alarms/computer security.

GETTING THE PRODUCT TO MARKET

Obviously, selling cannot occur unless the product gets to its market. Each of the resources discussed below depicts the wholesale or retail distribution landscape of the United States (and some neighboring countries, as indicated) with great precision and detail.

American Wholesalers & Distributors Directory. **Farmington Hills, MI: Gale Group. Annual. Print: $250. Contact: http://www.galegroup.com.**

This directory identifies more than 27,000 national, regional, and local wholesalers and distributors located throughout the United States and Puerto Rico. The marketer can use this information to discover new distribution channels or opportunities for product licensing (principal product lines are provided). Entries, organized according to 61 broad product categories, are arranged alphabetically by name of wholesaler/distributor. In addition to the customary contact information, entries also provide names of principal officers, total number of employees, estimated sales volume, and, when available, the Web address for an online product catalog. Indexing is by company name (alphabetically); by broad subject terms representative of each company's principal product line; by geographic region (state and city); and by SIC code. It is available online as part of the Gale's *Business and Company Resource Center.*

TIP: A Similar Directory, for Manufacturers' Representatives

As defined by the Manufacturers' Agents National Association (MANA), a manufacturer's representative is "an outsourced provider of field sales services to multiple manufacturers of complementary products." Normally working on commission, they subsidize their own expenses in exchange for a contractual agreement to be the exclusive agent of the manufacturers they represent in a particular region, market, or for specific accounts. To identify which manufacturers' agents represent which manufacturers and service companies, consult this source: *MANA Members Directory of Manufacturers' Sales Agencies* (Laguna Hills, CA: Manufacturers' Agents National Association. Annual). The online version, unfortunately available to members only, is updated daily, and searchable by territory, agency location, product classification, customers served, services offered, and keyword. Contact: http://www.manaonline.org/.

Sheldon's Major Stores & Chains & Resident Buying Offices. **Sarasota, FL: Phelon, Sheldon & Marsar, Inc. Annual. Print $200. Contact: PSMpublishing@aol.com (via e-mail).**

This directory, which has been published annually since 1885, is a premier guide to United States retail outlets; the current edition also has listings for Canadian and Mexican stores. Its coverage includes department stores and chains, home furnishing chains, women's specialty stores and chains, and resident buying offices for the retail outlets covered. The entries are coded to provide even more specialized identification of the stores, making it possible to zero in on such categories as college book stores, fabric store chains, gift stores and chains, jewelry stores and chains, sporting goods chains, and more. In Section 1, all stores and chains are listed alphabetically according to the following hierarchy: state, city, and store name. Each store listing includes all or part of the following information: store names, complete mailing address, telephone and fax numbers, number of employees, year established, annual sales volume, number of stores operated, resident buying office locations, executives and their titles, lines of merchandise sold and buyers' names for each line, and a list of accounts (stores and chains) represented. Indeed, few business directories of any kind offer such a wealth of contact names, from corporate officers to individual buyers.

Resident Buying Offices appear in Section 2, listed alphabetically by company names, first in New York City, followed by Los Angeles, and then by locations in other cities. Each listing includes all or part of the following information: company name, complete address, telephone and fax numbers, type of stores and chains served, executives and titles, lines of merchandise sold and buyers' names for each line, and a listing of accounts (stores and chains) represented. Further detail is provided by the resident buying office codes included with each entry; these enable the user to identify which firms may be "merchandise brokers/selling agents," as distinct from those which are resident buying offices only, or the buying office/corporate headquarters for an out of town store or chain. In Section 3, stores and chains are indexed alphabetically by name.

Shopping Center Directory. **Chicago, IL: National Research Bureau. Annual. Print $685/set or $355/volume. CD-ROM or Online (price varies). Contact: http://www.nrbonline.com/.**

This national directory, covering nearly 39,000 U.S. shopping centers and their 450,000-plus tenants, is issued in five volumes, one each for east, south, Midwest, and west regions, plus another for "Top Contacts," a listing of national headquarters. Volumes may be purchased individually. Four categories of shopping centers are identified: neighborhood "strip malls"; community strip centers; regional malls; and "super" regional malls. These encompass convenience centers, discount and factory outlet centers, home improvement centers, auto malls, and more. The extraordinarily comprehensive indexing is by name (alphabetically); by shopping center name; by Metropolitan Statistical Area (MSA); by city; by county; by "Gross Leasable Area" (GLA); by tenant mix; by space availability; by planned/proposed new centers; by expanding/renovating centers; and by major owner; leasing agent, or manager.

Thus, the researcher can quickly identify who the competition may be in a given geographic location, or what the mix of tenants may be in this or that shopping mall. This directory may also be used to map out sales or site visits; to find out where retail space may be available; to pinpoint undiscovered markets; to assess the financial risks of others; to fine-tune distribution channels; and more. The entire directory is also available in a CD-ROM version (which has additional features and can be networked for multiple users). It is also available by online subscription, through PlainVanillaShell.com (contact http://plainvanillashell.com).

TIP: A Source for Extensive Retail Data by City

Editor & Publisher Market Guide, an annual newspaper markets directory, is widely available in public and academic library reference collections. Its profiles of every U.S. and Canadian city that has a daily newspaper include a wealth of handy facts. "Principal" or "Neighborhood" shopping centers are named in section 12 of each city's entry; also, where available, "Nearby Shopping Centers," their distance in miles from downtown, and their largest constituent stores are named. The principal shopping days and whether stores are open evenings and Sundays are typically noted, as well. In Section 13, "Retail Outlets," the city's department, discount, variety, and chain drug stores are enumerated, along with chain supermarkets, fast food/chain restaurants, auto dealerships, and other chain retailers. Contact: http://www.editorandpublisher.com/.

Retail Tenant Directory. **Wilton, CT: Trade Dimensions. Annual. Print $355. Contact: http://www.Tradedimensions.com.**

Closely related to the *Shopping Center Directory* is this annual directory, which provides detailed information for more than 5,300 "actively expanding" retail chains in the United States and Canada, covering some 70 product categories. Along with the usual "company directory-style" information (which, for some entries, includes the name of the Marketing Manager), answers may be found to such questions as the following: What types of retail locations do they prefer? Which geographical areas are they located in currently, and which are they targeting? What kinds of co-tenants do they prefer? Indexes show which operating names go with which (parent) company names, square footage preferences, and regional preferences by type of retail category. Also, like the *Shopping Center Directory*, the *Retail Tenant Directory* is available by online subscription, as "Find a Tenant," through PlainVanillaShell.com (contact http://plainvanillashell.com).

REFERENCES

Hise, Richard T. 1986. "Trade Show." In *Beacham's Marketing Reference*, edited by Walston Beacham et al. Washington, DC: Research Publishing.

Incentive.com. 2003. "About Us." <http://www.incentivemag.com/incentive/about_us/index.jsp> (April 23, 2003).

Incentive Performance Center. 2002. "A Study of the Incentive Merchandise and Travel Marketplace, 2000." <http://www.incentivecentral.org/html/incentivemerch-study.asp> (April 23, 2003).

Kotler, Philip and Gary Armstrong. 2001. *Principles of Marketing.* 9th ed. Upper Saddle River, NJ: Prentice Hall.

Lewis, Gerald. 2002. "The Case for Innovative Loyalty Card Programs." *NPN, National Petroleum News* 94, no. 4 (April): 68-69.

U.S. Census Bureau.

_____ 2002. "1997 Economic Census, Wholesale Trade." http://www.census.gov/epcd/www/97EC42.HTM (April 30, 2003).

_____ 2002. "1997 Economic Census, Retail Trade." <http://www.census.gov/epcd/www/97EC44.HTM> (April 23, 2003).

_____ 2003. "2002 Economic Census: Glossary of Terms for the Economic Census." <http://help.econ.census.gov/econhelp/glossary/> (May 1, 2003).

Chapter 10

Direct Marketing and E-Commerce Sources

Topics

Direct Marketing
E-Commerce

Sources

State of the List Industry Report
Statistical Fact Book
Direct Marketing List Source
Direct Marketing Market Place
SRDS Interactive Advertising Source
DMNews.com
Gale Encyclopedia of E-Commerce
Plunkett's E-Commerce and Internet Business Almanac
E-Stats
ecommerce-guide.com
E-Business Research Center
eMarketer
Center for Research in Electronic Commerce

The theme of this chapter is "marketing outside the walls," and a brief history of Montgomery Ward, an American retail giant throughout

[Haworth co-indexing entry note]: "Direct Marketing and E-Commerce Sources." Diamond, Wendy, and Michael R. Oppenheim. Co-published simultaneously in *Journal of Business & Finance Librarianship* (The Haworth Information Press, an imprint of The Haworth Press, Inc.) Vol. 9, No. 4, 2004, pp. 221-236; and: *Marketing Information: A Strategic Guide for Business and Finance Libraries* (Wendy Diamond, and Michael R. Oppenheim) The Haworth Information Press, an imprint of The Haworth Press, Inc., 2004, pp. 221-236. Single or multiple copies of this article are available for a fee from The Haworth Document Delivery Service [1-800-HAWORTH, 9:00 a.m. - 5:00 p.m. (EST). E-mail address: docdelivery@haworthpress.com].

the 20th century, will flesh out the contours of the story. Non-store retailing and the marketing that drives it started in the United States when the first mail-order catalog–a single-sheet, illustrated price list, with ordering instructions–was introduced in Chicago by Aaron Montgomery Ward in 1872. Some thirty years later, that sheet had grown into a four-pound catalog, mailed to millions of Montgomery Ward customers throughout the country. The "Monkey Ward" Wish Book had become a staple of the American home.

Montgomery Ward did not go "bricks and mortar" until 1926 when its first retail store opened in Plymouth, Indiana. The mail-order catalog survived until 1985, just prior to the explosion of the electronic commerce era. Another catalog business, Montgomery Ward Direct, emerged in 1991, and lasted another five years. However, by December 2000, Montgomery Ward itself announced it was closing for good–and an amazing retail saga came to an end (*Hoover's Online* 2002 and Chicago Public Library 2001).

Hoover's Online defines "non-store retailing" as "companies engaged in the sale of various retail items using catalogs, mail order, the Internet, television, and other direct marketing media" (*Hoover's Online* 2002). Direct marketing, which has most commonly taken the form of direct mailing to prospective clients or customers, "is a mass medium that delivers an advertising message directly to individual prospects through the U.S. Postal Service or through private services" (Caballero 1986, 249). In recent years, electronic mail (e-mail) and the Internet have become major staging grounds for direct marketing, thus their pairing in this chapter.

According to the Direct Marketing Association's seventh annual *Economic Impact* study, conducted for the Association by Wharton Economic Forecasting Associates (WEFA), direct and interactive marketing expenditures rose to $196.8 billion in 2001, up 3.6% from $189.9 billion in 2000. Also in 2001, direct marketing retail sales grew 9%, to $1.86 trillion from $1.71 trillion in 2000. Business-to-consumer (B2C) marketers accounted for 48%, or $94.3 billion, of direct marketing spending in 2001, and are projected to grow 5.9% annually through 2006; business-to-business (B2B) spending should rise at a rate of 7.0% annually (DiPasquale 2002).

The objective of direct marketing is to alter the sales distribution chain–to bypass the wholesaler and the retailer and go directly to the customer. Direct marketing can take a variety of forms: (1) *direct mail* involves the use of letters and other promotional materials mailed to specific individuals; (2) *mail order*, where buyers contact sellers by mail, telephone, fax, or the Internet and order goods to be delivered directly to them; (3) *direct response marketing*, in which the target audience is asked to do something, such as send in a coupon, or make a telephone call; (4) *telemarketing*, the telemarketer telephones potential customers; and (5) *database marketing*, which involves contacting those customers whose records reside in an electronic database.

The popular preference for electronic mail over traditional mail delivery by the U.S. Postal Service has skyrocketed to the point that that the U.S. General Accounting Office, in its grim February 2002 analysis of the postal service, concluded that "USPS's basic business model is not sustainable" (U.S. General Accounting Office 2002, 45). As regularly rising postal rates continue to be part of the response to the Postal Service's shrinking financial fortunes, it is easy to see the appeal of "free" e-mail and the Internet for the next generation of direct marketing—hence, electronic commerce.

According to the Direct Marketing Association's 2001 *State of the E-Commerce Industry Report*, not only are direct marketers enjoying high returns from their current e-commerce activities, they are also planning to invest even more heavily in interactive media selling projects. Somewhat counter-intuitively, the survey also found that although direct marketers are getting better and better results using e-mail marketing, the "rich" e-mail (as opposed to "plain text" messages) and other Internet technologies, such as streaming video, are *not* contributing to that success. Additional relevant findings of the survey, as reported in the business press, underscore the prominence that e-commerce has developed among all types of direct marketing.

> Fifty-five percent of the 700 companies polled are earning a profit from their e-commerce operations; according to the survey, 83% said they expect that interactive media will have a positive impact on revenue by 2005. Fifty-nine percent of companies reported increased sales as a result of e-mail marketing promotions, while 65% said they rely on click-throughs to track the effectiveness of campaigns. Web sites are also being viewed as good e-commerce sales-lead vehicles, according to the survey. Fifty-seven percent said their sites are used for lead generation. Eighty-five percent of companies said they are using their Web sites for the marketing of information, while 61% are using sites to reach new clients. (Clark 2001, 2 and 25)

This chapter discusses basic information sources for direct marketing and e-commerce.

DIRECT MARKETING

***State of the List Industry Report.* New York: Direct Marketing Association. Annual. Print $495 (DMA members), $995 (nonmembers). Contact: http://www.the-dma.org/bookstore/cgi/displaybook?product_id= 009318.**

Formerly known as the *Annual List Usage Survey*, in 2002 this report changed title and greatly enhanced its scope beyond postal mail issues alone. In the first quarter of 2002, the DMA List/Database Council expanded its annual survey to include e-mail issues, the better to assess their impact on postal mail volume and frequency. The report covers the key issues confronting the direct marketing industry, and tracks trends in members' activities in the following areas: mailing patterns (i.e., mailing quantity, frequency, peak mailing time); use of outside and "housefile" names; response information; use of direct mail alternative distribution media; use of list rental marketing information; marketing database maintenance, strategies, and uses; cross-selling and upselling strategies; and customer service technologies.

***Statistical Fact Book.* New York: Direct Marketing Association. Annual. Print and Online $295 (nonmembers). Contact: http://www. the-dma.org/bookstore/cgi/bookstore.**

For the most extensively detailed portrait of the direct marketing industry "by the numbers," this compendium is *the* source to consult. Coverage is primarily for the United States, although there is a section devoted to international statistics. The following topics, with a representative sample of the content noted parenthetically, are covered in the latest edition: direct response advertising (percentage of marketing budget spent on direct marketing); direct mail (how consumers respond to direct mail); catalogs (comparative annual operating costs for catalog fulfillment centers); telephone (outbound consumer and business to business sales operation annual costs); print/promotion (coupon redemption rates by media); television/home shopping (infomercial production cost worksheet); interactive media (e-mail marketing expenditures); lists/databases (list of internal/external-prospect database values); consumer demographics (main reasons for no Internet use at home); business-to-business (businesses with active, purposeful Web sites); financial services (most and least preferred credit card marketing channel); circulation/books (insert card performance compared to prior year); nonprofit (nonprofit direct marketing jobs by industry); international (international direct marketing sales); customer service/fulfillment (customer relationship management development budget); U.S. Postal Service information (response rates to first-class advertising solicitations); and "Economic Impact: U.S. Marketing Today" (direct mail advertising expenditures by medium and market). Altogether, the text contains more than 400 charts and graphs, and offers indexing by topic and by source contact. This source is among those which are completely reproduced for inclusion in the *SRI Microfiche Library*, the companion to LexisNexis Academic and Library Solutions' print *Statistical Reference Index (SRI)* and Web-based *LexisNexis Statistical* (please see the discussion of *SRI* in Chapter 1, "Introduction to Sources and Strategies for Research on Marketing").

***Direct Marketing List Source.* Des Plaines, IL: Standard Rate & Data Service. Bimonthly. Print and Online $578 (annual subscription). Contact: http://www.srds.com/.**

To market your product most effectively, do you need to target detective agencies that have armored car services? You can find a mailing list of such customers in this print and online service, part of the SRDS "suite" of tools (see additional discussion in Chapter 7, "Advertising and Media Planning Sources"). This tool provides rental information for mailing lists, including sources, costs and other information that may be used to custom-tailor a list strategy for a direct marketing campaign. Formerly known as *Direct Mail List Rates and Data*, this SRDS resource contains some 38,000 listings for domestic and international list rental opportunities, arranged according to 223 business, consumer, and farm market classifications. A typical listing includes the following: date the information was last verified; personnel (i.e., contact person[s] for the list, along with complete contact information); a detailed description of the list, often including a gender breakdown; the source of the list; the types of selections available, with counts (e.g., number of recipients) for each; the commission and credit policy; the method(s) of addressing; and possible restrictions (i.e., a sample mailing piece may be required before the list may be purchased). Entries may also cover such items as a delivery schedule, fees and deposits, or test arrangements.

Indexes provide searching by market classification; specific mailing list title; "high-ticket" mail order buyers; "enhanced" lists (those that provide additional demographic or lifestyle information, to expand on the characteristics of particular market segments); and e-mail lists. An annual subscription includes 6 bi-monthly print issues and unlimited access to the online version, which is updated continuously. As would be expected, it provides instant access to Web sites for list brokers, managers, and compilers, as well as other data sources included in the entries.

TIP: Additional Mailing List Sources

- *Directory of Mailing List Companies: A Complete Guide to Mailing List Sources.* Biennial. Nyack, NY: Todd Publications.
- *National Directory of Mailing Lists.* Annual. CD-ROM. New York: Oxbridge Communications.

Direct Marketing Market Place. **New Providence, NJ: National Register Publishing. Annual. Print $325. Contact: http://www. dirmktgplace.com/.**

Subtitled "The Networking Source of the Direct Marketing Industry," the annual *Direct Marketing Market Place* (DMMP) lists some 16,000 individual contacts and more than 10,000 direct marketers, service firms, and suppliers. The directory is intended to be a "one-stop shopping" resource for both direct marketers and the companies whose services they use. Listings are provided for advertising agencies, broadcast and print media, copywriters, direct response and sales promotion agencies, graphic designers, list brokers, mailing houses, photographers, printers and research firms, and telemarketing firms. *DMMP* uses 19 categories of direct marketers, 15 categories of service firms and suppliers, and 5 categories of creative services. Suppliers and other firms that provide services to direct marketers can fine-tune their searches for prospective clients by identifying who spends the most money on direct marketing, as well as which media they are most likely to use. A typical entry will include number of employees; date of company founding; contact names; the amount of money a company allocates to its direct marketing budget, and the percentage of the advertising budget that is devoted to direct marketing. The location of service firms and suppliers may be found by using the geographic section; firms and contact names are also indexed. Additional features of the directory include industry statistics, listings of related books and periodicals, information about direct marketing associations and events, and more. This work is widely available in the business reference sections of public and academic libraries.

TIP: Direct Mail/E-Mail Campaign ROI Calculator

Marketing Today offers this handy Web tool, free of charge and with no registration required. To determine the "return on investment," or ROI, for a direct mail or e-mail campaign, the marketer enters program costs and projected program results under "Input" and clicks on "Calculate" to retrieve the estimated ROI and other pertinent details, such as cost per piece, cost per new customer, and more. Contact: http://www.marketingtoday.com/tools/roi_calculator.htm.

SRDS Interactive Advertising Source. **Des Plaines, IL: Standard Rate and Data Service. Quarterly. Print $581. Online (free access with annual print subscription). Contact: http://www.srds.com.**

This monthly publication, which identifies itself as "the marketing professional's complete source for interactive media and marketing opportunities," shows advertising rates offered by Web sites, including both business to business ("B2B") and consumer-oriented sites. Organization is by subject; an alphabetical index of Web sites by name is also included (published on yellow paper). Typically, entries include a profile, the names of key personnel, self-reported usage or circulation (i.e., the number of "hits" the site receives), audience profile, and the advertising rates for banners, keyword clusters, and sponsorship packages.

DMNews.com. **New York: Courtney Communications. ©2001. Online (fee varies). Contact: http://www.dmnews.com/cgi-bin/index.cgi.**

This "online newspaper of record for direct marketers," the Web version of *DM News*, offers daily news and feature articles about direct marketing, and many other valuable features. News coverage encompasses new direct marketing campaigns, the activities of both direct marketing clubs and associations as well as general advertising agencies, postal news, and legislative developments. An especially valuable feature is the "DM News Online List Directory," a continuously updated directory of direct mail lists, opt-in e-mail lists, and alternative media. The directory is impressively searchable by business lists, consumer lists, North American Industry Classification System (NAICS) code number, or keyword (including exact phrases). The business, consumer, and NAICS code number are already designated, and may be selected from drop-down boxes. Searches may be limited by media type (direct mail, e-mail list, or alternative media), or geographically by list location (i.e., by country). Searching the directory is free, and list owners, managers or compilers may enter unlimited basic listings in the Directory at no cost. Silver and Gold levels of enhanced listings can be purchased, in order to highlight special files. Also available is a searchable archive of articles, covering January 1998 forward; articles from the past 30 days are free online, grouped under 18 topical categories, including agency news, database and Internet marketing, "high-tech" direct marketing, and infomercials. Daily news updates via e-mail or a downloadable screensaver are available simply for the asking. Searching for articles (on the site) is free; the actual articles are not. *DMnews.com* also provides an events calendar and classified job ads.

TIP: States' "Do Not Call" Lists

The Federal Trade Commission's Telemarketing Sales Rule (Title 16, Part 310 of the *Code of Federal Regulations*) makes it illegal for a telemarketer to call parties who have specifically asked not to be called. Consumers can report offending telemarketers to their State Attorneys General. Accordingly, 26 states (as of April 1, 2003) maintain a "Do Not Call List," located on the DMA site. The list shows the effective date of the state law or regulation, and how to obtain the list (whether by telephone or via the Internet). Contact: http://www.the-dma.org/government/donotcalllists.shtml.

E-COMMERCE

A wealth of facts and figures about electronic commerce may be found in some of the direct marketing sources already discussed, such as the Direct Marketing Association's *Statistical Fact Book* and *DMnews.com*. Fittingly, many of the key resources for e-commerce information are found on the Web.

***Gale Encyclopedia of E-Commerce*. Edited by Jane A. Malonis. Farmington Hills, MI: Gale Group, 2002. Print $295. 1,000 pages.**

For a well-rounded, basic grounding in the world of electronic commerce, the student, researcher, or budding e-marketer would do well to consult this work. This two-volume guide covers, as noted in the introductory Highlights, the "topics and terms, companies, people, events, and legislation most relevant to the e-commerce industry" (*Gale Encyclopedia of E-Commerce* 2002, xi). The more than 470 alphabetically-arranged essays, written by business writers (though not individually attributed), range in length from about half a page (for example, "authentication") to nearly four pages (the entry on Ebay). Banner ads, brand building, encryption, internet metrics, shipping and shipment tracking, and Web site usability issues are only a few of the topics covered. Each entry concludes with cross-references and a bibliography of print and Web-based items for "Further Reading."

The table of contents lists each entry. The Master Index, at the end of volume 2, provides considerably enhanced access to all the contents of each volume. A chronology and timeline traces the history of e-commerce, in the broadest sense possible, from the 1904 patenting of the Fleming valve, the first vacuum tube, through the 2001 merger of corporate behemoths Time Warner and America Online (AOL). A companion work is the two-volume *Gale E-Commerce Sourcebook* ($195), a wide-ranging collection of such items as sample business plans, advertising trend data, company listings, and government agencies related to electronic commerce.

Plunkett's E-Commerce & Internet Business Almanac. Houston, TX: Plunkett Research, Ltd. Annual. Print $250 (includes CD-ROM). Contact: http://www.plunkettresearch.com/index.htm.

This work offers full-page profiles of the 400 largest and most successful U.S. Internet and e-commerce companies, arranged alphabetically by company name. Each entry typically includes the company's URL; type of business and description of business activities; sales and profits ranks; brief financial data; stock market ticker symbol; number of employees; executives' salaries, bonuses, and benefits; women and minority directors and officers; growth plans; brands and affiliates; "competitive advantage" (summarized in a sentence or two); contact names; telephone and fax numbers; and company locations. The indexing offers a wide array of access points: by company headquarters location, by state; by regions of the United States; by firms which have international locations; by companies described as "Hot Spots for Advancement for Women and Minorities"; and by subsidiaries, brand names, and selected affiliations. Also included are an alphabetical index by company name, and an index of companies by industry, with rankings within industry groups.

Additional content includes an electronic commerce glossary and chapters on such topics as B2C (business to consumer) e-business, trends in B2B (business to business e-commerce); online financial services; and trends in personal computers, Internet access, and Internet domains. The work is illustrated with charts and tables showing Internet business and e-commerce performance statistics and trends (for example, "largest online stock brokerages" or "fiber optic network speeds"). This Plunkett's Almanac (and others) are among the directory titles reproduced in full in the *SRI Microfiche Library* (see the discussion of the Direct Marketing Association's *Statistical Fact Book*, near the beginning of this chapter).

TIP: "Industry Research" Section of Plunkett Research Web Site

At the Industry Research section of its site, Plunkett provides "Market Research Channels" that offer an excellent grounding in a variety of those industries covered by its publications. Of interest to e-marketers are "Computers & Internet," "Retail," and "Telecommunications." The "Retail Industry Channel," for example, includes a glossary of retail terms, an executive-summary-style essay on "Retail Industry Trends/Retail Trade Analysis," a collection of retail industry statistics (recent and historical, but not current), and a very extensive collection of "Retail Industry Contacts and Associations," including addresses, telephone numbers, and Web sites (with helpful annotations). Contact: http://www.plunkettresearch.com/channels.htm.

E-Stats. U.S. Census Bureau, Dept. of Commerce. Washington, DC. Online (free). Contact: http://www.census.gov/eos/www/ebusiness614.htm.

This Census Bureau site is devoted exclusively to "Measuring the Electronic Economy" of the United States. It provides news releases, information on electronic commerce statistics-gathering methods, industrial classification systems, and the full texts of background papers which trace the development of electronic commerce measurement within the federal government. To date, the Census Bureau has collected electronic commerce data in four separate surveys, each of which focused on different measures of economic activity, such as shipments for manufacturing, sales for wholesale and retail trade, and revenues for service industries. Measures of total economic and e-commerce activity thus differ among the economic sectors, in both concept and definition. (The questionnaires used for most of the surveys are available at the site.) The Census Bureau's electronic commerce measures represent the value of goods and services sold online, whether over open networks such as the Internet, or over proprietary networks running systems such as Electronic Data Interchange (EDI). The data tables are provided in PDF format; the majority of the most recent tables are also offered in Excel spreadsheet format.

E-Stats does not cover the entire U.S. economy: agriculture, mining, utilities, construction, nonmerchant wholesalers, and about one-third of service-related industries are not included. Data for the most recent report (as of Spring 2003) were collected from more than 125,000 manufacturing, services, wholesale, and retail businesses that reflect about 70% of the economic activity measured in the 1997 *Economic Census.* These figures will undoubtedly change when the 2002 *Economic Census* is issued in 2003 or 2004. The *E-Stats* site also includes these features: a link to the NAICS home page; descriptions of the statistical methodology used; a "Frequently Asked Questions" (FAQ) section covering electronic commerce; and the names, telephone numbers, and e-mail addresses of Census Bureau staff experts for electronic commerce measurement.

TIP: More U.S. Government Information on E-Commerce–One-Stop Shopping

At *Uncle Sam E-Commerce*, the Government Publications Department of the University of Memphis library has conveniently gathered and annotated links to the most current U.S. government Web site–and some key non-governmental sources–dealing with electronic commerce. These are grouped by agency (Census Bureau, Federal Trade Commission, Justice Department, and many others); by publication (such as the Small Business Administration's *E-Commerce: Small Businesses Venture Online*); and by non-governmental resource (such as the Center for Research in Electronic Commerce at the University of Texas, *e-Marketer*, and the Electronic Payments Association). Contact: http://exlibris.memphis.edu/govpubs/ecomm.htm.

ecommerce-guide.com. **Jupitermedia Corporation**. ©**2003. Online (free). Contact: http://ecommerce.internet.com/.**

This site offers a broad range of free e-commerce information, including current, full-text "News and Trends"; an e-commerce glossary; an events calendar, listing upcoming trade shows and conferences; and a "Product Finder," a guide to e-commerce products and services in such categories as analysis, data management, networking, protection, site management, and more. Signed and dated "Product Reviews" include examinations and comparisons of such e-commerce tools as auction builders, commerce servers, payment solutions, portal sites, and storefront builders. The "How Do I?" section covers building an e-commerce site, attracting and retaining customers, getting paid, and securing the site.

TIP: An E-Commerce Reading List

Cunningham, Michael J. 2000. *B2B: How to Build a Profitable E-Commerce Strategy*. Cambridge, MA: Perseus.
Easton, Jaclyn. 2002. *Going Wireless: Transform Your Business with Mobile Technology*. New York: HarperBusiness.
Kalakota, Ravi; and Marcia Robinson. 2001. *E-Business 2.0: Roadmap for Success*, 2nd ed. Boston, MA: Addison-Wesley.
Lucas, Henry C. 2002. *Strategies for Electronic Commerce and the Internet*. Cambridge, MA: MIT Press.
Saloner, Garth, and A. Michael Spence. 2002. *Creating and Capturing Value: Perspectives and Cases on Electronic Commerce*. New York: John Wiley & Sons.
Smith, Dayle M. 2001. *The E-Business Book: A Step-by-Step Guide to E-Commerce and Beyond*. Princeton, NJ: Bloomberg Press.
Steingold, Fred. 2002. *How to Get Your Business on the Web: A Legal Guide to E-Commerce*. Berkeley, CA: Nolo Press.
Wind, Yoram, and Mahajan, Vijay. 2001. *Digital Marketing: Global Strategies from the World's Leading Experts*. New York: John Wiley & Sons.

The E-Business Research Center. **CXOMedia, Inc.** ©**1994-2003. Online (free). Contact: http://www.cio.com/research/ec/.**

This rich resource is "the executives' resource for doing business online." It offers a good deal of *CIO (Chief Information Officer) Magazine* content; provides recent articles from the magazine; a *CIO* article archive going back to September 1994, with many articles available in full text; business-to-business and business-to-consumer case studies (also reprinted from *CIO Magazine*); "Executive Summaries" of major e-commerce topics, much like white papers or tutorials (including bibliographies, with many of the cited sources linked, in turn, to full texts); current metrics (e-business performance and market share/market size); succinct and evaluative book reviews; an annotated events calendar, searchable by date (up to one year in advance) and by event focus (education, e-business, knowledge management, outsourcing, supply chain, and others); and libraries of Research Reports and White Papers, all available in full text.

TIP: Internet Advertising Information Sources

- *AdResource* offers "Internet Advertising and Promotion Resources." For example, the "Advertising" section provides annotated links to companies involved in "rich media," advertising design, networks, banner exchanges, and brokers and sales representatives. Other tools include a glossary of Internet advertising/e-commerce terms, an affiliate marketing reference guide, a CPM calculator (to calculate an Internet advertising campaign's costs per 1,000 impressions [CPM]), and an e-mail marketing reference guide. Links to current Internet advertising news stories are also provided. Contact: http://adres.internet.com.

- *Interactive Advertising Bureau* is the "only association dedicated to helping online, Interactive broadcasting, e-mail, wireless and Interactive television media companies increase their revenues." Free content in the "Resources and Research" section includes some fairly recent industry statistics and other data from *eMarketer* (described later). Registration (which is free) grants access to historical and recent (about six months old) IAB *Ad Revenue Reports* in full text. The "News" section of the site includes current and archived IAB press releases, which are rich sources of statistical data. Contact: http://www.iab.net/.

- *Nielsen//NetRatings* as NetRatings, Inc. (Nasdaq: NTRT) "provides the industry's global standard for Internet and digital media measurement and analysis." For subscribers, Nielsen/NetRatings furnishes such data as overall Internet traffic information, time spent on site, education/income/household status/profession/age of site visitors, overlap between two sites (i.e., who visits both sites), and much more. For nonsubscribers, the "Press Room" section of the site offers a goldmine of valuable data nuggets by way of its "Monthly Featured Analysis," press releases, and timely "Featured Data" from AdRelevance Analytics, AdRevelance Metrics, and NetView Usage Metrics. Contact: http://www.nielsen-netratings.com/.

***eMarketer*. New York: eMarketer, Inc. ©2003. Online (price varies). Contact:http://www.emarketer.com.**

Although a certain amount of its content is made available at no cost, *eMarketer* is essentially a subscription service that packages and delivers market research on Internet trends and user demographics, compiled from the published reports of more than 800 leading research firms, consultancies, government and nonprofit agencies worldwide. Sources for *eMarketer* range from the private (such as Accenture, Datamonitor, and Forrester Research, to name only three), to the public sector (such as the Federal Communications Commission, the Federal Trade Commission, and the U.S. Department of Commerce). Subscribers have access to the searchable and browsable "eStat Database," which offers more than 20,000 records and 300,000 datapoints on the Internet and e-business, and the "eMarketer Reports," in-depth analyses which typically range in length from 50-300 pages. Reports available as of Spring 2003 included "E-Commerce Trade & B2B Exchanges," "Security Online: Corporate & Consumer Protection," and "Privacy in the Information Age." Nonsubscribers may register with eMarketer to receive free research "nuggets" via e-mail, either weekly or daily. The free *eMarketer Daily* for April 18, 2003, for example, provided full-text (and graphics) articles on "Optimizing Online Ad Spending," "Factors Affecting Online Retail in 2002," and "Why People Aren't Online."

TIP: Additional "Don't-Miss" Sources of Internet/E-Commerce Statistics

* *CyberAtlas* is an exceptionally rich repository of Internet facts and figures, gathered from a wide range of secondary sources, and categorized into "The Big Picture," which includes the "Statistics Toolbox," and "Markets" (Advertising, Retailing, Small Business, and more). For more about CyberAtlas.com, see *Nua Surveys*, below. Contact: http://cyberatlas.internet.com.

- *Internet Economic Indicators* offers "Facts and Figures" on Internet development and users, the "Global Picture" of the same, and links to the "Media," "Government" sites, and "Internet Organizations" that provide major coverage of the Internet and related technology. Contact: http://www.internetindicators.com/index.html.
- *Nua Surveys* provides Internet business and demographic statistics by "Sectors" (advertising, e-commerce, marketing/brands, etc.); "Society" (government/legislation, online communities, privacy, etc.); "Tools" (access devices, e-mail, security tools, etc.); and "Demographics" (children, teenagers, seniors, women, general demographics, and usage patterns). Information is also presented by broad geographic area (e.g., Africa, Asia, Australia/New Zealand, Europe, Middle East, North America, Latin America). On April 15, 2003, a press release on InternetNews.com announced that CyberAtlas.com owner Jupitermedia had purchased Nua.com "for an undisclosed amount," with plans to turn *Nua Surveys* into a section of CyberAtlas.com. Contact: http://www.nua.com/surveys/.

Center for Research in Electronic Commerce. University of Texas at Austin. McCombs School of Business. Austin, TX. ©1994-2003. Online (free). Contact: http://cism.bus.utexas.edu/.

Established in the early 1990s (as the Center for Information Systems Management), the Center for Research in Electronic Commerce, part of the McCombs School of Business at the University of Texas, Austin, is among the premier research organizations in its field. That stature is amply reflected in the richness of the resources available at its site. These include the full texts of articles and working papers, a comprehensive FAQ on electronic commerce, news, and links to related publications and sites. Research reports and working papers are available in such categories as "Wireless and Mobile Commerce," "Business-to-Business (B2B) E-Commerce," "E-Business Value," "Supply Chain Management," and many more.

TIP: A Brief Internet Marketing Reading List

Bayne, Kim M. 2002. *Marketing Without Wires: Targeting Promotions and Advertising to Mobile Device Users.* New York: John Wiley & Sons.

Hanson, Ward. 2000. *Principles of Internet Marketing.* Cincinnati, OH: South-Western College Publishing.

Hofacker, Charles F. 2001. *Internet Marketing*, 3rd ed. New York: John Wiley & Sons.

Kaye, Barbara K., and Norman J. Medoff. 2001. *Just a Click Away: Advertising on the Internet.* Boston, MA: Allyn and Bacon.

Zedd, Robbin Lee, and Brad Aronson. 1999. *Advertising on the Internet.* New York: John Wiley & Sons.

TIP: Web Resources for E-Commerce and the Law

- *Advertising and Marketing on the Internet: Rules of the Road.* 2000. [Washington, DC]: Federal Trade Commission, Bureau of Consumer Protection. Contact: http://www.ftc.gov/bcp/conline/ pubs/buspubs/ruleroad.pdf.
- *Electronic Commerce and Internet Law Resource Center.* ©2002. Seattle, WA: Perkins Coie. Contact: http://www.perkinscoie. com/resource/ecomm/ecomm.htm.

REFERENCES

Caballero, Marjorie J. 1986. "Direct Mail." In *Beacham's Marketing Reference*, edited by Walston Beacham et al. Washington, D.C.: Research Publishing.

Chicago Public Library. 2001. "Chicago Timeline, 1872 Montgomery Ward: First Mail-Order House." <http://www.chipublib.org/004chicago/timeline/mtgmryward. html> (April 15, 2003).

Clark, Philip B. 2001. "Direct Marketers Profit from E-Commerce." *B to B*, no. 21 (November 26): 2 and 25.

DiPasquale, Cara B. 2002. "Direct Marketing Rose 3.6% in '01." *Advertising Age* 73, no. 23 (June 10): 8.

Gale Encyclopedia of E-Commerce. 2002. Farmington Hills, MI: Gale Group. *Hoover's Online.* 2003.

_____. "Montgomery Ward, LLC Historical Profile." <http://www.hoovers.com/ premium/profile/boneyard/2/0,5034,40322,00.html> (April 15, 2003).

_____. "Retail: Non-store Retailing." <http://www.hoovers.com/industry/description/ 0,2205,6390,00.html> (April 15, 2003).

U.S. General Accounting Office. 2002. *U.S. Postal Service: Deteriorating Financial Outlook Increases Need for Transformation: Report to Congressional Requesters.* Washington, DC: The Office.

Chapter 11

International Marketing Sources

Topics

Global Economic and Political Scan
Country-Specific Information
Understanding Culture and Values
Export Environment
Market Research
Advertising and Promotion
Selected U.S. Government Web Site Gateways

Sources

World Economic and Social Survey
World Economic Outlook
Global Competitiveness Report
Political Risk Yearbook
World Factbook
Country Study Series
Country Report (EIU)
Country Watch
CultureGrams
Exporters' Encyclopedia
Export Sales and Marketing Manual
Country Commercial Guides
Country Reports on Economic Policy and Trade Practices
Market Research Reports (U.S. International Trade Administration)

[Haworth co-indexing entry note]: "International Marketing Sources." Diamond, Wendy, and Michael R. Oppenheim. Co-published simultaneously in *Journal of Business & Finance Librarianship* (The Haworth Information Press, an imprint of The Haworth Press, Inc.) Vol. 9, No. 4, 2004, pp. 237-265; and: *Marketing Information: A Strategic Guide for Business and Finance Libraries* (Wendy Diamond, and Michael R. Oppenheim) The Haworth Information Press, an imprint of The Haworth Press, Inc., 2004, pp. 237-265. Single or multiple copies of this article are available for a fee from The Haworth Document Delivery Service [1-800-HAWORTH, 9:00 a.m. - 5:00 p.m. (EST). E-mail address: docdelivery@haworthpress.com].

http://www.haworthpress.com/web/JBFL
© 2004 by The Haworth Press, Inc. All rights reserved.
Digital Object Identifier: 10.1300/J109v09n04_03

Euromonitor International
WARC's *Pocket Books*
International Media Guides
Advertising Red Books–International Advertisers and Agencies
World Advertiser and Agency Database
World Advertising Trends
International Advertising and Marketing Information Sources
STAT-USA: *Globus/National Trade Data Bank*
USA Trade Online
U.S. Government Export Portal (Export.gov)
Export Advantage

Although the world may not be exactly a global village, it is most certainly a global shopping center. As the world grows smaller in time and space, it is essential to have a strategy for reaching the vast market beyond the United States.

Although other chapters in this book may include sources that include some section or aspect dealing with international business, this chapter focuses on fundamental information tools specifically directed toward exporting overseas. It does not cover other aspects of international business, such as importing, financing, transfer pricing, counter trade, taxation, etc. Sources are discussed in the same basic sequence as an international marketing plan is developed: scanning a global overview to select a target country; surveying information about the selected country; searching exporting and trade guides; and investigating market research tools for information on distribution channels, product pricing, advertising, retail spending, and customer segmentation. The chapter concludes with a selection of government Web sites that cover the full span of international marketing topics.

The fundamental "Four Ps of Marketing" (product, price, promotion, place) can be particularly challenging to define and investigate in the international environment, and their relative priority can be quite different from that of a domestic marketing plan. The element of "place" becomes primary; therefore the first decision–where to market the product–requires a scan of worldwide economic and political trends. The sources for a comprehensive overview of global issues range from such international agencies as the International Monetary Fund (IMF) and the United Nations (UN) to high-end private publishers, such as the Economist Intelligence Unit (EIU) and Euromonitor International.

The next step is to gain in-depth understanding of the target country's geographical, political, and population factors. Promoting a product requires a comprehensive economic, social and cultural understanding of the country, including government system, family patterns, religion and ethnicity, housing and health standards, literacy and media penetration, etc. Depending on the product, the marketer might also want to understand values and belief systems which impact purchasing patterns, cuisine, or communication styles.

Options abound for finding such descriptive information about countries. Many of the sources which provide global overviews and comparative data are also useful for information about specific countries; sometimes it will be possible to find both global and country-specific data in a single source. Note that in the "Global Scan" section we focus on sources for economic and political information; cultural and social factors are emphasized in the "Country Specific" and "Understanding Culture and Values" sections.

This step is followed by the "nitty-gritty" technical investigation of trade regulations, standards, business practices, and the other particulars that need to be dealt with when actually bringing a product into a foreign country. Many exporter's guides are available from the U.S. government; because they often provide a one-stop source of information for economic profiles, country descriptions, trade regulations, and market research, they are highlighted in a separate section. There are also private publishers that offer legal and documentation detail on customs, shipping requirements, tariffs, distribution channels, packaging and labeling, and even pricing, consumer segmentation, advertising, and other marketing issues.

Market research reports, industry analyses, and advertising information are just as necessary to the development of an international marketing plan as they are for domestic marketing. As mentioned previously, one of the best sources for this type of information is the U.S. government. Although not always free, the government's products are generally more accessible and inexpensive than those of private market research publishers. Except for specialized private market research publishers (like Euromonitor), these government market research reports provide the most detailed information on industry environment, competitive products, and the overall outlook for particular markets (such as "toys in Denmark" or "snack food in Argentina").

GLOBAL ECONOMIC AND POLITICAL SCAN

Sometimes the selection of an appropriate foreign market target is obvious due to geography, or language, or an invitation to bid. But frequently, the possibilities for selection of a target country or region are more open. In selecting the best opportunities, it is helpful to obtain an overview of the global picture. The following sources tackle the fundamental issue of how best to scan for general trends, macroeconomic statistics, and the kind of political climate required to determine the most favorable economic, political, social, and cultural environments in which to launch a product or service.

Various criteria may be used to identify foreign markets, to assess relative openness to foreign trade, to analyze an individual country's growth, and to evaluate the economic and political climate for a product. The marketer might prefer the fastest growing economy, or perhaps the country with the largest population. In any case, a comparative review provides the background, and often the specifics, needed to make marketing decisions.

***World Economic and Social Survey*. New York: United Nations. Department of Economic and Social Affairs. Annual. Print $10. Contact: http://www.un.org/esa/analysis/wess/.**

This annual report provides economic overviews which can help sort out the potential for growth in major regions of the world. It is the United Nations (UN) Secretariat's assessment of global economic and regional trends and issues. Some issues focus on specific topics (such as "A Globalizing World: Risks, Vulnerability and Opportunity" in 2001 and "Escaping the Poverty Trap" in 2000); in 2002 and 2003, the reports were entitled "World Economic Situation and Prospects." Each report also consistently includes regular features and statistics that are essential for analyzing the world economic situation. There is discussion of individual regions and countries, focusing on issues such as income, output, investment, and domestic demand. The macroeconomic data are succinctly explained, accessible to the business person not trained in the study of economics. Although individual countries are not given a focused treatment, many are mentioned specifically in the regional discussion. Likewise, there is discussion of the international trade and finance. These can be used by the marketer to assess areas where market entry is more or less difficult, or where there may be pent-up demand for imported products.

***World Economic Outlook*. Washington, DC: International Monetary Fund. Annual. Print $49. Online (free). Contact: http://www.imf.org/external/pubind.htm.**

The *World Economic Outlook* constitutes the "main instrument of the [International Monetary Fund's] global surveillance activities" (IMF

2002) and is part of its series, "World Economic and Financial Surveys." This longstanding annual print publication, now handily available in PDF on the Web, analyzes and projects economic developments at the global level, in individual countries, and in major country groups. Economic policies, economic developments, and future trends are emphasized.

Users should be aware that, because of the IMF's particular focus on emerging economies and countries in developing regions of the world, this source may not be as useful for North America and Europe as it is for Asia, Africa, and South America. Nonetheless, it is worthwhile for developed economies because those are usually discussed as a benchmark of global trends and comparisons. For instance, the first chapter of the 2002 edition discusses the North American, European, and Japanese economies in sections called "Economic Prospects and Policy Issues," "North America: A Strengthening Recovery," "Japan: Significant Challenges Remain," and "How Will the Recovery in Europe Compare with that in the United States?" Throughout, the regional discussions highlight trends in individual countries which can help the marketer make an informed decision.

The marketer can also make good use of the wealth of statistical data available on 183 member countries. The statistical appendix is arranged according to types of economies, so that "advanced economies" are grouped together, as are "developing economies" and "economies in transition." These groupings make it easy for the marketer to identify and compare likely target markets. Although much of the data for balance of payments, savings rates, and debt service are geared to the needs of economists, marketers will also find useful data. For example, there are various tables covering consumer price indexes, unemployment, and economic growth. The most useful information is probably in the narrative essays preceding the statistical appendix, which describe worldwide trends for advanced, developing, and transitional economies.

The IMF also publishes another series entitled "IMF Country Reports," available in PDF from the same Web site, which is discussed later under "Country-Specific Information."

***Global Competitiveness Report*. Geneva, Switzerland: World Economic Forum. Distributed by Oxford University Press. Annual. Print with CD-ROM $65. Contact: http://www.oup-usa.com/isbn/ 019521837X.html.**

Published since 1979, the *Global Competitiveness Report* is a collection of numeric indexes that rank 75 countries according to their capacity for economic growth over a period of time. This report offers the marketer an excellent measure of the comparative potential of individual countries by condensing essential marketing factors (such as openness to international trade, quality of infrastructure, quality of technology, labor market flexibility, government surplus/deficit, and regulation) into a single numeric index. Each chapter contains an introductory essay explaining the significance of each measure (e.g., technological advancement, innovative capacity, environmental regulation) as well as the ranking tables themselves. Although there is little or no narrative discussion of individual countries, each country profile includes a "national competitiveness balance sheet" which effectively summarizes key data. The marketer seeking more detailed information on international competitiveness should investigate the more expensive and extensive publications offered by the Institute of Management Development in Lausanne, Switzerland. Specifically, its *World Competitiveness Report* provides extensive narrative discussion and *World Competitiveness Yearbook* provides succinct statistical profiles in print or CD-ROM format.

Political Risk Yearbook. Syracuse, NY: PRS Group Inc. Annual. Print $2,600. CD-ROM $2600. Online (price varies). (Academic discounts are available.) Contact: http://www.prsgroup.com.

Political risk assessment is an essential step in evaluating access and potential problems in the international marketplace. The *Political Risk Yearbook* provides this information in an annual volume covering over 100 countries organized by regional groupings. Published in eight regional volumes, it can be purchased either as a set or as individual volumes. The publisher, PRS Group, specializes in the impact of political factors on the international business climate, and claims to supply information to over 80% of the world's top corporations as ranked by *Fortune* magazine (PRS Group Inc. 2002). It produces many publications in a range of prices and specialization, some suitable for academic libraries (at reduced prices) and others geared to the corporate market. Selected portions of the dataset are also available free at the Web site *Country Data* (http://www.countrydata.com).

Designed for the busy executive, the *Yearbook* presents each country report in a format that is easy to scan and absorb. Entries are consistently organized and include these sections: highlights, comments, analysis, forecast scenarios, political framework, economic policies and restrictions, trade and transfer policies, and social, historical and geographic background. Although most other general economic and social profiles discuss basic political structure and recent political events, this is the only service that provides short- and long-term forecasting for different scenarios based on possible regime and policy changes.

COUNTRY-SPECIFIC INFORMATION

The first step in selling a product or service overseas is learning about the environment. Background about the society and culture is needed, as well as facts and figures. Because so many different cultural factors impact the appeal and marketability of products, the marketer needs to look at such issues as literacy and education rates, technological development and infrastructure, the health care system, religions, and family patterns.

There are many options available at a wide range of levels and costs for any kind of country-specific information. There is a high degree of variability in the amount of information available for any given country, even within the same source: there might be excellent in-depth coverage for some countries and areas, but not for others. In many cases the best sources, that is, the most detailed and up-to-date, are expensive and are less likely to be available in public libraries or general university library collections. On the other hand, a tremendous amount of fundamental country information is widely available from governmental and non-governmental agency sources, but it may not be as well-presented, targeted, or specific as the more costly privately published sources. Many of these excellent sites are described later in this chapter in "Selected U.S. Government Gateways."

When reviewing country information sources, the marketer should focus on social and economic factors for an indication of demand. Mike Dwyer, an economist with the U.S. Department of Agriculture, advises:

> In gauging foreign demand, don't rely on per capita income numbers alone . . . A better indicator of demand, especially for high-value products, is the number of middle-class households and how fast they are expanding. This information is substantially harder to uncover than per capita income but it is a more insightful indicator of a market's export potential. (Dwyer 2001, 12)

Though it may be difficult to find an exact measurement for middle-class households, especially considering the different ways they might be defined, many of the sources listed here will prove useful. For instance, the CIA *World Factbook* gives a percentage of "population below poverty line." In addition, Euromonitor's many publications, which are discussed in the "Market Research" section of this chapter, offer measurements for "personal disposable income" which can be an indicator of middle class consumers.

World Factbook. Washington, DC: U.S. Central Intelligence Agency. Annual. Print $92. Online (free). Contact: http://www.odci.gov/cia/publications/factbook/index.html.

The CIA *World Factbook* is one of the most useful and easily accessed compendia of descriptive country information. It is prepared annually for the use of U.S. government officials, and its coverage, content, and style are designed to meet those particular needs. As well as fulfilling this function of providing factual background material from which other intelligence work flows, it also meets the needs of travelers, students, foreign investors, and marketers. It has been published and made available to the public in its current form since 1975.

In a brief, succinct, and easy-to-read format, the *Factbook* covers a prodigious amount of material about individual countries, arranged in simple alphabetic order. Each country's listing is organized with standard headings (Geography, People, Government, Economy, Environment, Transportation, Communications, etc.). Certain sections are of particular interest to the marketer. For example, when evaluating potential customer demand for a product, the entry in the "People" heading under "Age Structure" provides the population distribution according to age and gender, which helps determine whether a particular product would find a ready market. In the "Economy" heading, under "Household Income or Consumption," the marketer will find a figure representing data from household surveys, if available. This may be the only consumption data available for some countries. In addition, the figure that measures the percentage of "Population Below Poverty Line" indicates likely demand at the middle and upper ends of the income spectrum. Though fairly rudimentary, these figures can help the marketer select a country with adequate representation of population at the desired ranges of income and consumption.

Similarly, the section on "Communications," which covers media and other means of exchanging information, describes telephone, radio, television, and Internet services. Obviously, this information is essential for assessing promotion and advertising potential. And, under the

"Transportation" heading, the marketer can determine whether there is sufficient infrastructure to distribute a product. Additional headings cover descriptions of climate, terrain, natural hazards, language, ethnicity and religion. Thus, in little more than two or three pages, the CIA *World Factbook* provides the essential starting point for many international marketing projects.

To build up a more detailed country profile, there are other sources. In fact, there are so many, each with its own advantages, that it is worthwhile to ask a reference librarian at a local public or academic library for guidance. For instance, the *Worldmark Encyclopedia of the Nations* (Farmington Hills, MI: Gale Group; 10th edition, print) provides informative profiles of individual countries along with some special features. It includes extensive discussions of transportation, industry, energy and power, and science and technology sectors, which give important indications about market access and level of infrastructure in a country. For evaluating culture and literacy, there are descriptive profiles under such headings as social development, housing, education, libraries and museums, media, and recreation. Specific to the export marketing process, there is information on foreign trade and its role in the economy, as well as on customs and duties. Perhaps the most useful section for the marketer is the section on "domestic trade," which includes beneficial discussion of retailing, wholesaling, distribution channels, and stores. In the Philippines, for example, it is useful to know that that the island geography requires regional distribution centers, and that small stores typify retail trade in an economy where cash remains the primary means of commerce. The usual hours of trade are given, along with the fact that most advertising is local. Because this encyclopedia is not published annually, other more up-to-date sources should be consulted.

***Country Study Series (Area Handbook Program).* Washington, DC: Government Printing Office. Print (price varies). Online (free). Contact: http://lcweb2.loc.gov/frd/cs/cshome.html.**

The Web site contains online versions of hardcopy books produced by the Library of Congress for the U.S. Department of the Army. These extensive, detailed descriptions of countries are an excellent resource, but unfortunately they are not available in current editions for all countries. Because the primary purpose of the original program was to provide basic information on lesser-known (to Americans) regions and countries, the series does not include countries such as Canada, the United Kingdom, France, and other western nations. In addition, because the reports available on the Web were written between 1988 and

1998, they are not useful for current economic, political, and social developments. Despite these drawbacks, the *Country Studies/Area Handbooks* remain a good tool for the marketer because they interweave cultural factors into the discussion of politics, economics, and history. For instance, the report on Haiti discusses the increasing use of Creole and English rather than traditional French in the mass media and business settings, giving some useful clues for advertising effectiveness.

Country Report. London: Economist Intelligence Unit (EIU). Quarterly or continuous updates. Print \$455/per country. Online \$455/per country. (Single issues are also available for \$215.) Contact: http:// store.eiu.com.

For each of nearly 200 countries, the *Country Report* series analyzes political and economic developments. These are detailed, up-to-date reports on individual countries that offer extensive coverage of national, regional, and global events and their potential impact on business. The Economist Intelligence Unit (EIU) is probably the premier publisher of country analysis data. Their suite of products includes the *Country Profile* series (analyzes political, infrastructure, and economic trends over a longer term), the *Country Forecast* series (focuses on projections and future scenarios), and *Country ViewsWire* (a daily online service which includes coverage of social and cultural factors). Although the data can be used for performing the type of global scan described earlier, it is an expensive proposition. To cover the whole world one must purchase a subscription to reports for each country. Nonetheless, they are extremely valuable for the planning stage after a target country has been identified, when current, specific information is needed.

Each issue in the quarterly *Country Report* series contains approximately 40 pages of narrative and statistics for all covered countries. The narrative analysis offers discussion of recent trends and two-year forecasts of the political outlook, economic outlook, fiscal and monetary policy, and considerable assessment of the trends for inflation, growth, exchange rates, etc. The statistical tables are quarterly and annual, including approximately 150 data elements; 117 countries are covered in monthly updates to the time series.

The series is offered in two formats, both of which are standardized to make it easy to locate information and compare countries. The print subscription offers quarterly main reports and includes the "Country Profile," an annual reference compendium. The online format offers Internet delivery in quarterly reports, plus eight additional updates. One benefit of the online subscription is continuous updating, including e-mail alerts.

Country Watch: Website to the World. CountryWatch.com. Houston, TX. ©2003. Online (price varies). Contact: http://www. countrywatch.com.

Country Watch is a useful one-stop shop for many kinds of background information needed for international marketing. Geared to the academic market of schools, universities, and libraries, it contains descriptions of social, geographical, infrastructure, and governmental institutions along with up-to-date economic and political developments. The site is easy to use, and different amounts of information are available at different price levels.

At the free level, the searcher has access to a limited amount of country-specific information which is mostly compiled from government and public sources, such as basic descriptive statistics, political history, environmental issues, and foreign investment climate. For paid subscribers, there is more detailed information in the following categories: People & History, Geography, Economy, Agriculture, Energy, Metals, and Environment. Using Argentina as an example, this level of information describes the Spanish, Italian and Latin American heritage of the people and their religious orientation. In addition, one can learn that Argentina's population growth rate is the slowest in Latin America, one-third of the population lives in one major metropolitan area, and the rate of schooling and literacy is very high.

The marketer will also focus on the "Economy" section, which covers macroeconomic conditions and global ranking tables for trade, population, technology, and development. This analysis is still not as in-depth, specific, and detailed as that found in the EIU's *Country Reports* and related products. Rather, marketers must draw their own conclusions about the potential impact of macroeconomic conditions such as monetary policy, inflation, employment rates, and so on. It is useful to keep in mind that the narrative sections are credited to *CountryWatch.com*'s own analysts, using widely available sources such as the World Bank and the IMF and some proprietary sources (e.g., PRS Group's political risk measures). The statistical sections are primarily credited to standard sources as well, such as CIA *World Factbook*, IMF *International Financial Statistics*, *World Bank Development Data*, IMF *World Outlook*, and the UN *Monthly Bulletin of Statistics*. Thus, much of *CountryWatch*'s information is readily available from public and governmental sources, though there is a major benefit in the compilation and convenient access.

UNDERSTANDING CULTURE AND VALUES

Although most of the sources already discussed contain some information on history and culture along with facts and descriptions, they do not generally cover customs, manners, attitudes, and lifestyle, topics essential to the marketing process. For this type of qualitative information, look to the following sources.

***CultureGrams*. Lindon, UT: Axiom Press. Annual. Print with CD-ROM $130. Online (price varies). (Single country reports can be downloaded for $4 each.) Contact: http://www.culturegrams.com.**

CultureGrams offers brief reports describing the customs and lifestyles of 177 individual countries. Each four-page country report, written by natives or expatriates, presents a view of the manners and routines of daily life, as well as its general political and economic environment. Although primarily designed to meet educational needs, it is an easy-to-use, comprehensive resource for businesspeople, travelers, and anyone else who needs to understand the cultural aspects of other societies. Published in print since 1974, the title is updated annually and available in a variety of formats. Print may be selected in bound or loose-leaf editions. A CD-ROM version is available, and a site license can be arranged for online access. There are several possible packages, including individual country reports or regional sets.

Each report begins with an excellent general discussion of "The People," which incorporates language, religion, general attitudes, and personal appearance. Here one might learn, for example, that Hungarians have a sense of pride in their democratic and independent heritage, but are also somewhat pessimistic and cynical in their humor. Education is highly valued, professionals are well-respected, and women pay attention to appearance and enjoy wearing stylish clothing. In the section on "Customs and Courtesies," greeting, visiting, and eating habits are discussed, such the time of day the main daily meal is eaten. In the "Lifestyle" section, there is even more useful information for the marketer, including discussions of recreation and leisure, family size, working women, and whether unmarried adult children live with their parents. The "Commerce" and "Transportation and Communication" sections also include important information for marketing purposes, such as the presence of supermarkets, whether there is a national TV or radio channel, and the relative importance of regional media. Any or all of these factors could impact the marketing plan of a wide array of consumer products, from juice drinks to cosmetics to toys.

There are other sources which provide similar information about cultural norms and customs. One excellent choice is *Kiss, Bow, or Shake Hands: How to Do Business in Sixty Countries* by Terri Morrison, Wayne A. Conaway, and George A. Borden (Holbrook, MA: Bob Adams Inc., 1994, print). Here the emphasis is on customs that impact business, focusing on such aspects as negotiation styles and information processing. These are the types of factors that might influence the design of promotional materials or packaging. "Expanded" (additional content for 40 countries) and "special" editions (additional content for 65 countries) are available via the Web at http://www.getcustoms.com/database.html. These are updated at least twice yearly with material from the authors' other articles and books, including their *Dun & Bradstreet's Guide to Doing Business Around the World*. Aimed at the corporate market, the site-licensed products offer unlimited usage, downloading, and printing capacity.

Another useful book in this category is *Do's and Taboo's Around the World*, by Roger E. Axtell (New York, NY: John Wiley, 3rd ed, 1993, print). Chapters cover such topics as etiquette, body language, gift-giving, and idioms for individual countries and regions. The emphasis here is on protocol, customs, manners and gestures, to enable the marketer to avoid costly *faux pas* or missteps in package design, advertising images, or brand names.

TIP: ExecutivePlanet.com

A free Web site called *ExecutivePlanet.com* provides guides to business etiquette and culture in 35 countries that are among the U.S. top trading partners. Gift-giving, negotiating tactics, business entertaining, dress, and cross-cultural communication are among the business protocol topics that are treated. Contact: http://www.executiveplanet.com/community/default.asp.

EXPORT ENVIRONMENT

After the economic, social, and cultural setting for a product has been assessed, the next step is to investigate the rules and regulations for bringing the actual product into the selected country. The marketer must realize that importing any product into a foreign country is essentially an international event, and thus governments become involved with tariffs, regulations, and treaties. Labeling and packaging requirements vary widely across the world. Many products, such as food and cosmetics, are regulated but every country has different requirements. Even for those products which are not directly regulated, labeling, packaging, and documentation requirements will vary. It is often easier to utilize the services of a customs agent or broker, and sources are needed to locate reputable services.

***Exporters' Encyclopedia*. New York: Dun & Bradstreet International. Annual with updates. Print $568. Contact: http://www.dnb.com.**

The *Exporters' Encyclopedia* is a comprehensive compilation of the customs, tariffs, shipping, documentation, and packaging regulations for the most "nuts-and-bolts" aspects of an international marketing project. In addition, this excellent resource also provides general information about 200 individual countries, such as advertising media, business etiquette, and basic economic statistics. Dun & Bradstreet, the publisher, has been one of the world's leading sources of business information for over 160 years, offering a range of worldwide company information and other publications.

The book opens with a section entitled "The Export Order" which provides an extensive outline of the entire export process from solicitation to shipping, including a checklist of documents used in international trade, samples of documents, and a glossary. There are descriptions of the particulars that should be included in international correspondence, pricing and quotations, packing lists, bills of lading, certificates of origin, dock receipts, etc. Also discussed are technicalities of packaging and shipping methods, liability and insurance, and most importantly, receiving payment.

Section II, "Export Markets," is the largest section of the book, with extensive entries devoted to individual countries listed in alphabetical order. Each country listing is divided into the following sections: Country Profile, Communications, Key Contacts, Trade Regulations, Documentation, Marketing Data, Transportation, and Business Travel. The brief country profile includes population and demographics, language, time zone, currency, type of legal system, and weight and measures. Practical details of communications are covered, including dialing codes, mail regulations, and availability of service. The list of key contacts in embassies and trade associations both in the U.S. and the profile

country can be used effectively to confirm the viability of trading partners and for help in selecting a customs agent. There is detailed explica-
tion of "Trade Regulations" and "Documentation." Outlined under
these headings are the requirements regarding licensing, payment conditions, customs authorities, taxes, and miscellaneous duties, as well as
the documentation needed for various inspections and declarations. Under the heading "Marketing Data," there are discussions of laws, regulations, and rules for principal-agency relations, specialized rules of
government procurement (such as the "Anti-Mafia Certification" required by Italian legislation), consumer protection, product standards,
labeling and packaging requirements, and intellectual property rights.
Also included is a brief discussion of advertising, which covers such basic information as major TV channels and newspapers, the role of direct
marketing and mail order, restrictions regarding cash discounts, and advertising bans that may apply on special products such as tobacco.

The "Export Know-How" section covers more generalized export information: here are legal requirements and accepted commercial practice as outlined and preferred by the U.S. government, various treaty
agreements, and other companies. For example, there are discussions of
the Foreign Corrupt Practices Act, marking of origin for exported
goods, freight claims, letters of credit, the United Nations Convention
for the International Sale of Goods, U.S. export controls on software,
packing for export, and so on. The *Encyclopedia* contains an extensive
list of information sources and services, ranging from government as-
sistance to exporters to treaty organizations. Finally, there is a section
on "Transportation Data/Services" with U.S. ports, U.S. foreign trade
zones, and U.S. Customs Service Points of Entry. As a printed reference
book, it is designed for ease of use for quick-look-ups and extensive
study. It is kept up-to-date between annual editions by twice-monthly
supplements provided with sticky "red dots" that are interfiled in order
to alert the user to new material.

Some of the information available in *Exporters' Encyclopedia* can be
gathered using various U.S. government Web sites such as Tradenet.
gov and Export.gov, but it is convenient to have it compiled in a single
volume. There are also some similar commercial publications available,
but they are specialized, mostly legal tools. For instance, BNA (http://
www.bna.com), a legal publisher, produces *International Trade Reporter* and *Export Reference Library*, which are available in print,
CD-ROM or Internet. EIU (http://store.eiu.com), the market research
publisher, produces *Investing, Licensing and Trading Conditions*. Both

are more detailed but more expensive than Dun & Bradstreet's *Exporter's Encyclopedia*, which remains one of the most effective sources of its kind.

TIP: Export Information and Glossary from Dun & Bradstreet, Inc.

The International Business section of the Dun & Bradstreet Web page includes the "export decision" articles and "glossary" published in the *Exporter's Encyclopedia.* Contact: http://www.dnb.com/US/communities/intlbusiness/index.html?link=intlbusiness.

Export Sales and Marketing Manual. **John R. Jagoe. Minneapolis, MN: Export Institute USA. 2002. Print, CD-ROM, or online ($295). Print and CD-ROM ($395). 640 pages. Contact: http://www.exportinstitute.com.**

The Export Institute USA, as its name implies, specializes in providing information and consulting services to exporters, and also includes universities, trade associations, and government agencies among its clients. The *Export Sales and Marketing Manual*, written by the director of the Institute, covers the practical aspects of the export process, including chapters on identifying potential export markets, locating sales representatives, licensing and trade restrictions, pricing, export agency and distributor agreements, working with foreign freight forwarders, and payment options. The text is supported by tables, figures, charts, checklists, appendices, and a lengthy glossary.

Country Commercial Guides. **U.S. Department of State. Annual. Online. Contact: http://www.export.gov (free) or http://www.tradenet.gov (free) or http://www.usatrade.gov/website/ccg.nsf/ccghomepage?openform (free) or http://www.stat-usa.gov/ (by subscription).**

The *Country Commercial Guides* (CCGs) are lengthy reports that present an overview of a country's commercial environment, combining economic, political, business, and market analysis. Available online in PDF or HTML format, they are prepared annually by U.S. embassies with the participation of several other U.S. government agencies. CCGs are distributed by the Department of Commerce's International Trade Administration through many U.S. government Web sites, such as

Tradenet.gov, Export.gov, and Stat-USA: Globus/NTDB. They are an indispensable tool for the export market researcher because they cover a comprehensive range of essential topics specific to the marketing process in over 120 countries.

Each CCG focuses on one country and follows a consistent format. The 2002 chapter topics include economic trends, political environment, marketing U.S. products and services, leading sectors for U.S. exports, market research, trade regulations, investment climate, business travel, U.S. and country contacts, and more. Even though these guides include economic and political analysis found in other sources, the focus is on key marketing concerns.

For instance, taking the 2002 Argentina *Country Commercial Guide* as an example, the reader is informed in the "Political Environment" section that some U.S. companies have been adversely affected by unfair application of rules and regulations, although the overall climate encourages U.S. investment. In the same report, the section on "Marketing U.S. Products and Services" describes those factors that make Argentina different from other Latin American cultures, such as the large middle class and strong European heritage. In addition, it is noted that the Argentine version of Spanish is unusual in its many colloquialisms, and the marketer is advised to have all packaging, ads, and labels read by a native translator. The *Country Commercial Guides* are intended to give a general picture of the commercial environment; as such, they do not focus on single products or industries. Nonetheless, there is a great deal of useful information targeted to market analysis, such as customer segmentation and distribution channels. In the Argentina *Guide*, the report explains the differences between agents and distributors and when it is more advantageous to utilize one or the other in the Argentine environment. There is discussion of the retail network, the relative mix of mass-merchandisers versus traditional mom-and-pop stores, and which products are likely to be sold in each type.

Because they are free and provide so much useful information, the *Country Commercial Guides* should not be overlooked by anyone marketing products or services overseas.

TIP: *Country Commercial Guides*

A permanent electronic archive of *Country Commercial Guides* released before January 2001 is available at http://www.state.gov/www/about_state/business/com_guides/index.html.

***Country Reports on Economic Policy and Trade Practices*. U.S. Department of State. Annual. Online (Free). Contact: http://www. state.gov/business/.**

Prepared by the Department of State, the *Country Reports on Economic Policy and Trade Practices* go beyond marketing to focus on policy aspects of international trade. They provide a comparative analysis of economic policies and trade practices in individual countries. Opening with tables of economic statistics, each report includes sections on economic policy, exchange rates, debt management, and economic structure. These general issues are followed by a discussion of "significant barriers to U.S. Exports" in that particular country. For instance, in the 2002 report on South Korea, the marketer discovers that, although Korea's tariffs are modest, there is a significant impact from non-trade barriers such as non-transparent regulatory practices. Furthermore, for some toiletry and cosmetic products, the issue of testing is relevant, and the basic requirements are succinctly outlined. Other specifics are also noted: for instance, the Korean government requires that local films be shown in cinemas for a minimum number of days per year. A discussion of intellectual property and the protections afforded are also included, and the discussion of workers' rights and protections may be important for those involved in manufacturing.

TIP: *Country Reports on Economic Policy and Trade Practices*

A permanent electronic archive of *Country Reports on Economic Policy and Trade Practices* released prior to January 20, 2001 is available at http://www.state.gov/www/issues/economic/trade_reports.

MARKET RESEARCH

After developing a profile for the *place* aspect of the international marketing plan, including assessment of the economic, political, social, cultural, and commercial environments, the next step is the market research component. The issues of *product, pricing,* and *promotion* now become paramount and, to a marketer, these concerns may be more familiar. However, in terms of the sources available, there is both good news and bad news. First the bad news: consumer spending data, advertising rates, market share, and prices of competitors' products are not readily available for many foreign countries. Furthermore, the most consistently published sources are expensive, specialized tools designed for corporate and other research-level analysts. On the other hand, the good news is that the federal government also publishes extensive market research reports which *may* contain some of this information, although these governmental reports will not cover all products and industries in all countries.

Market Research Reports. U.S. International Trade Administration. Irregular. Online. Contact: http://www.export.gov (free) or http://www.tradenet.gov (free) or http://www.stat-usa.gov/ (by subscription).

The International Trade Administration produces various types of market research reports which are available at several Web sites. These reports are of two basic types: (1) market research by product and/or country, and (2) analyses of industry sectors. In general, the search interfaces and even the titles may vary. Nonetheless, the content of the reports is the same and an understanding of the underlying structure is helpful.

The market research reports by product or country are variously known as *International Market Insight* (IMI) reports and *Best Market Reports (BMR)*. These focus on market conditions in individual countries. The reports issued in the IMI series focus on specific products in specific countries. For instance, "The Sporting Goods Market in Belgium," dated January 3, 2000, is a six-page report offering an overview of general market characteristics. In addition to the fact that Belgians generally spend less than other Europeans in this product category, the discussion covers characteristics of major chain stores, including an extensive list of specific stores and the names of their buyers. Some reports in this series also contain statistics on purchasing patterns, market share, and customer demographics.

The *BMR* series provides comparative analysis and "snapshots of a given market segment." As part of their regular reporting, U.S. embassy personnel are required to assess the best market segment for U.S. exports in their particular country. Incorporated into longer reports like the *Country Commercial Guides*, these "best market" sections are later compiled along with those of other countries into the "Best Market Reports." Thus, the *BMR* on "Apparel," dated November 15, 1999, covers the clothing industry in six countries, with comparative data tables and brief narrative assessments of each.

Another type of industry-specific market analysis is provided in the *Industry Sector Analyses* (ISAs). These provide research about the major trading partners of the U.S. For example, the report entitled "Pet Product Market in France" (January 2, 2001) is 29 pages and contains extensive coverage of competitive issues such as price, distribution, domestic production, the relative position of U.S. and other countries' importers, customer tastes and buying habits, etc. Thus, the marketer can discover that the French consumer is price sensitive, has a preference for items with an amusing and funny character, and that the market for pet care products is expected to grow rapidly in the near future.

All of these various types of market research reports are arranged by country and by product, and the researcher can search or browse by sectors and countries. Even if the particular product is not given full treatment, it is worthwhile to consult reports about related products or industries. Some of the information about distribution channels, advertising, packaging, or pricing may be applicable for more than one product or service.

TIP: *Industry Canada*'s "Create Your Own Customized Market Reports"

Industry Canada provides an excellent interactive search interface for the U.S. Department of Commerce market reports. It is found under "Trade and Investment" at their Web site (http://strategis.ic.gc.ca). Contact: http://strategis.ic.gc.ca/SSG/bi18351e.html.

Included in the search are the following documents:

- *Market Research Reports* (multiple series)
- *Country Commercial Guides*
- *International Business Practices*
- *CIA World Factbook*

Euromonitor International. London. Contact: http://www.euro monitor.com.

Founded in 1972, Euromonitor is one of the largest publishers of international marketing data and analysis in the English language. Issued in numerous databases, online services, printed reference tools, and market research reports, Euromonitor's products offer the marketer information for all aspects of an international marketing research project, from fundamental economic statistics and country profiles to detailed consumer expenditure data for individual demographic groups in over 200 countries. This information is compiled from public sources such as national statistical offices, private sources such as industry and trade associations, and from Euromonitor's own primary research.

As one would expect, access to this data is not inexpensive. However, the options for purchase are diverse both in format and coverage. For instance, *World Marketing Data and Statistics* is a CD-ROM database of country information that allows users to construct detailed market profiles based on demographic and economic characteristics. With data manipulation functionalities such as charting, graphing, and spreadsheet display, it answers questions that help determine which country to select for marketing a specific product, such as "Which European country has the highest average monthly earnings?" (Denmark) and "How many microwave ovens were sold there in 1999?" (about 83,000 units).

The equivalent coverage of this database is available in print in *International Marketing Data and Statistics* (covering 161 non-European countries) and *European Marketing Data and Statistics*. With these two print titles, a marketer has handy, authoritative access to a wide range of social, economic, and lifestyle data for nearly all countries in the world. (These are aggregated electronically in the Web-based *Global Market Information Database*, described below.)

These volumes provide data on large and small countries, presented in clear spreadsheet-style tables and organized in separate sections (e.g., demographic trends and forecasts, consumer expenditure patterns, advertising patterns and media access, retail distribution). The tables of contents make it easy to locate a relevant topic or table, and sources are always noted. Although in some cases there are limited data for smaller countries, Euromonitor may be the sole source of whatever information may be available. For instance, the inclusion of data on type and number of retail outlets can be hard to obtain from other publications.

These two titles are also useful for determining the availability of middle class households in specific countries, as discussed earlier in this chapter under "Country-Specific Information." Under "Income and Earnings," there are tables expressing "personal disposable income," "average monthly earnings" and "gross personal income." In addition, data on key agricultural and industrial sectors are included, so marketers can assess infrastructure and technological support. An additional benefit is that the coverage includes long time series, which allows comparison and accuracy of datasets for analysis and forecasting. Note that the data concerning monetary value are generally reported in national currencies, except in some cases where originally reported in U.S. dollars.

Euromonitor also has two other print titles that are useful for analyzing consumer markets worldwide. *World Consumer Income and Expenditure Patterns* (3rd edition, 2002) provides detailed breakdown of consumer spending for 71 countries and worldwide, plus data on income and earnings. It contains 10 years of historical data. The *World Consumer Lifestyles Databook* (1st edition, 2002) is the first statistical book to focus on worldwide coverage for consumer preferences, activities, and interests, a key component in target marketing and customer segmentation.

For more extensive coverage, Euromonitor offers an integrated Web site with data from all of their business reference books and electronic datasets, including their many market research reports. Updated on a continual basis, the *Global Market Information Database (GMID)* is a subscription online service that provides a one-stop source of analysis and data on countries, markets, industries, products, and companies. Combining secondary and primary research, market data are developed by Euromonitor's analysts, drawing on official and semi-official sources and interviews with key manufacturers, retailers and wholesalers in each country covered.

The *GMID* offers information in the following modules: Country Data, Consumer Lifestyles, Consumer Market Sizes, Forecasts, Companies & Brands, Information Sources, Major Market Profiles, and Market Analysis. The coverage is both broad and deep. "Consumer Market Sizes" provides volume and value data from 1996-2001 for 330 consumer products (e.g., disposable paper products, furniture) for 52 countries.

The key advantages to the market research data found in the *GMID* and from any of the Euromonitor publications are specificity and time currency. Compared to the limited type of market research found in U.S. government reports such as *International Market Insight* or *Industry Sector Analysis*, Euromonitor tracks well over 300 consumer products, 209 countries, and over 1,000 data elements compiled on a regular basis. Thus, for most products in most countries, you can be confident about finding up-to-date market size and purchasing data. Concomitantly, because the "Country Data" section tracks demographic, economic and social background information for 209 countries, even if your particular product is not covered in a focused report, you can generally find relevant background information. For instance, in the hospital supply business, you might not find a report on "cotton swabs" or "sanitary disposal bags," but you could find rate of growth in hospital beds and medical care services.

TIP: Sources for International Market Share Data

- *World Market Share Reporter* (Farmington Hills, MI: Gale Group, 2001).
- *Global Market Share Planner* (Oxford, U.K.: Euromonitor). Available in print and online.
- *Market Share Tracker* (Oxford, U.K.: Euromonitor). Available in print and online.

TIP: *World Consumer Lifestyles Databook*

In 2002, Euromonitor International announced a new publication entitled *World Consumer Lifestyles Databook*. Available in print or on the Internet, it lets marketers segment consumers by demographics, socio-economic variables, lifestyles, product preferences, and buying habits. Coverage is provided for over 71 countries worldwide from 1990-2000. Contact: http://www.euromonitor.com.

WARC's *Pocket Books* **[series]. Henley on Thames, Oxfordshire, U.K.: World Advertising Research Center. Annual. Print $58. Contact: http://www.warc.com.**

These handy, digest-sized volumes are published in three editions covering The Americas, Europe, and Asia/Pacific. They are an affordable alternative to Euromonitor's more extensive publications, though not nearly as detailed. Focusing on the type of data needed by media professionals and marketers, they include country-by-country statistics for economic indicators, socio-demographic data, buying patterns, media consumption, and more. Some unusual data elements are offered, such as annual media cost inflation for TV, radio, magazines, newspapers, and cinema, and "weekly reach percentage" data for major demographic groups. The data are gathered from public sources and WARC's extensive database of content partners.

ZenithOptimedia (http://www.zenithmedia.com) publishes a similar set of guides entitled *World Market & MediaFact Pocket Books* (London. Annual. Print $105 each). These cover advertising, media, demographics, and economic information for countries in Eastern Europe, Western Europe, Asia/Pacific, the Americas, the Middle East, and Africa. Basic data on advertising costs and expenditures for various types of media (e.g., TV, radio, out-of-home, press) are included.

TIP: Company Directories by Country

- Corporate Information. Contact: http://www.corporateinformation.com.
- WAND Global Trade Directory. Contact: http://www.wand.com/wand/english/html/default.asp.

ADVERTISING AND PROMOTION

Many of the sources already discussed include brief coverage of information on advertising and promotion. For example, there is discussion of advertising venues and contacts in the *Country Commercial Guides*, *Exporters' Encyclopedia*, and U.S. government market research reports. As noted previously, Euromonitor and WARC publication materials include statistics on media access and advertising patterns. Further information needed for a full media placement plan and campaign design may be found in the following sources.

***International Media Guides*. Des Plaines, IL: SRDS Publications. Annual. $315 per volume. $739 for 3-volume set. $1,089 for 5-volume set. Contact: http://www.srds.com.**

The set of *International Media Guides* is an important English-language source of information on print publications in 200 countries. Over 20,000 publications are listed, including newspapers, business (i.e., trade) journals, and consumer magazines. Five individual regional titles comprise the set: *Business Publications: Asia-Pacific/Middle East/Africa*; *Business Publications: Europe*; *Business Publications: The Americas*, *Newspapers Worldwide*; and *Consumer Magazines Worldwide*. Each volume is organized by country, and publications are described according to geographic distribution, circulation numbers, frequency, readership, and editorial content. The entries provide basic advertising and editorial contacts, advertising rates (in U.S. dollars), and production specifications (in inches and millimeters). In addition to this series, SRDS also produces *Canadian Advertising Rates & Data*, and a two-volume Spanish-language set entitled *Mexican Audiovisual/ Print Media Rates & Data*. Both cover print, TV, radio and interactive media for those countries.

Advertising Red Books–International Advertisers and Agencies. **New Providence, NJ: LexisNexis. Annual. Print $659. Contact: http:// lexisnexis.com.**

The *Advertising Red Books–International Advertisers and Agencies* edition is a listing of companies which advertise and the agencies they employ. This source is especially useful for conducting an advertising campaign in a foreign country; it identifies existing advertisers and provides the marketer with descriptions and contact information for agencies. The 2000 edition contains listings for 3,500 advertisers and agencies in 124 countries, plus the names of over 20,000 executives from those companies. The criterion for inclusion is companies with an advertising budget of over $200,000. Thus, the directory has broad coverage, ranging from moderate-sized companies to large multinational corporations. This title is related to the *Advertising Red Books* and is incorporated into the CD-ROM edition of that title. In addition, the database is available at the Web site *Red Books Online* (http://www. redbooks.com) where the international and U.S. listings are searchable in one data file.

The main section of the print directory is an alphabetical listing by "advertiser," i.e., by company name. In addition, there are indexes by product or brand name, and by the name of the advertising agency. Each listing includes advertising expenditures by media, sales figures, brand name, and key agency contact names.

World Advertiser and Agency Database. **AdAge Global (Crain Communications). New York, NY. ©2000. Online (free). Contact: http:// www.adageglobal.com.**

The *World Advertiser and Agency Database* is a directory which includes approximately 500 advertisers' accounts and 25 agencies. Agency listings qualify if they are handled in five or more countries and are worth at least $5 million. Searches can be done by advertiser or agency name: a search on an agency name (McCann-Erickson Worldwide) shows brands represented and the associated countries; a search on an advertiser name (e.g., General Motors) shows all the agencies which represent it and the countries covered by each. In addition, the site includes several useful rankings and lists, such as Top Global Ad Markets, Top Agency Networks, Top World Brand Advertisers, etc.

World Advertising Trends. Henley on Thames, Oxfordshire, U.K.: World Advertising Research Center. Annual. Print $184. Contact: http://www.warc.com.

World Advertising Trends is a compendium of worldwide advertising statistics allowing comparison of ad spending data between countries. The publisher also publishes numerous other book titles and an online subscription database of articles, market research, and case studies with contributions from a wide range of content partners. This print title contains approximately ten years of trend data in a country-by-country format, covering size and share of total ad spending for TV, magazine newspaper, cinema, radio, and outdoor advertising. Selected data from this publication are available at the publisher's Web site.

International Advertising and Marketing Information Sources. Edited by Gretchen Reed. 2nd edition. Washington DC: SLA Advertising and Marketing Division, 2000. Print $36. 114 pages. Contact: http://www.sla.org.

This guidebook covers advertising sources in 40 countries, including professional associations, publications, media expenditures, ad tracking services, and agency/client directories. Arranged by region and country, contact information includes Web sites, e-mail and fax numbers. For some countries, not all information is available, and there is no index. The editor is the director of the information center at an international advertising, marketing and corporate communications agency.

TIP: Other Global Advertising Resources

- *Global Advertising Forecasts.* Annual. London: ZenithOptimedia. Contact: http://www.zenithmedia.com. (This report covers 58 countries with actual data through 2001 and forecasts to 2005.)
- Kloss, Ingomar. 2002. *More Advertising Worldwide.* Berlin: Springer Verlag. (This book contains contributions from international authors on advertising conditions in their respective countries. It many figures and tables.)

SELECTED U.S. GOVERNMENT WEB SITE GATEWAYS

Maintaining a healthy balance of trade is important to our economic growth, and therefore the federal government has long been in the business of helping U.S. companies sell products overseas. Many agencies and all the embassies have been charged with compiling practical documents such as those discussed previously (like the *Country Commercial Guides* and *Best Market Reports*), thereby making high quality information available at little or no cost. While there is considerable overlapping material, they are worthy of revisiting here because they meet a variety of needs and also provide some unique information. This section highlights features not discussed previously.

STAT-USA: Globus/National Trade Data Bank. Online. $175/year or $75/quarter. Contact: http://www.stat-usa.gov/.

STAT-USA: Globus/National Trade Data Bank (NTDB) has been available in libraries for many years. Managed by the U.S. Department of Commerce, and funded by user fees, it is a good general resource for international marketing research. For trade leads, the "NTDB Global Trade Directory" is a searchable database of worldwide manufacturers, resellers, and buyers. The "Commerce Business Daily" is a source of announcements of overseas contracts available for bidding. There are also national trade reports by country, foreign exchange rates, foreign agricultural market reports, and current press releases on international trade.

USA Trade Online. Online. $300/year or $75/month. Contact: http://www.usatradeonline.gov.

This is a subscription-based service which emanates from the STAT-USA division of the U.S. Department of Commerce. It offers the most current data on U.S. imports and exports with tables from the current and previous month. Retrospective coverage is generally about two years old. Designed for professional export marketers, the site lets users create custom reports on specific products. Using these data, marketers can discover emerging markets for products, compare exports on similar products, and monitor trends in specific countries. For a $75 monthly fee, the researcher can create custom reports with easy-to-use software. Though the data are compiled and accessed using the "Harmonized Schedule" of commodity codes, the user can easily find and select the correct code directly on the site using an intuitive system of expanding and collapsing lists. Thus, Toys, Games & Sports Equipment is expanded to select Dolls, Representing Human Beings, which in turn is expanded to Doll Garments & Accessories. Once the code has been selected, you may select from one or all ports of departure and all worldwide destinations or a particular partner country. Your result will provide the quantities and value of shipments in that product category. Data can be sorted by country or commodities, and custom tables can be printed, saved, and exported into a variety of formats.

TIP: Foreign Trade Statistics

For current and historical trade data, covering country balances, commodity and product categories, and state-by-state exports data, use the Census Bureau's Foreign Trade page. Contact: http://www. census.gov/foreign-trade/www/statistics.html.

U.S. Government Export Portal (Export.gov). Online (free). Contact: http://www.export.gov.

This free Web site also provides a broad spectrum of information specifically for exporters. Both experienced and novice exporters will find a variety of useful tools and services that would be hard–if not impossible–to find elsewhere. The "Basic Guide to Exporting" is a free book-length report, which covers topics such as developing an export strategy and marketing plan, financing, pricing, technology licensing, legal considerations and much more. Other sections provide links to consultants, export counseling, promotional services, and numerous information resources For example, under "Industry Sector Offices and Contacts," there is a contact list of government trade development analysts (names and e-mail addresses) for a broad range of industries and products, and a link to "Export Finance Matchmakers" (in various government agencies). Another link is "NAFTA Rules of Origin," which details how to qualify goods for preferential duty treatment.

Export Advantage. U.S. International Trade Administration. Office of Textiles and Apparel. Online (free). Contact: http://otexa.ita.doc.gov.

Export Advantage is described as a "one-stop resource for exporting U.S.-made textile and apparel products." Produced by the Office of Textiles and Apparel (OTEXA), of the International Trade Administration, Department of Commerce, it focuses on this single industry and compiles all relevant information while eliminating redundancy. The site contains market research, how-to-export guides, import quotas, directories of overseas buyers, trade events, trade data and agreements, and more.

TIP: Other Web Gateways for International Marketing Information

- *GlobalEdge*. Contact: http://globaledge.msu.edu
- *Virtual International Business & Economic Sources* (VIBES). Contact: http://libweb.uncc.edu/ref-bus/vibehome.htm
- *Marketing Resources Gateway*. University of Strathclyde Department of Marketing (Glasgow, Scotland). Contact: http://www.marketing.strath.ac.uk/dcd/Export_Marketing
- *Super Searchers Cover the World: The Online Secrets of Global Business Researchers.* Mary Ellen Bates. Contact: http://www.infotoday.com/supersearchers/sscw.htm

---

REFERENCES

Dwyer, Mike. 2001. "Developing Nations: Markets on the Grow." *AgExporter* 13, no. 4 (April): 12-16.

International Monetary Fund (IMF). 2002. "World Economic Outlook." <http://www.imf.org/external/pubs/ft/weo/2002/01/index.htm> (May 21, 2002).

PRS Group Inc. 2002. "Frequently Asked Questions." <http://www.prsgroup.com/commonhtml/faq.html#whatisprsgroup> (May 21, 2002).

PART VI

RESEARCHING PRICE, PACKAGING, AND PLACE

Chapter 12

Product Development, Packaging, Pricing, and Place

Topics

Product Development and Management
Packaging
Pricing
Place: Strategies of Distribution and Logistics

Sources

Product Development and Management Association
PDMA Handbook of New Product Development
Product Manager's Handbook
NewProductWorks
Packexpo.com
Packaginginfo.com
Rauch Guide to the U.S. Packaging Industry
Michigan State University, School of Packaging
The Marketer's Guide to Successful Package Design
Handbook of Package Engineering
Professional Pricing Society
The Strategy and Tactics of Pricing: A Guide to Profitable Decision-making
Pricing Policies and Strategies: An Annotated Bibliography
Value of a Dollar 1860-1999

[Haworth co-indexing entry note]: "Product Development, Packaging, Pricing, and Place." Diamond, Wendy, and Michael R. Oppenheim. Co-published simultaneously in *Journal of Business & Finance Librarianship* (The Haworth Information Press, an imprint of The Haworth Press, Inc.) Vol. 9, No. 4, 2004, pp. 269-284; and: *Marketing Information: A Strategic Guide for Business and Finance Libraries* (Wendy Diamond, and Michael R. Oppenheim) The Haworth Information Press, an imprint of The Haworth Press, Inc., 2004, pp. 269-284. Single or multiple copies of this article are available for a fee from The Haworth Document Delivery Service [1-800-HAWORTH, 9:00 a.m. - 5:00 p.m. (EST). E-mail address: docdelivery@haworthpress.com].

http://www.haworthpress.com/web/JBFL
Digital Object Identifier: 10.1300/J109v09n04_04

What Is a Dollar Worth?
Council of Logistics Management
LogisticsWorld, LogLink, LogisticsZone and *Virtual Logistics Directory*

The layperson often equates advertising with marketing, but students in introductory marketing courses learn that there are other aspects of marketing beyond the "P" of Promotion. Marketers also must consider the "Ps" of Product, Pricing, and Place. For these areas, marketers need to understand finance, accounting, engineering, materials science, transportation, and logistics in order to communicate with technical experts. They will routinely utilize formulas, models, internal company data, case studies, checklists, worksheets, and outside consultation, and therefore do not rely significantly on secondary, published sources. However, for effective utilization of these sources, relevant background knowledge is essential. Therefore this chapter includes more handbooks, workbooks, and integrated Web sites than other chapters in this book.

PRODUCT DEVELOPMENT AND MANAGEMENT

In *product development* (or NPD, "new product development") and *product management*, the product itself is the focus, rather than any particular marketing function. It is one of the most integrated areas of marketing, covering conceptualization, research, planning, packaging, production, profitability, and promotion. Although the "product" can be any manufactured item, or even a service sold to customers, the term usually refers specifically to packaged consumer goods such as food, beverages, cosmetics, toiletries, soaps, and the like. New product development is often an extension of established product lines and brands in large corporate settings. However, even the small entrepreneur can utilize established concepts and practices in NPD and product management for creating and sustaining a product or service. This section offers some sources that cover development and management of new and existing products.

Product Development and Management Association. Mount Laurel, NJ. ©1994-2002. Contact: http://www.pdma.org.

Like most professional associations, the Product Development and Management Association (PDMA) supports its members with information-disseminating activities such as conferences, discussion lists, continuing education, newsletters, and journals. In addition, PDMA is also actively involved with several knowledge-generating activities such as sponsorship of research competitions and awards to encourage academics to engage in new product research. The site contains several useful features also available to non-members. For example, the "Glossary of New Product Development Terms" is an online 28-page list of definitions adapted from several other publications.

The online bookstore identifies practical and authoritative works in the area of product management. The listing of titles is classified using the following categories: "Classics," "Best Practice," "Process and Strategy," "Organization and Teams," "Cycle Time," "Tools and Techniques," and "Industries and Topics." Most of the listings contain excerpts or full-text articles from recent reviews in the Association's research journal, *Journal of Product Innovation and Management (JPIM)*. Although the Association disavows a direct endorsement of the titles listed, it has excluded those that did not receive a positive review.

The Web site also contains full text articles from current and archived issues of *Visions*, a trade magazine for NPD professionals. The special section devoted to NPD practices provides methodology, tips, and techniques. The table of contents from the current issue of *JPIM* is also available. At the Web site itself, the full-text archive is accessible only to Association members. (However, the full-text of *JPIM* is available to subscribers through periodical databases such as Elsevier's *Science Direct*.)

PDMA Handbook of New Product Development. Edited by Milton D. Rosenau Jr., Abbie Griffin, George A. Castellon, and Ned F. Anschuetz. 2nd edition. New York: John Wiley and Sons, 1996. Print $120. 636 pages.

The former president of the Product Development and Management Association (PDMA), Milton D. Rosenau, is a co-editor of the *PDMA Handbook of New Product Development*. Containing 33 chapters written by academics and professional specialists in various aspects of product management, this handbook emphasizes aligning product development with overall strategic goals. The book offers in-depth coverage of practical and theoretical aspects, with cited references at the end of each chapter and a detailed index. It also contains several appendices that lift this book above the typical handbook level and make it useful as a reference tool. Appendix A is entitled "Role for Software," Appendix

B is a Glossary (some of which is included in the NPD Glossary on the PDMA Web site), and Appendix C contains Cumulative Indexes of abstracts, articles and book reviews from the literature.

***Product Manager's Handbook*. Linda Gorchels. 2nd edition. Lincolnwood, IL: NTC Business Books, 2000. Print $50. 240 pages.**

In typical handbook style, this book combines theory with practical examples and techniques. As the title suggests, there is an emphasis on the product manager's role and the functional skills needed for integrated product management, including advertising, strategy, development proposals, planning, pricing, and sales. The book presents sophisticated concepts and analytical tools in a comfortable format that includes many charts, checklists, and real-world case studies.

NewProductWorks. Ann Arbor, MI. http://www.newproductworks. com.

NewProductWorks (a division of the Arbor Strategy Group) is a consulting business which stimulates and assists companies in new product development activities. It primarily provides consulting services in research and development, marketing research, and marketing management for corporate clients in consumer products, as well as for attorneys specializing in patents, product liability, and intellectual property. The firm states that their core clients are manufacturers, marketers, and package design companies. They work closely with branding and marketing managers and with research and development professionals to help them generate creative product ideas.

One of its centerpiece activities is a unique resource with particular applications for labeling and packaging research. Entitled the NPW Product Collection, this is a storehouse of product *realia* of "new and once-new consumer packaged good products" housed in a large facility at company headquarters in Ann Arbor, Michigan (NewProductWorks n.d.). The collection represents products found in grocery stores and contains items going back as far as 1965. It is a growing collection and includes items like today's latest ketchup color and yoghurt flavor. The actual products can be viewed and investigated for ingredient composition, package features, and marketing claims, and NPW can provide studio photography and written product histories.

Since this is not a collection housed in a public institution such as a library or museum, access is limited. In order to determine what is in the collection, a database search needs to be requested, presumably for a fee; arrangements can then be made to view selected products in-person. Nonetheless, the firm recognizes that the collection provides an "interactive environment allowing for hands-on education in all areas of packaged goods," and they are willing to make the collection available to academic researchers or to provide tours for high school and college classes at a reasonable price (NewProductWorks n.d.). Photographs and discussions of some of the products from the collection are also available in a book authored by Robert (Bob) McMath, founder of NewProductWorks, entitled *What Were They Thinking: Marketing Lessons I Have Learned from over 80,000 New Product Introductions* (New York: Times Business Books, 1999). The Web site provides an interactive tour with photos of the facility, and there are conceptual outlines of new product development projects that may be useful as case studies for teaching purposes at the link entitled "NPW in Action" (http://www.newproductworks.com/helping_you/npw_in_action.html).

PACKAGING

As a result of changes in technology, globalization, and entrepreneurship, whole areas of product development and management, such as packaging, have grown into specializations of their own. Packaging is integral to the marketing aspects of consumer product development because it presents the public face and identity of a product. Packaging experts describe it as the most powerful sales tool for the majority of products that are not advertised. The editor of *BrandPackaging* magazine says, "packaging is the last three feet and last three seconds of your marketing program" (Swienek 2002). Coca Cola®'s classic bottle is a familiar example of how integral a package design can be to the brand identification of a product. Marketers working in package design must consider graphics, engineering, safety, transportation, and legal aspects. The package must not only meet marketing objectives, it must also fulfill the purpose of creating a safe physical environment in which to store and ship the product, which can be particularly crucial for food, drugs and other perishable materials. In addition, marketers must consider product reliability, label content, health claims, weight limits and many other issues which are controlled by laws and regulations. Further complicating the packaging picture is the fact that it involves many other industries, such as transportation, machinery, paper, glass, or plastic (Michigan State University School of Packaging 2002).

Like the marketing aspects of pricing, packaging is a topic that does not rely heavily on secondary sources, but marketing professionals may find the following sources useful.

***Packexpo.com*. Fairfax, VA. © 2002. Online (free). Contact: http://www.packexpo.com.**

This Web site is sponsored by and maintained as a for-profit joint venture between the Packaging Machinery Manufacturers Institute (PMMI) and Cendex, an online business-to-business service provider representing manufacturers of packaging machinery and related equipment. PMMI members are involved primarily with the engineering and technological aspects of packaging, but they must also consider the "communication-with-the-customer," or marketing, aspects.

Packexpo.com's primary focus is its business-to-business services. No registration is required to access the supplier directory, which includes more than 20,000 listings organized into seven major categories (e.g., components, containers, machinery, and materials). Products and services are described and there are links to information request forms. In addition, there is a Purchase Exchange which requires registration in order to issue a request-for-proposal (RFP) for a specific packaging job.

Beyond its business-to-business functions, Packexpo.com also offers a Discussion Forum, custom research, trade show listings, and many features for marketers seeking packaging news and industry background. There are sections devoted to breaking daily news, industry watch, and current and archived product announcements. The latest issue of *Packaging Digest* magazine is posted and available for no fee. For the student and general researcher, the *Packexpo.com* Web site also provides a very useful Reference section which contains various weights and measures calculators, definitions, glossaries, conversion charts and the like.

***Packaginginfo.com*. St. Charles, IL. ©1994-2002. Online (free). Contact: http://www.packaginginfo.com.**

This Web site offers access to the current and archived content of three leading trade journals in packaging: *Food & Drug Packaging, BrandPackaging, and Flexible Packaging*. These titles are part a group of publications produced by Stagnito Communications, which also includes *Beverage Industry, Candy Industry,* and other similar professional magazines. The user can enter any of the titles individually and select articles from the most recent issue or browse by date in the Issue Archive. In addition, there is an Advanced Search option for keyword access which enables searching either in one journal or across the suite of three. When an article is displayed, links to related articles in these publications are also provided.

Users should be aware that all the content on the Web site originates from articles in these journals. And there is another important caveat to consider when using this Web site. Clearly the editors are experts in the field of packaging and marketing of food products, but the fact that both print and Web content are available without subscription fees indicates that the journals are largely supported by advertising, and indeed, many of the companies mentioned in articles are also advertisers.

Rauch Guide to the U.S. Packaging Industry. 4th edition. Manchester Center, VT: Impact Marketing Consultants, Inc., 2002. Print (or CD-ROM) $595. 370 pages. Contact: http://www.impactmarket. com.

Formerly published by Rauch Associates, the 4th edition of the *Rauch Guide to the U.S. Packaging Industry* provides a concentrated overview and analysis of the packaging industry. Published in March 2002, it contains data for 2000 with forecasts to 2005. With 370 pages, 11 major sections, and over 100 tables, the *Guide* appraises the general packaging industry, as well as specific segments within it. According to the publisher, a "unique feature of the *Guide* is its ranking of the largest packaging companies" (*Impact Marketing* 2002). It offers a current and excellent picture of the economics of the industry as a whole, plus profitability and market share for specific companies, with extensive discussion of market size and structure, prices, major consumers, transportation patterns, and regulatory issues.

There is detailed coverage of paperboard, metal cans, glass, plastic, flexible packaging, closures, wood and other materials. Discussions include technological and research updates, competitive structure, capitalization and profitability, product uses, prices, and raw material use. Within each major product category, there are also sub-sections covering specific products. For example, in the chapter on paperboard, there are sub-sections for corrugated and solid boxes, folding cartons, sanitary food containers, etc. Importantly, each section also includes a list under "Sources of Information" so the researcher may find additional leads. Some of the information is gathered from other published sources, and this presentation compiles a wide array of scattered information into a single industry guide.

Michigan State University. The School of Packaging. East Lansing, MI. Contact: http://www.msu.edu/~sop.

As stated at the Web site, the School of Packaging at Michigan State University has a mission to provide research and education involving the packaging system. Currently comprised of sixteen faculty, it was founded in 1952 and confers Bachelor of Science and Master degrees. It is international in focus and offers extensive outreach, distance education, and other lifelong learning opportunities for packaging industry professionals.

The Web site is not a source per se, but may be an excellent lead for further information. Faculty experts can be contacted for more information about the packaging industry. There is also a link that describes the process for contracting with the School for research and testing services. For general purposes, the most useful leads will be found under "Other Packaging Related Sites." There are extensive links to trade and professional organizations covering a variety of industries related to packaging, such as the Fiber Box Association (http://www.fibrebox. org), the Council of Logistics Management (http://www.clm1.org), Glass Packing Institute (http://www.gpi.org), as well as those dealing with the packaging industry itself, such as World Packaging Organization (http://www.packinfo-world.org) and *Packaging Network* publication (http://www.packagingnetwork.com). Links for manufacturers and packaging user companies, publishing organizations, and college and university programs are also provided.

The Marketer's Guide to Successful Package Design. Herbert M. Meyers and Murray J. Lubliner. Lincolnwood, IL: NTC Business Books, 1998. Print $50.00. 320 pages.

Many books on package design emphasize design and technology, but this one focuses on finding the "right" package to create an effective image for the product within it. Originally issued by the Institute of Packaging Professionals, it covers marketing strategy, sales objectives, competitive research, graphic designer selection, managing the design process, the relationship to advertising, and legal issues. The guide's utility is enhanced by a complete chapter of analyzed case studies (called "Insights"), a glossary of terms, and a bibliography.

Handbook of Package Engineering. **Joseph F. Hanlon, Robert J. Kelsey, and Hallie E. Forcinio. 3rd edition. Lancaster, PA: Technomic Publishing Co. 1998. Print $160. 698 pages.**

This handbook is a reference source for factual information on the technical aspects of packaging materials and containers. Twenty-one chapters cover topics from general issues ("Laws and Regulations," "Packaging and the Environment") to specific materials ("Cushioning," "Plastics," "Films and Foils") with subsections covering history, design, labeling, and physical and chemical properties. Other topics include machinery design and selection, coatings and laminations, performance testing, aerosols, closures, fasteners, adhesives, cushioning, pouches, metallized films, aseptic packaging, plastic drums, and more. Extensive bibliographic references are included at the end of each chapter. In addition, there is an appendix of common mathematical conversions and a full index. This is the third edition of a classic guide originally written by Joseph Hanlon, now comprehensively updated and revised by Robert J. Kelsey and Hallie E. Forcinio.

TIP: Text for Certified Packaging Professional Examination

The text used for the Certified Packaging Professional examination is *Fundamentals of Packaging Technology* by Walter Soroka (Herndon, VA: Institute of Packaging Professionals, 1999). It is in textbook/workbook format, with material similar to the *Handbook of Package Engineering.* It contains end-of-chapter exercises, a 40-page glossary, and 300 illustrations.

PRICING

Pricing is a technical area involving finance and accounting, but it is also the most direct way that a business communicates to customers. Although customer segmentation, branding, and advertising are all effective tools for positioning a product, it is ultimately *price* that tells the customer whether the product is upscale, economy, status-conscious, reliable, and a worthwhile purchase. Setting the price is a complex business decision that applies theoretical and mathematical scenarios using both internal and external data in order to balance financial profit with strategic marketing objectives. Many of the primary decision factors are derived from proprietary company information such as sales volume and production cost. Other parts of the decision necessitate an under-standing of market conditions, competitors' positions, and legal re-quirements, and these rely on the published data sources for industry and market research discussed in other chapters in this book. Addition-ally, primary market research is sometimes required, and price setting may involve shopping surveys and focus groups.

This section provides sources for both the theoretical and strategic aspects of pricing from a marketing point of view. In addition, it in-cludes some external sources for price data which can supplement inter-nal market research and shopping surveys.

Professional Pricing Society. Atlanta, GA. Contact: http://www. pricing-advisor.com.

The Professional Pricing Society is an international association sup-porting pricing executives and decision makers with conferences, work-shops, a monthly newsletter, quarterly journal, Web site discussion groups, consulting, and a range of job-related services. Members in-clude marketing, pricing, and management professionals in large and mid-sized companies from diverse industries and countries.

As part of its workshop program, the Society formerly published an excellent series of pricing workbooks under the imprint "The Pricing Advisor." Although no longer in print (Smith 2002), these workbooks may be available in libraries. In particular, two titles authored by Eric G. Mitchell, former Pricing Society president, are worth noting. *The Complete Pricing Workbook* (1990) is described as a "workbook on the pricing process [with] chapters on pricing research, financial tools, value-added pricing, and the price management process." *Profitable Pricing Strategies Workbook* (1990) focuses further on such marketing aspects as boosting profit margins, penetrating existing markets, open-ing new markets, and taking market share from the competition. For more recent books on pricing topics, the Society's Web site lists a vari-ety of titles from commercial publishers, along with brief reviews and descriptions.

The Society's Web site itself is a source of information, especially for members, but also for the general public. Each month a special fea-ture article or slide presentation is offered. In April 2002, the *Pricer's Salary Survey Results* were posted. In June 2001, the feature was titled "Discretion versus Valor: How to Manage an Aggressive Competitor." White papers, case studies, and articles on pricing issues are also avail-able. Many are written or presented by the Society's corporate sponsors, and although they have a promotional function, they also provide useful reading from people in the field. Sample topics include "Gaining Competitive Advantage Through Pricing" (from Revenue Technologies) and "Why Not Raise Your Prices" (from Strategic Pricing Group Inc.). In addition, the Pricing Society's Web site provides a demonstration area where industry software can be downloaded, tested and compared.

***The Strategy and Tactics of Pricing: A Guide to Profitable Decision Making.* Thomas T. Nagle and Reed K. Holden. 3rd edition. Upper Saddle River, NJ: Prentice Hall, 2002. Print $65. 400 pages.**

Although not a typical handbook, this practical guide is often found on professional marketers' lists of useful pricing books. Written in a straightforward style, it presents the concepts needed to integrate pricing into marketing strategy. Topics include using price to influence purchase decisions; financial analysis; segmented pricing for various customers; price competition; pricing psychology; and legal and ethical aspects. Practical examples are integrated with numerous formulas and theories, making it an effective learning tool. With its extensive bibliographic notes, appendices and indexing, it is also a useful reference work.

***Pricing Policies and Strategies: An Annotated Bibliography.* Chicago: American Marketing Association, 1982. 110 pages.**

Published over 20 years ago, this small volume provides a snapshot of the available literature on pricing issues from the late 1960s and 1970s. It will primarily be useful to those seeking early writing on the marketing aspects of pricing. Covering all aspects of the pricing decision, from economics and finance to marketing, it is a classified listing of annotated journal literature and a few monographs. It is no longer available but can be found in libraries.

***Value of a Dollar 1860-1999.* Scott Derks, ed. Millerton, NY: Grey House Publishing, 1999 Millennium Edition. Print $135. 493 pages.**

This intriguing reference book provides the student or researcher with historical prices on typical consumer goods and services. Derived from advertisements, catalog copy, and federal statistics, the information is presented in chronological chapters. Each chapter covers a five-year time span and includes a historical snapshot and chronology, a summarized report on per capita consumer prices nationwide, investment returns, jobs from classified listings, average wages, regional reports of food prices, priced items from advertisements, and other representative items tracked annually. Although this work is probably most likely to be useful to academics and students of social and economic history, it provides relatively recent data useful to the marketer seeking typical price points for products and services.

What Is a Dollar Worth? Federal Reserve Bank of Minneapolis. Contact: http://minneapolisfed.org/research/data/us/calc/.

This Web site is a handy Consumer Price Index (CPI) calculator that enables the user to determine how much a certain item would cost in today's dollars by using the CPI to account for the inflationary increase in prices. It is possible to key in a price and any purchase date since 1913. Using 1989 and a price of $400 as an example, you would find out that an equivalent would cost $578.39 in 2002. This quick tool can be used in two ways: to calculate a standard inflation measurement for specific prices, or to determine whether a specific price has risen faster or slower than the standard rate of inflation.

TIP: International Issues in Pricing

Pricing decisions for the overseas market are just as individualized as they are for the domestic market, and will vary according to the product, company, and market environment. However, international pricing requires consideration of important additional factors. The following sources provide technical and practical information for export pricing decisions.

- Export Institute USA. "Ask the Experts." Washington, DC. ©2002. Online (free). Contact: http://www.exportinstitute.com/askthe_experts.htm. (This site contains a section entitled "Pricing Competitively in World Markets." In addition, the Export Institute publishes *Export Sales and Marketing Manual* in print and CD-ROM with extensive discussion of international pricing techniques.)
- U.S. Small Business Administration. *Business Development Success Series*. Volume 1 "Starting a Business." Updated July 12, 2001. Contact: http://www.sba.gov/gopher/Business-Development/Success-Series/Vol1/Trad/trad7.txt. (This federal government site contains a useful overview of pricing methods used in international marketing contexts.)

- U.S. Trade Administration. "Chapter 11: Pricing, Quotations, and Terms." *Basic Guide to Exporting*. 1998-1999. Contact: http://www.unzco.com/basicguide/index.html. (This Web publication, developed by the U.S. Trade Administration in conjunction with Unz & Co., is also available at the *U.S. Government Export Portal* http://www.export.gov.)

PLACE: STRATEGIES OF DISTRIBUTION AND LOGISTICS

The fourth "p" represents *Place*, which in marketing terms can be defined as "getting the product to the buyer," that is, the *placement with*, or *distribution to* the customer. Sometimes called "supply chain management," this terminology points out the need for a strategy to fulfill the demand created by all the other marketing activities. "While the focus of many marketing activities is on demand creation, the primary focus of physical distribution is the fulfillment of customer demand" (McGinnis 1986, 643). Today's marketers have many distribution and supply chain options: they can market directly using mail order, Internet, or infomercials, or they can distribute their product indirectly through wholesalers and retailers. The choice depends not only on marketing objectives, but also on product stability, packaging concerns, cost of sales, and more. For example, a specialty food product might require a short distribution chain with manufacturer's representatives offering the product to distributors at trade shows. In order to carry out a strategy, marketing managers typically interact with experts from a variety of fields, and therefore need to understand such technical areas as transportation, logistics, warehousing, packaging, title transfer, inventory information systems, interim financing, and payment systems.

In this book we devote whole chapters to specific channels of distribution, such as direct marketing, retailing, and international marketing. Here we will consider sources that address the fields of distribution and logistics as a whole, again focusing primarily on those topics that relate to the information needs of marketers.

Council of Logistics Management. Oak Brook, IL. Online (free). Contact: http://www.clm1.org.

This source is the Web site for the Council of Logistics Management (CLM), a non-profit organization supporting the communication, research, and education needs of professionals in the fields of distribution and logistics. It is explicitly not a trade association, social organization, or high density market for suppliers of logistics products and services and does not endorse legislation or "engage in matters where members may have contrary interests" (Council of Logistics Management n.d.). CLM's self-defined mission is research and education.

Starting in 1997, CLM replaced its printed *Annual Bibliography of Logistics Management* with the *Online Logistics Bibliography*. It is updated weekly and contains over 30,000 abstracts and citations from periodicals and journals published since 1993. It provides both basic and advanced search interfaces, with keyword, Boolean and limited field searching options. Additionally, there is a count of word-occurrence in the database which can help identify the most frequently used terms, boosting retrieval results. A listing of all periodicals indexed is also provided.

As a research and education tool, the Web site provides a number of useful resources for logistics students and professionals. Since 1996, CLM has also developed a set of case studies which can be downloaded in PDF versions. These range from traditional logistics problems to e-business issues and are useful to both practitioners and academics alike. In a series called *Logistics Trends*, CLM co-publishes the *Annual State of Logistics Report* with CASS Corporation. Other titles in this series are for sale and vary in cost and coverage. Some examples include the Annual *Compensation Survey/Logistics Management* ($575), *American Trucking Trends* ($79), and *Armstrong's Guide to Third-Party Logistics Providers & Dedicated Contract Carriers* ($245). CLM also publishes the *Journal of Business Logistics*, conference proceedings, and numerous other special reports.

TIP: CLM Definitions

The Council of Logistics Management (CLM) provides definitions of logistics and supply chain management. Contact: http://www.clm1.org/aboutus/aboutus_policy.asp.

TIP: Some Logistics Industry Publishers

- Armstrong & Associates, Inc. Contact: http://www.3PLogistics.com/.
- Cass Info. Contact: http://www.cassinfo.org. (Their annual State of Logistics Report is available at http://www.cassinfo.com/bob_pc_2002.html.)
- Leonard's Guides. Contact: http://www.leonardsguide.com/.

TIP: Web Sites for Supply Chain Research

- Supply Chain Council. Contact: http://www.supply-chain.org.
- Center for Supply Chain Research. Smeal College of Business. Pennsylvania State University. Contact: http://www.smeal.psu. edu/cscr/.

***LogisticsWorld*. Las Vegas, NV. ©1995-2000. Online (free). Contact: http://www.logisticsworld.com.**

The complexity of the logistics industry and its wide variety of options for transportation, warehousing, storage, and inventory control, often requires marketers to seek information about potential suppliers and vendors. Consequently, there are a number of business-to-business sites on the Web that provide directory listings. *LogisticsWorld* is one of the largest and most extensive. It contains descriptive and contact information from companies and organizations, based on each company's own submissions of information. Free features include a searchable glossary of terms, a look-up tool for military and government acronyms, an extensive list of definitions of the term "logistics," Harmonized tariff schedules, and a reading list with descriptions and reviews.

Other Web sites with similar features, like vendor directories, book reviews, authored articles, glossaries, and trade show schedules include *LogLink* (http://loglink.com), *LogisticsZone* (http://www.logisticszone. com), and *Virtual Logistics Directory* (http://www.logisticsdirectory. com/main.htm). In addition to offering similar information and features, all these sites are primarily designed as promotion vehicles for companies offering services to industry.

REFERENCES

Council of Logistics Management. n.d. "Do's and Don'ts of CLM." <http://www.clm1. org/aboutus/aboutus_policy.asp> (April 17, 2003).

Impact Marketing. 2002. "U.S. Packaging Industry to Lag Economy, but Opportunities Abound." <http://www.impactmarket.com/Guides/Packaging/Packaging_Press_ Release.pdf> (April 17, 2003).

McGinnis, Michael A. 1996. Physical Distribution. In *Beacham's Marketing Reference*, edited by Walston Beacham et al. Washington, D.C.: Research Publishing.

Michigan State University School of Packaging. 2002. "General Information: What Is Packaging." <www.msu.edu/~sop/what_is_packaging.html> (April 17, 2003).

Professional Pricing Society. [n.d.] "Top Pricing Resource Publications." <http://www.pricing-advisor.com/res_book.htm> (April 17, 2003).

NewProductWorks.com [n.d.]

_____. "The NPW Difference: The Product Collection." <http://newproductworks.com/npw_difference/product_collection.html> (July 9, 2002).

_____. "Helping You." <http://newproductworks.com/helping_you/clients_who_benefit.html> (July 9, 2002).

Smith, Maveita. "Pricing Advisor Publications," April 8, 2002, personal e-mail.

Swienek, Bob. 1994-2002. "The Editor's Perspective on: Why Brand Packaging?" <http://www.packaginginfo.com/EditorDetail.asp?id=161> (April 9, 2002).

PART VII

SPECIAL TOPICS

Chapter 13

Sources for Special Topics:
Social Marketing, Nonprofit Organizations,
Services Marketing,
and Legal/Ethical Issues

Topics

Social Marketing
Marketing for Nonprofit and Public Organizations
Services Marketing
Legal and Ethical Issues in Marketing

Sources

Social Marketing Institute
Tools of Change
Social Marketing Network
National Social Norms Resource Center
California Nonprofit Corporation Book
Internal Revenue Code, Sections 501-530
Handbook of Services Marketing and Management
Delivering Quality Service: Balancing Customer Perceptions and Expectations
Marketing Ethics Web Sites

[Haworth co-indexing entry note]: "Sources for Special Topics: Social Marketing, Nonprofit Organizations, Services Marketing, and Legal/Ethical Issues." Diamond, Wendy, and Michael R. Oppenheim. Co-published simultaneously in *Journal of Business & Finance Librarianship* (The Haworth Information Press, an imprint of The Haworth Press, Inc.) Vol. 9, No. 4, 2004, pp. 287-299; and: *Marketing Information: A Strategic Guide for Business and Finance Libraries* (Wendy Diamond, and Michael R. Oppenheim) The Haworth Information Press, an imprint of The Haworth Press, Inc., 2004, pp. 287-299. Single or multiple copies of this article are available for a fee from The Haworth Document Delivery Service [1-800-HAWORTH, 9:00 a.m. - 5:00 p.m. (EST). E-mail address: docdelivery@haworthpress.com].

http://www.haworthpress.com/web/JBFL
Digital Object Identifier: 10.1300/J109v09n04_05

Advertising Law & Ethics
Robinson-Patman Act. 15 U.S.C.A. 13 (a-f)
Uniform Commercial Code
Journal of Public Policy and Marketing

The topics discussed in this chapter represent prominent developments and concerns in the field of marketing. They are topic areas that are best researched in books, journal articles, and textbooks, and this chapter provides guidance in using these sources.

SOCIAL MARKETING

Social concern is an increasingly important development in the field of marketing. In a then-controversial article published in 1969, Philip Kotler and Sidney J. Levy conceptualized marketing as a fundamental human activity, one that goes beyond the realm of merely selling goods and services (Kotler and Levy 1969). After developing this theoretical base for social marketing, Dr. Kotler, a world-renowned marketing expert, then went on to develop practical techniques and strategies for many different kinds of nonprofit marketing.

The field of social marketing focuses on changing societal attitudes and behavior by applying the powerful tools available to commercial marketing. Originally utilized mainly for health and wellness campaigns (high blood pressure, anti-tobacco), it is now also used to affect crime and other social problems (domestic violence awareness, anti-drug campaigns). Social marketing incorporates most of the basic activities and principles of general marketing: the target market must be defined, a campaign must be developed, media buying decisions must be made, and so on. However, when marketing concepts are applied outside the commercial world of product and customer, some unique issues are encountered.

Social Marketing Institute. Washington, DC. Online (free). Contact: http://www.social-marketing.org.

Developed by Dr. Alan R. Andreason of Georgetown University, one of the leading academics in the field of social marketing, the Social Marketing Institute was organized to bring research together with frontline best practices in the field. The Web site offers case studies in the form of "success stories," full text research papers, and links to other related resources. Users may register to receive updates on news and events. Dr. Andreason is also the editor of *Ethics in Social Marketing* (Washington, DC: Georgetown University Press, 2001), which is a collection of essays addressing ethical problems and solutions in social marketing.

Tools of Change. Ottawa, Canada. ©1996-1999. Online (free). Contact: http://www.toolsofchange.com.

The *Tools of Change* Web site is designed to promulgate the principles of community-based social marketing. The primary sponsors are Canadian government agencies (HealthCanada and Environment Canada) and Cullbridge Marketing and Communications, with participation from several other supporting sponsors. The site is designed to be a resource for those trying to replicate the "best practices" of successful programs. It offers a toolkit of techniques, case studies, and a planning guide for designing campaigns to improve people's health and environmentally-sustainable behavior. The site is updated continuously and is freely available, but regular users may wish to register for access to an interactive tool for creating a customized plan.

Social Marketing Network. HealthCanada. Ottawa, Canada. Online (free). Contact: http://www.hc-sc.gc.ca/hppb/socialmarketing/resources/index.html.

This Web site is provided by HealthCanada as a resource for social marketing practitioners and researchers. A link to a step-by-step tutorial guides the user through the process of planning and then implementing a social marketing program. Topics such as audience analysis, strategy and tactics, measurement, assessment, and scheduling and budgeting are covered. There is another link to a bibliography of published research up to 1998. Citations are listed by topic, and most are annotated with a brief abstract. The site also offers case studies and several full text documents, including a primer of social marketing.

National Social Norms Resource Center. De Kalb, IL. ©2001. Online (free). Contact: http://www.socialnorm.org.

The marketing of "social norms," a burgeoning sub-field of social marketing, is primarily focused on the risk behaviors of college students and young adults. It is defined as "the use of the methods of social marketing to correct a target population's misperception of the norm, thereby positively influencing its behavior" (NSNRC 2001). Its purpose is to publicize facts which counteract the peer pressure that is often mistaken for "conventional wisdom" by young people. Many successful campaigns have focused on communicating the "social norm" that most students really drink less than is commonly believed.

The National Social Norms Resource Center Web site (NSNRC) provides a set of useful resources for those researching and designing social norms campaigns. There is a six-page bibliography of the social norms approach which lists scholarly articles from academic journals, books, and conference proceedings. Many of these citations are linked directly to online full text versions. For the practitioner, there are sample posters from a variety of college campuses, and "Guidelines for Creating Media," a seven-step program for effective advertising campaigns.

TIP: A Reading List for Social Marketers

Andreasen, Alan R., Editor. 2001. *Ethics in Social Marketing.* Washington DC: Georgetown University Press. (See also "Social Marketing Institute" at http://www.social-marketing.org.)

Bloom, Paul N. and Gregory T. Gundlach, Editors. 2001. *Handbook of Marketing and Society.* Thousand Oaks, CA: Sage Publications.

Journal of Public Policy & Marketing. 2002. Special Issue on Social Marketing Initiatives. 21:1 (Spring).

Kotler, Philip, Ned Roberto, and Nancy Lee. 2002. *Social Marketing: Improving the Quality of Life.* 2nd edition. Thousand Oaks, CA: Sage Publications.

Siegel, Michael and Lynne Doner. 1998. *Marketing Public Health: Strategies to Promote Social Change.* Gaithersburg, MD: Aspen Publishers.

Weinrich, Nedra Kline. 1999. *Hands-on Social Marketing: A Step-by-Step Guide.* Thousand Oaks, CA: Sage Publications. (See also "Weinrich Communications" at http://www.social-marketing.com.)

TIP: Seminal Works in the Development of Social and Nonprofit Marketing

Fox, Karen F.A. and Philip Kotler. 1980. "The Marketing of Social Causes: The First Ten Years," *Journal of Marketing* 44 (Fall): 24-33.

Kotler, Philip and Sidney J Levy. 1969. "Broadening the Concept of Marketing." *Journal of Marketing* 33 (January): 10-15.

Kotler, Philip and Gerald Zaltman. 1971. "Social Marketing: An Approach to Planned Social Change." *Journal of Marketing* 35 (July): 3-12.

Shapiro, Benson. 1973. "Marketing for Nonprofit Organizations," *Harvard Business Review* (September, October): 223-32.

MARKETING FOR NONPROFIT AND PUBLIC ORGANIZATIONS

> Marketing is that function of the organization that can keep in constant touch with the organization's consumers, read their needs, develop "products" that meet these needs and build a program of communications to express the organization's purposes. (Kotler and Levy 1969, 15)

After the theoretical basis for social marketing was established, the concept was readily accepted by the numerous organizations and institutions that carry out social, artistic, educational, economic, and political programs. The marketing function in the public and nonprofit sectors utilizes many of the same concepts and sources as private sector marketing, and therefore many of the sources listed throughout this book will be useful to those involved in nonprofit and public organizations. However, there are also many differences in managing the customer-relationship and marketing function in such nonprofit sectors as education, the arts, public transportation, social services, and government. The "Four Ps" of the standard marketing mix must be re-defined for an environment in which profitability is not the main concern. Maintaining a "customer" focus, fulfilling the mission, and effective outreach take on paramount importance when applying the philosophy, processes, and tools of marketing.

In marketing for a nonprofit enterprise, there are actually two types of "marketing" going on: (1) marketing to fulfill the mission and reach the clientele, and (2) activities designed specifically to generate revenue. For both types, basic marketing concepts apply: the nonprofit marketer must identify the customer, segment the right market, undertake market and competitive industry research, develop a desirable product or service in an appealing package, and finally, design and implement effective media and public relations campaigns. None of these functions is unique, but there are some background sources that help focus on the particular challenges of the nonprofit and public environment.

California Nonprofit Corporation Book. **3rd edition. Berkeley, CA: Nolo Press, 2001. Print $60. 384 pages.**

Despite the focus indicated by the title, this book actually contains all the materials needed to apply for and obtain federal (Internal Revenue Status) nonprofit status. The book also includes sample material for preparing Articles of Incorporation, organizational bylaws and the like for nonprofit organizations.

Internal Revenue Code. Sections 501-530: Exempt Organizations. **Contact: http://caselaw.lp.findlaw.com/casecode/uscodes/26/toc.html.**

This is the part of the Internal Revenue Code (IRC) that defines a nonprofit organization. The IRC is found in the *United States Code*, Title 26, Subtitle A ("Income Taxes"), Chapter I ("Normal Taxes and Surtaxes"), Subchapter F ("Exempt Organizations"), Part I ("General Rule"). Section 501(3) (c) covers the majority of charitable, religious, and scientific organizations, and educational institutions. Other sections are concerned with different types of civic and social organizations that are also exempt from normal income tax requirements. Of special importance to marketers, Part III ("Taxation of Business Income of Certain Exempt Organization") discusses the taxation of income generated from sales and other activities not related directly to the organization's primary purpose.

TIP: Exempt Organizations

Forms and publications related to official exempt organization status can be downloaded from the IRS Web site. Contact: http://www.irs.gov.

TIP: A Selected Reading List for Nonprofit Marketers

Andreasen, Alan R. and Philip Kotler. 2003. *Strategic Marketing for Non-Profit Organizations*. 6th edition. Upper Saddle River, NJ: Prentice Hall.

Seminik, Richard J. and Gary J. Bamossy. 1994. *Advances in Non-profit Marketing*. Greenwich, CT: JAI Press.

Lovelock, Christopher H. and Charles B. Weinberg. 1984. *Marketing for Public and Nonprofit Managers*. New York: John Wiley & Sons.

Hutton, Stan. 2002. *"Marketing for Nonprofit Organizations"* (About.com Guide to Nonprofit Charitable Orgs). <http://nonprofit.about.com/cs/npomarketing> (August 8, 2002).

Stern, Gary J. and Elana Centor. 2001. *Marketing Workbook for Nonprofit Organizations Volume I: Develop the Plan*. 2nd edition. St. Paul, MN: Amherst H. Wilder Foundation.

SERVICES MARKETING

With the decline of the manufacturing economic base and the ascendance of the commercial service sector in the U.S. economy, the field of services marketing has grown into a full discipline in its own right. Examples of major service sectors include tourism and leisure, financial management, information technology, geographic mapping, executive placement, and many others. Service businesses have traditionally posed challenges for marketers because they are immensely diverse and, unlike product marketing, they deal in intangible benefits and values. Scholars of services marketing have attempted to define the complexities of services management: services offer intangible benefits; customers are involved in the production process; people are part of the product; products are not subject to standardization, are hard to evaluate, have no inventories, and their value is time sensitive; and distribution channels are variable. In fact, they speak of the "8 Ps" of integrated service management which recognize four additional decision variables in the marketing mix. In addition to the standard "4Ps" of product, price, place, and promotion, the "8Ps" include process, productivity and quality, people, and physical evidence (Lovelock and Wright 2001, 13).

***Handbook of Services Marketing and Management*. Teresa A. Swartz and Dawn Iacobucci, editors. Thousand Oaks, CA: Sage Publications, 2000. 521 pages.**

This handbook provides researchers and practitioners a foundation in basic theory and the ways it is expressed in latest practice. The contributing authors are well-known academic contributors in the fields of services marketing and management. Because the book is intended for practitioners as well as scholars, the writing style is "conceptual but not esoteric" (Swartz and Iacobucci 2000, 3).

The *Handbook of Services Marketing and Management* is organized into six major sections: the services setting, demand management, excellence and profitability, service recovery, service relationships, and the firm. The book includes both in-depth chapters as well as focused "mini" chapters, so that it offers broad coverage of many topics. It is useful as a reference tool due to the extensive chapter bibliographies, name index, and subject index.

Delivering Quality Service: Balancing Customer Perceptions and Expectations. **Valarie A. Zeithaml, A. Parasuraman, and Leonard L. Berry. New York: Free Press. 1990. Print. 226 pages.**

This book presents a groundbreaking model ("SERVQUAL") which has since become a standard method by which companies, marketing managers, and empirical researchers measure customer service success.

The authors identify several factors which customers ranked as the most important for quality of service. These include tangibles (facilities, equipment, personnel, communications); responsiveness (helpfulness and promptness); reliability (dependability and accuracy); assurance (that employees are knowledgeable and courteous); and empathy (understanding customer needs) (Zeithaml, Parasuraman, Berry 1990, 21-23). The model provides a two-part measure of customer perceptions and expectations, enabling marketers to segment their customer base into groups with different service expectations.

Their SERVQUAL survey instrument can be used by almost any type of organization to identify and correct areas in which adjustment is needed to increase customer satisfaction.

TIP: A Reading List on Services Marketing

Journal of Services Marketing. Bradford, U.K.: MCB University Press. 7 issues/year. $1,329. (Full text articles from 1994 to present are available online in the databases *Emerald Library* and *ABI/INFORM*. The journal is also indexed and abstracted in a number of periodical databases, including Gale's *General Reference Center, Ingenta*, and OCLC First Search's ArticleFirst.)

Lovelock, Christopher H. and Lauren Wright. 2002. *Principles of Service Marketing and Management.* 2nd edition. Upper Saddle River, NJ: Prentice Hall. (This is a popular textbook on the topic.)

Swartz, Teresa A. and Dawn Iacobucci. 2000. *Handbook of Services Marketing and Management.* Thousand Oaks, CA: Sage Publications.

Zeithaml, Valarie and Mary Jo Bitner. 2003. *Services Marketing.* 3rd edition. New York, NY: McGraw Hill-Irwin. (This textbook is geared to graduate students and executives.)

LEGAL AND ETHICAL ISSUES IN MARKETING

Because the purpose of marketing is to persuade and influence, there are concomitant legal, moral and ethical issues. Advertising and sales promotions have traditionally been the focus of these concerns, and they are regulated by the Federal Trade Commission (FTC). Other areas of marketing also raise questions dealing with the unscrupulous gathering and use of information; privacy has become an area of increasing concern due to the growth of our technological capabilities in database marketing and the Internet.

TIP: FTC's Advertising Policy and Guidelines

See the section of the FTC Web site on Advertising Policy and Guidelines at http://www.ftc.gov/bcp/guides/guides.htm.

Ethics and values are key issues in almost every area of marketing specialization. This is evident in the various codes of ethics or standards of practice adopted by corporations and professional associations to guide their employees and members. One prominent example is the American Marketing Association's Code of Ethics, which begins, "Members of the AMA are committed to ethical professional conduct." The Code then details marketers' responsibilities and general guidelines for conduct, and specifies particular points relevant to five specialized marketing areas: product development and management; promotions; distribution; pricing; and marketing research. Finally, the Code states, "Any AMA member found to be in violation of any provision of this Code of Ethics may have his or her Association membership suspended or revoked" (American Marketing Association 2002).

Similarly, the American Marketing Research Association maintains codes and professional standards for data collection, opinion research, Internet ethics, etc. The degree of the Association's commitment to its standards may be judged by its enforcement statement. There are three levels of sanctions for violations: censure, suspension, or expulsion, including permanent loss of membership (American Marketing Research Association 2000-2002). Codes of ethics may be found on most, if not all, professional association Web sites.

TIP: A Reading List About Marketing Ethics

Laczniak, Gene R. and Patrick E. Murphy, eds. 1985. *Marketing Ethics: Guidelines for Manager.* Lexington, MA: Lexington Books.
Schlegelmilch, Bodo. *Marketing Ethics: An International Perspective.* 1997. (Advanced Marketing Series) London: International Thomson Business Press.

There is a close relationship between ethics and the law, in that it is law which makes the ethics or values enforceable. In the ethical/legal context, the following sources are useful for anyone involved in marketing.

***Marketing Ethics Web Sites.* Marketing Education Review. University of Louisville. Louisville, KT. ©1999. Online (free). Contact: http://www.cbpa.louisville.edu/mer/ethics_websites.htm.**

This site provides a listing of Web links on the topic of marketing and ethics. There are educational sites listing syllabi and course readings. In addition, links to the codes of conduct promulgated by the important professional associations are included, such as those of the American Marketing Association, the Marketing Research Association, the Direct Marketing Association, and the European Society for Opinion and Marketing Research (ESOMAR). The site also links to numerous company and organizational examples.

***Advertising Law & Ethics.* Department of Advertising. University of Texas at Austin. Online (free). Contact: http://advertising.utexas. edu/research/law/index.html.**

Along with many other advertising-related resources, the Department of Advertising at the University of Texas-Austin provides an encyclopedic overview of advertising ethics at its Web site. This research guide contains sections on the First Amendment, trademark and copyright, deception, subliminal appeals, tobacco and alcohol, and more. Most of these sections contain background, definitions, bibliographies, the text of laws and regulations, and links to related information.

Robinson-Patman Act. 15 U.S. Code 13 (a-f)

The *Robinson-Patman Act* is a 1936 statute "aimed at price discrimination which . . . prohibits a seller of commodities from selling comparable goods to different buyers at different prices, except in certain defined circumstances" (*West's Encyclopedia of American Law* 1998, 9: 48-49). The act applies only to tangible goods, not to services such as loans, insurance, electricity, and advertising. It has been criticized over the years and the number of enforcement actions has declined, but it is still an important piece of sales law of which marketers should be aware.

TIP: *LAWMALL.com*

Lawmall.com is subtitled "A Unique Antitrust Website for Fighting Unlawful Price Discrimination (under the Robinson-Patman Act), Wal-Mart Expansion, Globalization Concerns and Related Matters, Including Prosecutorial Abuse." The site focuses on lawsuits and other documents related to the Robinson-Patman Act. Site developer Carl E. Person is an attorney practicing in New York. Contact: http://www.lawmall.com.

Uniform Commercial Code. **LII: Legal Information Institute. Cornell Law School. Ithaca, NY. Contact: http://www.law.cornell.edu/ucc/ucc.table.html.**

In the United States, commercial law is governed by the individual states. Therefore, the states, not the Federal government, are the primary source of law on commercial transactions in the U.S. The *Uniform Commercial Code* (UCC) is a set of suggested laws that states have elected to adopt.

> In all 50 states and the District of Columbia at least some of that commercial law is based on the *Uniform Commercial Code* (U.C.C.). A joint project of the American Law Institute and the National Conference of Commissioners on Uniform State Laws,

the first version of the U.C.C. was a "1952 Official Text." While one of several versions of the U.C.C. has now been adopted, at least in part by each of the states, not all states have adopted the most recent version and many states have amended some of the "uniform" provisions. As a consequence, the provisions of the U.C.C. appearing here are not, in fact, the uniform law of the U.S. (LII 2002)

The UCC contains articles covering sales, leases, commercial paper, bank deposits, funds transfers, letters of credit, bulk transfers, warehouse receipts, investment securities, and secured transactions. The Cornell University LII Web site contains a useful state-by-state guide to which versions of individual articles have been adopted by which states. There is also a Uniform Consumer Credit Code designed to protect consumers' credit transactions.

TIP: Legal issues specific to advertising are covered at these Web sites, which are fully described in Chapter 7, "Advertising and Media Planning Sources."

- *Advertising Law* http://www.arentfox.com/quickGuide/quickguide.html.
- *AdLaw* http://www.adlaw.com/.

Journal of Public Policy and Marketing. **University of Florida. Warrington College of Business. Gainesville, FL. Semi-Annual. Contact: http://bear.cba.ufl.edu/centers/jppm.**

One of the American Marketing Association's family of journals, the *Journal of Public Policy and Marketing* (JPPM) chronicles and analyzes the broader impact of marketing on consumer welfare and economic performance, as well as relevant policies and actions taken by the various branches of government that affect marketing practice and consumers (*JPPM* 2002). In addition to full-length articles, *JPPM* publishes book reviews, plus commentaries and viewpoints in its Policy Watch section. Recent issues have covered a range of topics including Internet marketing, tobacco advertising, sports marketing, FTC regulations, green marketing practices, online privacy, and credit card marketing to college students. In Spring 2002, a special issue on "Social Marketing" was published, including an article discussing ethics.

REFERENCES

American Marketing Association. 2002. "About the AMA/Code of Ethics." <http://www.marketingpower.com> (April 17, 2003).

American Marketing Research Association. 2000-2002. "Codes & Guidelines" <http://www.mra-net.org/codes/index.cfm> (April 17, 2003).

Journal of Public Policy and Marketing (JPPM). 2002. Gainesville, FL: University of Florida. Warrington College of Business <http://bear.cba.ufl.edu/centers/jppm> (April 17, 2003).

Kotler, Philip and Sidney J. Levy. 1969. "Broadening the Concept of Marketing." *Journal of Marketing* 33 (January): 10-15.

Legal Information Institute (LII). "Uniform Commercial Code." <http://www.law.cornell.edu/ucc/context.html> (April 17, 2003).

Lovelock, Christopher and Lauren Wright. 2001. *Principles of Service Marketing Management,* 2nd edition. Upper Saddle River, NJ: Prentice Hall.

National Social Norms Resource Center (NSNRC). 2001. <http://www.socialnorm.org/faqs.html> (April 17, 2003).

Swartz, Teresa A. and Dawn Iacobucci. 2000. *Handbook of Services Marketing and Management.* Thousand Oaks, CA: Sage Publications.

West's Encyclopedia of American Law. 1998. s.v. "Robinson-Patman Act." St. Paul, MN: West Publishing Co.

Zeithaml, Valerie, A. Parasuraman, and Leonard L. Berry. 1990. *Delivering Quality Service: Balancing Customer Perceptions and Expectations.* New York: Free Press.

Appendix
Selected Glossaries

Subject or Focus	Chapter(s)	Source
Ad copy and campaigns	7	SRDS publications
Branding terms	3	*Brandchannel.com*
Demographics	5 and 6	New Strategist publications (e.g., *American Marketplace, Racial & Ethnic Diversity*, etc.)
Economic Census (2002 terms)	9	U.S. Census Bureau
E-Commerce & Internet Advertising	10	*Plunkett's E-Commerce & Internet Business Almanac*; *Ecommerce-guide.com*; *AdResource*
Exporting; international trade	11	*Exporters' Encyclopedia*; Dun & Bradstreet Web site; *Export Sales and Marketing Manual*
Logistics	12	*LogisticsWorld*
Magazine publishing & circulation	7	Magazine Publishers of America
Marketing	1	*Blackwell Encyclopedic Dictionary of Marketing*; *Dictionary of Marketing and Advertising*; *Marketing: The Encyclopedic Dictionary*; *The Marketing Glossary*
Market Research	4	*Dictionary of Market Research Terms (IMRI)*; *Dictionary of Social and Marketing Research*; *Dictionary of Marketing Research*
Media buying	7	SRDS publications
Packaging	12	*Packexpo.com*; *Marketer's Guide to Successful Package Design*; *Fundamentals of Packaging Technology*
Product development	12	Product Development and Management Association; *PDMA Handbook of New Product Development*
Retail terminology	9	*Plunkett's Retail Industry Almanac*; *Plunkett's Research Industry Channel*

[Haworth co-indexing entry note]: "Appendix. Selected Glossaries." Diamond, Wendy, and Michael R. Oppenheim. Co-published simultaneously in *Journal of Business & Finance Librarianship* (The Haworth Information Press, an imprint of The Haworth Press, Inc.) Vol. 9, No. 4, 2004, p. 301; and: *Marketing Information: A Strategic Guide for Business and Finance Libraries* (Wendy Diamond, and Michael R. Oppenheim) The Haworth Information Press, an imprint of The Haworth Press, Inc., 2004, p. 301. Single or multiple copies of this article are available for a fee from The Haworth Document Delivery Service [1-800-HAWORTH, 9:00 a.m. - 5:00 p.m. (EST). E-mail address: docdelivery@haworthpress.com].

http://www.haworthpress.com/web/JBFL
© 2004 by The Haworth Press, Inc. All rights reserved.
Digital Object Identifier: 10.1300/J109v09n04_06

Title Index

"A Unique Antitrust Website for
  Fighting Unlawful Price
  Discrimination, Wal-Mart
  Expansion, Globalization
  Concerns and Related
  Matters, Including
  Prosecutorial Abuse," 297
"A View on the Future of Branding,"
  89
AAAA. *See* American Association of
  Advertising Agencies (AAAA)
AAAAgency Search, 164
ABI/FORM, 27,29,61,125,136,141,
  144,294
ABI/FORM database, 81
ABI/INFORM, 9-10,23-24
A.C. Nielsen Media Research, 166
Accenture, 234
ACORN, 132,144
ACS. *See American Community Survey
  (ACS)*
Ad Revenue Reports, 233
Ad*Access, 176-178
AdAge Data Center, 173
AdAge Global, 261-262
Adfacts, 176
"AdFolio," 164
AdForum.com, 164,180
ADIs. *See* Areas of Dominant Influence
  (ADIs)
AdLaw, 184
AdLaw.com, 164
AdNetTrackUS, 175
Ad$pender, 175
AdRelevance Analytics, 234
AdRelevance Metrics, 234
AdResource, 233
AdReview.com, 180

AdTelligence, 175
Advertiser Magazine, 28
Advertisers edition, 159
*Advertising Age Encyclopedia of
  Advertising*, 179-180
Advertising Age magazine, 146,161,
  171,173,179,180
Advertising Agencies, 160
"Advertising Effectiveness Survey," 182
Advertising Growth Trends (AGT), 172
*Advertising Growth Trends (AGT):
  Inflation Adjusted Analysis of
  Ad Spending*, 172
Advertising Law, 184-185
Advertising Law & Ethics, 296-297
Advertising Law Internet Site, 184
Advertising Manager's Handbook, 11,
  185
Advertising Ratios & Budgets (ARB),
  171-172
Advertising Red Book, 136
*Advertising Red Books–International
  Advertisers and Agencies*, 261
Advertising Research Foundation (ARF),
  144,181-182
Advertising World, 180,186
Adweek Directory, 164
AFF. *See American FactFinder (AFF)*
Agencies ComPile.com, 164
Agencies edition, 159
"Agency Preview," 164
Agency Redbook, 164
Agency Responsibilities index, 160-161
Agriculture, 59
AGT. *See Advertising Growth Trends
  (AGT)*
Alacra, Inc., 27-28
"All in One Media Directory," 193

Almanac of Business and Financial Ratios, 60
AltaVista, 32
AMA. *See* American Marketing Association (AMA)
AMACOM, 18
America Online (AOL), 32,229
American Association of Advertising Agencies (AAAA), 161,164, 169-170,185-186
American Society of Association Executives Gateway, 66
American Booksellers Association, web site for, 62
American Booksellers Association Research and Statistics web site, 65
American Business Disc, 75-76
American Community Survey (ACS), 112,116-117
American Demographics magazine, 125
American FactFinder (AFF), 55,114
American Housing Survey, 112
"American Indian and Alaska Natives–an Untapped Emerging Majority Market," 141
American Institute of Certified Public Accountants, 171-172
American Law Institute, 297
American Marketing Association (AMA), 5,17,35,142,197, 279,296
　Code of Ethics of, 295
American Marketing Research Association, 296
American Marketplace: Demographics and Spending Patterns, 124
American Men: Who They Are and How They Live, 124
American Statistics Index (ASI), 32,65
American Stock Exchange, 72-73
American Trucking Trends, 282
American Wholesalers & Distributors Directory, 217

"Amusement, Gambling, & Recreation Industries," 47
ANA. *See* Association of National Advertisers (ANA)
Annual Bibliography of Logistics Management, 282
Annual Consumer Show Report, 211
Annual List Usage Survey, 224
Annual Report to Shareholders (ARS), 77
Annual State of Logistics Report, 282
Annual Survey of Manufactures, 46, 57-58
AOL. *See* America Online (AOL)
Apple Computer, 87,178
ARB. *See Advertising Ratios & Budgets (ARB)*
Arbor Strategy Group, 272
Areas of Dominant Influence (ADIs), 192
Arent Fox Attorneys at Law, 184-185
ARF. *See* Advertising Research Foundation (ARF)
ARF Youth Research Council, 144
Armstrong's Guide to Third-Party Logistics Providers & Dedicated Contract Carriers, 282
ARS. *See* Annual Report to Shareholders (ARS)
ARS Group, 183-184
ARS Group Web site, 183-184
ARS Persuasion, 183
ASI. *See American Statistics Index (ASI)*
ASI Market Research, 184
"Ask the Experts," 280
Associated Press, 216
Association of National Advertisers (ANA), 169-170
Associations Unlimited, 66
Axiom Press, 248-249

Bacon's Information, Inc., 193
Bank and Finance, International companies, 73

Barron's, 26
"Basic Guide to Exporting," 281
Basic Marketing: A Managerial Approach, 6
Beacham's Marketing Reference, 19
Bernan Press, 59-60,118
Best Customers: Demographics of Consumer Demand, 120
Best Market Reports (BMR), 255
"Best Practice: The Principles of Effective Advertising for Dotcoms," 89
Best Practice Tools, 183
Beverage Industry, 274
Bibliography of Research and Writings on Marketing and Advertising to Children, 146-147
Bill Communications, Inc., 209
BizMinder.com, 60
"BizSector Creative Reviews," 164
BizStats.com, 60
Blackwell Publishers, 18
BLS. *See* Bureau of Labor Statistics (BLS)
BMR. *See* Best Market Reports (BMR)
Bob Coen's Insider's Report, 172-173
"Bonus" Information, in *Red Books*, 163
Bowker, 191-193
BPI. *See* Buying Power Index (BPI)
BPI Communications, 166
Brand Name Indexes, in Advertisers *Red Books*, 163
Brandchannel.com, 88-89
BrandLine, 101
BrandPackaging magazine, 273,274
Brands and Their Companies, 85
BrightPlanet, 33
"Broadening the Concept of Marketing," 36
BrokerLine, 101
"Building Corporate Reputation," 198
Bureau of Labor Statistics (BLS), 115
Burrelle's Information Services, 191, 193-194
Burrelle's Media Directory, 191

Business & Company Resource Center, 25,75
Business & Industry, 24-25,27,29,30, 81,98,125,136,141
Business & Management Practices, 10
Business and Company Resource Center, 81,84,85,217
Business Development Success Series, 280
Business Information: How to Find It, How to Use It, 13,29
Business Management Practices, 98
Business Periodicals, 25
Business Periodicals Index, 21
Business Publication Advertising Source, 165
Business Publications: Asia-Pacific/ Middle East/Africa, 260
Business Publications: Europe, 260
Business Publications: The Americas, 260
Business Rankings Annual, 80-81,81
Business Source Corporate, 24
Business Source Elite, 24
Business Source Premier, 24,61,81, 125,136,141
Business Statistics of the United States, 59-60
Business Week, 64,89
Business Wire, 194,216
Business/Marketing/Market Research Suppliers category, 105
"Business-to-Business (B2B) E-Commerce," 235
Buyers Guide, 209
Buying Power Index (BPI), 133

CACI Marketing Systems, 131
California Nonprofit Corporation Book, 292
Canadian Advertising Rates & Data, 261
Candy Industry, 274
Capital Changes Reports, 84

"Career Seekers," 198
"Case Studies," 9
Cases in Marketing Management, 10
CASS Corporation, 282
CBP. *See County Business Patterns
    (CBP)*
CCGs. *See Country Commercial Guides
    (CCGs)*
Cendex, 274
Census Bureau, 54-55,56,57,58,112,114,
    115,116,212-215,230-231
Census Bureau reports, 119
Census Bureau Special Report, 137
Census Bureau Web site, 55
Census Bureau's Metropolitan
    Statistical Areas (MSAs), 121
Census of Housing, 116
Census of Manufactures, 57
Census of Manufacturing, 58
Census of Population, 116
Census of Population and Housing,
    112
Census of Retail Trade, 112,214
Census of Wholesale Trade, 112,214
*Center for Research in Electronic
    Commerce*, 235
Central Intelligence Agency (CIA),
    244-245,247
Chambers of Commerce, 76
*Children and Adolescents in the Market
    Place: Twenty-Five Years of
    Academic Research*, 147
"CI Strategies and Tools," 79
CIA. *See* Central Intelligence Agency
    (CIA)
*CIO (Chief Information Officer)
    Magazine*, 232-233
Claritas, Inc., 133
Class/Brand $, 176
CLM. *See* Council of Logistics
    Management (CLM)
"Clutter Study," 170
CMR, 174-176
Coca Cola, 87,273

Code of Ethics, of AMA, 295
Code of Federal Regulations, 228
College of Journalism and
    Communication, at University
    of Florida, 200-201
Columbia Books, 66
"Commerce Business Daily," 263
*Commercial Closet: The World's
    Largest Collection of Gay
    Advertising*, 150-151
Commercial Closet Association, 150-151
Commodity Line Sales, 213,214
Communications World, 200
Companies and Their Brands, 85
Company/Brand, 176
CompanyLine, 101
"Comparative Company Analysis," 51
CompBook, 28
*Compensation Survey/Logistics
    Management*, 282
Competia, 66
"Competitive Advertisements
    Collection," 177
*Competitor Intelligence: How to Get
    It, How to Use It*, 79
Competitrack, 176
CompletePlanet, 33
Congressional Voting Scorecards, 216
Consumer Expenditure Survey, 112,119
Consumer Expenditures, 132-133
*Consumer Magazine Advertising
    Source*, 128,165
Consumer Magazines Worldwide, 260
Consumer Price Index (CPI) calculator,
    280
Consumer Products, 99
"Copy Research Validity Project," 182
Cornell Law School, 297-298
Cornell University LII Web site, 298
Council Annual Report, 198
Council of Logistics Management
    (CLM), 276,281-282
Council of Public Relations Firms
    (CPRF), 197
Council of Public Relations Firms
    (CPRF) Web site, 196

Country Commercial Guides (CCGs), 252-253,255,260

Country Data, 242

Country Forecast series, 246

Country Profile series, 246

Country Report, 246,247

Country Reports on Economic Policy and Trade Practices, 254

Country Studies/Area Handbooks, 246

Country Study Series, 245-246

Country ViewsWire, 246

Country Watch: Website to the World, 247

CountryLine, 101

CountryWatch.com, 247

County and City Data Book: A Statistical Abstract Supplement, 118

County and City Extra: Annual Metro, City, and County Data Book, 118

County and City Extra: Special Decennial Census Edition, 118

County Business Patterns (CBP), 56,57

Courtney Communications, 227-228

CPI calculator. *See* Consumer Price Index (CPI) calculator

CPRF. *See* Council of Public Relations Firms (CPRF)

CPS. *See* Current Population Survey (CPS)

Crain Communications, 161,173

Crain Publications, 180

"Create Your Own Customized Market Reports," of *Industry Canada*, 256

Credit Suisse First Boston, 53,102

"Cross-Client Index," 195

Cullbridge Marketing and Communication, 289

CultureGrams, 248-249

Current Industrial Reports, 46,57,58

Current Population Reports, 115

Current Population Survey (CPS), 112, 115,118,119

Customer Service Week Web site, 208

CXOMedia, Inc., 232-234

CyberAtlas.com, 235

Dartnell Corporation, 185,207-208

Dartnell's Advertising Manager's Handbook, 185

Dartness's 30th Sales Force Compensation Survey 1998-1999, 207-208

"Data about American Consumers," 124

Data Query Manager (DQM), 33

Datamonitor, 53,234

Datastar, 27

Delivering Quality Service: Balancing Customer Perceptions and Expectations, 294

Demographic Sourcebooks, 131-133

Department of Advertising, at University of Texas, at Austin, 296-297

Department of Commerce, 52,58,139, 230-231,234,263

International Trade Administration of, 252-253

OTEXA of, 264-265

Department of Economic and Social Affairs, of UN, 240

Department of Marketing, 34

"Designated market areas (DMAs)," 121,127-128,140

"Developing Your E-Mail Marketing Lists," 212

Dialog, 9,26-27,27,100

Dialog, 26-27,53,194

Dictionary of Marketing and Advertising, 18

Dictionary of Marketing Research, 93

Dictionary of Marketing Terms, 5

Dictionary of Social and Marketing Research, 93

Digital Millennium Copyright Act (DMCA) of 1998, 15

Direct Mail List Rates and Data, 225

"Direct Marketing," 212

Direct Marketing Association, 222,
    223,224,296
Direct Marketing List Source, 128,165,
    225-226
*Direct Marketing Market Place
    (DMMP)*, 226
Directory of Associations, 66
Directory of Corporate Affiliations,
    70-71
*Directory of Multicultural Relations
    Professionals and Firms*, 139
*Directory of Premium, Incentive, &
    Travel Buyers*, 207,208
Directory of Public Relations Firms,
    195-196
"Discretion *versus* Valor: How to
    Manage an Aggressive
    Competitor," 278
Disney, 87
"DM News Online List Directory," 227
DMA List/Database Council, 224
DMAs. *See* "Designated market areas
    (DMAs)"
DMCA of 1998. *See Digital
    Millennium Copyright Act
    (DMCA) of 1998*
DMMP. *See Direct Marketing Market
    Place (DMMP)*
DMNews.com, 227-228,228
"Do Not Call" lists, 228
Donnelley Marketing, 76
Do's and Taboo's Around the World,
    249
Douglas Publications, Inc., 208
Dow Jones & Reuters, 25-26
Dow Jones Business News, 216
DQM. *See Data Query Manager (DQM)*
Duke University, 176-178,179
Dun & Bradstreet Information
    Services, 73
Dun & Bradstreet International, 250-252
*Dun & Bradstreet's Guide to Doing
    Business Around the World*,
    249

Dun & Bradstreet's Sales and Marketing
    Solutions, 209

Easy Demographics Software, Inc., 125
EBSCO Information Services, 24
"E-Business Value," 235
ECCH. *See* European Case Clearing
    House (ECCH)
ECNext Knowledge Center, 98-99,99
ECNextInc., 98-99
"E-Commerce Trade & B2B
    Exchanges," 234
ecommerce-guide.com, 232
Economic Census, 54-55,56,58,59,
    214,219
Economic Census data, by zip code, 56
Economic Census reports, 57
Economic Censuses, 46,118
*Economic Census–Wholesale and
    Retail Trade Sectors*, 212-214
"Economic Impact: U.S. Marketing
    Today," 225
Economic Impact study, 222
Economist Intelligence Unit (EIU), 27,
    53,238,246
EDGAR database, 77
EDI. *See* Electronic Data Interchange
    (EDI)
Editor & Publishers Market Guide, 219
Educational Marketer, 29
EIU. *See* Economist Intelligence Unit
    (EIU)
"Electronic Data Gathering, Analysis,
    and Retrieval (EDGAR)," 77
Electronic Data Interchange (EDI), 231
Elsevier Science, 271
eMarketer, 233,234
eMarketer, Inc., 234
eMarketer Daily, 234
"eMarketer Reports," 234
Emerald, 10
Emerald Library, 294
EMMC. *See Encyclopedia of Major
    Marketing Campaigns
    (EMMC)*

Employment and Earnings, 115
Encyclopedia of Advertising, 179-180
Encyclopedia of American Industries,
  49-50,62,65
Encyclopedia of Associations, 66
*Encyclopedia of Business Information
  Sources*, 17,62-63,66
Encyclopedia of Consumer Brands,
  85-86
*Encyclopedia of Corporate Names
  Worldwide*, 88
*Encyclopedia of Major Marketing
  Campaigns (EMMC)*, 178-179
Environment Canada, 289
Environmental Protection Agency
  (EPA), 46,67
EPA. *See* Environmental Protection
  Agency (EPA)
EPM Communications, 96-97,141
EPM Consumer Segmentation Survey,
  125
Equifax, 126
eReleases.com, 194
ESOMAR. *See* European Society for
  Opinion and Marketing
  Research (ESOMAR)
ESRI BIS, 131,132
ESRI Business Information Solutions,
  131-133
Establishment and Firm Size, 213
"eStat Database," 234
E-Stats, 230-231
Ethnic Media Directory, 138
Ethnic NewsWatch, 142
Ethnics in Social Marketing, 289
Euromonitor, 61,98,260
Euromonitor International, 238,256-259
European Case Clearing House
  (ECCH), 10
*European Marketing Data and
  Statistics*, 257
European Society for Opinion and
  Marketing Research
  (ESOMAR), 296
E-Watch Internet Monitoring, 197

Executive Planet.com, 249
*Experts on Gay, Lesbian, Bisexual,
  Transsexual, and Transgendered
  Policy-relevant Research*, 149
Export Advantage, 264-265
"Export Finance Matchmakers," 264
Export Institute, USA, 252,280
Export Reference Library, 251
Export Sales and Marketing Manual,
  252,280
Exporter's Encyclopedia, 250-252,260
Export.gov, 253
Extensible Markup Language (XML),
  34

Factiva, 25-26,30,102,141,144,194
"Factors Affecting Online Retail in
  2002," 234
FCC. *See* Federal Communications
  Commission (FCC)
Federal Communications Commission
  (FCC), 234
Federal Reserve Bank, 52
  of Minneapolis, 280
Federal Trade Commission (FTC),
  234,295
Federal Trade Commission (FTC)
  updates, 184
Federal Trade Commission's
  Telemarketing Sales Rule, 228
"Fertility of American Women," 115
Fiber Box Association, 276
Films for the Humanities & Sciences, 36
*Finance, Insurance & Real Estate
  USA*, 59
"Find a PR Firm," 196
FINDEX, 96
*FINDEX: The Worldwide Directory of
  Market Research Reports,
  Studies, and Survey*, 96,97
Finding Market Research on the Web,
  94,96
First Search's ArticleFirst, 294
Fishing, 59

Fitzroy Dearborn, 179-180
Five Technologies to Watch, web site
    for, 65
Flexible Packaging, 274
Food & Drug Packaging, 274
Food Institute, 53
Food Marketing Institute, web site for,
    62
Forbes, 64
Forestry, 59
Forrester Research, 234
Fortune, 64
Fortune 1000, 76
"Four Ps of Marketing," 238
Free Press, 294
Freedonia, 98
FTC. *See* Federal Trade Commission
    (FTC)
FTC updates, 184
Fuld & Company, 66
*Fuld & Company Competitive
    Intelligence Guide*, 66
Fuld & Company Web site, 79
*Fundamentals of Packaging
    Technology*, 277

"Gaining Competitive Advantage
    Through Pricing," 279
Gale Encyclopedia of E-Commerce,
    228-229
Gale Group, 17,24-25,29,49-50,53,
    58-59,61,62-63,66,75,80-81,
    82-86,98,178-179,211,217,
    228-229
Gale Group databases, 98
Gartner Group, 52,53
*Gay Directory of Authoritative
    Resources (GAYDAR)*, 149-150
Gay Media Database, 149
"Gay Purchasing Power a Significant
    Force, Major Study Reveals,"
    151-152
*GAYDAR (Gay Directory of Authoritative
    Resources)*, 149-150
Gebbie Press, 193

Gebbie's, 193
Gebbie's Web site, 193
General Business File, 53
General Motors (GM), 180
General Reference Center, 294
Geographic index, 160
Geographical Mobility, 115
Geographical Mobility report, 115-116
Georgetown University, 288
GeoVALS, 131
GLA. *See* "Gross Leasable Area (GLA)"
Glass Packing Institute, 276
GLINN Media Corporation, 149
Global Competitiveness Report, 241-242
*Global Market Information Database
    (GMID)*, 257,258
Global Market Share Planner, 61
Globus/NTDB, 253,263
Glossary(ies), 301
Glossary of Market Research Terms, 93
"Glossary of New Product Development
    Terms," 271
GLVensus Partners, 151-152
GM. *See* General Motors (GM)
GMID. *See Global Market Information
    Database (GMID)*
Google, 10,32,33,34
Google Directory, 105
Google Web Directory, 66
Government Printing Office, 245-246
Government Publications Department,
    of University of Memphis
    library, 231
*Great Writings in Marketing: Selected
    Readings Together with the
    Authors' Own Retrospective
    Commentaries*, 36-37
Green Book, 144
*Green Book: The Worldwide Directory
    of Market Research Companies
    and Services*, 103-104
Greenfield Online, Inc., 105-106
Grey House Publishing, 279-280
"Gross Leasable Area (GLA)," 219

GSociety, 151
"Guidelines and Standards for Measuring
    the Effectiveness of PR
    Programs, 201

Hall, Dickler, Kent, Goldstein, & Wood,
    LLP, 184
Handbook of Marketing, 11
Handbook of Package Engineering, 277
*Handbook of Services Marketing and
    Management*, 293-294
HAPPI (Household and Personal
    Products Industry) Online,
    web site for, 62
Harvard Business Online, 10
Health Canada, 289
"Health Insurance Coverage," 116
"Hiring a Public Relations Firm: A
    Guide for Clients," 198
Hispanic Media & Market Source, 140
Hispanic Study, 141
Holmes Report, 198
"Home Computers and Internet Use,"
    116
Hoover's, Inc., 71-72,97
*Hoover's Handbook of American
    Business*, 71-72
*Hoover's Handbook of Emerging
    Companies*, 72
*Hoover's Handbook of Private
    Companies*, 72
Hoover's Handbook of World Business,
    72
Hoover's Online, 72,222
Hospitality Net, web site for, 62
"Hot Spots for Advancement for Women
    and Minorities," 229
House Agencies, 160
Household and Personal Products
    Industry (HAPPI) Online,
    web site for, 62
Household Food Consumption Survey,
    112

"How to Measure Your Results in a
    Crisis," 201
"How We Are Changing: The
    Demographic State of the
    Nation," 116
Howard University, 139
HTML (Hyper Text Markup Language),
    34
H.W. Wilson, 25
Hyper Text Markup Language
    (HTML), 34

IABC. *See* International Association of
    Business Communicators
    (IABC)
IABC Research Foundation, 200
IEBM. *See International Encyclopedia
    of Business and Management
    (IEBM)*
IEBM Encyclopedia of Marketing,
    18-19,36
*IEBM International Encyclopedia of
    Marketing*, 5
IGLSS. *See* Institute for Gay and Lesbian
    Strategic Studies (IGLSS)
IMF. *See* International Monetary Fund
    (IMF)
"IMF Country Reports," 241
IMI reports, 255
Impact Marketing Consultants, Inc.,
    275-276
IMRMall.com, 98
Incentive Magazine, 209
"Index of Newspapers by ADI," 192
Index to International Statistics, 65
"Index to Products & Services Section
    Headings," 74
Industry Canada, "Create Your Own
    Customized Market Reports,"
    256
*Industry Insider Trade Association
    Research*, 53
"Industry Quick Reports," 55
Industry Quick Reports, 174

"Industry Research" section, of Plunkett
    Research Web site, 230
Industry Sector Analyses (ISAs), 256
Industry Sector Analysis (ISAs), 258
Industry Sector Notebooks, 67
"Industry Sector Offices and Contacts,"
    264
Industry Surveys, 50-51,52
    Standard & Poor's, 62,65
Information Advisor, 99
Information Resources, Inc., 52
InfoTech Trends, web site for, 62
InfoUSA, 75-76
Ingenta, 294
"Innovation Center," 198
Insider's Report, 172-173
Insight Media, 36
Institute for Gay and Lesbian Strategic
    Studies (IGLSS), 149-150
Institute of Management Development,
    242
Institute of Packaging Professionals,
    276
Institute of Public Relations (IPR),
    200-201
Interactive Advertising Bureau, 233
Interactive Advertising Source, 165
Interbrand, 88-89
Internal Revenue Code (IRC), 292
*International Advertising and Marketing
    Information Sources*, 262
International Association of Business
    Communicators (IABC), 200
*International Brands and Their
    Companies/International
    Companies and Their
    Brands*, 85
International Customer Service
    Association, 208
International Data Corporation, 52
*International Directory of Company
    Histories*, 83-84
*International Encyclopedia of Business
    and Management (IEBM)*, 36

International Financial Statistics, 247
International Index of Statistics (ISI), 32
International Journal of Advertising, 28
*International Journal of Market
    Research*, 28
International Market Insight (IMI), 258
International Market Insight (IMI)
    reports, 255
*International Marketing Data and
    Statistics*, 257
International Media Guides, 260-261
International Monetary Fund (IMF),
    238,240-241,247
International News Distribution, 197
International Trade Administration, of
    Department of Commerce,
    OTEXA of, 264-265
International Trade Reporter, 251
International Tradeshow Directory,
    210
"Internet Advertising and Promotion
    Resources," 233
Internet Economic Indicators, 235
Internet Explorer, 32
Internet Intelligence Index, 66,79
"Internet Organizations," 235
Internet Service Provider (ISP), 32,34
InternetNews.com, 235
Investext, 25
Investext database, 102
Investext Investment Research, 53
Investext's Research Bank Web, 100
*Investing, Licensing and Trading
    Conditions*, 251
Invisible Web, 33
IPR. *See* Institute of Public Relations
    (IPR)
IRC. *See Internal Revenue Code (IRC)*
ISAs. *See Industry Sector Analyses
    (ISAs)*
ISI. *See International Index of Statistics
    (ISI)*
ISP. *See* Internet Service Provider (ISP)

J. Walter Thompson Company
 Archives, 177
John W. Harman Center for Sales,
 Advertising, and Marketing
 History, 176-178,179
John Wiley & Sons, 18,79,271-272
Jolly Green Giant, 186
Journal of Advertising Research, 6
Journal of Business Logistics, 282
*Journal of Product Innovation and
 Management (JPIM)*, 271
*Journal of Public Policy and
 Marketing (JPPM)*, 298
Journal of Services Marketing, 294
JPIM. *See Journal of Product Innovation
 and Management (JPIM)*
JPPM. *See Journal of Public Policy
 and Marketing (JPPM)*
Jupitermedia Corporation, 231,235
"Just Do It," 178

Kalorama Academic, 101
Kalorama Information LLC, 97
*Kids These Days '99: What Americans
 Really Think About the Next
 Generation*, 146
*Kiss, Bow, or Shake Hands: How to
 Do Business in Sixty
 Countries*, 249
KnowThis.com, 34

LAWMALL.com, 297
Lehman Brothers, 53
Leo Burnett Worldwide, 186
Lexibot, 33
Lexington Books, 146-147
LexisNexis, 261
LexisNexis, 26,53,102,144,194
LexisNexis Academic and Library
 Solutions, 30,225
LexisNexis database, 65
LexisNexis Group, 26,70-71,159-165

LexisNexis Statistical, 32,225
Library and Knowledge Center, 138
Library of Congress, 245
*Lifestyle Market Analyst (LMA): A
 Reference Guide for Consumer
 Market Analysis*, 126-128
Little Black Book of Research Resources,
 105
Local Evening News, 170
Logistics Trends, 282
Logistics World, 283
Logistics Zone, 283
LogLink, 283

M + A Verlag fuer Messen, Ausstellungen
 und Kongresse GmbH, 210
"Magazine and Internal Publications
 Directory," 192
Magazine Publishers of America
 (MPA), 167,182
Magazine Publishers of America
 (MPA) Web site, 174
Mainsail Interactive Services, 198
Major Marketing Campaigns Annual,
 178
Major Topic Index, 147
MANA. *See* Manufacturers' Agents
 National Association
 (MANA)
*MANA Members Directory of
 Manufacturers' Sales
 Agencies*, 217
Manufacturers' Agents National
 Association (MANA), 217
*Manufacturing & Distribution USA
 (MDUSA)*, 58-59
*Mapping Census 2000: The Geography
 of U.S. Diversity*, 137
"Marital Status and Living
 Arrangements," 115
"Market Research Channels," 230
Market Research Reports, 255-256
Market Share Reporter, 61,67

Market Share Reporter: An Annual Compilation of Reported Market Share Data on Companies, Goods, and Services, 82

Marketer's Guide to Media, 140,167, 168,169

MARKETFULL, 100

Marketing: The Encyclopedic Dictionary, 18

Marketing Classics: A Selection of Influential Articles, 36-37

Marketing Education Review, 296

Marketing Ethics Web Sites, 296

Marketing Information: A Professional Guide, 17

Marketing Manager's Handbook, 11

"Marketing Myopia," 36

Marketing News, 5,63,197

Marketing Research Association, 296

Marketing Resource Gateway, 34

Marketing Science Institute (MSI), 35, 37

Marketing to Ethnic Consumers: An Annotated Bibliography, 142

Marketing to the Emerging Majorities, 141

Marketing to Women, 141

Marketing Today, 227

"Marketing Virtual Library," 34

MarketingPower.com, 197

MarketLooks, 102

MarketResearch.com, 96,97-98,101-102

MarketResearch.com, 96,97-98,99, 101-102,136,140,141,145

MarketResearch.com Academic, 102

MarketResearch.com collection, 96

MarkIntel Market Research, 53

Maydream, 180

McCann-Erickson WorldGroup Web site, 172

McCombs School of Business, at University of Texas, 235

McDonald's, 87

McFarland, 88

MDOL ("Media Directory Online"), 191

"Measuring the Electronic Economy," 230

"Measuring the Mix: Quantifying the Sales Impact of Magazine Advertising," 182

Media Buying Services, 160

"Media Directory Online" (MDOL), 191

Media Placement Guide: How to Work with Editors and Enjoy It, 196

Media Planning and Buying Calculations, 168

Mediamark Research, Inc. (MRI), 129, 144,169

MediaPost, 168

Mediaweek Multimedia Directory, 168

MEMRI database, 129

Merchandise Line Sales, 213

Mergent, Inc., 72-73

Mergent Industrial Manual, 72

Mergent Manuals, 72-73,84

Mergent Online, 73

Merrill Lynch, 53,102

MetricMedia Group, 51-52

Metro Business Patterns, 56

Metropolitan Statistical Area (MSA), 219

Mexican Audiovisual/Print Media Rates & Data, 261

Michigan State University, 276
   School of Packaging at, 276

Microsoft Excel, 33

Microsoft Word, 33

"Million Dollar Database," 73

"Million Dollar Database Lite," 73

"Million Dollar Database Premier," 73

Million Dollar Directory, 73

Millward Brown International, 184

MindBranch, Inc., 99

Mindbranch.com, 97,99

Mining & Construction USA, 59

Minority Buying Power in the New Century, 139

Miscellaneous Subjects, 213
"Money Income in the United States," 116
MONITOR, 144
"Monkey Ward" Wish Book, 222
Montgomery Ward, 222
Montgomery Ward Direct, 222
Monthly Bulletin of Statistics, 247
"Moody's Manuals," 72,84
Morgan Stanley Dean Witter, 53,102
Mouse Tracks: The List of Marketing Lists, 35
MPA. *See* Magazine Publishers of America (MPA)
MPA Web site. *See* Magazine Publishers of America (MPA) Web site
MRI. *See* Mediamark Research, Inc. (MRI)
MSA. *See* Metropolitan Statistical Area (MSA)
MSI. *See* Marketing Science Institute (MSI)
MSW Research, 184
Multex, 54,102-103
Multicultural Marketing News, 138
Multicultural Marketing Resources, 138
Municipal and Government entities, 73
Museum of Broadcast Communications, 179

"NAFTA Rules of Origin," 264
NAICS. *See* North American Industry Classification System (NAICS)
NAICS code. *See* North American Industry Classification System (NAICS) code
"National Business Statistics," 60
National Conference of Commissioners on Uniform State Laws, 297
National Consumer Survey data, from Simmons, 129
National Customer Service Week, 208

National Gay Newspaper Guild (NGNG), 151
National Paint and Coatings Association, web site for, 62
National Register Publishing, 226
National Research Bureau, 218-219
National Restaurant Association, 66
  web site for, 62
National Retail Federation (NRF), 215-216
National Social Norms Resource Center (NSNRC), 289-290
National Social Norms Resource Center (NSNRC) Web site, 290
National Sporting Goods Association, web site for, 62
National System Ad Tracking, 176
National Trade and Professional Associations of the United States, 66
NCM. *See* New California Media (NCM)
NetAdvantage, 50
NetRatings, Inc., 233
Netscape, 32
NetView Usage Metrics, 234
Network Evening News, 170
New California Media (NCM), 138
"New Coke," 190
New Strategist, 125
New Strategist Publications, 123-125, 137
New York AMA Communications Services, Inc., 103-104
New York Stock Exchange, 71
New York University Press, 86-87
New York Weekly, 52
NewProductWorks, 272-273
Newsline, 101
"Newspaper Directory," 192
Newspapers Worldwide, 260
Newsweek, 146
NGNG. *See* National Gay Newspaper Guild (NGNG)
Nielsen Media Research Media Market, 121

Nielsen/NetRatings, 233-234
Nike, "Just Do It" of, 178
1999 National Consumer Survey for Colleges and Universities, 128-130
"1984," 178
1994 Yankelovich MONITOR Perspective on Gays/Lesbians, 136
1997 Economic Census, 137
"1952 Official Text," 298
Nolo Press, 292
NOP World, 144
North American Industry Classification System (NAICS), 55,58,82,213
North American Industry Classification System (NAICS) code, 74,75, 76,172, 227-228,231
Notable Corporate Chronologies, 84
NPW Product Collection, 272
NRF. *See* National Retail Federation (NRF)
NSNRC. *See* National Social Norms Resource Center Web site (NSNRC)
NTC Business Books, 272,276
NTC Publishing Group, 87-88
NTC's Dictionary of Trade Name Origins, 87
NTDB. *See STAT-USA: Globus/National Trade Data Bank (NTDB)*
"NTDB Global Trade Directory," 263
Nua Surveys, 235
Nua.com, 235

OCLC First Search, 10
O'Dwyer's, 195-196
O'Dwyer's Directory of Corporate Communications, 195
O'Dwyer's Directory of Public Relations Executives, 195
O'Dwyer's Directory of Public Relations Firms, 195-196

Office of Textiles and Apparel (OTEXA), of International Trade Administration, of Department of Commerce, 264-265
"1-2-3 Success! Build Your Personal Brand and Expand Your Success," 89
Online Logistics Bibliography, 282
Online Trade Show Press Kit, 197
"Optimizing Online Ad Spending," 234
OpusComm Group, 151
OrgScience Web Site, 10
Oryx Press, 29
OTC Industrial, 73
OTC Unlisted, 73
OTEXA. *See* Office of Textiles and Apparel (OTEXA)
"Other Packaging Related Sites," 276
Outdoor Industry Association, web site for, 62
Oxford University Press, 241-242

Pacific News Service, 138
Packaging Digest, 274
Packaging Machinery Manufacturers Institute (PMMI), 274
Packaging Network, 276
Packaginginfo.com, 274-275
Packexpo.com, 274
Parenting, 146
PDF (Portable Document Format), 33,34
PDMA. *See* Product Development and Management Association (PDMA)
PDMA Handbook of New Product Development, 271-272
Penn Well Publishing Co., 37
Personal Communications Industry Association, 53
Personnel index, 160
"Pet Product Market in France," 256

PHC. *See* Population and Housing
    Count/Characteristics (PHC)
Phelon, Sheldon & Marsar, Inc., 218
PIB. *See* Publishers Information
    Bureau (PIB)
Pillsbury Doughboy, 186
Places, Towns, and Townships, 118
Plunkett Research, Ltd., 229-230
Plunkett Research Web site, "Industry
    Research" section of, 230
Plunkett's Almanac, 230
*Plunkett's E-Commerce & Internet
    Business Almanac*, 229-230
Plunkett's Retail Industry Almanac,
    216
Plunkitt Research, Ltd., 216
PMMI. *See* Packaging Machinery
    Manufacturers Institute
    (PMMI)
Pocket Books, of WARC, 259-260
Political Risk Yearbook, 242-243
Population and Housing Count/
    Characteristics (PHC), 112
Portable Document Format (PDF), 33,34
PortalB, 27
Postscript, 33
PowerPoint, 33,102
PR Buyer's Guide, 196
PR Newswire, 194,216
PR Tactics, 199
*Predicast's Overview of Markets and
    Technology (PROMT)*, 25
Prentice Hall, 36-37,185,279
Pricer's Salary Survey Results, 278
*Pricing Policies and Strategies: An
    Annotated Bibliography*, 279
Pricing Society, 278
"Privacy in the Information Age," 234
PRIZM, 133,144
Product Development and Management
    Association (PDMA), 270-271
Product Manager's Handbook, 272
Professional Pricing Society, 278-279
Profile of the Dry Cleaning Industry,
    67

Profile of the Printing Industry, 67
*Profile of the Shipbuilding and Repair
    Industry*, 67
*Profile of the Wood Furniture and
    Fixtures Industry*, 67
*Profitable Pricing Strategies
    Workbook*, 278
Profound, 100
Profound, 100-101
Profound's Market Briefings, 101
*PROMT (Predicast's Overview of
    Markets and Technology)*, 25
ProQuest, 9-10,23-24,97,101,142
PRS Group, Inc., 242-243
PRSA. *See* Public Relations Society of
    America (PRSA)
PRSA Blue Book, 199
*PRSA Red Book: A Directory of the PRSA
    Counselor Academy*, 199
PRSA's Code of Professional Standards
    for the Practice of Public
    Relations, 199
PRSSA. *See* Public Relations Student
    Society of America (PRSSA)
P60 Consumer Income and Poverty, 115
P20 Population Characteristics, 115
P23 Special Studies, 115
Public Agenda, 146
"Public Data Query," 120
Public Relations Firms, 160
Public Relations Handbook, 11
Public Relations Society of America
    (PRSA), 139,199-200
Public Relations Student Society of
    America (PRSSA), 199
Public Use Microdata Samples
    (PUMS), 117,120
Public Utilities, 73
Publishers Information Bureau (PIB),
    182
Publist, 168
PUMS. *See Public Use Microdata
    Samples (PUMS)*
Purchase Exchange, 274

Quarterly Report of Tradeshow Statistics, 211
QuickTake.com, 105-106
  guides and templates of, 106
Quirk's Marketing Research Review, 104-105
Quirks.com, 104-105

Racial and Ethnic Diversity: Asians, Blacks, Hispanics, Native Americans, and Whites, 124,137
Radio Advertising Source, 165
Rand McNally's Commercial Atlas & Marketing Guide, 122-123,133
Rauch Associates, 275
Rauch Guide to the U.S. Packaging Industry, 275-276
Reader's Guide to Periodical Literature, 21
Red Books, 26
  "Bonus" Information in, 163
Red Books Online, 261
Reed Business Information, 211
Reed Elsevier, 26
Reference USA, 75-76
Research Alert Yearbook, 96-97,142
Research Bank Web, 53-54,102
Research Line, 100
Research Publishing, 19
Research Sourcebook, 104
ResearchInfo.com, 104
ResearchLine, 101
Resources on Using the Case Method in Business & Management Education, 10
"Retail Benchmarks," 60
"Retail Industry Channel," 216
"Retail Industry Contact Information," 216
"Retail Industry Contacts and Associations," 230
"Retail Industry Statistics," 216

"Retail Industry Trends/Retail Trade Analysis," 216,230
Retail Tenant Directory, 220
Retail Trade Survey, 112,214-215
Reuters, 216
Right Site, 125
Rivendell Marketing Company, Inc., 151
RMA Annual Statement Studies, 60
Robertson Stephens, 53
Robinson-Patman Act. 15 U.S. Code 13 (a-f), 297
Roper ASW, 98,144-145
Roper Reports Consumer Insights program, 144
Roper Youth Report, 144-145

Sage Publications, 293-294
Sales & Marketing Management magazine, 120-123,133
Sales Promotion Agencies, 160
Sales Promotion Handbook, 11
Salomon Smith Barney, 53
Schonfeld & Associates, 163,172
School of Packaging, at Michigan State University, 276
Science Direct, 271
SEC. *See* Securities and Exchange Commission (SEC)
Securities and Exchange Commission (SEC), 77,171
"Security Online: Corporate & Consumer Protection," 234
Selig Center for Economic Growth, of Terry College of Business, at University of Georgia, 139
Semiannual Computer Show and Electronics Report, 211
Semiannual Medical Show Report, 211
"Services and Suppliers" section, 161
Services Industries USA, 59
SERVQUAL, 294

Sheldon's Major Stores & Chains & Resident Buying Offices, 218

Shopping Center Directory, 218-219, 220

S.I. Newhouse School of Communications, at Syracuse University, 151

SI: SpecialIssues.com, 63

SIC. *See* Standard Industrial Classification (SIC)

SIC code. *See* Standard Industrial Classification (SIC) code

SIC system. *See* Standard Industrial Classification (SIC) system

SIC/NAICS code, 81

Simmons, *National Consumer Survey* data from, 129

Simmons Kids Study, 145

Simmons Market Research, 141,151

Simmons Market Research Bureau (SMRB), 97,128-130,145

Simmons' National Consumer Survey, 145

Simmons Teen Study, 145

"Six Online Services PR Firms Should Provide for Every Client," 198

"65+ in the United States Current Population Report," 116

SLA Advertising and Marketing Division, 262

"Small Business Industries," 60

SMAs. *See* Census Bureau's Metropolitan Statistical Areas (MSAs)

SMRB. *See* Simmons Market Research Bureau (SMRB)

Social Marketing Institute, 288-289

Social Marketing Network, 289

Source Book of Multicultural Experts, 138

Source Index, 82

Sourcebook of County Demographics, 132

Sourcebook of ZIP Code Demographics, 132

Special Markets Index, 160

Spending Potential Index (SPI), 133

SPI. *See* Spending Potential Index (SPI)

Sporting Goods Manufacturers, 53

SQUAD Media Market Guide, 168-169

SRDS. *See* Standard Rate & Data Service (SRDS)

SRDS Business Publication Advertising Source, 63

SRDS Interactive Advertising Source, 227

SRDS Publications, 260-261

SRI. *See Statistical Reference Index (SRI)*

SRI Consulting Business Intelligence, 130-131

SRI Microfiche Library, 31,225,230

Stagnito Communications, 274

Standard & Poor's, 50-51

   Industry Surveys of, 62,65

Standard & Poor's Corporation, 74

Standard & Poor's Register of Corporations, Directors and Executives, 74

Standard Directory of Advertisers, 159

Standard Directory of Advertising Agencies, 159

Standard Industrial Classification (SIC), 172

Standard Industrial Classification (SIC) code, 71,73,75,76

Standard Industrial Classification (SIC) code categories, 82

Standard Industrial Classification (SIC) system, 55

Standard Rate and Data Service (SRDS), 126-128,140,165-169, 225-226,227

Standards of Practice for Advertising Agencies, 185-186

"Starting a Business," 280

State of the E-Commerce Industry Report, 223

State of the Industry Report, web site
for, 65
State of the List Industry Report, 224
State of the Nation (SOTN), of
STAT-USA, 58
"States, Counties, and Places in the
Late 1990s," 118
*Statistical Abstract of the United
States*, 97
Statistical Fact Book, 224-225,228,230
Statistical Reference Index (SRI), 30,
65,225
Statistical Universe, 32,65
STAT-USA, 58
STAT-USA: Globus/NTDB, 253,263
Stradegy2, 175
*Strategic Marketing Problems: Cases
and Comments*, 10
Strategy Research Corporation, 140-141
Strathclyde University, 34
Study of Media and Markets, 128
Subscription databases, 136
*Summary of Commentary on Current
Economic Conditions*, 58
Supermarket Facts: Industry Overview
2001, web site for, 65
"Supply Chain Management," 235
Survey of Buying Power, 133
*Survey of Buying Power and Media
Markets*, 120-123
"Survey Templates," 106
"Survey Writing Tips Guide," 106
Syracuse University, S.I. Newhouse
School of Communications
at, 151

TableBase, 29,61,98,125,136,141
TableBase databases, 81
Target Market News, 139-140
Target2, 175
Taylor Nelson Sofres Company, 174-176
Taylor Nelson Sofres' media
monitoring network, 175

Technomic Publishing Co., 277
Tele-Nacion, 141
*Television Commercial Monitoring
Report*, 169-170
"Ten Attention-Getting Ways to Use
E-Mail Lists," 212
Terry College of Business, Selig Center
for Economic Growth, at
University of Georgia, 139
Texas A&M University, 146
The Advertising Council, 146
The Advertising Red Book–Advertisers,
160
Brand Name Indexes, 163
*The Advertising Red Book–Advertisers
Business Classification*,
161-162
The Advertising Red Book–Agencies,
160,161
The Advertising Red Book–Geographic,
161,162
The Advertising Red Books, 159-165
The African American Market, 140
"The American Trademark Index," 74
*The Blackwell Encyclopedic Dictionary
of Marketing*, 18
The Buying Power of Black America,
139-140
"The Communication Function in
Small Businesses," 200
The Complete Pricing Workbook, 278
"The Concept of the Marketing Mix," 36
The Dialog Corporation, 100-101
The E-Business Research Center, 232-234
*The Green Book: A Select Guide to
Industry Services*, 199
"The Impact of the Internet on Public
Relations and Business
Communication," 198
*The Marketer's Guide to Successful
Package Design*, 276
The Marketing Glossary, 18
*The Millennials: Americans Under
Age 25*, 124

The New Competitor Intelligence: The Complete Resource for Finding, Analyzing, and Using Information About Your Competitors, 79
The Pierian Press, 147
"The Pricing Advisor," 278
The Red Books, 159,160
"The Sporting Goods Market in Belgium," 255
The Strategist, 200
The Strategy and Tactics of Pricing: A Guide to Profitable Decision Making, 279
The Ultimate 2000: Directory of Ethnic Organizations, Ethnic Media, and Scholars from the Chicago Metropolitan Area, 138
The Video Source Book, 36
The World's Greatest Brands, 86-87, 88-89
"The World's Top 100 Brands," 87
"The World's Top Brands by Sector," 87
"37 Ways to Improve Your User Conference Brochure," 212
Thomas Publishing Co., 74
Thomas Register of American Manufacturers, 74
Thomson Corporation, 27,102
Thomson Financial, 53
Thomson Research, 73
Time Warner, 229
Tools of Change, 289
Top 10 Agencies by U.S. Media Billings, 161
Top Agency Networks, 262
Top Global Ad Markets, 262
Top World Brand Advertisers, 262
Trade Dimensions, 220
Trade Name Origins, 87-88
Trade Shows Worldwide: An International Directory of Events, Facilities, and Suppliers, 211

Tradenet.gov, 253
"Tradeshow Directory," 211
"Tradeshow Trends," 211
Tradeshow Week Online, 211
Transportation, 73
Transportation and Public Utilities USA, 59
Travel Industry Association of America, web site for, 62
TSNN.com, 212
"TV and Radio Directory," 192
2001 Gay/Lesbian Consumer Online Census, 151-152
2001 Industry Documentation and Rankings, 198
2001 Youth Research Sourcebook, 144
Tylenol, 190

UCC. *See Uniform Commercial Code (UCC)*
UN. *See* United Nations (UN)
"Uncle Sam," 178
Uncle Same E-Commerce, 231
Understanding the Census: A Guide for Marketers, Planners, Grant Writers and Other Data Users, 112
Uniform Commercial Code (UCC), 297-298
Uniform Resource Locator (URL), 34
United Nations (UN), 238,247
    Department of Economic and Social Affairs of, 240
United Nations (UN) Convention for International Sale of Goods, 251
United States Code, 292
United States Summary Reports, 112
Universal McCann, 172-173
University of Florida
    College of Journalism and Communication of, 200-201
    Warrington College of Business at, 298

University of Georgia, Terry College
    of Business, Selig Center for
    Economic Growth, 139
University of Memphis library,
    Government Publications
    Department of, 231
University of Texas
    at Austin, 296-297
    Department of Advertising at,
    186,296-297
    McCombs School of Business at,
    235
URL (Uniform Resource Locator), 34
U.S. Agency Brands Ranked by Gross
    Income, 161
U.S. Bureau of Economic Research, 52
U.S. Bureau of Labor Statistics, 119
U.S. Business Reporter, 51-52
U.S. Census Bureau. *See* Census Bureau
U.S. Customs Service Points of Entry,
    251
U.S. Department of Agriculture, 243
U.S. Department of Commerce, 52,58,
    139,230-231,234,263
    International Trade Administration
    of, OTEXA of, 264-265
U.S. Department of Commerce market
    reports, 256
U.S. Department of State, 254
U.S. Department of the Army, 245
U.S. General Accounting Office, 223
U.S. Government, "Uncle Sam" of, 178
U.S. Government Export Portal, 264
U.S. government research reports, 260
U.S. Hispanic Market Report, 140-141
U.S. International Trade Administration,
    255-256,264-265
U.S. Market Trends and Forecasts, 61,82
U.S. Postal Service, 222,223,225
U.S. Small Business Administration, 280
U.S. Sourcebook of Advertisers, 163
U.S. Trade Administration, 281
USA Trade Online, 263-264

VALS Survey, 130-131
Value Line Investment Survey, 52
Value of a Dollar 1860-1999, 279-280
VALUESCOPE, 144
Video Monitoring Services (VMS), 176
Virtual Logistics Directory, 283
Visions, 271
VMS (Video Monitoring Services), 176
VNU Business Publications, 167

Wall Street Journal, 23-24,25,26,64,146
WARC. *See* World Advertising Research
    Center (WARC)
*Ward's Business Directory of U.S. and
    Public Companies*, 75
Warrington College of Business, at
    University of Florida, 298
Washington Retail Insight, 216
Webdata.com, 33
WEFA. *See* Wharton Economic
    Forecasting Associates (WEFA)
West Chester University, 34
West's Encyclopedia of American Law,
    297
Wharton Economic Forecasting
    Associates (WEFA), 222
What Is a Dollar Worth?, 280
*What Were They Thinking: Marketing
    Lessons I Have Learned from
    over 8,000 New Product
    Introductions*, 273
*Where to Go Who to Ask (A Gale Ready
    Reference Handbook)*, 18
Who Owns Whom, 161
Wholesale and Retail Trade USA, 59
"Why Not Raise Your Prices," 279
"Why People Aren't Online," 234
"Wireless and Mobile Commerce," 235
WireLine, 101
Working Paper Series, 37
Working Press of the Nation (WPN),
    191-193
Workplace Population, 133
*World Advertiser and Agency
    Database*, 261-262

World Advertising Research Center
  (WARC), 28,259-260,262
Pocket Books of, 259-260
World Advertising Trends, 262
World Bank, 247
World Bank Development Data, 247
World Competitiveness Report, 242
World Competitiveness Yearbook, 242
*World Consumer Income and
  Expenditure Patterns*, 258
World Consumer Lifestyles Databook,
  258,259
"World Economic and Financial
  Surveys," 241
World Economic and Social Survey, 240
World Economic Outlook, 240-241
"World Economic Situation and
  Prospects," 240
World Factbook, 244-245, 247
*World Market & MediaFact Pocket
  Books*, 260
World Market Share Reporter, 61
World Marketing Data and Statistics,
  257
World Outlook, 247
World Packaging Organization, 276

*Worldmark Encyclopedia of the
  Nations*, 245
World's Top 50 Advertising
  Organizations, 161
*Worldwide Directory of Focus Group
  Companies and Services*,
  103-104
WPN. *See Working Press of the Nation
  (WPN)*

.xls., 27-28
XML (Extensible Markup Language),
  34

Yahoo, 32
Youth Markets Alert, 141

Zapdata, 209
Zapdata.com, 57
ZenithOptimedia, 260
Zip code, economic census data by, 56
Zip Code Business Patterns, 56
Zogby International, 151

Subject Index

AAAA. *See* American Association of
    Advertising Agencies (AAAA)
A.C. Nielsen Media Research, 166
Accenture, 234
Acronym(s), WWW–related, 34
AdAge Data Center, 173
AdAge Global, 261-262
ADI. *See* Areas of Dominant Influence
    (ADI)
AdRelevance Analytics, 234
AdRelevance Metrics, 234
Advertisement(s), historical, 176-180
  collections of, 178
Advertiser(s)
  defined, 158
  locating of, 159-165
Advertising, 260-262
  defined, 158
  handbooks on, 185-186
  history of, 158
  legal issues on, web sites for, 298
  measurement in, reading on, 183
  outdoor, advertising rates and cost
    data for, 169
  PR *vs.*, 190
  web gateways on, 185-186
Advertising agencies, 160
  departments of, 158
  locating of, 159-165
  rankings of, finding of, 161
  types of, 160
Advertising and media planning sources,
    157-187
Advertising expenditures, 170-174
Advertising industry data, 170-174
Advertising information sources, on
    Internet, 233-234
Advertising law, 184-185

Advertising Law Internet Site, 184
Advertising rates, for TV, radio, and
    outdoor advertising, 169
Advertising ratios, 170-174
Advertising research, 181-184
Advertising Research Foundation
    (ARF), 144,181-182
Advertising resources, global, 262
Agency Responsibilities index, 160-161
Alacra, Inc., 27-28
AltaVista, 32
AMA. *See* American Marketing
    Association (AMA)
AMACOM, 18
Amazon, 21
America Online (AOL), 32,229
American Association of Advertising
    Agencies (AAAA), 161,164,
    169-170,185-186
American Booksellers Association,
    web site for, 62
American Booksellers Association
    Research and Statistics web
    site, 65
American Community Survey, 114
American Consumer Survey (ACS), 117
  narrative profiles of, 117
American Law Institute, 297
American Marketing Association
    (AMA), 5,17,35,142,197,279,
    296
  Code of Ethics of, 295
  web site of, 21
American Marketing Research
    Association, 296
American Stock Exchange, 72-73
ANA. *See* Association of National
    Advertisers (ANA)

Andreason, A.R., 288,289
Annual report(s), of companies, 77-78
    free web sites for, 77
Annual Report to Shareholders (ARS),
    77
Anschuetz, N.F., 271
AOL. *See* America Online (AOL)
Apparel and Accessory Store Sales, 121
Apple Computer, 87,178
Arbitron radio and television ratings, 7
Arbor Strategy Group, 272
Areas of Dominant Influence (ADI),
    123,192
Arent Fox Attorneys at Law, 184-185
ARF. *See* Advertising Research
    Foundation (ARF)
ARF Youth Research Council, 144
ARS. *See* Annual Report to
    Shareholders (ARS)
ARS Group, 183-184
ARS Group web site, 183-184
Article(s), as information resource, 19-21
ASI Market Research, 184
Associated Press, 216
Association of National Advertisers
    (ANA), 169-170
Association web sites, examples of
    industry facts, figures, and
    reports available from, 65
Axiom Press, 248-249
Axtell, R.E., 249

B2B. *See* Business-to-business (B2B)
B2C. *See* Business-to-consumer (B2C)
Bacon's Information, Inc., 193
Baker, M.J., 5,18-19
Banking(s), of companies, 80-83
BAR. *See* Broadcast Advertisers Reports
    (BAR)
Barksdale, H.C., 17
Barnes and Noble, 21
BDI. *See* Brand Development Index
    (BDI)
Beacham, W., 19

Benchmarking, advertising-related, 181
Berkman, R.I., 96
Bernan Press, 59-60, 118
Bernhardt, K.L., 10
Berry, L.L., 294
Best Market Reports (BMR), 255
Bill Communications, Inc., 209
Blackwell Publishers, 18
Block, T.B., 11
BLS. *See* Bureau of Labor Statistics
    (BLS)
Bly, R.W., 185
BMR. *See* Best Market Reports (BMR)
Boettcher, J., 49
Book(s)
    as information resource, 19-21
    in online library catalogs, case
        studies in, 9
Boolean combinations, in periodical
    indexes, 23
Boolean connectors, 99
Booth, C., 10
Borden, G.A., 249
Bowker, 191-193
BPI. *See* Buying Power Index (BPI)
BPI Communications, 166
Brand(s), 84-89
Brand Development Index (BDI), 168
Brand Name Indexes, in Advertisers
    Red Books, 163
Brand Power, components of, 86-87
Brewer, C.A., 137
BrightPlanet, 33
Broadcast Advertisers Reports (BAR),
    174
Bureau of Labor Statistics (BLS), 115
Burrelle's Information Services, 191,
    193-194
Bushko, D., 185
Business information
    overview of, 6-11
    staying current with, 16-17
Business libraries, 11-12
Business Nation's business book review
    service, web site of, 21
Business periodical databases, 23-25

Business/Marketing/Market Research
    Suppliers category, 105
Business-to-business (B2B) sites, 227
Business-to-business (B2B) spending,
    222
Business-to-consumer (B2C) marketers,
    222
Buyers Guide, 209
Buying Power Index (BPI), 121,133

CACI Marketing Systems, 131
Calculator(s)
    CPM, 233
    direct mail/e-mail campaign ROI, 227
Campaign(s), historical, 176-180
Carter, D.E., 87
Case studies, findings of, 9-10
CASS Corporation, 282
Castellon, G.A., 271
Catalog(s)
    library, large, available free on Web,
      20
    online library, books in, case studies
      in, 9
Category Development Index (CDI),
    168
CDI. *See* Category Development Index
    (CDI)
Cendex, 274
Census(es), Economic, 118
CENSUS 2000 data products,
    introduction to, 114
Census Bureau, 43,54-55,56,57,58,
    111,112,114,115,116,
    212-215, 230-231
    demographic data from, 111-119
    MSAs of, 121
    Public Use Presentation Library of,
      114
Census Bureau reports, 119
Census Bureau Special Report, 137
Census Bureau Web site, 55
Census data, 111
    sampling *vs.* complete counts in,
      112

Central Intelligence Agency (CIA),
    244-245,247
Certified packaging professional
    examination, text for, 277
Chambers of Commerce, 76
Chandler, T.M., 147
Children, marketing to, 143-148
    ethical issues on, resources for, 148
    policy issues on, resources for, 148
    reading list about, 147-148
Choudhury, P., 142
Christ, P., 34
CIA. *See* Central Intelligence Agency
    (CIA)
Claritas, Inc., 133
Classic texts, as information resource,
    36-37
Clemente, M.N., 18
CLM. *See* Council of Logistics
    Management (CLM)
CMR, 174-176
CMSAs. *See* Consolidated
    Metropolitan Statistical Areas
    (CMSAs)
Coca Cola, 87,273
Code(s), industry, 47-49
Code of Ethics, of AMA, 295
Coen, R.J., 172
College of Journalism and
    Communication, at University
    of Florida, 200-201
Columbia Books, 66
Commercial Closet Association,
    150-151
Company(ies)
    annual reports of, 77-78
      free web sites for, 77
    bankings of, 80-83
    directories of, 70-76
      by country, 260
    history of, 83-84
      sources of, 84
    market share of, 80-83
    name origins of, 88
    research basics of, 70

sources about, 69-84
10-K forms of, 77-78
Competia, 66
Competitive intelligence, 78-80
    mining for, 79
    in public corporate filings, unearthing
        of, 78
    reading list for, 80
Conaway, W.A., 249
Consolidated Metropolitan Statistical
        Areas (CMSAs), 113,121,127
Consumer data
    ethnic–related, web sites with, 143
    lifestyle market–related, web sites
        with, 143
Consumer expenditure data, access of,
        120
Consumer Price Index (CPI) calculator,
        280
Consumer Product category, 99
Consumer Products, 99
Consumer-oriented sites, 227
"Copy Research Validity Project," 182
Copyright, 15-16
Cornell Law School, 297-298
Cornell University LII Web site, 298
Cost data, for TV, radio, and outdoor
        advertising, 169
Cost-per-rating-point (CPP), 168
Cost-per-thousand (CPM), 168
Council Annual Report, 198
Council of Logistics Management
        (CLM), 276,281-282
    definition of logistics and supply
        chain management of, 282
Council of Public Relations Firms
        (CPRF), 197
Council of Public Relations Firms
        (CPRF) web site, 196
Country-specific information, 243-247
Courtney Communications, 227-228
CPI calculator. *See* Consumer Price
        Index (CPI) calculator
CPM. *See* Cost-per-thousand (CPM)
CPM calculator, 233

CPP. *See* Cost-per-rating-point (CPP)
CPRF. *See* Council of Public Relations
        Firms (CPRF)
CPS. *See* Current Population Survey
        (CPS)
Crain Communications, 161,173
Crain Publications, 180
Credit Suisse First Boston, 53,102
Cui, G., 142
Cullbridge Marketing and
        Communication, 289
Culture, understanding of, 248-249
Current Population Surveys, 118
Customer segmentation, 134
Customer Service Week web site, 208
Customized research, on web, 103
CXOMedia, Inc., 232-234
CyberAtlas.com, 235

Darney, A.J., 58
Dartnell Corporation, 11,35,185,
        207-208,208
"Data Mining," to obtain expensive
        market research data, 145
Database(s), periodical, as information
        resource, 21-23
Database marketing, 223
Datamonitor, 53,83,234
DeBrandt, K.A., 118
Demographic data, from Census Bureau,
        111-119
Demographic niches, marketing sources
        for, 135-153
Demographic sources, 109-126
    with enhanced marketing features,
        119-125
Demographics, reading list on, 134
Department of Advertising, at University
        of Texas, at Austin, 296-297
Department of Commerce, 52,58,139,
        230-231,234,263
    International Trade Administration
        of, 252-253
    OTEXA of, 264-265

Department of Economic and Social Affairs, of UN, 240
Department of Marketing, 34
Derks, S., 279
Designated Market Areas (DMAs), 121,123,127,140
"Developing Your E-Mail Marketing Lists," 212
Dialog, 26-27,27,100
Diamond, W., xix
Dictionary(ies)
   as information resource, 18
   of market research terminology, 93
Dilenschneider, R.L., 11
Direct mail, 222
Direct mail/e-mail campaign ROI calculator, 227
Direct marketing, 224-228
"Direct Marketing," 212
Direct Marketing Association, 222,223,224,296
Direct marketing sources, 221-236
Direct response marketing, 223
Directory(ies)
   of companies, 70-76
   of market research firms, 103-105
   of media contacts, 191-193
   of press contacts, 191-193
Disney, 87
Distribution, strategies of, 281-283
DMA List/Database Council, 224
DMAs. *See* Designated Market Areas (DMAs)
Donnelley Marketing, 76
Douglas Publications, Inc., 208
Dow Jones & Reuters, 25-26
Dow Jones Business News, 216
Duke University, 176-178,179
Dun & Bradstreet, Inc., export information and glossary from, 252
Dun & Bradstreet Information Services, 73
Dun & Bradstreet International, 250-252

Dun & Bradstreet's Sales and Marketing Solutions, 209
DVDs, as information resource, 35-36
Dwyer, M., 243

Easy Demographics Software, Inc., 125
EBI. *See* Effective buying income (EBI)
EBSCO Information Services, 24
ECCH. *See* European Case Clearing House (ECCH)
ECNextInc., 98-99
E-Commerce, 228-236
   law and, web sources for, 236
   reading list on, 231
   U.S. Government information on, 231
E-Commerce sources, 221-236
E-Commerce statistics, "Don't Miss" sources of, 234-235
Economic census(es), 118
Economic census data
   use of, 56
   by zip code, 56
Economist Intelligence Unit (EIU), 27, 53,238,246
EDGAR database, 77
EDI. *See* Electronic Data Interchange (EDI)
Edsel, 86
Effective buying income (EBI), 121
Egolf, K., 179
EIU. *See* Economist Intelligence Unit (EIU)
Electronic Data Interchange (EDI), 231
Elsevier Science, 271
eMarketer, Inc., 234
Encyclopedia(s), as information resource, 18-19
Enis, B.M., 36
Environment, export, 249-254
Environment Canada, 289
Environmental Protection Agency (EPA), 46,67
EPA. *See* Environmental Protection Agency (EPA)

EPM Communications, 96-97,141
Equifax, 126
eReleases, for press release services, 194
eReleases.com, 194
ESOMAR. *See* European Society for
      Opinion and Marketing
      Research (ESOMAR)
ESRI BIS, 131,132
ESRI Business Information Solutions,
      131-133
Establishment, defined, 213
Ethic(s), marketing, reading list on, 296
Ethical issues
   on marketing, 295-298
   on marketing to children and youth,
      resources for, 148
Ethnic groups, marketing to, 137-143
Ethnicity, consumer data related to, web
      sites with, 143
Euromonitor, 61,98,260
Euromonitor International, 238,256-259
European Society for Opinion and
      Marketing Research
      (ESOMAR), 296
Evatt, D., 200
E-Watch Internet Monitoring, 197
Exempt organizations, 292
Export environment, 249-254
Export information, from Dun &
      Bradstreet, Inc., 252
Export Institute, USA, 252,280
Export.gov, 253
Extensible Markup Language (XML),
      34

Fair use, 15-16
FCC. *See* Federal Communications
      Commission (FCC)
Federal Communications Commission
      (FCC), 234
Federal Information Processing
      Standard (FIPS), 123
Federal Reserve Bank, 52
   of Minneapolis, 280

Federal Trade Commission (FTC),
      234,295
   advertising policy and guidelines
      of, 295
Federal Trade Commission (FTC)
      updates, 184
Federal Trade Commission's
      Telemarketing Sales Rule, 228
Fiber Box Association, 276
Field searching, in periodical indexes, 22
Films for the Humanities & Sciences, 36
Financial ratios, sources for, 61
FIPS. *See* Federal Information
      Processing Standard (FIPS)
First Search's ArticleFirst, 294
Fischer, C.A., 18
Fitzroy Dearborn, 179-180
Five Technologies to Watch, web site
      for, 65
Fleming valve, 229
Food Institute, 53
Food Marketing Institute, web site for,
      62
Food Store and Gasoline Service Stations
      Sales, 121
Forcinio, H.E., 277
Foreign trade statistics, 264
Forrestal, D.J., 11
Forrester Research, 234
Fortune 1000, 76
"Four Ps of marketing," 5,6
Free Leads, 209
Free Press, 294
Free web aggregators, 97-99
Freedonia, 98
Frerichs, G., 11
FTC. *See* Federal Trade Commission
      (FTC)
Fuld & Company, 66
Fuld & Company web site, 79
Fuld, L.M., 79

Gale Group, 17,24-25,29,49-50,53,
      58-59,61,62-63,66,75,80-81,
      82-86,98,178-179,211,217,
      228-229

Gale Group databases, 98
Gaquin, D.A., 118
Garfield, B., 180
Gartner Group, 52,53
Gay(s), marketing to, 149-153
  reading list for, 152
Gebbie Press, 193
Gebbie's web site, 193
General business periodical databases,
  for industry data, 61
General Motors (GM), 180
Geographic index, 160
Geographic sources, 109-126
Geographical Mobility, 115
Geographical Mobility report, 115-116
Geography Quick Reports, 55
Georgetown University, 288
Glass Packing Institute, 276
GLINN Media Corporation, 149
Global advertising resources, 262
Global economic and political scan,
  239-243
Glossary(ies), 301
  from Dun & Bradstreet, Inc., 252
  of market research terminology, 93
  of media buying and magazine
    publishing terms, 167
GLVensus Partners, 151-152
GM. *See* General Motors (GM)
Goldstucker, J.L., 17
Google, 32,33,34
Google Web Directory, 66
Gorchels, L., 272
Gordon, H., 11
Government information, 67
Government Printing Office, 245-246
Government Publications Department,
  of University of Memphis
    library, 231
Government web sites gateways, 263-265
Greenfield Online, Inc., 105-106
Grey House Publishing, 279-280
Griffin, A., 271
GSociety, 151

Hall, Dickler, Kent, Goldstein, &
  Wood, LLP, 184
Handbook(s)
  advertising-related, 185-186
  locating of, 11
  marketing, selected, 11
Hanlon, J.F., 277
HAPPI (Household and Personal
  Products Industry) Online,
    web site for, 62
Harvard Business School, 10
Health Canada, 289
Heide, C.P., 207
Heinzerling, B.M., 147
Hise, R.T., 19
Holden, R.K., 279
Hoover's, Inc., 71-72,97
Hospitality Net, web site for, 62
House Agencies, 160
Household and Personal Products
    Industry (HAPPI) Online,
      web site for, 62
Howard University, 139
HTML (Hyper Text Markup Language),
  34
Humphries, J.M., 139
H.W. Wilson, 25
Hyper Text Markup Language (HTML),
  34

IABC. *See* International Association of
    Business Communicators
    (IABC)
IABC Research Foundation, 200
Iacobucci, D., 293
IGLSS. *See* Institute for Gay and Lesbian
    Strategic Studies (IGLSS)
IGLSS web site, 150
IMF. *See* International Monetary Fund
    (IMF)
IMI reports, 255
Impact Marketing Consultants, Inc.,
    275-276
Incentive Federation, 206

Industry, *vs.* market, 42
Industry codes, 47-49
Industry data, general business
        periodical databases for, 61
Industry scan, sources for, 41-67
Industry-specific information, 62
Information
    business
        overview of, 6-11
        staying current with, 16-17
    country-specific, 243-247
    government, 67
    logo, 84-89
    regulatory, 67
Information Resources, Inc., 52
Information sources
    articles, 19-21
    books, 19-21
    classic texts, 36-37
    dictionaries, 18
    DVSs, 35-36
    encyclopedias, 18-19
    marketing, guides to, 17-18
    periodical databases, 21-23
        business-related, 23-25
    professional organizations on
        WWW, 35
    scholarly material, 36-37
    specialized business search systems,
        25-28
    statistics, 28-32
    tables, 28-32
    videos, 35-36
    WWW, 32-34
InfoTech Trends, web site for, 62
InfoUSA, 75-76
Insight Media, 36
Institute for Gay and Lesbian Strategic
        Studies (IGLSS), 149-150
Institute of Packaging Professionals,
        276
Institute of Public Relations (IPR),
        200-201
Intelligence, competitive, 78-80. *See
        also* Competitive intelligence

Interbrand, 88-89
International Association of Business
        Communicators (IABC), 200
International Customer Service
        Association, 208
International issues in pricing, 280-281
International Market Insight (IMI)
        reports, 255
International market share data, sources
        for, 259
International marketing information,
        web gateways for, 265
International marketing sources, 237-265
International Monetary Fund (IMF), 238,
        240-241,247
International News Distribution, 197
International Thomson Business Press,
        18-19
International Trade Administration, of
        Department of Commerce,
        OTEXA of, 264-265
Internet, 15,209
Internet advertising information
        sources, 233-234
Internet Explorer, 32
Internet Intelligence Index, 66,79
Internet Service Provider (ISP), 32,34
Internet/E-Commerce statistics, "Don't
        Miss" sources of, 234-235
InternetNews.com, 235
Investment research reports, 52-54,
        102-103
Invisible Web, 33
IPR. *See* Institute of Public Relations
        (IPR)
ISP. *See* Internet Service Provider
        (ISP)

J. Walter Thompson Company Archives,
        177
Jagoe, J.R., 252
Jargon, WWW–related, 34
John W. Harman Center for Sales,
        Advertising, and Marketing
        History, 176-178,179

John Wiley & Sons, 18,79,271-272
Jolly Green Giant, 186
Journal(s), trade, 62-64
Jupitermedia Corporation, 231,235
"Just Do It," 178

Kalorama Information LLC, 97
Kelsey, R.J., 277
Kerin, M.A., 10
Keyword searches, *vs.* subject heading
    searches, 20
Keyword searching, in periodical
    indexes, 22
Kinnear, T.C., 10
Kochan, N., 86
Koschnick, W.J., 93
Kotler, P., 288

Lavin, M.R., 13,29,47
Law
    advertising, 184-185
    E-Commerce and, web sources for,
        236
LCSH. *See* Library of Congress Subject
    Headings (LCSH)
Leading National Advertisers (LNA),
    174,176
Legal issues
    advertising-related, web sites for, 298
    in marketing, 295-298
Lehman Brothers, 53
Leo Burnett Worldwide, 186
Lesbian(s), marketing to, 149-153
    reading list for, 152
Levy, S.J., 11,288
Lewis, B.R., 18
Lexington Books, 146-147
LexisNexis, 261
LexisNexis Academic and Library
    Solutions, 30,225
LexisNexis database, 65
LexisNexis Group, 26,70-71,159-165
Library(ies), business, 11-12
Library and Knowledge Center, 138

Library catalogs, large, available free
    on Web, 20
Library of Congress, 20,245
Library of Congress Subject Headings
    (LCSH), 20
Lifestyle markets, consumer data
    related to, web sites with, 143
Lifestyle sources, 126-134
Littler, D., 18
LNA. *See* Leading National
    Advertisers (LNA)
Local Evening News, 170
Logistics
    CLM definition of, 282
    strategies of, 281-283
Logistics industry publishers, 282
Logo information, 84-89
Lubliner, M.J., 276

M + A Verlag fuer Messen,
        Ausstellungen und Kongresse
        GmbH, 210
Magazine Publishers of America (MPA),
        167,182
Magazine Publishers of America (MPA)
        web site, 174
Magazine publishing, terminology
        related to, glossaries of, 167
Mail order, 222-223
Mailing list sources, 226
Mainsail Interactive Services, 198
Major Topic Index, 147
Malonis, J.A., 228
MANA. *See* Manufacturers' Agents
        National Association
        (MANA)
Manufacturers' Agents National
        Association (MANA), 217
Manufacturers' representatives,
        directory for, 217
Market(s)
    lifestyle, consumer data related to,
        web sites with, 143
    Media, 123
    niche, publishers and market research
        firms focusing on, 153

product delivery to, 217-220
vs. industry, 42
Market research, 254-260
    primary, 93-94
    secondary, 93-94
    terminology related to, dictionaries
        and glossaries of, 93
    WWW in, 95
Market research data, expensive, "Data
    Mining" to obtain, 145
Market research firms
    directories of, 103-105
    focus on niche markets, 153
    well-known, 100
Market research reports, 255-256
    described, 92-93
    industry analysis in, 54
    selection of, 94-95
    sources for, 91-106
Market share, of companies, 80-83
Marketer(s)
    business-to-consumer, 222
    nonprofit, reading list for, 292-293
    social, reading list for, 290
Marketing
    to children, 143-148
        ethical issues on, resources for,
            148
        policy issues on, resources for,
            148
        reading list about, 147-148
    database, 223
    defined, 291
    direct, 224-228
    direct response, 223
    ethic(s) of, reading list on, 296
    ethical issues in, 295-298
    to gays and lesbians, 149-153
        reading list for, 152
    legal issues in, 295-298
    to multicultural and ethnic groups,
        137-143
    niche, 135-153
    nonprofit, development of, seminal
        works in, 290-291

for nonprofit and public
    organizations, 291-293
    reading list on, 201
    research on, sources and strategies
        for, 3-37
    services, 293-295
        reading list on, 294-295
    social, 288-291
        development of, seminal works
            in, 290-291
    target, 111
    to teens, reading list about, 147-148
Marketing concepts, checklist for,
    xxi-xxvi
Marketing Education Review, 296
Marketing handbooks, selected, 11
Marketing information sources, guides
    to, 17-18
Marketing mix, "four Ps" of, 5,6
Marketing Research Association, 296
Marketing Science Institute (MSI),
    35,37
Marketing source, international, 237-265
Marketing terms, geography of, 123
MarketingPower.com, 197
MarketResearch.com, 96,97-98,101-102
Marlow-Ferguson, R., 49
Master Index, 71
Maydream, 180
McCann-Erickson WorldGroup web
    site, 172
McCarthy, E.J., 6
McCombs School of Business, at
    University of Texas, 235
McDonald's, 87
McDonough, J., 179
McFarland, 88
McMath, R., 273
McNeal, J.U., 146
MDOL ("Media Directory Online"),
    191
Media buying, terminology related to,
    glossaries of, 167
Media buying services, 160
    directories for, 165

Media contacts, directories of, 191-193
"Media Directory Online" (MDOL), 191
Media Market(s), 123
Media Market Rankings, 121
Media monitoring services, 193-194
Media planning and buying, 165-170
Media Planning and Buying
    Calculations, 168
Media planning sources, 157-187
Media research, web sites with, 143
Mediamark Reporter, guides to using,
    130
Mediamark Research, Inc. (MRI),
    129,144,169
MEMRI database, 129
Mercer, D., 18
Mergent, Inc., 72-73
Merrill Lynch, 53,102
MetricMedia Group, 51-52
Metro and Media Market Totals, 122
Metropolitan Statistical Areas (MSAs),
    55,113,123,219
    of Census Bureau, 121
Meyers, H.M., 276
Michigan State University, 276
    School of Packaging at, 276
Microsoft Excel, 33
Microsoft Word, 33
Millward Brown International, 184
MindBranch, Inc., 99
Mitchell, E.G., 278
Mitchell, S., 120
MLS. *See* Multiple Listing Service (MLS)
MONITOR, 144
Monography collections, case studies
    in, 10
Montgomery Ward, 222
Montgomery Ward Direct, 222
Morgan Stanley Dean Witter, 53,102
Morrison, T., 249
MPA. *See* Magazine Publishers of
    America (MPA)
MRI. *See* Mediamark Research, Inc.
    (MRI)
MSAs. *See* Metropolitan Statistical
    Areas (MSAs)

MSI. *See* Marketing Science Institute
    (MSI)
MSW Research, 184
Multicultural groups, marketing to,
    137-143
Multicultural marketers, book list for,
    143
Multicultural Marketing Resources,
    138
Multi-industry overviews, 49-52
Multiple Listing Service (MLS), 7
Munter, P., 172
Museum of Broadcast
    Communications, 179

NAFTA. *See* North American Free Trade
    Agreement (NAFTA)
Nagle, T.T., 279
NAICS code. *See* North American
    Industrial Classification
    System (NAICS) code
    where to look up, 48,49
National Conference of Commissioners
    on Uniform State Laws, 297
National Customer Service Week, 208
National Gay Newspaper Guild
    (NGNG), 151
National Paint and Coatings
    Association, web site for, 62
National Register Publishing, 226
National Research Bureau, 218-219
National Restaurant Association, 66
    web site for, 62
National Retail Federation (NRF),
    215-216
National Social Norms Resource
    Center (NSNRC), 289-290
National Social Norms Resource Center
    (NSNRC) web site, 290
National Sporting Goods Association,
    web site for, 62
NCM. *See* New California Media (NCM)
Neilsen's Direct Market Areas, 169
NetLibrary, 19

NetRatings, Inc., 233
Netscape, 32
NetView Usage Metrics, 234
Network Evening News, 170
New California Media (NCM), 138
"New Coke," 190
New Strategist, 125
New Strategist Publications, 123-125,137
New York AMA Communications
    Services, Inc., 103-104
New York Public Library, Science,
    Industry and Business
    Library of, 12
New York Stock Exchange, 71
New York University Press, 86-87
NewProductWorks, 272-273
News, web sites with, 143
NGNG. *See* National Gay Newspaper
    Guild (NGNG)
Niche market(s), publishers and market
    research firms focusing on, 153
Niche marketing, 135-153
Nielsen Media Research Media Market,
    121
Nielsen/NetRatings, 233-234
Nike, "Just Do It" of, 178
1994 Yankelovich MONITOR
    Perspective on Gays/
    Lesbians, 136
Nolo Press, 292
Nonprofit marketers, reading list for,
    292-293
Nonprofit marketing, development of,
    seminal works in, 290-291
Nonprofit organizations, marketing
    for, 291-293
NOP World, 144
North American Free Trade
    Agreement (NAFTA), 47
North American Industrial Classification
    System (NAICS) code, 172,
    227-228,231
North American Industry Classification
    System (NAICS), 47,55,58,
    82,213

North American Industry Classification
    System (NAICS) code, 74,75,76
NPW Product Collection, 272
NRF. *See* National Retail Federation
    (NRF)
NSNRC. *See* National Social Norms
    Resource Center Web site
    (NSNRC)
NTC Business Books, 272,276
NTC Publishing Group, 87-88
Nua.com, 235

O'Dwyer's, 195-196
Office of Textiles and Apparel
    (OTEXA), of International
    Trade Administration, of
    Department of Commerce,
    264-265
Online library catalogs, books in, case
    studies in, 9
Online Trade Show Press Kit, 197
Oppenheim, M.R., xix
OpusComm Group, 151
Oryx Press, 29
OTEXA. *See* Office of Textiles and
    Apparel (OTEXA)
Outdoor advertising, advertising rates
    and cost data for, 169
Outdoor Industry Association, web site
    for, 62
Oxford University Press, 241-242

Pacific News Service, 138
Packaging, 273-277
Packaging Machinery Manufacturers
    Institute (PMMI), 274
Parasuraman, A., 294
PDF (Portable Document Format), 33,34
PDMA. *See* Product Development and
    Management Association
    (PDMA)
Penn Well Publishing Co., 37

Periodical articles, case studies in, 9-10
Periodical databases
general business, 23-25
as information resource, 21-23
Periodical indexes, features found in, 22-23
Personal Communications Industry Association, 53
Personnel index, 160
Peterson, R.A., 10
PHC. *See* Population and Housing Count/Characteristics (PHC)
Phelon, Sheldon & Marsar, Inc., 218
PIB. *See* Publishers Information Bureau (PIB)
Pillsbury Doughboy, 186
Place, strategies of distribution and logistics, 281-283
Plunkett Research, Ltd., 229-230
Plunkett Research web site, "Industry Research" section of, 230
Plunkett's Almanac, 230
Plunkitt Research, Ltd., 216
PMMI. *See* Packaging Machinery Manufacturers Institute (PMMI)
Policy issues, on marketing to children and youth, resources for, 148
Population and Housing Count/ Characteristics (PHC), 112
Portable Document Format (PDF), 33,34
Postscript, 33
PowerPoint, 33,102
PowerPoint presentations, 114
PR. *See under* Public relations (PR)
Prentice Hall, 36-37,185,279
Press clipping services, 193-194
Press contacts, directories of, 191-193
Press release services, eReleases for, 194
Pricing, 277-281
international issues in, 280-281
Pricing Society, 278
Primary Metropolitan Statistical Areas (PMSAs), 113

Primary research, 93-94
on web, 105-106
Print publications, new strategist web site for, 124
Product(s)
market delivery of, 217-220
name origins of, 88
Product development, 269,270-273
Product Development and Management Association (PDMA), 270-271
Product management, 270-273
Professional associations
PR–related, 196-201
on WWW, as information resource, 35
Professional Pricing Society, 278-279
Profound, 100
Promotion, 260-262
ProQuest, 23-24,97, 101,142
PRS Group, Inc., 242-243
PRSA. *See* Public Relations Society of America (PRSA)
PRSA's Code of Professional Standards for the Practice of Public Relations, 199
PRSSA. *See* Public Relations Student Society of America (PRSSA)
PSMAs. *See* Primary Metropolitan Statistical Areas (PMSAs)
Psychographic sources, 126-134
Public Agenda, 146
Public corporate filings, competitive intelligence in, unearthing of, 78
Public organizations, marketing for, 291-293
Public relations (PR)
advertising *vs.*, 190
described, 189-191
directories for, 165
for multicultural communications, 139
professional associations in, 196-201
reading list on, 201

Public relations (PR) firms, 160
   locating of, 195-196
Public Relations Society of America
   (PRSA), 139,199-200
Public relations (PR) sources, 189-202
Public Relations Student Society of
   America (PRSSA), 199
Public Use Microdata Samples (PUMS),
   117,120
Public Use Microdata Samples (PUMS)
   files, 113,117
Public Use Presentation Library, Census
   Bureau of, 114
Publication searches, in periodical
   indexes, 23
Publisher(s), focus on niche markets, 153
Publishers Information Bureau (PIB),
   182
PUMS files, 113-117
Purchase Exchange, 274

Quantitative data, 54-61

Radio, advertising rates and cost data
   for, 169
Radio Expenditure Reports (RER), 174
Radio TV Reports (RTV), 174-175
Ranally Metro Area (RMA), 123
Ratcliffe, T.A., 172
Rauch Associates, 275
Realtor(s), MLS of, 7
Reed Business Information, 211
Reed Elsevier, 26
Reed, G., 262
Regulatory information, 67
Request-for-proposal (RFP), 274
RER. *See* Radio Expenditure Reports
   (RER)
Research
   advertising, 181-184
   market, 254-260
   on marketing, sources and strategies
      for, 3-37
   media, web sites with, 143

primary, on web, 105-106
   supply chain, web sites for, 283
Research Publishing, 19
Research strategies, 12-15
   steps in, 15
Resource(s), 131
Retail, defined, 216
Retail data, 212-216
   by city, source for, 219
Return-on-investment (ROI),
      advertising-related, 181
Reuters, 216
RFP. *See* Request-for-proposal (RFP)
Riggs, T., 178
Rivendell Marketing Company, Inc., 151
RMA. *See* Ranally Metro Area (RMA)
Robertson Stephens, 53
Robinson, W.A., 11
Robinson-Patman Act, 297
ROI. *See* Return-on-investment (ROI)
Room, A., 87,88
Roper ASW, 98,144-145
Roper Reports Consumer Insights
      program, 144
Rosenau, M.D., Jr., 271
Rosenberg, J.R., 18
RTV. *See* Radio TV Reports (RTV)
Russell, C., 120,137

Sage Publications, 11,293-294
Sales management, reading on, 209
Sales promotion(s), directories for, 165
Sales Promotion Agencies, 160
Sales prospect lists, creation of, free
      web source for, 209
Salomon Smith Barney, 53
Scholarly materials, as information
      resource, 36-37
Schonfeld & Associates, 163,172
Schonfeld's data, source for, 171
School of Packaging, at Michigan
      State University, 276
Science, Industry and Business Library
      (SIBL), of New York Public
      Library, 12

Search engines, finding trade associations using, 66

SEC. *See* Securities and Exchange Commission (SEC)

Secondary research, 93-94

Securities and Exchange Commission (SEC), 77,171

Segmentation, 111
customer, 134

Self-orientation, 131

Selig Center for Economic Growth, of Terry College of Business, at University of Georgia, 139

Seminal works, in development of social and nonprofit marketing, 290-291

Services marketing, 293-295
reading list on, 294-295

SERVQUAL, 294

S.I. Newhouse School of Communications, at Syracuse University, 151

SIBL. *See* Science, Industry and Business Library (SIBL)

SIC. *See* Standard Industrial Classification (SIC)

SIC system. *See* Standard Industrial Classification (SIC) system

SIC/NAICS code, 81

Simmons
guides to using, 130
National Consumer Survey data from, 129

Simmons Market Research (SMR), 141,151

Simmons Market Research Bureau (SMRB), 97,128-130,145

Simmons' National Consumer Survey, 145

SLA Advertising and Marketing Division, 262

SMAs. *See* Census Bureau's Metropolitan Statistical Areas (MSAs)

SMR. *See* Simmons Market Research (SMR)

SMRB. *See* Simmons Market Research Bureau (SMRB)

Social marketers, reading list for, 290

Social marketing, 288-291
development of, seminal works in, 290-291

Social Marketing Institute, 288-289

Soroka, W., 277

Source Index, 82

Special Markets Index, 160

Special topics, sources for, 287-299

Specialized business search systems, as information resource, 25-28

Spending, business-to-business, 222

Spending Potential Index (SPI), 133

SPI. *See* Spending Potential Index (SPI)

Sporting Goods Manufacturers, 53

SRDS. *See* Standard Rate & Data Service (SRDS)

SRDS Publications, 260-261

SRI Consulting Business Intelligence, 130-131

St. James Press, 93

Stagnito Communications, 274

Standard & Poor's, 50-51,74
Industry Surveys of, 62,65

Standard Industrial Classification (SIC) code, 71,73,75,76

Standard Industrial Classification (SIC) code categories, 82

Standard Industrial Classification (SIC) system, 47,49,55,172

Standard Rate and Data Service (SRDS), 126-128,140,165-169, 225-226,227

Stansfield, R.H., 11

STAT ("Search-term-and-text"), 98

State of the Industry Report, web site for, 65

State of the Nation (SOTN), of *STAT-USA*, 58

Statement of Principle SOP 93-7, 171-172

Statistics, 54
  as information resource, 28-32
Strategist web site, for print
  publications, 124
Strategy Research Corporation, 140-141
Strathclyde University, 34
Strawser, C.J., 59
Subject heading searches, *vs.* keyword
  searches, 20
Subject searching, in periodical indexes,
  22
Subscription databases, 136
Subscription web aggregators, 100-102
Suchan, T.A., 137
Summary Files, 113,114
Supermarket Facts: Industry Overview
  2001, web site for, 65
Supply chain management, CLM
  definition of, 282
Supply chain research, web sites for,
  283
Swartz, T.A., 293
SWOT analysis, industry research for,
  45
Syracuse University, S.I. Newhouse
  School of Communications
  at, 151

Table(s), as information resource, 28-32
Target Market News, 139-140
Target marketing, 111
Taylor Nelson Sofres Company, 174-176
Taylor Nelson Sofres' media monitoring
  network, 175
Technomic Publishing Co., 277
Teens, marketing to, reading list about,
  147-148
Telemarketing, 223
Television (TV), advertising rates and
  cost data for, 169
"Ten Attention-Getting Ways to Use
  E-Mail Lists," 212

10-K forms, 77-78
Terry College of Business, Selig Center
  for Economic Growth, at
  University of Georgia, 139
Texas A&M University, 146
The Advertising Council, 146
The Dialog Corporation, 100-101
The Pierian Press, 147
The Red Books, 160
"37 Ways to Improve Your User
  Conference Brochure," 212
Thomas Publishing Co., 74
Thompson, H.A., 37
Thomson Corporation, 27,102
Thomson Financial, 53
Thomson Research, 73
Time Warner, 229
Tongren, H.N., 19
Tooke, A.H., 96
Top 10 Agencies by U.S. Media
  Billings, 161
Top Agency Networks, 262
Top Global Ad Markets, 262
Top World Brand Advertisers, 262
Total quality management (TQM),
  advertising-related, 181
Total Retail Sales, 121
TQM. *See* Total quality management
  (TQM)
Tracking services, 174-176
Trade association web sources, 64-66
Trade Dimensions, 220
Trade journal articles, finding industry
  overviews in, 64
Trade journals, 62-64
Trade shows, 210-212
Tradenet.gov, 253
"Tradeshow Directory," 211
"Tradeshow Trends," 211
Travel Industry Association of America,
  web site for, 62
Truax, E., 180
Truncation, in periodical indexes, 22
Tylenol, 190

UN. *See* United Nations (UN)
"Uncle Sam," 178
Uniform Resource Locator (URL), 34
United Nations (UN), 238,247
    Department of Economic and
        Social Affairs of, 240
United Nations (UN) Convention for
        International Sale of Goods,
        251
United States Summary Reports, 112
Universal McCann, 172-173
University of Florida
    College of Journalism and
        Communication of, 200-201
    Warrington College of Business at,
        298
University of Georgia, Terry College
        of Business, Selig Center for
        Economic Growth, 139
University of Memphis library,
        Government Publications
        Department of, 231
University of Texas
    at Austin, 296-297
    Department of Advertising at,
        186,296-297
    McCombs School of Business at, 235
URL (Uniform Resource Locator), 34
U.S. Agency Brands Ranked by Gross
        Income, 161
U.S. Bureau of Economic Research, 52
U.S. Bureau of Labor Statistics, 119
U.S. Census Bureau. *See* Census Bureau
U.S. Constitution, 111
U.S. Customs Service Points of Entry,
        251
U.S. Department of Agriculture, 243
U.S. Department of Commerce, 52,58,
        139,230-231,234,263
    International Trade Administration
        of, OTEXA of, 264-265
U.S. Department of Commerce market
        reports, 256
U.S. Department of State, 254
U.S. Department of the Army, 245

U.S. General Accounting Office, 223
U.S. Government, "Uncle Sam" of, 178
U.S. Government information, on
        E-Commerce, 231
U.S. Government research reports, 260
U.S. International Trade Administration,
        255-256,264-265
U.S. Postal Service, 222,223,225
U.S. Small Business Administration,
        280
U.S. Trade Administration, 281
U.S Government agencies, 47

Value(s), understanding of, 248-249
VALUESCOPE, 144
Valve(s), Fleming, 229
Van Minden, J.J.R., 93
Video(s), as information resource, 35-36
Video Monitoring Services (VMS), 176
VMS (Video Monitoring Services), 176
VNU Business Publications, 167

WARC. *See* World Advertising
        Research Center (WARC)
Ward, A.M., 222
Warrington College of Business, at
        University of Florida, 298
Web aggregators
    free, 97-99
    subscription, 100-102
Web gateways, advertising-related,
        185-186
Web sites
    critical evaluation of, criteria for, 14
    industry-specific, 62
Webdata.com, 33
WEFA. *See* Wharton Economic
        Forecasting Associates
        (WEFA)
Weitz, B.A., 11
Wensley, R., 11
West Chester University, 34

Wharton Economic Forecasting
    Associates (WEFA), 222
Who Owns Whom, 161
Wholesale data, 212-216
Wholesale Trade, 55
Wildcard(s), in periodical indexes, 22
Working Paper Series, 37
World Advertising Research Center
    (WARC), 28,259-260,262
    Pocket Books of, 259-260
World Bank, 247
World Packaging Organization, 276
World Wide Web (WWW),
    xvi,xvii,xviii,4,32-34
    case studies in, 10
    customized research on, 103
    jargon and acronyms related to, 34
    large library catalogs available free
        on, 20
    in market research, 95
    primary research on, 105-106
    professional organizations on, as
        information resource, 35
    trade association sources on, 64-66

World's Top 50 Advertising
    Organizations, 161
WWW. *See* World Wide Web
    (WWW)

XML (Extensible Markup Language),
    34

Yahoo, 32
Youth, marketing to, 143-148
    ethical issues on, resources for, 148
    policy issues on, resources for, 148

Zapdata, 209
Zeithaml, V.A., 294
ZenithOptimedia, 260
Zip codes, 123
    economic census data by, 56
Zogby International, 151

For Product Safety Concerns and Information please contact our EU
representative GPSR@taylorandfrancis.com Taylor & Francis Verlag GmbH,
Kaufingerstraße 24, 80331 München, Germany

Printed and bound by CPI Group (UK) Ltd, Croydon, CR0 4YY

06/05/2025

01861450-0001